Illustrated TCP/IP

Matthew Naugle

Wiley Illustrated Network Series

Series Editor: Matthew Naugle

Illustrated TCP/IP

Matthew Naugle

WILEY COMPUTER PUBLISHING

John Wiley & Sons, Inc.
New York • Chichester • Weinheim • Brisbane • Singapore • Toronto

Publisher: Robert Ipsen
Editor: Marjorie Spencer
Assistant Editor: Margaret Hendrey
Managing Editor: Frank Grazioli
Associate New Media Editor: Mike Sosa
Production Assistant: Liz Adams
Text Design & Composition: Benchmark Productions, Inc.

Designations used by companies to distinguish their products are often claimed as trademarks. In all instances where John Wiley & Sons, Inc., is aware of a claim, the product names appear in initial capital or all capital letters. Readers, however, should contact the appropriate companies for more complete information regarding trademarks and registration.

This book is printed on acid-free paper. ∞

This publication is designed to provide accurate and authoritative information in regard to the subject matter covered. It is sold with the understanding that the publisher is not engaged in rendering professional services. If professional advice or other expert assistance is required, the services of a competent professional person should be sought.

Library of Congress Cataloging-in-Publication Data:

Naugle, Matthew G.
    Illustrated TCP/IP / Matthew Naugle.
       p. cm. –– (Wiley illustrated networks series)
    Includes index.
    ISBN 0-471-19656-8 (alk. paper)
    1. TCP/IP (Computer network protocol) 2. Computer networks.
  I. Title. II. Series.
  TK5105.585.N38   1998
  004.6'2––dc21   98-8271
                                                                        CIP

Printed in the United States of America.
10 9 8 7 6 5 4 3 2 1

This book is dedicated to a good friend of mine, for whom I continue to have great admiration. His tireless instruction of limitless boundaries will forever be remembered. His thoughts and ideas were given to me years ago, but I continue to use them successfully everyday.

This book is dedicated to John J. (JJ) Anderson.

How to Use This Book

With the amount of information we are forced to consume everyday, it would be nice to simply skim over a few sentences in a paragraph to get the key points of the topic. That is what the Illustrated Network books are about. Each page has a graphic and concise text that makes key points quick to learn and review.

Like all books in the Illustrated Network series, this one is very detailed, yet it is written in way that makes it easy to comprehend. Eighty percent of what is commonly written about is filler information. What this book does is extract the twenty percent of the required information and places this information in an easy to use format. A similar format is used quite often with training material. As we all know, training must be done is a very structured and concise fashion and it must be delivered within a limited window of time. I have taken this quick learning concept further by using a combination of a text book and a training manual—producing the format of this book.

This book is built specifically to be used as both a reference manual and a text book. There is no reason to read it from cover to cover. A topic can simply be turned to and quickly learned without having to read the whole book.

The back of the book contains a CD. The graphics containing all the key points of the lessons are provided on this CD. You can use the graphics to create a customized training slide show, or use them in a classroom setting in conjunction with the book. The files are in a Microsoft PowerPoint presentation. The version of PowerPoint used is PowerPoint 97. Simply start your PowerPoint application and open one of the files on the CD corresponding to the information in the book.

Contents

Acknowledgments

Two people made this book possible, Margaret Hendrey and Marjorie Spencer. I provided the information, but it was the continuous work of these two that produced this book. The amount of work it takes to put something like this together covers a long time and without these individuals' assistance, this book would not have been the same.

Part One

Introduction to the TCP/IP Protocol

1 Transmission Control Protocol/Internet Protocol

The TCP/IP protocol suite is being used for communications, whether for voice, video, or data. There is a new service being brought out for voice over IP at a consumer cost of 5.5 cents per minute. Radio broadcasts are all over the Web. Video is coming, but the images are still shaky and must be buffered heavily before displaying on the monitor. However, give it time. All great things are refined by time, and applications over TCP/IP are no exception.

Today, you will not find too many data communications installments that have not implemented or have not thought about the TCP/IP protocol. TCP/IP is becoming so common that it is not so much a matter of selecting the TCP/IP protocol stack as it is selecting applications that support it. Many users do not even know they are using the TCP/IP protocol. All they know is that they have a connection to the Web, which many people confuse with the Internet. We'll get into the details of the differences later, but for now, you just need to understand that the Web is an *application* of the Internet. The Web uses the communications facilities of the Internet to provide for data flow between clients and servers. The Internet is not the Web and the Web is not the Internet.

In the 1970s, everyone had some type of WANG machine in their office. In the 1980s and early 1990s, Novell's NetWare applications consumed every office. Today, NetWare continues to dominate the network arena with its installed based of client/server network applications. However, the TCP/IP protocol

> ## Transmission Control Protocol/Internet Protocol
>
> - The protocol suite of TCP/IP is becoming the world's most widely implemented network protocol.
> - 1970s—WANG
> - 1980s—SNA / Novell NetWare
> - 1990s—Novell and TCP/IP
> - TCP/IP combined with the Web browser is creating a new type of client/server network operating system.

and Internet browsers, such as NetScape's Navigator and Microsoft's Internet Explorer, and Web programming languages are combining to produce powerful corporate networks known as *intranets*, which mimic the facilities of the Internet but on a corporate scale. Intranets from different companies or simply different sites can communicate with each other through the Internet. Consumers can access corporate intranets through an *extranet*, which is simply part of the corporate intranet that is available to the public. A great example of this is electronic commerce, which is what you use when you purchase something via the Internet. Directory services are provided through Domain Name Services (DNSs) Microsystems. File and print services are provided in many different ways. Finally, the ultimate in full connectivity is the Internet, which allows the corporate intranets to interconnect (within the same corporation or different corporations), providing global connectivity unmatched by any network application today.

Therefore, within a short time (possibly 1998), very powerful applications will be built that utilize the TCP/IP software suite that will eventually rival NetWare at the core.

Introduction (continued)

2

Introduction (continued)

- TCP/IP is portable.
  - Runs on different computer operating systems
  - Addressing is handled on a global assignment
- Novell is supporting TCP/IP.
  - Native TCP/IP support
  - IntraNetWare — (native support with release 5.0)
- Microsoft is supporting TCP/IP.
  - Native
  - Client/server support with NT

Another key factor of TCP/IP is *extensibility*. How many people can you name that use NetWare out of their house to allow for corporate connectivity or for commercial connectivity? Yes, programs such as remote node and remote control allow for NetWare clients to be accessed remotely, but not as seamlessly as with TCP/IP. TCP/IP allows you to move your workstation to any part of the network, including dialing in from any part of the world, and gain access to your network or another network. This brings up another point: How many networks interact using NetWare? Theoretically, with TCP/IP you can access (excluding security mechanisms for now) any other TCP/IP network in the world from any point in the world. Addressing in TCP/IP is handled on a global scale to ensure uniqueness. Novell attempted global addressing but failed. Novell addresses are unique to each private installation, such as a single company, but are probably massively duplicated when taken as a whole (all installations). I know many installations with the Novell address of 1A somewhere in their network. Not everyone is going to renumber their network for uniqueness, but one trick is to match the 32-bit address of TCP/IP subnets to your Novell network. Convert each octet of the 32-bit address of TCP/IP into hex and use that as your NetWare address.

Novell has entered the TCP/IP fray with its IntranetWare and support for native IP. IntraNetWare allows NetWare workstations to access TCP/IP resources. As of version 5.0, IntraNetWare is going away in name only and another version of NetWare is supposed to allow for NetWare to run directly on top of TCP/IP (this is known as native TCP/IP support).

Microsoft and its emerging NT platform can also use TCP/IP as a network protocol. Two flavors are available:
- Native TCP/IP and its applications (TELNET, FTP, etc.)
- RFC compliant (RFC 1001 and 1002) TCP, which allows file and print service

This enables the ability to telnet from an NT server or workstation and transfer files to that workstation or server using native TCP/IP. For file and print services in a TCP/IP environment, NT can be configured to use NetBIOS over TCP/IP. This enables NT to be involved in a routed network. NT can run many other protocols as well, but that is beyond the scope of this book.

Introduction (continued)

- Novell continues to dominate the client/server environment.
- Mainframes are continually upgraded and being used more often.
  - Web interfaces to mainframe data
  - Some mainframe functions have been converted to Unix platforms
- TCP/IP is an extensible protocol.

However, this does not mean that the other protocols (beyond TCP/IP) are being disbanded. Novell NetWare continues to run with the IPX protocol. As of this writing, NetWare is still the best constructed client server platform available. Tens of thousands of programs have been written directly to the NetWare interface and it is used in corporate networks, schools, and state, local, and federal governments. These users are not going to disconnect their NetWare networks and move to TCP/IP over night. NetWare will be around for a great length of time, albeit in a diminishing role (start the arguments!).

Most Fortune 1000 companies still depend on large mainframes for their day-to-day processing. The early 1990s and late 1980s were interesting times when many corporations were convinced that smaller Unix platforms using a distributed (client/server) architecture could replace their "antiquated" SNA networks. Wrong! Although some networks have converted to this architecture, many have not. There are many factors involved here. Time and money play an important role, but the rule continues to be, "if it ain't broke, don't fix it." Huge applications such as the airline reservation system and the banking system are built using the SNA architecture, and even if a perfect solution is found, it will take years to convert these programs over to a new system. SNA is still being used, and I have even supported some sites that have reverted back to SNA mainframes, which were best suited to their particular situation. Today, there are Web servers that front IBM mainframes as well. IBM fully supports the TCP/IP protocols and there is a 3270 terminal emulation program known as TN3270 that allows for 3270 terminal emulation over the TCP/IP protocol. All of this is beyond the scope of this book, but remember, TCP/IP is very popular; however, protocol schemes are still in existence, still provide many benefits, and will continue to be used for years to come.

From this, one would tend to think that the TCP/IP protocol was developed by a large-scale R&D center like that of IBM or DEC. It wasn't. It was developed by a team of research-type people, comprised of college professors, graduate students, and undergraduate students from major universities. This should not be hard to believe. These individuals are the type who not only enjoy R&D work, but also believe that, when problems occur, the fun starts.

Many years from now we will look back on the TCP/IP protocol as the protocol that provided the building blocks of future data communications. However, take notice: TCP/IP is an extensible protocol. It is fully functional today, but the work on the project continues. There are over 75 working groups of the Internet Engineering Task Force (IETF, explained in a moment), and as new needs continue to arise for the Internet, new working groups are formed and new protocols will emerge. In fact, the IP version of the existing protocol (known as IPv4, or IP version 4) will be replaced. IP version 6 (IPv6) is currently being implemented around the Internet. It will be a few years before a complete switchover takes place, but it is a great example of the extensible protocol.

4 TCP/IP and Other Protocols

While the ARPAnet (and later the Internet) was being built, other protocols such as System Network Architecture (SNA) and protocols based on XNS (there are many proprietary versions) prevailed. Client/server applications that allowed for file and print services on personal computers were built using protocols based on XNS such as Novell NetWare (using IPX) and Banyan VINES. SNA was alive and well in the mainframe, and DECnet controlled the minicomputer marketplace. DEC also supported LAT

TCP/IP and Other Protocols

- ARPAnet built at the same time as SNA and XNS networks.
- XNS supported Novell, Banyan, and most other networking devices.
- WAN access limited to X.25 and vendor proprietary solutions.
- DEC continued to support DECnet/LAT.
- LAN media as Ethernet, Token Ring, and FDDI.

(Local Area Transport) for terminal servers, which supported printers as well. DECnet started out before commercial Ethernet, and DEC's minicomputers were connected together via local interfaces. Later, around 1982, DEC started to support Ethernet but still with the DECnet protocol.

All of these protocols could run over Ethernet, Token Ring, or FDDI. In this respect, they did openly support the LAN protocol. However, disregarding the LAN protocol, these protocols were proprietary; in other words, *vendor dependent*. However, other protocols beyond TCP/IP are proprietary, and the internals of those systems are known only to their respective company owners. Users and network administrators were held to proprietary network environments and proprietary network applications, which deterred network development and enhancement in all corporate environments. Just because a vendor supported XNS, did not mean that it would interoperate with other vendors running XNS. Running XNS on one system did not guarantee compatibility of communication to any other system except for the same vendor's. This was good for the vendor, but it tended to lock users into one vendor.

The only public Wide Area Network (WAN) access was X.25, and not everyone supported all features 100 percent, which lead to compatibility problems. All of us remember X.25 as a slow (primarily 9.6 kbps or 19.2 kbps) WAN access protocol. (This is not bashing the X.25 protocol. There were many valid reasons for running it at the slower network speeds, like error correction and control, and faster speeds such as T1 were not available for data connection transfers.)

Alternatively, leased lines based on proprietary protocols of the network vendors were an option, but that only allowed the corporate networks to be interconnected. Ethernet was also available, but host interfaces and standardized network protocols were not readily available.

The Internet started as a research facility and to link the government to the research facilities as well. It remained this way until about 1992. Only a handful of people knew about the Internet, and the Internet had nothing really to offer the commercial world. Engineers and scientists loved the Internet. No one knew of the advantages of the TCP/IP protocol. It was not until the GUI interface was developed that the Internet took off, and the TCP/IP protocol came with it. Therefore other protocols such as SNA and Novell NetWare sprouted in corporate America. Basically, there was no other choice.

5 Other Protocols (continued)

One of the better protocols was AppleTalk. Much like a Macintosh computer, it was very costly to implement. Seriously, I happen to like the AppleTalk protocol. AppleTalk was actually the software and LocalTalk was the hardware. It was Apple's version of networking Mac computers, and, except for the wiring, it was free. The protocol was simple to install and use. It was built into every Mac. Cables were simply needed to hook up Apple computers to a simple network, and file and print services were built in as well. It was known as true peer-to-peer, for each workstation could see every other workstation, and each workstation could be a server and share any of its resources. Each node ran the name service. Each node picked its own physical address. Even dialing in to an AppleTalk network was easy using the AppleTalk Remote Access (ARA) protocol, and it made it look like you were a local node on the AppleTalk network. It soon became a very popular method of hooking together Mac computers into a network. However, AppleTalk was not envisioned as a protocol to handle large internets of Apple computers, and the inefficiencies of the protocol soon arose. It was about as close as you could come to a network operating system that allowed for simplicity and ingenuity. AppleTalk had one problem: scalability. Try building a large AppleTalk network, not an easy task, if not impossible.

TCP/IP eliminated proprietary network operating systems; however, not intentionally. Again, it was built for a different purpose. TCP's

> ## Other Protocols (continued)
>
> - AppleTalk (software) and LocalTalk (hardware) were built into every Mac.
>   - Very robust protocol but not scalable
>   - Each node had a naming service
>   - Network IDs were dynamic (seed router)
>   - Node IDs were dynamic
>   - Remote access was fully integrated as a remote node
> - TCP/IP eliminated the proliferation of proprietary network operating systems.
>   - Any hardware and software platform could communicate
> - TCP/IP was completely open to any vendor to write code to.
> - TCP/IP is the protocol of choice for future network systems.

beginnings were rough (interoperability issues) and, in fact, TCP/IP was not the original protocol of the ARPAnet. But the protocol stabilized and the interoperability between different computers and operating systems became a reality. For example, a DEC system running the VMS operating system combined with TCP/IP running as the network operating system can communicate with a Sun Microsystems' Unix workstation running TCP/IP. The two systems can communicate by taking advantage of the protocol and the specific applications written for the protocol, primarily by being able to log on to one another and transfer files between the two across a network.

When interconnecting computers and their operating systems with TCP/IP, it does not matter what the hardware architecture or the operating systems of the computers are. The protocol will allow any computer implementing it to communicate with another. The methods used to accomplish this are discussed in the following sections.

Suffice it to say, the TCP/IP protocol is the protocol of choice for future network installations.

The Origins of TCP/IP

6

The Origins of TCP/IP

- A TCP/IP network is heterogeneous.
- Popularity due to:
  - Protocol suite part of the Berkeley Unix operating system
    - College students worked with it and then took it to corporate America
  - In 1983, all government proposals required TCP/IP
  - The Web graphical user interface
- TCP/IP has the ingenious ability to work on any operating platform.
- TCP/IP has easy remote access capabilities.

A TCP/IP network is generally a heterogeneous network, meaning there are many different types of network computing devices attached. The suite of protocols that encompass TCP/IP were originally designed to allow different types of computer systems to communicate as if they were the same system. It was developed by a project underwritten by an agency of the Department of Defense known as the Advanced Research Projects Agency (DARPA).

There are many reasons why the early TCP/IP became popular, three of which are paramount. First, DARPA provided a grant to allow the protocol suite to become part of Berkeley's Unix system. When TCP/IP was introduced to the commercial marketplace, Unix was always mentioned in every story about it. Berkeley Unix and TCP/IP became the standard operating system and protocol of choice for many major universities, where it was used with workstations in engineering and research environments. Second, in 1983, all U.S. government proposals that included networks mandated the TCP/IP protocol. (This was also the year that the ARPAnet was converted to the TCP/IP protocol. Conversions in those days happened within days. That was when the Internet was small.)

And third, a graphical user interface was developed to allow easy access with the system. TCP/IP or its applications can be a difficult protocol to use if you have not had experience with it. Finding information on the Internet was a formidable task. Before the browser, TCP/IP applications were accessed from a command line interface with a few basic applications that allowed you to call a remote system and act as a remote terminal, transfer files, and send and receive mail. Some companies of these applications built graphical interfaces to the applications, but they were still rough and would not have gained commercial success. The browser hid all the complexities of the TCP/IP protocol and its applications and allowed for graphics to appear as well as text, and by clicking on either the graphics or text, we could place ourselves anywhere on the Internet (within security reasons!). It also allowed for easier access to information on the Internet.

Based on those points, it was not very long before everyone knew of the capability of the protocol to allow dissimilar systems to communicate through the network—all this without a forklift upgrade to mainframes, minis, and personal computers. It simply bolted on to existing computer devices. TCP/IP became a very popular network operating system that continues today.

TCP/IP originated when DARPA was tasked to bring about a solution to a difficult problem: allowing different computers to communicate with one another as if they were the same computer. This was difficult, considering that all computer architectures in those days (the early 1970s) were highly guarded secrets. Computer manufacturers would not disclose either their hardware or software architectures to anyone. This is known as a *closed* or *proprietary* system.

The architecture behind TCP/IP takes an alternative approach. TCP/IP developed into an architecture that would allow the computers to communicate without grossly modifying the operating system or the hardware architecture of the machine. TCP/IP runs as an application on those systems.

However, before TCP/IP, the original result was known as the Network Control Program (NCP). The protocol was developed to run on multiple hosts in geographically dispersed areas through a packet switching internet known as the Advanced Research Project Agency network—ARPAnet. This protocol was primarily used to support application-oriented functions and process-to-process communications between two hosts. Specific applications, such as file transfer, were written to this network operating system. The ARPAnet was taken down in 1993. The Internet that we run today was built during the ARPAnet time, but as a parallel network.

In order to perpetuate the task of allowing dissimilar government computers to communicate, DARPA gave research grants to the

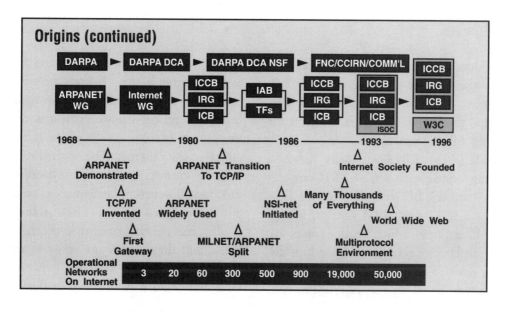

University of California at Los Angeles (UCLA), the University of California at San Bernadino (UCSB), the Stanford Research Institute (SRI), and the University of Utah. A company called BBN provided the Honeywell 316 Interface Message Processors (IMPs, which have evolved into today's routers), which provided the internet communications links. In 1971, the ARPAnet Networking Group dissolved, and DARPA took over all the research work. The first few years of this design proved to be an effective test, but had some serious design flaws, so a research project was developed to overcome these problems. The outcome of this project was a recommendation to replace the original program known as NCP with another called Transmission Control Program (TCP). Between the years of 1975–1979, DARPA had begun the work on the Internet technology, which resulted in the TCP/IP protocols as we know them today. The protocol responsible for routing the packets through an internet was termed the *Internet Protocol*. Today, the common term for this standard is *TCP/IP*.

With TCP/IP replacing NCP, the NCP application-specific programs were converted to run over the new protocol. The protocol became mandated in 1983, when ARPA demanded that all computers attached to the ARPAnet use the TCP/IP protocol.

8 Origins (continued)

In 1983, the ARPAnet was split into two networks: the Defense Data Network (DDN), also known as the MILNET (military network), and the DARPA Internet, a new name for the old ARPAnet network.

Outside of the ARPAnet, many networks were being formed, such as CSNET (Computer Science Network); BITNET (Because It's Time Network) used between IBM systems; UUCP (User to User Copy), which became the protocol used on USENET (a network used for distributing news); and many others. All of these networks were based on the TCP/IP protocol, and all were interconnected using the ARPAnet as a backbone. Many other advances were also taking place with Local Area Networks using Ethernet, and companies began making equipment that enabled any host or terminal to attach to the Ethernet. The original route messengers, known as IMPs (Interface Message Processors), were now being made commercially and were called *routers*. These routers were smaller, cheaper, and faster than the ARPAnet's IMPs, and they were more easily maintained. With these devices, regional networks were built and could now hook up to the Internet.

Origins (continued)

- In 1983, ARPAnet was split into two networks.
  - Defense Data Network (DDN) or MILNET
  - The DARPA Internet—new name for the ARPAnet
- In 1985, NSFnet was established to allow five supercomputer sites to be accessed by scientists.
- Outside the ARPAnet, many "regional" networks based on TCP/IP were built.
  - CSNET (Computer Science Network)
  - BITNET (Because It's Time Network, IBM)
  - UUCP (User to User Copy), which became USEnet
- All were connected via the ARPAnet backbone.
- Original routers were called Interface Message Processors (IMPs).

could establish a physical link to the NSFnet backbone could gain access to it. In 1990, the NSFnet was upgraded to 45-Mbps links.

Once the word of NSFnet spread, many regional networks sprang up, such as NYSERnet (New York State Educational Research Network), CERFnet (named for California Educational Research Network and not Vint Cerf), and others. The regional networks were supported at their level and not by the NSF.

However, commercial access to the Internet was still very limited.

One experiment that was successful, CSNET (computer science network), provided the foundation for the NSF to build another network that interconnected five supercomputer sites. The five sites were interconnected via 56-kbps lines. This was known as NSFnet. However, the NSF also stated that if an academic institution built a community network, the NSF would give it access to the NSFnet. This would allow both regional access to the NSFnet and the regional networks (based on the TCP/IP protocol) to communicate with one another. The NSFnet was formally established in 1986. It built a large backbone network using 56-kbps links, which were later upgraded to T1 links (July 1988). Anyone who

The NSFnet was found to be very useful beyond its conception of linking super-computers to academic institutions. In 1987, NSF awarded a contract to MERIT Network (along with IBM and MCI) to upgrade the NSFnet to T1 and to link six regional networks, the existing five supercomputer centers, MERIT, and the National Center for Atmospheric Research into one backbone. This was completed in July 1988. In 1989, a nonprofit organization known as ANS (Advanced Network and Services, Inc.) was spun off from the MERIT team. Its goal was to upgrade the NSFnet to a 45-Mbps backbone and link together 16 regional sites. This was completed in November 1991.

More commercial entities were springing up building regional networks via TCP/IP as well. To allow these entities access to the backbone, a concept known as the Commercial Internet eXchange (CIX) was built. This was a point on the backbone that allowed commercial regional networks access to the academic NSFnet backbone.

The original ARPAnet was expensive to run and interest inside DARPA began to wane. Major promoters of the ARPAnet had left DARPA to take positions elsewhere. It was taken completely out of service in 1989, and what emerged in its place is what we know as the Internet. The term *Internet* was coined as an abbreviation to the Internet Protocol (IP).

> **Origins (continued)**
> - The original ARPAnet was taken out of service in 1989.
> - Internet backbone supported by NSFnet using 56-kbps lines.
> - NSFnet upgraded to 45-Mbps backbone.
> - In 1993, NSF granted out the operation of the backbone to various companies to continue running it.
> - Most operations of the Internet are run by private companies and not the government.

The NSFnet was basically a mirror image of the ARPAnet, and they were running in parallel. Regional networks based on the TCP/IP protocol were interconnected via NSFnet, which had connections to the ARPAnet. More connections were being made through NSFnet because it was higher speed, easier to hook into, and less expensive.

It was determined that the original network, the ARPAnet, should be shut down. Sites on the ARPAnet found new homes within the regional networks or as regional networks. NSFnet provided the backbone for interconnection of these regional networks.

Origins (continued)

Origins (continued)

- Today, any company can build a backbone based on TCP/IP.
- Connections to other backbones are provided through peering points known as Network Access Points (NAPs).
- Internet Service Providers allow for anyone to connect to the Internet through Points of Presence (POPs).
  - Essentially, a location in any city that can accept a phone call from a user's modem. The line is then connected to a network that provides access to the Internet.
- Running TCP/IP does not require access to the Internet.

Word quickly spread about the Internet and around 1993, and NSF decided it could not continue supporting the rapid expansion directly and produced contracts for outsourcing the continuation of the Internet. Many companies responded to the call, and the functional responsibilities of running the Internet were given to many different companies. In place of the NSFnet would be a concept called *Network Access Points*, points located throughout the United States through which companies that built their own backbones could interconnect and exchange route paths. Also with this came the concept of *peering*. NAPs provided access to other backbones, and by peering with another backbone provider, a provider allowed their backbone to

be used by another provider to move their customers' traffic. There was a lot of controversy with this concept: Who should a backbone provider peer with or not peer with? Why should a provider let another provider use its backbone as a transit for its customers for free? The answer: because NSF stated this and the issue was tabled.

NAPs are basically the highest point in the Internet. In this way, many backbones would be privately built, and all would be interconnected through the NAPs. Initially, there were four official NAPs, but this number has grown by an additional 13 (with more being added) as of this writing. Even with the commercialization of the Internet, no one company owned any part of the Internet, and everyone associated with the Internet had to abide by the rules in place. External companies simply provided a specific service required to run the Internet. For example, Network Solutions, Inc. was granted the right to control the domain name registration. However, it does not own this capability. Network Solutions is still under the authority of the Internet Assigned Numbers Authority run by Jon Postel (as of this writing) at the University of Southern California. AT&T was granted the right to host many document databases required by the Internet user community. Eventually, all the functions of running the Internet were contracted out by NSF. Any company (with lots of money) can build a backbone. To provide access to others, its backbone must be connected to others at the NAP. Individual backbone providers then interconnect multiple connections known as Points of Presence, or POPs, which are where the individual user or business connects to the Internet. In April of 1995, the NSFnet backbone was shut down, and the Internet was up and running as we know it today.

One last distinction of TCP/IP: Running the protocol on any network does not require a connection to the Internet. TCP/IP may be

installed on as few as two network stations or on as many as can be addressed (possibly millions). When a network requires access to the Internet, the network administrator must call his or her local registry (or Internet Service Provider [ISP]) to place a request for access and be assigned an official IP address.

11   The World Wide Web

Great application programs and intercommunication have been available on the Internet for dozens of years, so why all the hype since 1994? The Web came to us in 1994 (commercially) and allowed for everyone to work on the Internet, even though many had no idea what they were working on. The browser became the interface, a simple-to-use interface, and this was the start of the commercialization of the Web. This is when "corporate" money became involved. However, the idea started out way back in 1981 with a program called Enquire, developed by Tim Berners-Lee. A pro-

gram known as Mosaic was released in November 1993 as freeware written by the cofounder of NetScape, Marc Andreeson, at the U.S. National Center for Supercomputer Applications (NCSA). Mosaic allowed text and graphics on the same Web page and was the basis for NetScape's Navigator browser and Microsoft's Internet Explorer.

First and foremost, the Web allows anyone, especially nontechnical people, instant access to an infinite amount of information. You can get stock reports, information from a library, order a book, reserve airline tickets, page someone, find that long-lost friend through the yellow pages, order a data line for your house, check your credit card statement, check on the availability of that one-and-only car, provide computer-based training, or attend a private (video and audio) meeting. And yes, you can send an email.

All this and still more! Unlike other online services such as CompuServe, Prodigy, and America Online (at the time), anyone can create a Web page as well—not too hard to do, the language to create a Web page is pretty much English. Millions of ideas are available, and there is a pulldown menu in the browser that allows you to see the source code (the basic instructions that tell the Web server how to format a page) of any Web page. By 1995, companies known as Internet Service Providers (ISPs) were advertising their ability to put you on the Web for a low price of $19.95. In fact, today, most professional ISPs give you space on their servers (a small amount, but enough to get started) for you to create your Web page, at no charge!

Point and click to access any information that you would like; you do not have to know an operating system to move around the Web. No other "cyberspace" provider has the rich simplicity of the browser. One click and you can be on a server in Japan, video conference to California, send an email to your friend in England, or plan a vacation to Breckenridge, Colorado. Other online providers had information, but it was the simplicity and combination of text and still pictures on the same page that catapulted the Web into every home.

Virtually anything that you want to check on, you can do on the Web and you do not have to remember IP addresses, directory commands for DOS and Unix, file compression, executing the TAR command, printing to a postscript printer, and so on. Simply stated, the Web allows everyone access to network data with a simple click of the mouse.

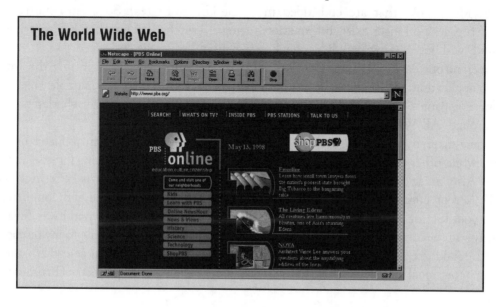

The World Wide Web

12 The Web (continued)

On the application front, more and more applications are being written towards (or have embedded) the most common Internet interface: a browser. A browser allows the Internet to be accessed graphically using icons and pictures and a special text language known as Hypertext Markup Language, or HTML. For platform independence in writing applications for the Web, the Java language was created.

What is the downfall of the Internet? No, connectivity is generally not the problem. ISPs can be a problem, but even they are manageable. The biggest problem with the Internet is its biggest asset: information.

You may find yourself scratching your head while traveling the Internet. Anyone can create content and post it, so there is a lot of old information on the Internet. Web pages are not kept up. Web pages are not written correctly and contain too many slow-loading graphics. Many links that are embedded in other Web pages no longer exist. Information is posted without having validity checks. Remember, no one entity owns the Internet or the Web application.

Some companies with Web pages are no longer around. All Web pages are not created equal; some take an eternity to write to your browser, while others take a minimal amount of time. Also, all ISPs are not created equal. An ISP is your connection to the Internet. Test out your ISP for service and connectivity. I recently switched from a major ISP to a local ISP and found 4x improvement in speed. However, the local ISP does not provide

---

The Web (continued)

- The biggest asset of the Web is its biggest downfall:
  - Information
- There is a tremendous amount of information on the Web.
- Information on the Web can be posted by anyone.
- However:
  - Many Web pages are not kept up
  - Many are not written correctly (minutes to build a screen)
  - Information is old and out of date
  - Information is not documented
  - Incredibly hard to search for simple items due to more than 50 million Web sites available
  - Search engines bring back many undesired Web pages which require advanced searching techniques

---

national service (local phone numbers around the United States). So when I started traveling, I switched to another ISP that has both national coverage and speed.

Be careful when scrutinizing the Internet. Make sure the data is reputable (i.e., can be verified). There are many charlatans on the Internet posting fiction.

The Internet really introduced us to the concept of trying something for free. For us old timers, we expected this. Postings to the Internet were always free and commercialism was a no-no. Years ago, when I was developing software, the Internet came to my rescue many times with postings of source code that assisted in my development projects. This source code was available for free and often the person who posted it did not mind an occasional email with a question or two. Another concept that the Internet was not used for was known as *shareware*, where the free samples of applications range from severely crippled (lacking many of the full-version features such as printing abilities) to the full-blown version of the software. The Web combined the two concepts, and the marketing concept really took hold when the Internet came into the business world. Every business sponsoring a Web page will give you something if you purchase something—a very old concept brought to life again via the Internet.

The Web (continued)　13

The Web (continued)

- Old-style marketing.
  - "Give away the razor and sell the razor blades"—Gillette
- Shareware programs.
  - The old concept of "try before you buy"
- Free programs.
  - Many diversified programs and interactive Web pages
- The 1-800 service for data.
  - Most companies have a Web page

Most of us try a free sample before purchasing. This is still known as shareware, and payment is expected, which leads to another big problem for the Internet: How and when do you charge for something? Most users expect to surf the Internet, pick up what they want for free, and then sign off. Sorry folks, we don't live in a free world, and eventually you must pay. Unfortunately, there are those out there who continue to download software and not pay for it. Bad, bad, bad. If this continues, shareware will not be available, and you will end up with a pay-first, try-later attitude.

Another problem of the Internet is the spread of viruses. Protect your workstation with some type of antiviral software before downloading anything from the Internet. Most protection schemes are dynamic in that they are constantly checking for viruses even during an email download or a file transfer. Here is where the other online providers do have an advantage. Private online providers such as America Online and CompuServe make every effort to test uploaded software and generally do not allow for content to be written to their

servers. You will find those services more protected and watched over than the Internet. The Internet has truly tested the first Amendment of the Constitution: the right to free speech.

The Internet is still the best thing going. Applications from all types of businesses are available on the Internet. Today, many experiments are on the Web as well, including audio/visual applications such as movies, radio, and even telephone access.

14 Internet, Intranets, and Extranets

We all know what the Internet is—at least I hope so. An *intranet* is a TCP/IP based internet used for a business' *internal* network. Intranets can communicate with each other via connections to the Internet, which provides the backbone communication; however, an intranet does not need an outside connection to the Internet in order to operate. It simply uses all the TCP/IP protocols and applications to give you a "private" internet.

When a business exposes part of its internal network to the outside community, it is known as an *extranet*. You may have used this extranet

Internet, Intranets, and Extranets

- The Internet is a complex organization of networks managed by companies that provide access to international resources through the use of the TCP/IP protocol suite.
- An intranet uses the TCP/IP protocols and applications based on the Internet but in a corporate environment.
- An extranet is the sharing of a corporate intranet (maybe just a piece of it) with the outside world.
  - E-commerce is an example of an extranet

when browsing through a web page at General Electric or ordering some diskettes via a reseller's Web page. You will not have complete access to a corporate network, but merely a part of it that the business wants you to have access to. The company can block access on its routers and put *firewalls* (a piece of software or hardware that allows you access to resources based on a variety of parameters such as IP addresses, port numbers, domain names, etc.) into place that force you to have access only to a subset of its intranet.

Who Governs the Internet? 15

Who governs the protocol, the Internet, and the Web? First off, let's make it clear that no one company or person owns the Internet. In fact, some say that it is a miracle that the Internet continues to function as well as it does. Why is this hard to believe? Well, in order to function, the Internet requires the complete cooperation of thousands of companies known as Internet Service Providers (ISPs), telecommunications companies, standards bodies such as IANA, application developers, and a host of other resources. The one main goal is to provide ubiquitous information access, and anyone who tries to divert the Internet to his or her own advantage is usually chastised. However, this is becoming more diluted now that ISPs are duking it out for traffic patterns. Furthermore, all those who participate in the Internet, including all companies that have IP connections to the Internet, must abide by the rules. Imagine that: Millions of people all listening to one set of rules.

Refer to slide 15. The TCP/IP protocol suite is governed by an organization known as the Internet Activities Board (IAB). In the late 1970s, the growth of the Internet was

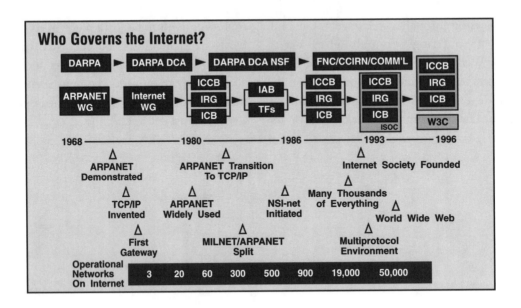

accompanied by a growth in the size of the interested research community, representing an increased need for coordination mechanisms. Vint Cerf, then manager of the Internet Program at DARPA, formed several coordination bodies: an International Cooperation Board (ICB) to coordinate activities with some cooperating European countries centered on Packet Satellite research; an Internet Research Group, which was an inclusive group providing an environment for general exchange of information; and an Internet Configuration Control Board (ICCB). The ICCB was an invitational body to assist Cerf in managing the burgeoning Internet activity.

In 1983, continuing growth of the Internet community demanded a restructuring of the coordination mechanisms. The ICCB was disbanded and, in its place, a structure of Task Forces was formed, each focused on a particular area of the technology (e.g., routers, end-to-end protocols, etc.). The Internet Activities Board (IAB) was formed from the chairs of the Task Forces.

By 1985, there was a tremendous growth in the more practical/engineering side of the Internet. This resulted in an explosion in the attendance at the IETF meetings. This growth was complemented by a major expansion in the community. No longer was DARPA the only major player in the funding of the Internet. In addition to NSFnet and the various U.S. and international government-funded activities, interest in the commercial sector was beginning to grow. Also in 1985, there was a significant decrease in Internet activity at DARPA. As a result, the IAB was left without a primary sponsor and increasingly assumed the mantle of leadership.

The growth continued, resulting in even further substructure within both the IAB and IETF. The IETF combined Working Groups into Areas, and designated Area Directors. An Internet Engineering Steering Group (IESG) was formed of the Area Directors. The IAB recognized the increasing importance of the IETF, and restructured the standards process to explicitly recognize the IESG as the major review body for standards. The IAB also restructured so that the rest of the Task Forces (other than the IETF) were combined into an Internet Research Task Force (IRTF), with the old task forces renamed as research groups. The growth in the commercial sector brought with it increased concern regarding the standards process itself. Starting in the early 1980s (and continuing to this day), the Internet grew beyond its primarily research roots to include both a broad user community and increased commercial activity. Increased attention was paid to making the process open and fair. This coupled with a recognized need for community support of the Internet eventually led to the formation of the Internet Society in 1991, under the auspices of the Corporation for National Research Initiatives (CNRI).

In 1992, the Internet Activities Board was reorganized and renamed the Internet Architecture Board, operating under the auspices of the Internet Society. A more "peer" relationship was defined between the new IAB and IESG, with the IETF and IESG taking a larger responsibility for the approval of standards. Ultimately, a cooperative and mutually supportive relationship was formed among the IAB, IETF, and Internet Society, with the

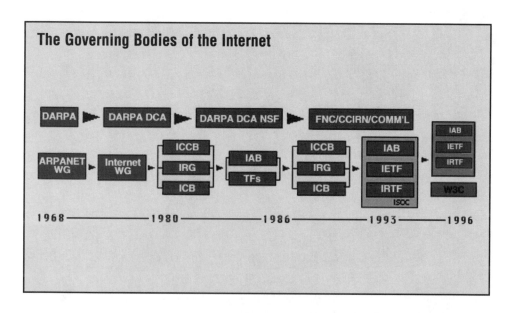

The Governing Bodies of the Internet

Internet Society taking on as a goal the provision of service and other measures that would facilitate the work of the IETF.

This community spirit has a long history beginning with the early ARPAnet. The early ARPAnet researchers worked as a close-knit community to accomplish the initial demonstrations of packet switching technology described earlier. Likewise, the Packet Satellite, Packet Radio, and several other DARPA computer science research programs were multicontractor collaborative activities that heavily used whatever available mechanisms there were to coordinate their efforts, starting with electronic mail and adding file sharing, remote access, and eventually, World Wide Web capabilities.

An Overall View of the Internet

This slide depicts the Internet backbone and shows the overall topology of a national ISP. All of the connection points (shown as cities) are places where the provider has a serial connection to another one of its sites. Located below these connection points are points-of-presence (POP), connection points for dial-in and leased-line users. Local users are connected at POPs by the connection points shown on this map and throughout the rest of the Internet.

The Internet is a connection of networks. Multiple national ISPs are interconnected through a concept of *peering*. There are points on the Internet where national ISPs connect and allow for routing tables to be shared and allow ubiquitous access to the Internet for all users.

An Overall View of the Internet

■ The following is an example of one national ISP backbone

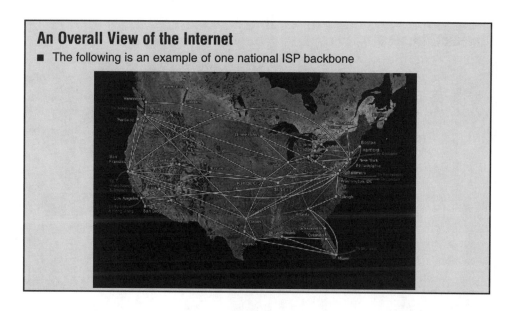

Internet Timeline

R efer to slide 18.

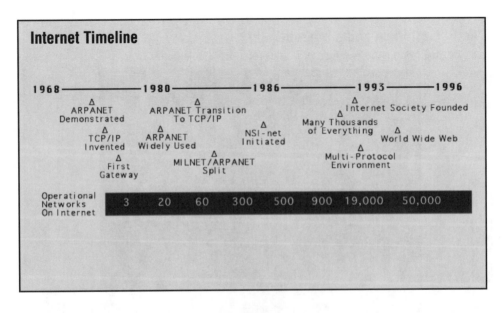

Circuit and Packet Switching

19

> ## Circuit and Packet Switching
>
> - Circuit switching provides for a prebuilt path that is reserved for the length of the call.
> - Packet switching determines a route based on information in the header of the packet. The packet is switched dynamically and multiple data packets may take the same route.
> - Packet switching is viable for all types of data, whether voice, video, or store-and-forward data.

TCP/IP allowed for open communications to exist and for the proliferation of LAN-to-LAN and LAN-to-WAN connectivity between multiple operating environments. Its topology and architecture, however, were not based on the methods employed by the phone company: circuit switching.

The phone company (AT&T, before the breakup) basically laughed at the idea of a packet switched network and publicly stated that it could never work. A network whose transmitted information can find its own way around the network? Impossible! A network in which every transmitted packet of information has the same chance for forwarding? The phone company maintained its stance that circuit switching was the only method that should be used for voice, video, or data. Circuit switching by definition provided guaranteed bandwidth and, therefore, Quality of Service. At that time, the phone company was correct, but only for voice. Voice and video cannot withstand delay beyond a small time frame (about 150 milliseconds, or 0.150 seconds), but data could! In packet switching, the path is found in real time, and each time the path should be the same, but it may not be. Still, the information will get from point A to point B.

There are many differences between circuit switching and packet switching. One is that in circuit switching, a path is prebuilt before information is sent, whereas packet switching does not predefine or prebuild a path before sending information. For example, when you make a phone call, the phone company physically builds a circuit for that call. You cannot speak (transmit information) until that circuit is built. This circuit is built via hardware. This path is a physical circuit through the telephone network system; however, the phone company is currently employing other technologies to allow for "virtual circuit switching" through technologies such as Asynchronous Transfer Mode, or ATM (beyond the scope of this book). For our comparison, a voice path is prebuilt on hardware before information is passed. No information is contained in the digitized voice signal to indicate to the switches where the destination is located. Each transmitting node has the same chance in getting its information to the receiver.

In packet switching, the information needed to get to the destination station is contained in the header of the information being sent. Stations, known as *routers*, in the network read this information and forward the information along its path. Thousands of different packets of information may take the exact same path to different destinations.

Today we are proving that not only is packet switching viable, it can be used for voice, video, and data. Newer, faster stations on the network along with faster transmission transports have been invented. Along with this are new Quality of Service protocols that allow priorities to exist on the network. This allows certain packets of information to "leapfrog" over other packets of information to become first in the transmission.

20 TCP/IP Protocol Documents

Complete details of a Request for Comments (RFC) document are contained in RFC 1543. If TCP/IP is such an open protocol, where does one find out information on the protocol and other items of interest on the Internet? RFCs define the processing functions of this protocol, and these documents are available online or may be purchased. Online, they may be found on any of the three registries: InterNIC (US), RIPE (Europe), and APNIC (Asia Pacific).

For example, point your Web browser to http://ds.internic.net/rfc/rfc-index.txt and review

TCP/IP Protocol Documents

- Review RFC 1583.
- TCP/IP technical documents are known as Request for Comments, or RFCs.
- Can be found at any of the three registries
  - APNIC (Asia), RIPE (Europe), INTERNIC (U.S.)
  - Point your browser to: ds.internic.net/RFC/rfcxxxx.txt
  - Replace the x with the RFC number
- Systems engineers should read at a minimum: RFCs 1812, 1122, and 1123.

the latest index (updated almost daily) of RFCs. My suggestion is that you save this as a file in your local computer. You will return many times to this document to find more information about a particular aspect of a protocol. Use the Find tool under the Edit pulldown menu to provide a search. Be careful: Just because you type in a word, the search engine may not find specifically what you are looking for, so you may have to know a few things before venturing forth, but for the most part, this is the best method of weeding through the RFCs.

After finding an RFC, change *rfc-index* on the URL to *rfcxxxx.txt*, where x is the RFC number, and you now have the RFC online. I suggest that you save the RFCs that you will return to the most on your local directory—they can take some time to download.

A majority of individuals are trusting the statements of a company's implementation of the TCP/IP protocols more than what is written in an RFC. The RFC is the definitive document for the TCP/IP protocol suite. I asked some systems engineers who I know two things:

- When was the last time you reviewed a question by reading an RFC?
- Have you read RFC 1812, 1122, and 1123?

The answer to the first question is generally, "I don't know" (occasionally, I got the response, "Hey Matt, get a life!"), and the answer to the second question is, "What's in those RFCs?" How any systems engineers can claim that they know the TCP/IP protocol (as always indicated on their résumés, along with knowledge of 100 other protocols and applications) without having read these three RFCs? The Web makes it so easy to review an RFC: Simply point your browser to ds.internic.net/rfc/rfcxxxx.txt, or for an index to ds.internic.net/rfc/rfc-index.txt. Get the RFC electronically, save it, and then use the search commands to find what you are looking for.

21 Why Study the RFCs?

It may seem trivial, but I have expanded this section of the book because everyone seems to be getting away from the RFCs. Also, many people are still getting into the TCP/IP protocol who may have never seen an RFC before.

The Request for Comments are papers (documents) that define the TCP/IP protocol suite. They are the Internet's technical (mostly) documents; I say "mostly" for some are intellectually humorous (e.g., "A View from the 21st Century" by Vint Cerf, RFC 1607). An RFC can be written and submitted by anyone; However, any document does not automatically become an RFC. A text document becomes a draft RFC first. At this point it is considered a public document. A peer review process is then conducted over a period of time and comments are continually made on the draft. It will then be decided whether or not it becomes an RFC.

Steve Crocker wrote the first RFC in 1969. These memos were intended to be an informal, fast way to share ideas with other network researchers. RFCs were originally printed on paper and distributed via snail mail (postal). As the File Transfer Protocol (FTP) came into use, the RFCs were prepared as online files and accessed via FTP. Existing RFCs (as of this writing) number over 2200 and contain information on any aspect of any Internet protocol.

Why Study the RFCs?

- Request for Comments technically define a protocol for the Internet and are informational, or even humorous.
- The first RFC was written by Steve Crocker.
  - Sent via "snail mail" until FTP came along
- An RFC can be submitted by anyone.
  - Does not automatically become an RFC
  - First enters as an RFC draft with no number associated
  - Must follow the instructions for authors detailed in RFC 1543

Development engineers read these documents and produce applications based on them.

For systems engineers, most of the RFCs do not need to be studied. However, for a basic understanding of the TCP/IP protocol suite, three RFCs must be read. Therefore, in the spirit of the RFC action words, "you MUST read RFCs 1122, 1123, and 1812 before being able to state that you understand the TCP/IP protocol suite." There are many RFCs, but the majority can be summed up in those three RFCs. The reading is not difficult, and many things are explained.

Submitting an RFC

Submitting an RFC

- Anyone can submit an RFC according to RFC 1543.
    - A major source for RFCs is the Internet Engineering Task Force (IETF), which now has over 75 working groups
- The primary RFC, including all diagrams, must be written in 7-bit ASCII text.
- The secondary publication may be in postscript.
    - Primarily used for clarity
- Once issued, RFCs do not change.
    - Updated by new RFCs
    - RFCs can be obsoleted but their numbers are never used again
- As TCP/IP evolves, so does the RFC.

Memos proposed to be RFCs may be submitted by anyone. One large source of memos that become RFCs comes from the Internet Engineering Task Force (IETF). The IETF working groups (WGs) evolve their working memos (known as Internet Drafts, or I-Ds) until they feel they are ready for publication. Then the memos are reviewed by the Internet Engineering Steering Group (IESG) and, if approved, are sent by the IESG to the RFC Editor. The primary RFC must be written in ASCII text. This includes all pictures, which leads to some interesting images! The RFC may be replicated as a secondary document in PostScript (this must be approved by the author and the RFC editor). This allows for an easy-to-read RFC, including pictures.

The primary RFC, however, is always written in ASCII text. Remember: Simplicity and availability for all is the overall tone of the Internet. Therefore, in order to interact in a digital world, it is mandatory that everyone have at least ASCII terminal functions either through a computer terminal or on a PC.

The format of an RFC is indicated by RFC 1543, "Instructions to Authors," and also shown in slide 22. Each RFC is assigned a number in ascending sequence (newer RFCs have higher numbers, and they are never reassigned). Once issued, RFCs do not change. Revisions may be made to the RFCs, but revisions are issued as a new RFC. But do not throw out that old RFC. Some of the newer RFCs only replace part of the older RFC such as replacing an appendix or updating a function. They may also simply add something to the older RFC. This is indicated by an "updated-by:" statement on the first page. If a new RFC completely replaces an RFC, the new RFC has "Obsolete: RFC XXXX" in the upper-left corner of the RFC. The index of RFCs, indicated by the URL given earlier, contains the information about updates.

The RFCs are continuing to evolve as the technology demands. This allows for the Internet to become the never-ending story. For example, the wide area network connection facility known as the Frame Relay specification is becoming very popular, and there are RFCs to define how to interface TCP to the frame relay protocol. RFCs also allow refinements to enhance better interoperability. As long as the technology is changing, the RFCs must be updated to allow connection to the protocol suite. IPv6 is well documented with many RFCs.

As of this writing, the IETF now has in excess of 75 working groups, each working on a different aspect of Internet engineering.

Each of these working groups has a mailing list to discuss one or more draft documents under development. When consensus is reached on a draft, a document may be distributed as an RFC.

23   RFC Updates

The RFC announcements are distributed via two mailing lists: the "IETF-Announce" list, and the "RFC-DIST" list. You don't want to be on both lists.

To join (or quit) the "IETF-Announce" list, send a message to:

IETF-Request@cnri.reston.va.us

To join (or quit) the "RFC-DIST" list, send a message to:

RFC-Request@NIC.DDN.MIL

RFC Updates

- To join or quit the IETF-Announce list, send an email to:
  - IETF-Request@cnri.reston.va.us

- To join or quit the RFC-DIST list, send an email to:
  - RFC-Request@NIC.DDN.MIL

First page. Refer to slide 24. **Network Working Group.** The traditional heading for the group that founded the RFC series. This appears on the first line on the left-hand side of the heading.

Request for Comment: nnnn. Identifies this as a request for comments and specifies the number. Indicated on the second line on the left side. The actual number is filled in at the last moment before publication by the RFC Editor.

Author Name. The author's name (first initial and last name only), indicated on the first line on the right side of the heading.

Author Organization. The author's organization (company name, college division, etc.), indicated on the second line on the right side.

Submission Date. This is the month and year of the RFC publication. Indicated on the third line on the right side.

Obsoletes/Updates. If this RFC updates or obsoletes another RFC, it is indicated in the third line on the left side of the heading.

Category. The category of this RFC, one of: Standards Track, Informational, or Experimental. This is indicated on the third (if there is no Obsoletes/Updates indication) or fourth line on the left side.

RFC Format

Running header

Network Working Group

Request for Comment <place number here>

Obsoletes/Updates: <Place RFC number here>

Category:

Author Name (first initial and last name)

Author Organization

Submission Date

Title

Status of this memo

Abstract

Table of Contents

Running Footer

Title. The title appears, centered, below the rest of the heading. If there are multiple authors, and if the multiple authors are from multiple organizations, the right-side heading may have additional lines to accommodate them.

Running headers. The running header in one line (on page 2 and all subsequent pages) has the RFC number on the left (RFC NNNN), the title centered (possibly an abbreviated title), and the date (month, year) on the right.

Running footers. The running footer in one line (on all pages) has the author's last name on the left and the page number on the right ([Page N]).

Status section. Each RFC must include on its first page the "Status of this Memo" section, which contains a paragraph describing the type of RFC.

The content of this section will be one of the three following statements:

Standards track. "This document specifies an Internet standards track protocol for the Internet community, and requests discussion and suggestions for improvements. Please refer to the current edition of the 'Internet Official Protocol Standards' (STD 1) for the standardization state and status of this protocol. Distribution of this memo is unlimited."

Experimental. "This memo defines an experimental protocol for the Internet community. This memo does not specify an Internet standard of any kind. Discussion and suggestions for improvement are requested. Distribution of this memo is unlimited."

Informational. "This memo provides information for the Internet community. This memo does not specify an Internet standard of any kind. Distribution of this memo is unlimited."

RFC Format (continued)

```
Network Working Group                                    M. Horowitz
Request for Comments: 2228                          Cygnus Solutions
Updates: 959                                                 S. Lunt
Category: Standards Track                                   Bellcore
                                                       October 1997


                        FTP Security Extensions

Status of this Memo

   This document specifies an Internet standards track protocol for the
   Internet community, and requests discussion and suggestions for
   improvements.  Please refer to the current edition of the "Internet
   Official Protocol Standards" (STD 1) for the standardization state
   and status of this protocol.  Distribution of this memo is unlimited.

Copyright Notice

   Copyright (C) The Internet Society (1997).  All Rights Reserved.

Abstract
```

Other RFC Format Requirements

Introduction section. Each RFC should have an Introduction section that (among other things) explains the motivation for the RFC and (if appropriate) the applicability of the protocol.

Discussion. The purpose of this RFC is to focus discussion on particular problems in the Internet and possible solutions. No proposed solutions in this document are intended as standards for the Internet. Rather, it is hoped that a general consensus will emerge as to the appropriate solution to such problems, leading eventually to the adoption of standards.

Interest. This RFC is being distributed to members of the Internet community in order to solicit their reactions to the proposals contained in it. While the issues discussed may not be directly relevant to the research problems of the Internet, they may be of interest to a number of researchers and implementers.

Status report. In response to the need for maintenance of current information about the status and progress of various projects in the Internet community, this RFC is issued for the benefit of community members. The information contained in this document is accurate as of the date of publication, but is subject to change. Subsequent RFCs will reflect such changes. These paragraphs need not be followed word for word, but the general intent of the RFC must be made clear.

References section. Nearly all RFCs contain citations to other documents, and these are listed in a References section near the end of the RFC. There are many styles for references, and the RFCs have one of their own.

Other RFC Format Requirements

- Introduction.
  - Each RFC should have an Introduction section that (among other things) explains the motivation for the RFC and (if appropriate) describes the applicability of the protocol described
- RFC text.
  - The body of the RFC
- Discussion.
  - The purpose of this RFC is to focus discussion on particular problems in the Internet and possible solutions
- Acknowledgments.
  - This is where the author may place individual acknowledgment of others
- References.
  - Nearly all RFCs contain citations to other documents, and these are listed in a References section near the end of the RFC. There are many styles for references, and the RFCs have one of their own.

Security considerations section. All RFCs must contain a section near the end of the document that discusses the security considerations of the protocol or procedures that are the main topic of the RFC.

Author's address section. Each RFC must have at the very end a section giving the author's address, including the name and postal address, the telephone number, a FAX number (optional), and the Internet email address.

Other RFC Format Requirements (continued)

- Security considerations.
  - All RFCs must contain a section near the end of the document that discusses the security considerations of the protocol or procedures that are the main topic of the RFC.
- Author's address.
  - Each RFC must have at the very end a section giving the author's address, including the name and postal address, the telephone number, a FAX number (optional), and the Internet email address.

Requirements in RFCs

The first RFCs led to ambiguity in the protocol; not everyone reads and interprets alike. Therefore, most RFCs have the following to indicate precisely what should be implemented and what is optional:

MUST. This word or the adjective "REQUIRED" means that the item is an absolute requirement of this specification.

MUST NOT. This phrase means the item is an absolute prohibition of this specification.

SHOULD. This word or the adjective "RECOMMENDED" means that there may exist valid reasons in particular circumstances to ignore this item, but the full implications should be understood and the case carefully weighed before choosing a different course.

SHOULD NOT. This phrase means that there may exist valid reasons in particular circumstances when the listed behavior is acceptable or even useful, but the full implications should be understood and the case carefully weighted before implementing any behavior described with this label.

MAY. This word or the adjective "OPTIONAL" means that this item is truly optional. One vendor may choose to include the item because a particular marketplace requires it or because it enhances the product. Another vendor may omit the same item.

Requirements in RFCs

- MUST—The word or adjective "REQUIRED" means that the item is an absolute requirement of this specification.
- MUST NOT—This phrase means the item is an absolute prohibition of this specification.
- SHOULD—The word or the adjective "RECOMMENDED" means that there may exist valid reason in particular circumstances to ignore this item, but the full implications should be understood and the case carefully weighed before choosing a different course.
- SHOULD NOT—This phrase means that there may exist valid reasons in particular circumstances when the listed behavior is acceptable or even useful, but the full implications should be understood and the case carefully weighed before implementing any behavior described with this label.
- MAY—This word or the adjective "OPTIONAL" means that this item is truly optional. One vendor may choose to include the item because a particular marketplace requires it or because it enhances the product, while another vendor may omit the same item.

29 TCP/IP: The Protocols (covered in this book) and the OSI Model

The best way to introduce TCP/IP is by looking at it through the ISO OSI model. I am not going to discuss the OSI model and its layer functions here. I am placing the protocol of TCP/IP into this model to show you where the protocol suite sits in this model.

Let's start with understanding the functions and protocols by studying their placement in the OSI model. This slide shows that the protocol suite of TCP/IP has its place in the OSI model. The heart of the TCP/IP network protocol is at layers 3 and 4. The applications for this protocol (file transfer, mail, and terminal emulation) run at the session through the application layer.

As you can see, this protocol runs independently of the data-link and physical layer. At these layers, the TCP/IP protocol can run on Ethernet, Token Ring, FDDI, serial lines, X.25, and so forth. It has been adapted to run over any LAN or WAN protocol. TCP/IP was first used to interconnect computer systems through synchronous lines and not high-speed local area networks. Today, it is used on any type of media. This includes serial lines (asynchronous and synchronous) and high-speed networks such as FDDI, Ethernet, Token Ring, and Asynchronous Transfer Mode (ATM).

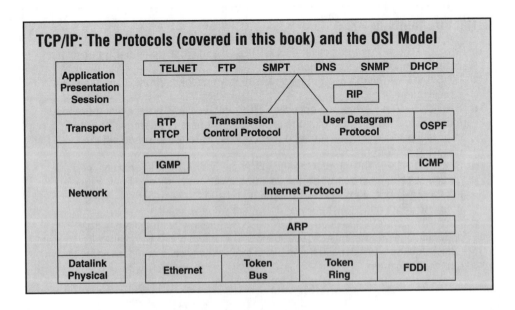

The Protocol Suite, According to This Book

1. The Internet Protocol (IPv4 and IPv6):
   RIP, RIP2, OSPF, ICMP, IGMP, RSVP, and ARP
2. The Transport Control Protocol and the User Datagram Protocol (TCP and UDP)
3. The suite of specific applications specifically developed for TCP/IP:

   TELNET

   File Transfer Protocol (FTP)

   Trivial File Transfer Protocol (TFTP)

   Domain Name Service (DNS)

   Simple Mail Transfer Program (SMTP)

   Real Time Protocol (RTP)

Real Time Control Protocol (RTCP)

Boot Protocol (BOOTP)

Dynamic Host Configuration Protocol (DHCP)

Simple Network Management Protocol (SNMP)

There are many other applications that run on a network using the TCP/IP protocol suite that are not shown here. Included in this listing are the applications that are defined in the RFCs and are usually included in every TCP/IP protocol suite that is offered. However, newer applications or protocols for TCP/IP are sometimes not included.

The Protocol Suite, According to This Book

- TCP/IP is a family of protocols.
  - Internet Protocol (IPv4 and IPv6)
    - RIPv1, RIPv2, OSPF, ICMP, IGMP, RSVP, ARP
  - Transport Control Protocol and the User Datagram Protocol
    - TCP and UDP
  - Suite of applications
    - TELNET
    - File Transfer Protocol (FTP)
    - Trivial File Transfer Protocol (TFTP)
    - Domain Name Server (DNS)
    - Simple Mail Transfer Protocol (SMTP)
    - Real Time Protocol (RTP)
    - Real Time Control Protocol (RTCP)
    - Bootstrap Protocol (BOOTP)
    - Dynamic Host Configuration Protocol (DHCP)

31   IP Overview

The Internet Protocol (IP) is situated at the network layer of the OSI model and is designed to interconnect packet switched communication networks to form an internet. It transmits blocks of data called *datagrams* received from the IP's upper-layer software to and from source and destination hosts. It provides a best effort or connectionless delivery service between the source and destination— connectionless in that it does not establish a session between the source and destination before it transmits its data. This is the layer that is also responsible for the IP protocol addressing.

In order to allow for multiple IP networks to interoperate, there must be a mechanism to provide flow between the differently addressed systems. The device that routes data between different IP addressed networks is called a *router*, which is often erroneously thought of as being the only function of the IP layer. It is not, and this is explained in more detail later. The router is basically a traffic cop. You tell the traffic cop where you want to go and he points you in the right direction. Routers contain ports that are physical connections to networks. Each of these ports must be assigned a local address. With more than one router, each router must know the others' configured information. We could configure all the IP addresses and their associated ports on a router statically, but this is a very time-consuming and nonefficient method. Therefore, we have protocols that distribute the IP address information to each router. These are called *routing*

IP Overview

- IP is designed to interconnect packet switched communication networks to form an internet.
- It transmits blocks of data known as datagrams received from IP's upper-layer software to and from hosts.
- IP provides best-effort or connectionless delivery service.
- IP is responsible for addressing.
- Two versions of IP: version 4 and version 6.
- Network information is distributed via routing protocols.

---

protocols. The two main types for IP networks are RIP (Routing Information Protocol, version 1 or 2) and OSPF (Open Shortest Path First). Both are known as Interior Gateway Protocols (IGPs), protocols that run within a single autonomous systems. An autonomous system is a collection of networks and routers that is under one administrative domain. For example, if you work for the Timbuktu Company and you have seven regional offices in the United States, all communication between those offices is accomplished via routers all running RIP. You have one domain known as Timbuktu.com; therefore, all the networks and routers and computer equipment is under one administrative domain. Connection to the outside world via the

Internet (which is another domain) allows communication with another company that is under another administrative domain.

You should be aware there are two version of IP: IPv4 (version 4, the current IP) and IPv6 (version 6, the experimental IP). IPv4 continues to operate admirably, but has become strained with "patches" to make it continue to work. The latest is the address scheme and IPv6 was partially motivated by the inability to scale and the exhaustion of IP Class B addresses. IPv6 is a natural evolution of IP and extends the address space to 128 bits and cleans up a lot of unused functions.

IGPs, EGPs, and Routing Protocols 32

IGPs, EGPs, and Routing Protocols

- There is a difference between a routing protocol and a routable protocol.
  - A routing protocol is one that is used to propagate route path information on a network
  - A routable protocol is one that has the ability to be routed as opposed to a nonroutable protocol such as NetBIOS
- IGPs are used as routing protocols within an AS.
- EGPs are used as routing protocols between ASs.

There are two classifications of propagating information: Interior Gateway Protocols (IGP) and Exterior Gateway Protocols (EGP). An IGP is a routing protocol that propagates information inside one autonomous system. An EGP is a routing protocol that propagates information between autonomous systems.

In order for data to be moved across an internet, information on the location of the networks must be propagated throughout the network. This is the introduction to the difference between a routing protocol and a routable protocol. IP is a *routable* protocol. Propagating information throughout the network as to the location of the networks is known as a *routing* protocol. Don't confuse the two.

I know that I keep using the term *autonomous system* (AS). Yes, it is defined as a network that is under a single administrative control, but let's define that a little—and yes, it does get a little blurry. Before the plethora of ISPs, anyone connected to the Internet was assigned an address and used a special protocol (then known as EGP) to connect to the Internet. Therefore, that connection became known as an *autonomous system*, and routes for that network were known on the Internet using EGP (yes, the acronym for the protocol is the same one used for the definition of the protocol). Autonomous systems were simply entities connected to the Internet. They were given a special AS number, and EGP knew how to route this data. An AS could mean a four-user office with a single Internet connection, a network as large as the one used by General Motors, or an Internet Service Provider (ISP). So don't get confused by the term *autonomous system.*

Today, ISPs rule the connection to the Internet and an AS is more blurry. The new protocol that controls routes on the Internet is known as Border Gateway Protocol (BGP), and it is an EGP (as opposed to an IGP). However, only certain ISPs need this protocol; all others are simply connections (hierarchical) off of their upstream ISP. So AS takes on a new meaning. For our purposes, yes, it still means a single customer network, but for the Internet, it is generally the upper-end ISP. Many IP networks are simply running as part of their ISP AS.

Introduction to Routing Protocols (RIP)

Introduction to Routing Protocols (RIP)

- Rooted in the early days of the ARPAnet.
  - Historically tied to the Xerox XNS network operating system
- IP is a routable protocol, it needs a routing protocol to route between subnets.
- It is known as a distance vector protocol.
- It builds a table of known networks, which is distributed to other routers.
- A hop is one router traversed.

There are a few protocols that handle for a single autonomous system. RIP is the easier of the two (RIP or OSPF) and came from the Xerox Network System (XNS) protocol. The origins of RIP are based in the origins of the Internet, but historically it came from Xerox and its XNS protocol. RIP was freely distributed in the Unix operating system and, because of its simplicity, gained widespread acceptance. Unfortunately, there are many deficiencies associated with this protocol, and there have been many "patches" applied to it to make it work more reliably in large networks. For smaller networks, the protocol works just fine.

Since, IP is a *routable protocol*, it needs a *routing protocol* to enable it to route between networks. RIP is known as a *distance vector* protocol. Its database (the routing table) contains two fields needed for routing: a vector (a known IP address) and the distance (how many routers away) to the destination. Actually, the table contains more fields than that, but we will discuss that later.

RIP simply builds a table in memory that contains all the routes that it knows about and the distance to that network. When the protocol initializes, it simply places the IP addresses of its local interfaces into the table. It associates a cost with those interfaces and that cost is usually set to 1 (explained in a moment). The router will then solicit (or it may wait for information to be supplied to it) information from other routers on its locally attached subnets. Eventually, as other routers report (send their tables) to other routers, each router will have the information needed about all routes on its subnets or internetwork.

Any IP datagrams that must traverse a router in the path to its destination is said to have traversed one hop for each router traversed. Therefore, when a router receives a packet and examines the destination address in the datagram, it will then perform a table lookup based on that destination address. The router will also find the port associated with this destination address in the database and will forward the datagram out of that port and onward to the final destination. In RIP, all routers compute their tables and then give each other their tables (just the IP network address and the cost). Routers that receive this table will add the cost assigned to the incoming interface (received port) to each of the entries in the table. The router then decides whether to keep any of the information in the received table. This information is then passed to other routers.

34 Introduction to Routing Protocols (OSPF)

OSPF is also routing protocol, but it does not compare to RIP with the exception that it, too, is an IGP. Of course, let's be fair. In the beginning, when the Internet was created, the processors that we had were nowhere near the power of what we have today. In fact, a Honeywell 516 minicomputer was used as the first router (then called an Internet Message Processor, or IMP). The only micro-CPU in those days was the Z80 from Zilog. RIP worked great on the routers that we had at that time. It had very low overhead (computationally speaking). OSPF is a great protocol, but at the time of RIP, there was no machine that could run it economically.

Today, with the faster processors and plentiful memory, OSPF is the routing protocol of choice (for open routing protocols, that is). It is very efficient when it comes to the network, although it is a complicated protocol and is very CPU intensive when it builds its routing table.

OSPF is an IGP protocol. It exchanges routing information within a single autonomous system (described as those networks and

Introduction to Routing Protocols (OSPF)

- OSPF is an IGP routing protocol.
- Operates differently than RIP.
- Used on small, medium, and large networks.
  - Most beneficial on large, complex networks
- It is a link-state protocol.
  - It maintains the knowledge of all links (interfaces) in the AS
- The link information is flooded to all other routers in the AS (or area).
  - All routers receive the same link information
- All routers compute their own tables based on the link information.

algorithm runs and produces a shortest-path tree based on the metrics, using itself as the root of the tree. The information this produces is used to build the routing table.

routers grouped into a single domain under one authority). It can be used in small, medium, or large internetworks, but the most dramatic effects will be readily noticed on large IP networks. As opposed to RIP (a distance vector protocol), OSPF is a link-state protocol. It maintains the state of every link in the domain, and information is *flooded* to all routers in the domain. Flooding is the process of receiving the information on one port and transmitting it to all other active ports on the router. In this way, all routers receive the same information. This information is stored in a database called the *link-state* database, which is identical on very router in the AS (or every area if the domain is split into multiple areas). Based on information in the link-state database, an algorithm known as the Dykstra

35 Other IP-Related Protocols

The Internet Control Message Protocol (ICMP) is an extension of the IP layer. This is the reason that it uses an IP header and not a UDP (User Datagram Protocol) header. The purpose of ICMP is to report or test certain conditions on the network. IP delivers data and has no other form of communication. ICMP provides some error reporting mechanism for IP. Basically, it allows internet devices (hosts or routers) to transmit error or test messages. These error messages may be that a network destination cannot be reached or they may generate/reply to an echo request packet (PING, explained later).

The Internet Group Management Protocol (IGMP) is an extension of the IP protocol that allows for multicasting to exist for IP. The multicast address already existed for IP but there was not a control protocol to allow it to exist on a network. IGMP is a protocol that operates in workstations and routers and allows the routers to determine which multicast addresses exist on their segments. With this knowledge, routers can build multicast trees allowing multicast data to be received and propagated to their multicast workstations. IGMP headers are used as the basis for all multicast routing protocols for IPv4.

RSVP is called the *resource reservation protocol* and allows some semblance of Quality of Service (QoS) to exist using IP. It used to be we could increase the speed of a network to allow more bandwidth on which to fit hungry applications. With that capability, QoS was essentially ignored. However, bandwidth can-

---

Other IP-Related Protocols

- ICMP is an extension of the IP protocol.
  - IP is connectionless
  - Possible to have errors but they are not reported by IP
  - ICMP allows for internet devices to transmit error or test messages
- IGMP is also an extension of the IP protocol.
  - Allows for multicast to operate on an internetwork
  - Allows hosts to identify the groups they want to the router
- RSVP is an entrance to providing QoS on an IP internet.
  - Allows devices to reserve resources on the network
- ARP provides the ability to translate between 48-bit physical-layer addresses and 32-bit IP addresses.

---

not continually expand. The Internet was not provisioned for Quality of Service, and RSVP is the first attempt to allow for it. Its benefits are apparent in multicasting applications, but it can be used with unicast applications as well. It allows stations on the network to reserve resources via the routers on the network.

ARP is not really part of the network layer; it resides between the IP and data-link layers. It is the protocol that translates between the 32-bit IP address and a 48-bit Local Area Network address. ARP is only used with IPv4; IPv6 has no concept of ARP. Since IP was not intended to run over a LAN, an address scheme was implemented to allow each host and network on the internet to identify itself. When TCP/IP was adapted to run over the LAN, the IP address had to be mapped to the 48-bit datalink or physical address that LANs use, and ARP is the protocol that accomplishes it.

Introduction to Transport Layer Protocols   36

Introduction to Transport Layer Protocols

- TCP provides for reliable data transfer using sequence numbers and acknowledgments.
- UDP provides a simple connectionless transport layer to allow applications access to the IP.
- RTP and RTCP are framework protocols that are usually incorporated into an application.
    - It is placed at the transport layer software to work alongside TCP

Since IP provides for a connectionless delivery service of TCP (Transmission Control Protocol) data, TCP provides application programs access to the network, using a reliable connection-oriented transport-layer service. This protocol is responsible for establishing sessions between user processes on the internet, and also ensures reliable communications between two or more processes. The functions that it provides are to:

1. Listen for incoming session establishment requests

2. Request a session to another network station
3. Send and receive data reliably using sequence numbers and acknowledgments
4. Gracefully close a session

The User Datagram Protocol (UDP) provides application programs access to the network using an unreliable connectionless transport-layer service. It allows the transfer of data between source and destination stations without having to establish a session before data is transferred. This protocol also does not use the end-to-end error checking and correction that TCP uses. With UDP, transport-layer functionality is there, but the overhead is low. It is primarily used for those applications that do not require the robustness of the TCP protocol; for example, mail, broadcast messages, naming service, and network management.

The Real Time Protocol (RTP) and the Real Time Control Protocol (RTCP) allow for real-time applications to truly exist on an IP network. RTP resides at the transport layer and works alongside the TCP protocol, and is a replacement for the TCP protocol for real-time applications. RTCP is the protocol that provides feedback to the RTP application and lets the application know how things are going on the network. The protocols are actually frameworks more than protocols and are usually included in the application itself rather than residing as a separate protocol that has an interface.

Data is not the only information that is being passed around on the Internet. Multimedia applications such as voice and video are moving from experimental status to emerging. However, voice and video cannot simply be placed on a connectionless, packet switched network. They need some help, and RTP, along with RTCP, provides this help. This in conjunction with RSVP is paving the way for real-time applications on the Internet.

Introduction to the TCP/IP Standard Applications 37

Introduction to the TCP/IP Standard Applications

- TELNET—Provides remote terminal emulation.
- FTP—Provides a file transfer protocol.
- TFTP—Provides for a simple file transfer protocol.
- SMTP—Provides a mail service.
- DNS—Provides for a name service.
- BOOTP/DHCP—Provides for management of IP parameters.

Remote terminal emulation is provided through the TELNET protocol. For new users of the TCP/IP protocol, this is not Telenet, a packet switching technology using the CCITT standard X.25. It is pronounced TELNET. This is an application-level protocol that allows terminal emulation to pass through a network to a remote network station. TELNET runs on top of the TCP protocol and allows a network workstation to appear as a local device to a remote device (i.e., a host).

The File Transfer Protocol (FTP) is similar to TELNET in terms of control, but this protocol allows for data files to be reliably transferred on the Internet. FTP resides on top of TCP and uses it as its transport mechanism. TFTP is a simplex file transfer protocol (based

on an unreliable transport layer called UDP), and is primarily used for boot loading of configuration files across an internet.

The Simple Mail Transport Protocol (SMTP) is an electronic mail system that is robust enough to run on the entire Internet system. This protocol allows for the exchange of electronic mail between two or more systems on an internet. Along with a system known as Post Office Protocol, individual users can retrieve their mail from centralized mail repositories.

The Domain Name Service (DNS) is a centralized name service that allows users to establish connections to network stations using human-readable names instead of cryptic network addresses. It provides a name-to-network address translation service. There are many other functions of DNS, including mail server name to IP address translation. Mail service would not exist if not for the DNS.

The Boot Protocol (BOOTP) and Dynamic Host Configuration Protocol (DHCP) allow for management of IP parameters on a network. These protocols do not provide for router configurations but endstation configurations. BOOTP was the original protocol that provided not only a workstation's IP address but possibly its operating image as well. DHCP is best known for its management allocation scheme of IP addresses and is a superset of BOOTP that provides extended functions of IP as well as IP address management.

38 The Internet Protocol (IP)

Now that the introductions are over, let's get into the technical details of the TCP/IP protocol suite. The main goal of IP is to provide interconnection of subnetworks (the interconnection of networks, explained later) to form an internet in order to pass data. The IP protocol provides four main functions:

1. basic unit for data transfer,
2. addressing,
3. routing, and
4. fragmentation of datagrams.

The Internet Protocol (IP)

- IP's main function is to provide for the interconnection of subnetworks to form an internet in order to pass data.
- The functions provided by IP are:
  - Basic unit for data transfer
  - Addressing
  - Routing
  - Fragmentation of datagrams

---

39 Connectionless, Best-Effort Delivery Service

The IP layer provides the entry into the delivery system used to transport data across the Internet. Usually, when anyone hears the name IP, he or she automatically thinks of the networks connected together through devices commonly known as *routers*, which connect multiple subnetworks together. It is true the IP performs these tasks, but the IP protocol performs many other tasks, as mentioned previously. The IP protocol runs in all the participating network stations that are attached to subnetworks so that they may

---

Connectionless, Best-Effort Delivery Service

- Implements two functions: addressing and fragmentation.
- IP encapsulates data handed to it from its upper-layer software with its headers.
- IP delivers data based on a best effort.
  - Transmits an encapsulated packet and does not expect a response
- IP receives data handed to it by the datalink.
  - Decapsulates a packet (strips its headers off) and hands the data to its upper-layer software

---

submit their packets to routers or directly to other devices on the same network. It resides between the datalink layer and the transport layer. IP also provides for connectionless data delivery between nodes on an IP network.

The primary goal of IP is to provide the basic algorithm for transfer of data to and from a network. In order to achieve this, it implements two functions: *addressing* and *fragmentation*. It provides a connectionless delivery service for the upper-layer protocols. This means that IP does not set up a session (a virtual link) between the transmitting station and the receiving station prior to submitting the data to the receiving station. It encapsulates the data handed to it and delivers it on a *best-effort* basis. IP does not inform the sender or receiver of the status of the packet; it merely attempts to deliver the packet and will not make up for the faults encountered in this attempt. This means that if the datalink fails or incurs a recoverable error, the IP layer will not inform anyone. It tried to deliver (addressed) a message and failed. It is up to the

upper-layer protocols (TCP, or even the application itself) to perform error recovery. For example, if your application is using TCP as its transport layer protocol, TCP will time-out for that transmission and will resend the data. If the application is using UDP as its transport, then it is up to the application to perform error recovery procedures.

IP submits a properly formatted data packet to the destination station and does not expect a status response. Because IP is a connectionless protocol, IP may receive and deliver the data (data sent to the transport layer in the receiving station) in the wrong order from which it was sent, or it may duplicate the data. Again, it is up to the higher-layer protocols (layer 4 and above) to provide error recovery procedures. IP is part of the network delivery system. It accepts data and formats it for transmission to the datalink layer. (Remember, the datalink layer provides the access methods to transmit and receive data from the attached cable plant.) IP also retrieves data from the datalink and presents it to the requesting upper layer.

40   Data Encapsulation by Layer

IP will add its control information (in the form of headers), specific to the IP layer only, to the data received by the upper layer (transport layer). Once this is accomplished, it will inform the datalink (layer 2) that it has a message to send to the network. At the network layer, encapsulated data is known as a *datagram* (rumor has it that this term was coined referring to a similar message delivery system known as the telegram). This datagram may be transferred over high-speed networks (Ethernet, Token Ring, FDDI). When the datalink layer adds its headers and trailers it is called a *packet* (a term referring to a small package). When transmitted onto the cable, the physical layer *frames* (basically with signaling information such as the preamble for Ethernet or the flag field for Frame Relay and X.25) the information it has received from the

datalink layer; therefore, it is called a *frame*. For most of us, the terms *frame* and *packet* are interchangeable. If you want to get into an argument about those terms you need to go find the people who are still arguing about baud and bits per second (bps). For simplicity, considering that the primary focus of the book is network protocols over high-speed networks, packets and frames will be synonymous. Frames will not be mentioned unless the original specification mandated that term. It is important to remember that IP presents datagrams to its lower layer (the datalink layer). When I talk about a datagram, I am specifically talking about the IP layer. When I talk about a packet, I am specifically talking about the access layer (data link and physical).

The IP protocol does not care what kind of data is in the datagram. All it knows is that it

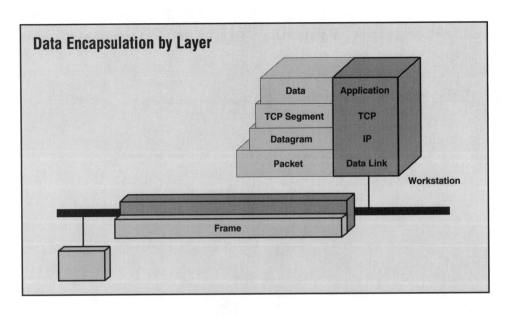

must apply some control information, called an IP header, to the data received from the upper-layer protocol (presumably TCP or UDP) and try to deliver it to some station on the network or internet.

The IP protocol is not completely without merit. It does provide mechanisms on how hosts and routers should process transmitted or received datagrams, or when an error should be generated, and when an IP datagram may be discarded. To understand the IP functionality, a brief look at the control information it adds (the IP header) to the packet will be shown.

IPv4 Header

41

There are many header fields in the IP header, each with a defined function to be determined by the receiving station. The IP header is shown here, encapsulated in an Ethernet packet.

The first field is the VERS, or version, field. This defines the current version of IP implemented by the network station. Version 4 is the latest version. The other versions out there are in experimental stages, or the experiments are finished and the protocol did not make it or was used to test version 6. There are three versions of IP that are running today: 4, 5, and 6. Most do not believe that version 5 is out there but it is; it is known as the Streams 2 protocol. The following information was taken from RFC 1700.

Assigned Internet Version Numbers

Decimal	Keyword	Version	References
0	Reserved		
1–3	Unassigned		
4	IP	Internet Protocol	RFC791
5	ST	ST Datagram Mode	
6	IPv6	RFC 1883	
7	TP/IX	TP/IX: The Next Internet	
8	PIP	The P Internet Protocol	
9	TUBA	TUBA	
10–14	Unassigned		
15	Reserved		

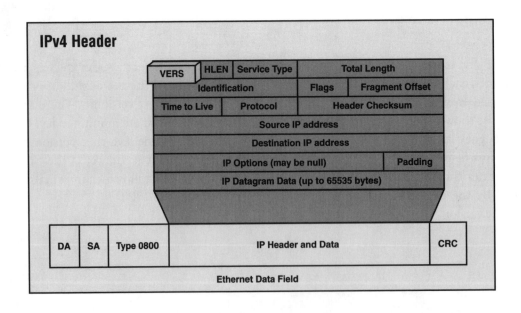

Header Length, Service Type, and Total Length Fields

The length of the IP header (all fields except for the IP data field) can vary. Not all the fields in the IP header need to be used. Fields are measured in the amount of 32-bit words. The shortest IP header will be 20 bytes; therefore, this field would contain a 5 (20 bytes = 160 bits; 160 bits/32 bits = 5). This field is necessary, for the header can be variable in length depending on the field called *options*. IPv6 has a static-length header field.

The service field was a great idea, but it is rarely used and is usually set to 0. This was a entry that would allow applications to indicate the type of routing path they would like (the key point here is that the application chooses this field). For example, a real-time protocol would choose low delay, high throughput, and high reliability—a file transfer does not need this. A TELNET session could choose low delay with normal throughput and reliability. There is another side to this story, however. The router must support this feature as well and this usually means building and maintaining multiple routing tables. The Service type is made up of the following fields: precedence, delay, throughput, and reliability. However, supporting this field caused the router to support multiple routing tables per router, and this complication never progressed with the router vendors. This precedence bits of the service field may have an entry of zero (normal precedence) and up to 7 (network control), which allows the transmitting station's application to indicate to the IP layer the priority of sending the datagram. This is combined with the D (delay), T (throughput), and R (reliability) bits. This field is known as a Type of Service (TOS)

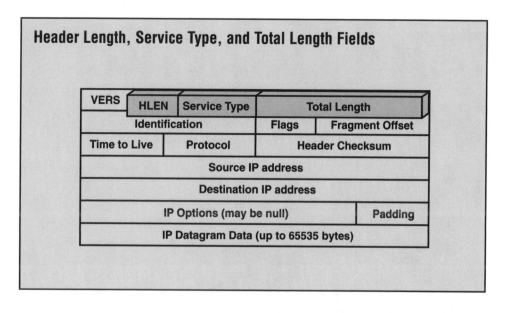

Header Length, Service Type, and Total Length Fields

VERS	HLEN	Service Type	Total Length	
Identification			Flags	Fragment Offset
Time to Live		Protocol	Header Checksum	
Source IP address				
Destination IP address				
IP Options (may be null)			Padding	
IP Datagram Data (up to 65535 bytes)				

identifier, and these bits indicate to a router which route to take:

D bit. Request low delay when set to 1

T bit. Request high throughput when set to 1

R bit. Request high reliability when set to 1

For example, if there is more than one route to a destination, the router could read this field to pick a route. This becomes important in the OSPF routing protocol, which is the first IP routing protocol to take advantage of this. If the transaction is a file transfer, you may want to set the bits to 0 0 1 to indicate that you do not need low delay or high throughput, but you would like high reliability. TOS fields are set by applications (i.e., TELNET or FTP) and not routers. Routers only read this field, they do not set this field. Based on the information read, routers will select the optimal path for the datagram. It is up to the TCP/IP application running on a host to set these bits before transmitting the packet on the network. It does require a router to maintain multiple routing tables—one for each type of service.

The total length is the length of the datagram (not packet) measured in bytes (this field allots for 16 bits, meaning the data area of the IP datagram may be 65535 bytes in length). IPv6 allows for a concept known as *jumbo datagrams*. Remember, TCP may not always run over Ethernet, Token Ring, and so on. It may run as a channel attached to a Cray supercomputer that supports much larger data sizes.

Fragmentation

- Different media allows for different-sized datagrams to be transmitted and received.
- Fragmentation allows a datagram that is too large to be forwarded to the next LAN segment to be broken up into smaller segments to be reassembled at the destination.
- The fragmentation occurs at the router that cannot forward it to the next interface.
- Applications should use path MTU discovery to find the smallest datagram size.
  - Do not depend on the router

A great idea, but basically discouraged, is the capability of fragmentation. There may be times when a packet transmitted from one network may be too large to transmit on another network. The default datagram size (the data and IP headers but not the Ethernet packet headers of the physical frame headers or trailers), known as the path MTU, or Maximum Transmission Unit, is defined as the size of the largest packet that can be transmitted or received through a logical interface. This size includes the IP header but does not include the size of any Link Layer headers or framing (Reference RFC 1812). It defaults to 576 bytes when the datagram is to be sent remotely (off the local subnet). Many IP datagrams are transmitted at 576 bytes, a recommended standard size, instead of queuing the max MTU size.

But why cripple networks that support large packets? If a TCP connection path is from FDDI to Token Ring, why should the default datagram size be only 576 bytes when these media types support much larger packet sizes? The answer is, it shouldn't, but we cannot guarantee that any intermediate media types between the Token Ring and the FDDI support those large sizes. For example, suppose the source is a Token Ring station and the destination is an FDDI station. In between the two stations are two Ethernet networks that support only 1518-byte packets. There are no tables in the routers or workstations that indicate media MTU (maximum transmission unit). There is a protocol (path MTU discovery, RFC 1981 for IPv6 and 1191 for IPv4) that allows for this, but under IPv4 it is optional whether the router and workstations implement it. Therefore, to be safe, instead of implementing RFC 1191, a transmitting station will send a 576-byte datagram or smaller when it knows the destination is not local.

Another example is when a host is initialized on an Ethernet, it can send a request for a host server to boot it. Let's say the bootstrap host is on an FDDI network. The host sends back a 4472-byte message, and this is received by the bridge. Normally, the bridge will discard the packet because bridges do not have the capability of fragmenting an IP datagram. Therefore, some bridge vendors have placed the IP fragmentation algorithm in their bridges to allow for something like this to occur. This is a great example of how proprietary (albeit based on an standard) implementation of certain protocols can benefit the consumer.

Although a router will fragment a datagram, it will not reassemble it. It is up to the receiving host to reassemble the datagram. Why? Well, considering the implication of

CPU and memory required to reassemble every datagram that was fragmented, this would be an overwhelming feature of the router. If there were 2000 stations communicating all using fragmentation, it could easily overwhelm a router, especially in the early days.

44 Fragmentation (continued)

A fragmented IP datagram contains the following fields:

Identification. Indicates which datagram fragments belong together so datagrams do not get mismatched. The receiving IP layer uses this field and the source IP address to identify which fragments belong together.

Flags. Indicate whether more fragments are to arrive or no more data is to be sent for that datagram (no more fragments).

Whether or not to fragment a datagram (a don't-fragment bit). If a router receives a

packet that it must fragment to be forwarded and the don't-fragment bit is set, then it will discard the packet and send an error message (through a protocol known as ICMP, discussed later) to the source station.

Offset. Each IP header from each of the fragmented datagrams is almost identical. This field indicates the offset (in bytes) from the previous datagram that continues the complete datagram. In other words, if the first fragment has 512 bytes, this offset would indicate that this datagram starts the

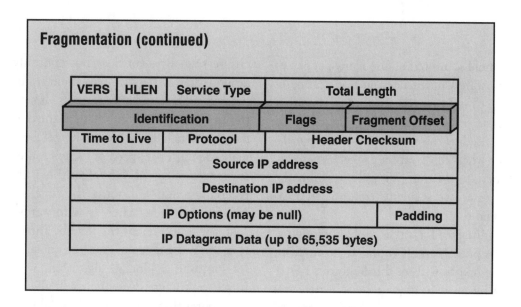

513th byte of the fragmented datagram. It is used by the receiver to put the fragmented datagram back together.

Using, the total length and the fragment offset fields, IP can reconstruct a fragmented datagram and deliver it to the upper-layer software. The total length field indicates the total length of the original packet, and the offset field indicates to the node that is reassembling the packet the offset from the beginning of the packet. It is at this point that the data will be placed in the data segment to reconstruct the packet.

45 Time to Live (TTL)

This field seems to confuse many people, so let's state what it does up front. Time to Live (TTL) indicates the amount of time that a datagram is allowed to stay on the network. It is not used by the routers to count up to 16 to know when to discard a packet. There are two functions for the TTL field: to limit the lifetime of a TCP segment (transmitted data) and to end routing loops.

The initial TTL entry is set by the originator of the packet, and it varies. To be efficient, a routing update will set this field to a 1 (RIP will). Why set it to anything else, when that update is sent only to its local segments? Multicast protocols set it to many different sizes to limit the scope of the multicast. For normal usage, many applications set it to 32 or 64 (2 and 4 times the size of a RIP network). Time to live is a field that is used by routers to ensure that a packet does not endlessly loop around the network. This field (currently defined as the number of seconds) is set at the transmitting station and then, as the datagram passes through each router, it will be decremented. With the speed of today's routers, the usual decrement is 1. One algorithm is that the receiving router will notice the time a packet arrives, and then, when it is forwarded, the router will decrement the field by the number of seconds the datagram sat in a queue waiting for forwarding. Not all algorithms work this way. A minimum decrement will always be 1. The router that decrements this field to 0 will discard the packet and inform the originator of the datagram (through the ICMP protocol) that the TTL field expired and the datagram did not make it to its destination.

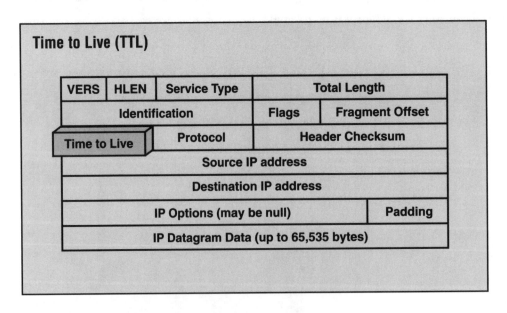

Time to Live (TTL)

VERS	HLEN	Service Type	Total Length	
Identification			Flags	Fragment Offset
Time to Live		Protocol	Header Checksum	
Source IP address				
Destination IP address				
IP Options (may be null)				Padding
IP Datagram Data (up to 65,535 bytes)				

The time-to-live field may also be set to a certain time (i.e., initialized to a low number like 64) to ensure that a packet stays on the network for only a set time. Some routers allow the network administrator to set a manual entry to decrement. This field may contain any number from 0 to 255 (an 8-bit field).

Protocol and Checksum Fields 46

What IP asks here is, who above me wants this data? The protocol field is used to indicate which higher-level protocol should receive the data of the datagram (i.e., TCP, UDP, OSPF, or possibly other protocol). This field allows for multiplexing. There are many protocols that may reside on top of IP. Currently, the most common transport implementations are TCP and UDP. If the protocol field is set to a number that identifies TCP, the data will be handed to the TCP process for further processing. The same is true if the frame is set to UDP or any other upper-layer protocol. This field becomes very apparent to anyone who troubleshoots networks. Simply stated, it allows for IP to deliver the data (after it strips off and processes its fields) to the next intended protocol.

The second field is a Cyclic Redundancy Check (CRC) of 16 bits. How this number is arrived at is beyond the scope of this book, but the idea behind it is to ensure the integrity of the header. A CRC number is generated from the data in the IP data field and placed into

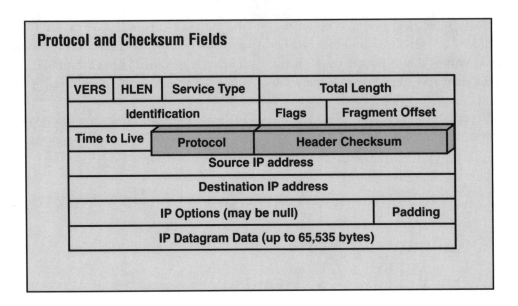

this field by the transmitting station. When the receiving station reads the data, it will compute a CRC number. If the two CRC numbers do not match, there is an error in the header and the packet will be discarded. Stretching it, you may think of this as a fancy parity check. As the datagram is received by each router, each router will recompute the checksum. Why change it? Because the TTL field is changed by each router the datagram traverses.

This field is found on IPv4 packet headers. It contains information on source routing (nothing to do with Token Ring), tracing a route, timestamping the packet as it traverses routers, and security entries. These fields may or may not be in the header (which allows for the variable length header). It was found that most of these features were not used or were better implemented in other protocols, so IPv6 does not implement them as a function of the IP header.

Source routing is the ability of the originating station to place route information into the datagram to be interpreted by routers. Router will forward the datagram based on information in the source route fields, and in some cases, it will be blind. The originator indicates the path it wishes to take, and the routers must

obey, even if there is a better route. There are two types: loose source route (LSR) and strict source route (SSR).

The difference between the two is relatively simple. Routes (IP addresses) are placed in a field of the IP header. The IP addresses indicate the route the datagram would like to take to the destination. Loose source route allows a router to forward the datagram to any router it feels is correct to service the next route indicated in the source route field. A complete list of IP addresses from the source to the destination is probably not in the IP header, but some points in the Internet should be used to forward the datagram. For example, IP multicast uses LSR for tunneling its IP multicast datagrams over the nonmulticast-enabled IPv4 Internet. Strict source routing forces a router

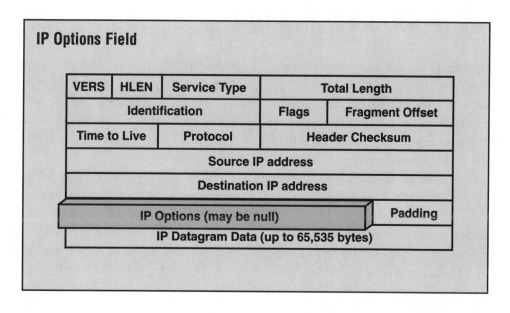

IP Options Field

VERS	HLEN	Service Type	Total Length	
Identification			Flags	Fragment Offset
Time to Live		Protocol	Header Checksum	
Source IP address				
Destination IP address				
IP Options (may be null)			Padding	
IP Datagram Data (up to 65,535 bytes)				

to forward a datagram to its destination completely based on the routes indicated by the source route field.

The Traceroute is a very useful utility. It allows the echoing of the forwarding path of a datagram. With this option set, the points to which the datagram is routed are echoed back to the sender. This allows you to follow a data-gram along a path. It is very often used in troubleshooting IP networks. If you have Windows 95, you have this utility. Type in (DOS prompt) "tracert <IP address>" and watch the echo points on your screen.

IPv6 eliminated this field and those functions that were not used or were better implemented by other protocols.

48 Source and Destination Address Fields

The next fields are the source and destination address fields. These fields are very important for they identify the individual IP network and station on any IP network. These are particularly important, for users will be most aware of this when starting their workstation or trying to access other stations without the use of a domain name server or an up-to-date host file. These fields indicate the *originator* of the datagram, the *final* destination IP address that the packet should be delivered to, and the IP address of the station that originally transmitted the packet. All hosts on an IP internet will be identified by these addresses. IP addressing is extremely important and a full discussion follows. Currently, these addresses are set to 32 bits, which allows for over 4 billion addresses.

This may sound like a lot of addresses but unfortunately, many mistakes were made in assigning IP addresses to corporations and individuals. The mistakes were made unknowingly, for this protocol suite took off by surprise. This is fully discussed at the end of this

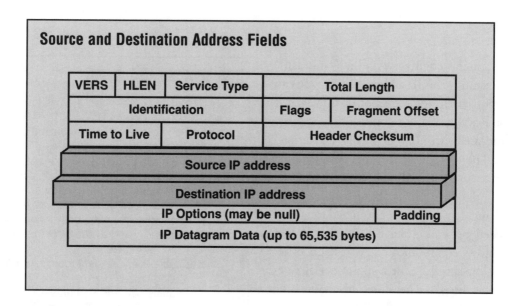

Source and Destination Address Fields

VERS	HLEN	Service Type	Total Length	
Identification			Flags	Fragment Offset
Time to Live		Protocol	Header Checksum	
Source IP address				
Destination IP address				
IP Options (may be null)			Padding	
IP Datagram Data (up to 65,535 bytes)				

section. There are two types of addresses: class-less and classful. Both types will be presented.

IPv6, the next version of IP (currently being implemented as autonomous islands in the sea of IPv4), allows for 128 bits of address, which basically allows for thousands of billions of hosts to be numbered. Also, with IPv6, an efficient allocation scheme was developed to hand out IPv6 addresses as well.

49   The IP Address Scheme

Every systems engineer who understands IP, understands the IP address scheme. It can be the most confusing aspect of IP, however, it must be learned. Do not confuse this addressing structure with that of media (Ethernet) address. The ideas and concepts that evolved the protocol of TCP/IP were devised separate from any datalink protocols of Ethernet and Token Ring. Hosts were not attached to a local high-speed network (like Ethernet or Token Ring). Hosts communicated with each other through low-speed, point-to-point serial lines (telephone lines). Therefore, an addressing scheme to identify TCP/IP hosts and where they were located was implemented. The addressing scheme used to identify these hosts is called the 32-bit IP address. This is also known as a protocol address.

There are two types of network addressing schemes used with IP:

Classless. The full address range can be used without regard to bit reservation for classes. This type of addressing scheme is primarily not used in direct host assignment. The scheme is directly applied to the routing tables of the Internet and ISPs.

Classful. The original (RFC 791) segmentation of the 32-bit address into specific classes denoting networks and hosts.

The fun part is that the range of addresses (32 bits for IPv4) available are used for both classless and classful addressing. Most of us will never have to worry about the classless range of IP addressing, for it is used on the Internet

---

The IP Address Scheme

- Two types of addressing schemes for IPv4:
    - Classful (based on RFC 791)—The original style of addressing based on the first few bits of the address
        - Generally used in customer sites
    - Classless—The new style of addressing that disregards the Class bits of an address and applies a variable 32 prefix (mask) to determine the network number
    - Generally used by the global routing tables and ISPs
    - Enables very efficient routing, smaller routing tables
    - Enables efficient IP address allocation (to the ISPs) and assignment (to the ISP customer)

---

itself and not on customer networks. It provides an easy method with which to reduce the routing tables and allow large address ranges to be provided to the ISPs. The first part of this section will deal with classful, since it started first and is continuing to be used on many networks. It is confusing, but keep reading.

The second part of this section will deal with classless addressing and the concepts of CIDR (Classless InterDomain Routing), Variable Length Subnet Masks (VLSM), and supernetting.

Classful Addressing—The Original Address Scheme

Classful Addressing—The Original Address Scheme

- Based on RFC 791.
- An addressing scheme based on a simple hierarchy.
- Class of address determined by the first few bits of the address.
- Uses the dotted decimal notation system.
- Allocated by the Internet Registry.
- All addresses ultimately owned by the IANA.

Many, many years ago, RFC 760 introduced IP. The beginnings of the IP addressing scheme were very simple and flat. This RFC didn't have a concept of classes (not to be confused with classless IP of today); addressing was an 8-bit prefix that allowed as many as 200+ networks and a lot of hosts per network. RFC 791 obsoletes RFC 760 and this RFC included the concept of IP address classes. Back then, it was easy to change addressing schemes for there were but a few hosts on the entire network. RFC 950 introduced us to subnetting and RFC1518 introduced the CIDR (classless) protocol. There have been many enhancements to the original IP addressing scheme, but they continue to operate on the bases of Class and Classless.

Addressing's purpose was to allow IP to communicate between hosts on a network or on an internet. Classful IP addresses identify both a particular node and a network number where the particular node resides on an internet. IP addresses are 32-bits long, separated into four fields of 1 byte each. This address can be expressed in decimal, octal, hexadecimal, and binary. The most common IP address form is written in decimal and is known as the *dotted decimal notation* system.

There are two ways that an IP address is assigned; it all depends on your connection. If you have a connection to the Internet, the network portion of the address is assigned through an Internet Service Provider. Yes, there are three addresses assigned for private addressing. But for a connection to the Internet, at least one address must be defined as a public address assigned to you by the ISP.

To identify all hosts on your network with public address, the ISP will only provide the network range (a continuous IP network address segment) that you may work with. It will not assign host numbers nor assign the network numbers to any part of your network. If your network will never have a connection to the Internet, you can assign your own addresses, but it is highly recommended that you follow RFC 1918 for the private assignment. These are Class A, Class B, and Class C address assignments for private use.

51 IP Address Format

Each host on a TCP/IP network is uniquely identified at the IP layer with an address that takes the form of <netid, hostid>. The address is not really separated and is read as a whole. The whole address is always used to fully identify a host. There is no separation between the fields. In fact, when an IP address is written, it is hard to tell the distinction between the two fields without knowing how to separate them.

The following shows the generalized format of an IP address:

<Network Number, Host Number> in the form of xxx.xxx.xxx.xxx

In decimal, the address range is 0.0.0.0 through 255.255.255.255. 128.4.70.9 is an example of an IP address. When looking at this address, it is hard to tell which is the network number and which is the host number, let alone a subnet number. Except for the first byte, any of the bytes can indicate a network number or host number. The first byte always indicates a network number. In order to understand how this is accomplished, let's look first at how IP addresses are divided.

Each byte (or in Internet terms, an octet) is 8 bits long, naturally! Each of the bytes, however, can identify a network, a subnetwork, or a host.

As shown in the slide, there are 32 bits separated into 4 bytes that are used to represent an IP address. The network number can shift from the first byte to the second byte to the third byte. The same can happen to the host

---

IP Address Format

- Uniquely identifies both the network and the host in one address.
- Uses the form:
  <Network ID Host Number>
- The address is 32 bits in length which is further separated into 4 bytes of 8 bits each.
  xxxxxxxx.xxxxxxxx.xxxxxxxx.xxxxxxxx
- There are five classes of addresses: A–E.

---

portion of the address. xxx represents a decimal number from 0 to 255 (the reason for three xs).

IP addresses are divided into five classes: A, B, C, D, and E. RFC 791, which classified these types, did so without the foregoing knowledge of subnets. The classes allowed for various amounts of networks and hosts to be assigned. Classes A, B, and C are used to represent host and network addresses. Class D is a special type of address used for multicasting (for example, OSPF routing updates use this type of address as well as IP multicast). Class E is reserved for experimental use.

For those trying to figure out this addressing scheme, it is best if you also know the binary numbering system and are able to convert between decimal and binary. Finally, IP addresses are sometimes expressed in hexadec- imal and it is helpful to know. IPv6 uses only hexadecimal. The most common form for IPv4 is decimal. This book shows most addresses in binary and decimal.

Identifying a Class   52

For network and host assignment, Classes A through C are used. Class D is not used for this, and Class E is never assigned. Referring to the slide, we can see how the classes are actually defined. How does a host or internet device determine which address is of which class? Since the length of the network ID is variable (dependent on the class), a simple method was devised to allow the software to determine the class of address and, therefore, the length of the network number.

The IP software will determine the class of the network ID by using a simple method of reading the first bit(s) in the first field (the first byte) of every packet. IP addresses contain 4 bytes. The slide shows an address in binary. If you are not familiar with binary, I suggest you study up on it, for understanding addressing, especially classless addressing, can only be figured out by converting the address to binary.

The slide breaks the IP address down into its binary equivalent. If the first bit of the first

Identifying a Class

Address Identifier	Network Address	Host Address

Class A

0	7 bits of network address	24 bits of host address
	First byte	Last three bytes

Class B

10	14 bits of network address	16 bits of host address
	First two bytes	Last two bytes

Class C

110	21 bits of network address	8 bits of host address
	First three bytes	Last byte

Class D

1110	Multicast address in the range of 224.0.0.0 - 239.255.255.255

Class E

11110	Class E - Reserved for future use

byte is a 0, it is a Class A address. If the first bit is a 1, then the protocol mandates reading the next bit. If the next bit is a 0, then it is a Class B address. If the first and second bits are 1 and the third bit is a 0, it is a Class C address. If the first, second, and third bits are 1, the address is a Class D address and is reserved for multicast addresses. Class E addresses are reserved for experimental use.

53

Class A addresses take the 4-byte form <network number.host.host.host>, bytes 0, 1, 2, and 3. Subnetting has not been introduced here yet! Class A addresses use only the first of the 4 bytes for the network number. Class A is identified by the first bit in the first byte of the address. If this first bit is a 0, then it identifies a Class A address. The last 3 bytes are used for the host portion of the address.

Class A addressing allows for 126 networks (using only the first byte) with up to 16,777,214 million hosts per network number. The range for Class A is 1–126. With 24 bits in the host fields (last 3 bytes), there can be 16,277,214 hosts per network (again, disregarding subnets). This is actually $(2^{24}) - 2$. We subtract 2 because no host can be assigned all 0s (reserved to indicate a default route, which will be explained later) and no

host can be assigned all 1s. For example, 10.255.255.255 is not allowed to be assigned to a host, although it is a valid address. Yes, this is a broadcast address.

If all 7 bits are set to 1 (starting from the right), this represents 127 in decimal, and 127.x.x.x is reserved as an internal loopback address and cannot be assigned to any host as a unique address. This is used to indicate whether your local TCP/IP stack (software) is up and running. The address is never seen on the network. You may want to look at your machine IP addresses (usually by typing netstat –r at the command line) and you will notice that every machine has 127.0.0.1 assigned to it. The software uses this as an internal loopback address. You should not see this address cross over the LAN (via a protocol analyzer such as a Sniffer.) In fact,

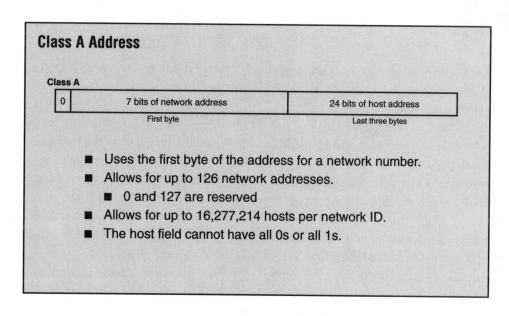

Class A Address

Class A

0	7 bits of network address	24 bits of host address
	First byte	Last three bytes

- Uses the first byte of the address for a network number.
- Allows for up to 126 network addresses.
  - 0 and 127 are reserved
- Allows for up to 16,277,214 hosts per network ID.
- The host field cannot have all 0s or all 1s.

127.anything is proposed as the loopback. 127.1.1.1 delivers the same results as 127.0.0.1. Think about it. A whole address range assigned to one function: loopback. The problem is, if we tried to change it, it would probably cause mayhem on the millions of hosts that currently use IP.

Today, Class A addresses are being handed out through a different method involving Internet Service Providers that uses the Classless InterDomain Routing Protocol (CIDR), which is explained at the end of this section. When you get a Class A address, you will be told to subnet it appropriately (you will be told what the subnet address is). You will not get the whole Class A address. A good question here: How much of the address space does a Class A address define? (Hint: Do not think of it as a Class address but do use the first bit to answer the question). Give up?

54   Class B Address

Okay, the answer is, 50 percent of the available address space is defined by Class A. How? Change the address Class bits to binary. Since the address is defined by the first bit alone and the next 31 bits are disregarded, it represents 50 percent of the available bits for address assignment (for those scratching their heads, it is 2^{31} bits, which is 50 percent of the address space). Don't think in a class-oriented environment. I simply asked how much of the address space can be defined by using 1 bit. This will become more apparent in the classless routing section.

Class B addresses take the form <network number.network number.host.host>, for bytes 0, 1, 2, and 3. This is the most requested class of address and is the easiest to assign subnets to. Class B addresses use the first 2 bytes of the 4 bytes for the network number and the last two fields for the host number. It is identified by the first 2 bits of the first byte. If the first bit is a 1, then the algorithm checks the second bit. If the second bit is a 0, this will identify a Class B address.

This allows for 16,384 network numbers (10111111.11111111.host.host or (2^{14}), with each network number capable of supporting 65,534 ($2^{16} - 2$) hosts (net.net.11111111.111 11110). Wait, there are 16 bits in the first two fields, this should allow for 65,535 networks. Since Class B reserves the first 2 bits to identify the class type (in binary, a 10xxxxxx in the first field), there are limited address numbers that may be used in the first field (valid range becomes 2^{14}). This translates to 128–191 (in decimal) as the allowable network numbers in the first field. Since the first field identifies the class, the second field is free to use all 8 bits, and can range from 0 to 255. The total range

for network numbers for Class B addresses is 128 to 191 (in the first field), 0 to 255 (in the second field), and xxx.xxx (x represents the host ID) in the third and fourth fields. This is the most popular class of addresses.

It provides the largest range of addressing possibilities. However, unless companies have handed in their Class B addresses, this class is exhausted and they are no longer given out.

Okay, let's try again. How much of the available address space is defined by Class B's reserved first 2 bits? The answer is on the next page.

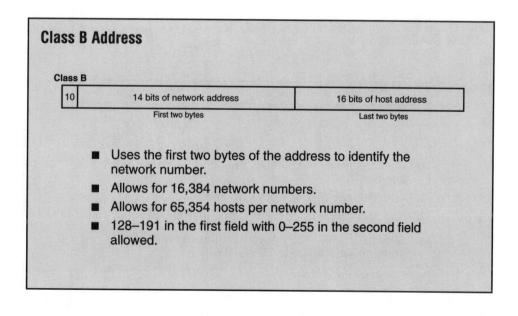

Class B Address

Class B

| 10 | 14 bits of network address | 16 bits of host address |

First two bytes   Last two bytes

- Uses the first two bytes of the address to identify the network number.
- Allows for 16,384 network numbers.
- Allows for 65,354 hosts per network number.
- 128–191 in the first field with 0–255 in the second field allowed.

55 Class C Address

For those who answered "25 percent," this is correct. With the first two bits reserved, this leaves 30 bits for address assignment. 230 is 25 percent of the available address space.

Class C takes the form of <network number .network number.network number.host>, bytes 0, 1, 2, and 3. Class C addresses use the first 3 out of 4 bytes of the address for the network number and the last field for the host number. This allows lots of networks with a fewer hosts per network. A Class C address is identified by the first 3 bits of the first field. If the first and second bits are 1s and the third bit is a 0, this will identify a Class C address (110xxxxx). Since the first 3 bits in the first field will always be a 110xxxxx, the allowable network range is 192–223 in the first field. This allows for 2,097,152 ($2^{n}21$) possible network addresses. All of the bits in the second and third fields are allowed to be used (including all 0s and 1s). Therefore, the whole allowable range for Class C network addresses is 192 to 223 (in the first field), 0 to 255 (in the second field), and 0 to 255 (in the third field). The last field will range from 1 to 254 for host assignment. This allows 2,097,152 network numbers, each capable of supporting 254 hosts (all 0s and all 1s are still reserved no matter what type of routing and addressing you are using). No host can be assigned a 0 or all 1s as its address. Class C addresses allow only 254 hosts per network number. Notice that the largest number in the first field may go up to 223. Any number over 223 in the first field will indicate a Class D address. Class D addresses are reserved as multicast addresses.

Class C addresses are the most commonly assigned by the NIC. Class B addresses have

Class C Address

Class C

110	21 bits of network address	8 bits of host address
	First three bytes	Last byte

- Uses the first three bytes of the address for the network number.
- The first byte ranges from 192–223.
- The second and third bytes range from 0–255.
- Allows for 2,097,152 network addresses with each address allowing up to 254 hosts.

been exhausted. Therefore, ISPs and regional Internet Registries are assigning Class C and Class A (with subnets).

Okay, yep, one more question: "How much of the address space is defined by Class C's bit reservation of 110?"

Class D Address   56

For those who answered 12.5 percent, you are correct. This is the odd thing. There are millions of Class C addresses (networks), but they only represent 12.5 percent of the available address space. Again, get those calculators out.

Class D addresses are special addresses and are known as multicast addresses. This address type is assigned to a group of network workstations and is not assigned to represent a unique address. They are used to send IP datagrams to a group, but not all of the hosts on a network. Multicasting has many uses, includ-

ing being used for addressing router update messages as well as delivering data, video, and voice over IP. Using a multicast address is a more efficient way of "broadcasting" rather than using a broadcast address, for the upper-layer software will not always be interrupted every time a broadcast packet arrives. Multicasting is different than broadcasting. With broadcasting, every station that receives the broadcast packet will automatically pass it to the upper-layer software without regard to the address. Every station that receives a broadcast packet must process it.

With a multicast address, each individual IP station must be willing to accept the multicast IP address before the transport-layer software will be interrupted. Each NIC will register a MAC layer multicast address on its adapter card, just like a unicast address (the IP address to Ethernet mapping of a multicast address is shown in a moment). In this way, the NIC can discard a packet without interrupting the upper-layer software (in most cases, anyway, some duplication of multicast addresses

exist, and this too is shown in a moment). The NIC is already set up to receive a broadcast packet. This is one address known as FF-FF-FF-FF-FF-FF.

As of this writing, RFC 1700 (assigned numbers) fully explains the mapping of Class D addresses to MAC addresses and it also indicates assigned multicast addresses and registered multicast addresses.

Multicasting is completely covered in another section of this book.

Class D Address

Class D

1110	Multicast address in the range of 224.0.0.0–239.255.255.255

- Reserved by IANA for multicast use.
- Address range 224.0.0.0 through 244.0.0.255 is reserved.
- Multicast datagrams are sent to a group of workstations.
- This IP address is mapped to a physical address (assigned in the NIC card).

For most of us, Classes A through D is what we will be working with. We will never have to dabble in the classless society of addresses. Classes A through D will be around for a long time and IPv6, although adopted, is still quite a few years away. IPv6 does not understand the concept of class networking and supplies enough addresses for millions of years to come—enough to supply an IP address for all those refrigerators and washers and dryers. (Don't laugh, this will happen. Why? Think of maintenance, or being able to control things in your house via your browser. Forget to turn off some lights or set the security up? The possibilities are endless.)

For those newbies, the easiest way to remember IP class addresses is this: The *first byte* will always identify the *class address*.

Whether you have converted to binary or are looking at the address in its dotted decimal form, the first byte gives it away. A is the *first letter* in the alphabet, and therefore a Class A network address is only the *first byte*, leaving the last three fields for host addressing. B is the *second letter* in the alphabet, and therefore the network portion of the address is the first *2 bytes* of the address, leaving the last two fields for host address. C is the *third letter* in the alphabet, and the network portion takes up the first *3 bytes* of the address and leaves one field for host addresses. As for remembering which number is associated to which class, the only field that is important is the first field. Memorize the starting network number for each class.

Classes A–D Review

- Network hosts can be assigned a Class address of Class A–D.
  - These are simply a grouping of addresses that indicate host and address assignment
- Class A has the network number in the first byte of the address and the last three bytes are assigned to the host.
- Class B has the network number in the first two bytes of the address and the last two bytes are assigned to the host.
- Class C has the network number in the first three bytes of the address and the host is assigned to the last byte.
- Class D is a multicast address.
- A is the first letter of the alphabet and therefore the network number is assigned the first byte.
- B is the second letter and therefore has the network number assigned to the first two bytes.
- Class C is the third letter and therefore has the network number assigned to the first three bytes.

The classes are

Class A: 0–127

Class B: 128–191

Class C: 192–223

Class D: 223–239

Reserved: 240–254

58   Subnetting

Now that IP address assignment has been shown, let's further confuse the issue by looking at subnet masks. Another name for subnet masks is extended network prefix. This book will continue to use the well-known name of subnetting. Subnetting is explained in RFC 950.

Implementing classes in network numbers gave us some hierarchical structure to the Internet. Using class assignment, you could select a network number based on the number of hosts that are on or will be on your network.

But the range was very limited. Class A gave you a lot of hosts but just a few networks. Class B was the one picked to allow for a balance of hosts and networks, and Class C allowed many networks and a few hosts. Not much choice, either you had a lot of networks or a lot of hosts. The most requested network number was Class B; however, many Class B assignments were not fully used—really hard to have 65,535 hosts on a single network. Too many Class C addresses filled up routing tables and most did not fully use all 254 host addresses.

Furthermore, some sites were requesting multiple addresses to fulfill their needs.

Not many Class A addresses were handed out. In fact, after about 63 assignments, Class A assignments were not handed out at all. Class B addresses were popular and were the most frequently asked for address class. What's the deal with Class C addresses? With only 254 hosts available for assignment, many Class C addresses have to be assigned. Again, using Class assignment, the routing tables started to fill up and most of the bits were wasted when implemented. It was like being given a five-passenger car, but you never had anyone in the other seats. In short, subnetting allows for tremendous efficiency not only in Internet routing tables but also on customer networks as well. It allows us to assign some of the bits normally used by the host portion of the address and reassign these bits to the network portion of the address. This is accomplished for the reasons that follow.

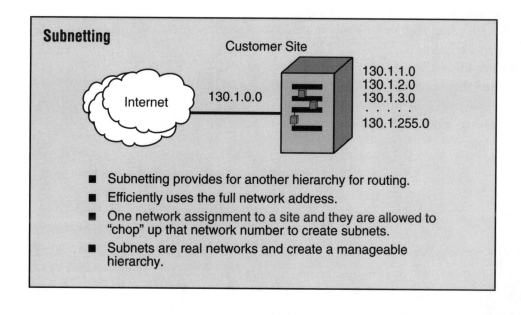

Subnetting

Customer Site

Internet   130.1.0.0

130.1.1.0
130.1.2.0
130.1.3.0
. . . . .
130.1.255.0

■ Subnetting provides for another hierarchy for routing.
■ Efficiently uses the full network address.
■ One network assignment to a site and they are allowed to "chop" up that network number to create subnets.
■ Subnets are real networks and create a manageable hierarchy.

59 Reasons for Subnetting

As network numbers were assigned, many sites were implementing routing on their local sites. This had many benefits. You could have many networks at your site (using RFC 791), but the problem was that you had to be given multiple network addresses (Class A, Class B, or Class C) to accomplish this. This started to fill up the ARPAnet routing tables and created other problems as well.

Many networks that accessed the Internet were creating their own home-grown subnetted environments, and many were beginning to be implemented. Before all networks ceased communicating because of incompatibilities, RFC 950 was released, defining a standard method for subnetting an IP address. A network mask that covers simply the network portion of the address is known as the *natural* mask (no portion of the address is subnetted).

The slide shows a subnetted network topology connected to the Internet. It is assigned a Class B address and uses an 8-bit subnet mask. The Internet knows of the IP address 130.1.0.0. It does not know the subnets involved. This allows the Internet address (routing) tables to remain smaller.

Subnet masks are used in routers and network stations.

Reasons for Subnetting
- Most IP address assignments were not used very efficiently.
    - Having millions of hosts for Class A and 254 hosts for Class was not working very well
- Many sites were requesting multiple network numbers due to variable amounts of networks at their sites.
- Many networks were implementing proprietary subnets.
- RFC 950 defined the adopted subnet method.

Any of the classes can be subnetted, although some are easier than others. The slide shows the three classes of networks, each with an address. This time, each of the addresses has been assigned a subnet mask. A mask is a series of bits that are applied (known as ANDing) to a portion of the address. This portion is what we are subtracting from the original address. It indicates how many bits we are masking out of the original host portion of an address to use as a subnet address. A subnet address is a real network number, but simply a network under the class address. Subnet masks are variable in length and move from the first host bit to the last. In other words, they move to the right of the address. Moving a mask to the left of the network address, beyond its natural mask, is known as supernetting (this concept will be discussed in a moment).

In this example of the Classes A and B addresses, I have shown all available bits following the network ID portion of the address used to indicate a subnet. The Class C address uses the first 3 bits of the host portion of the address for the subnet. With any of the addresses, any of the host bits (except for 2 bits at the end of the address; there must be at least one host on a network) may be used for subnetting. For example, a Class B address may use all of the third octet and 2 bits of the fourth octet for subnetting. This would give 1024 possible subnetwork numbers—yes, 1024. Those who are paying attention here should have caught the fact that in order to have 1024 subnet addresses we must use all 0s and all 1s in the subnet field as valid subnet addresses. This may seem contrary to host and network ID assignment, but it is not. All 0s and all 1s are allowed

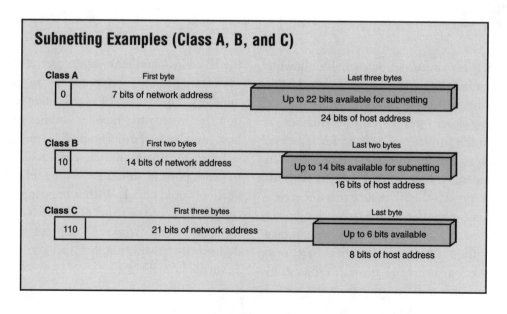

Subnetting Examples (Class A, B, and C)

Class A — First byte: 0 | 7 bits of network address — Last three bytes: Up to 22 bits available for subnetting — 24 bits of host address

Class B — First two bytes: 10 | 14 bits of network address — Last two bytes: Up to 14 bits available for subnetting — 16 bits of host address

Class C — First three bytes: 110 | 21 bits of network address — Last byte: Up to 6 bits available — 8 bits of host address

to be used in the subnet portion of any address (they still cannot be used in the host or network portions of the address as unique addresses). Refer to RFC 1812. This causes problems with subnet broadcasts, which I'll explain later. Using the preceding example (10-bit subnet on a Class B), each subnet can support up to 62 hosts (63 would indicate a broadcast).

Subnet considerations:

1. Hosts and routers must implement subnetting (there is a way around this discussed under Proxy ARP) and locally must have the same mask.
2. The router must be able to distinguish between all 1s as a subnet address and a subnet broadcast.
3. In some situations, the routing update protocol must support it.

61 More Subnet Examples

Subnetting confiscates unused bits, allowing for more efficient use of an address. Subnetting allows for more efficient use of addressing space and lowers the number of routes in the Internet routing tables. The bits are taken away from host assignment and given back to identify a subnet of a network address. The slide depicts this. The subnet is a real network. It is a subnet under the network number. With subnetting a Class B address, we can take any amount of the bits in the third byte, or 6 bits of the fourth byte (1 through 8 bits; they should be contiguous, starting from the left) of

the IP address and make them part of the network number (a subnet under the network number). The format of the IP address would now be: <network number, subnet number, host number>. For example, if the address assigned to a particular host is 130.1.5.1, the network portion would be 128.1 and the host portion would be 5.1. With subnetting (assuming all 8 bits of the third field were consumed for a subnet address), the address would be defined as network number 130.1 and subnet 5, with a host ID of 1.

Subnetting a Class B address is easy when you subnet the entire third octet. However, it becomes difficult when you subnet only a portion of the third octet. Suppose the first 5 bits (starting from the left; they should start from the left and remain contiguous going to the right) are reserved in the third field for assigning subnet numbers. What subnets do we have now? Convert those first 5 bits of that octet to binary. All five of those bits are now assigned to the subnet number and may not be used for host IDs. Five bits yields 32 subnet numbers (2^5). Now, the big challenge: Identify those numbers!

If we start from the left and go 5 bits to the right, we get X.X.11111000.X as a network number (we don't care what is in the X). The binary numbers are taken literally and will yield subnets in multiples of 8 (8 is the first binary bit set to a 1). This gives us 0, 8, 16, 24, 32, 40, 48, 56, 64, 72, 80, 88, 96, 104, 112, 120, 128, 136, 144, 152, 160, 168, 176, 184, 192, 200, 208, 216, 224, 232, 240, 248.

You really must completely understand binary before heading into this area.

More Subnet Examples

Original Network and Host		(Full 8 bits) Subnet Mask	Network Subnet Host		
130.1	5.1	255.255.255.0	130.1	5	1

- We recovered some of the unused host bits and made them into a subnet.
- This reduces the amount of hosts we can have.

(Five bits)
xxxxxxxx.xxxxxxx.11111000.xxxxx
Subnet mask 255.255.248.0

Subnet starts at 0 and increases in multiples of 8 for a range of 2^5.

Physical and Logical Addresses

A subnet can be complicated to figure out. The address fields do not allow for more than 255 to be placed in each field. However, it is possible to have host 257 on your network. Host 257 is not written into the address, but using the subnet mask, we can physically have a host 257 on a single network.

Do not confuse the addresses. A subnetted address is still read as if subnetting has not been turned on. It is not written differently. For example, if the address is 130.1.9.1 and the subnet mask is 255.255.248.0, then it is network 130.1, subnet 8, and host 257.

The point here is that you must make sure that you know the subnet mask before trying to determine the host, subnet, and network.

Physical and Logical Addresses

		Subnet	Host
1 0 0 0 0 0 1 0	0 0 0 0 0 0 0 1	0 0 0 0 1 0 0 1	0 0 0 0 0 0 0 1
130	1	9	1

Subnet Mask 255.255.248.0

Logical Address is:

    Network: 130.1.0.0

    Subnet: 8

    Host: 257

Physically, the host is number 257 on this subnet.
But this is only on paper.

Not sure about the previous example? Let's break it out. To identify the subnets is a little tricky. The previous slide is shown again. As you can see, the vertical line separating the host and subnet portions of the address is the dividing line. The first bit in the subnet portion of the address is set to 1. The subnet would not be 1. In calculating the value of the subnet, the whole third field is taken into consideration. Therefore, since that bit is set, it is actually a binary 8 (the fourth bit). Therefore, the first subnet number will be a 0. Each subsequent subnet will be a multiple of 8.

In the previous example with each of those subnetwork numbers, we could possibly have 2046 hosts per subnetwork number. This is a little more realistic than not subnetting. Not subnetting gives us 65,534 hosts. We were assigned one IP address and, with subnetting, we were able to make better use of the address without having to reserve more addresses (network numbers). Also, with subnetting, only one IP address is in the Internet routing tables, even though we have 32 subnets on our network. The Internet routing tables do not care about subnets. We used one Class B network number and have 32 subnets available to us from the one Class B network. Without subnetting, we would have one network number and up to 65,534 hosts assigned to it.

How did we get 32 possibilities? Using 5 bits for the subnet mask gives us 32 possible combinations (0 to 31), or $2^n 5$. Remember, we can move the mask anywhere in the 14 available bits. The subnet mask could have used all 8 bits in the third octet, which would give us 256 subnet numbers (all 0s and all 1s being allowed).

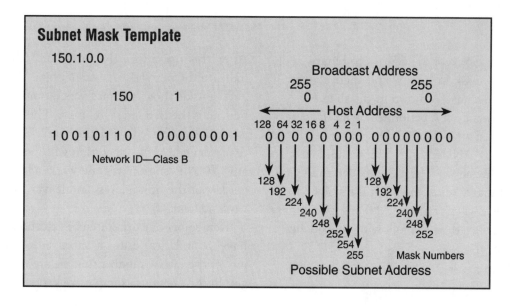

How do we write a subnet mask? It is always written in decimal and shows the number that will be used to mask the bits. For example, let's use the IP address 130.40.132.3. Using the first 5 bits of the first host field (the third octet) yields 248 (convert the first 5 bits to binary 11111000). The byte is read as a whole 8 bits even though part of it is used for the subnet and part for host assignment. This means the subnet mask for that IP address will be 255.255.248.0 in decimal. This is the mask that we have assigned to the network address of 130.40.132.3. We will always use 255 in the network potion of the subnet mask. The 248 is used to tell the network station to use the first 5 bits (5 bits binary is 248 decimal) of the network address, not for a host ID, but for a subnet. It tells a network station which bits to use for a subnet mask. The remaining 11 bits (the remaining 3 bits of the third octet and 8 bits of the fourth octet) should be used for the host ID. This allows for 32 subnets with 2046 hosts on each subnet.

Therefore, the IP address of 130.40.132.3, with a subnet mask of 255.255.248.0, yields the network number 130.40, subnet number 128, and host ID 1027.

64   An Example Conversion

(Hint: Convert the address to binary, apply the mask in binary, and then convert it back to decimal as shown in the slide.)

An operation is performed on an IP address. It is called a bit-wise AND operation. The IP address is ANDed with the subnet mask to allow the network station to determine the subnet mask. Yes, some math is involved here. Basically, when you are ANDing two binary numbers together, the following rule applies:

1. 1 AND 1 = 1
2. 1 AND 0 = 0
3. 0 AND 0 = 0

After this operation, the bits that "fall out" indicate the network and subnet bits.

The slide shows the mask operation. At the bottom is the IP address in binary. This address is logically ANDed with the mask. The bits that drop out of this operation will indicate to any TCP/IP station the network address. It masks out the host address and leaves the network address.

Remember one other item: Even though we have boundaries, using a short subnet mask moves the binary number that we are trying to get. In the previous example, we kept using the bits in the third octet as if they were part of the fourth octet. That is how we came up with 257. Since the mask was shorter than all 8 bits in the third octet, when figuring out the addressing, we continued to use the bits of the third octet as if they were part of the fourth octet. This makes the last bit of the third octet the 256 bit (binary) for the fourth octet. Be careful, using this same example, we must clear our heads and start over when figuring out what numbers are now assigned to the subnet. After we have figured out the host number, we then apply the mask, just like new, back on the third octet and look for the subnets. If it is a 7-bit subnet, then after we convert to binary, we number the last bit in the third octet as the first bit of the subnet numbering scheme, however, not actually part of the subnet number itself.

Sounds confusing but try a few more.

Class A addresses can use the second, third, or fourth (not the whole fourth field) field for subnets.

Class B addresses can use the third or fourth (not the whole fourth field) field for subnets.

Class C is tricky. The only field left is the single host field (one byte). Subnetting this is allowed, but you can only use up to 6 of the bits in the fourth field. You need to have a couple of hosts somewhere!

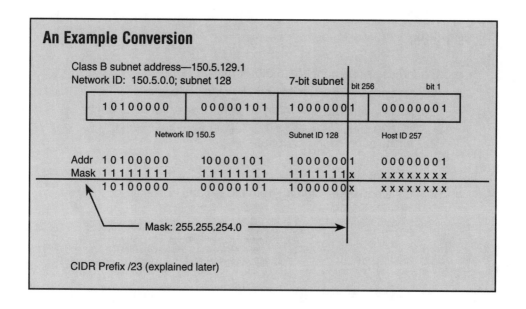

65 Let's Try One

You have been assigned an address of 150.5.0.0. You need 75 subnets with at least 75 hosts per subnet. What is the acceptable subnet mask?

The first step is to find out how many bits are needed for 75 subnets. In binary, 6 bits represent 64 possible subnets (2^n6). Not enough. Seven bits is 128 (0 inclusive) and this is the number of bits that we will use. Plus it gives us room for expansion. This leaves 9 bits for hosts, which allows for 510 hosts per subnet.

We start to assign subnets from the left and work to the right. We assign the hosts from the right and work to the left.

You must also define the broadcast address for a subnet. If you wanted to send something to all hosts on a subnet then the hosts field must be set to all 1s. With this subnet mask, there are 9 bits of 1s for an all-hosts broadcast address.

Another example (not shown in the slide) would be to define the mask for a network to support 40 hosts per subnet using the class address 195.1.10.0. First, we determine that this address is a Class C address and that only the last octet can be used for subnetting. Forty hosts is represented by 2^n6, which allows for 60 hosts. This may seem like a lot, but the nearest mask would be 2^n5, which would give us 30 possible host IDs, and this is not enough. Forty converted to binary is 101000. However, in the conversion we must remain contiguous and we cannot interleaf host and subnet bits. Therefore, we move the left 6 bits and then we can consume all 5 bits to the right. However, this only leaves 2 bits for a subnet. We can have 4, 2 bits left, subnets with 62 (2^n6) −2 hosts per subnet. If the site needed more subnets, we would have to assign more Class C addresses to the site.

Let's Try One

- IP address assignment 150.5.0.0.
- Requirements of 75 subnets and 75 hosts per subnet.
- First set is to find out how many bits are needed for 75 subnets.
  - $2^n5 = 30$ and 2^n6 is 64; $2^n7 = 128$, therefore we need 7 bits to subnet for 75 subnets
  - This leaves 9 bits for host assignment (16–7), which allows for 510 hosts
- Subnets are masked starting from the left and hosts are configured starting from the right.

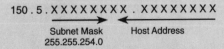

$$150 . 5 . XXXXXXXX . XXXXXXXX$$

Subnet Mask → ← Host Address
255.255.254.0

Subnet Bits

This slide provides a review of the availability of bits used for subnets.

Subnet Bits

Class A subnetted address—10.0.0.0

00001010	x x x x x x x x	x x x x x x x x	x x x x x 00

Network ID - 10   Subnet ID may use up to 22 bits

Class B subnetted address—128.2.0.0   Subnet ID may use up to 14 bits

10000000	00000010	x x x x x x x x	x x x x x 0 0

Network ID 128   Network ID 2

Class C subnetted address—193.2.8.0   Subnet ID may use up to 6 bits

00001010	00000010	00001000	x x x x x 00

Network ID 193   Network ID 2   Network ID 8

---

67 Subnet Restrictions

Subnets are good allowing for a more efficient use of the address bits, but when using a routing update protocol such as RIP version 1, you must be careful about assigning a subnet mask. This protocol only allows you to assign one mask per network number. Subnet masks allows for efficiency of address space, but there are possible problems. Under a restriction of one subnet mask per network, ID can still cause inefficiencies. For example, a serial line (a telephone connection) between two sites needs only two host IDs. But with the restriction of only one subnet mask, we will still not make great use of all the bits. Under this circumstance, we would have subnet down to two bits to make the most efficient use of the address (we only need two hosts). But this will not allow us to use the address for host assignment on the LAN (unless we only have

two hosts on the LAN). As you will see later, the best option is to allow variable-length subnet masks. In other words, move the mask around on different subnets that have different requirements. This is good, but you must make sure that the routing protocol (RIP, RIPv2, OSPF, etc.) understands this as well. Point blank, RIP does not, but RIPv2 does. OSPF does. Why? Routing updates have the subnet mask included in the update (it is in the link-state advertisement for OSPF). RIP does not include any subnet masks for routing entries in its table.

When using the RIPv1 routing protocol (explained later), the subnet mask must remain the same throughout a single Class B assignment. For example, if the network assignment is 130.1.0.0 and the subnet mask assigned is 255.255.255.0, the subnet mask must remain

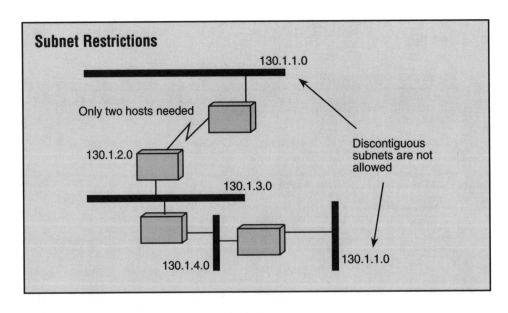

the same throughout the 130.1.0.0 network. If the network address changes (for example, to 131.1.0.0), the subnet mask may also change for this new network number.

RIP version 2 and OSPF do not have this restriction because they broadcast their subnet masks in the table with the network IDs (more on this in a moment).

Subnet Mask Decisions 68

Subnet Mask Decisions
- Subnetting is based on the following:
  - Hosts
  - Subnets
  - Serial lines
  - Expansion
  - Mergers
  - Routing protocol (RIP v1 or v2, OSPF)

Let's say you are assigned one network number and you are using RIP version 1. Although we are introducing this concept here, it is covered in more detail later. It is provided here to give you an understanding that under certain conditions, certain decisions have to be made. The subnet mask must be the same throughout your network, unless you change network IDs. You must make a decision on how large the subnet mask should be. How many hosts per subnet will there be? What about expansion? These are issues you must consider when assigning a subnet mask. With RIPv1, it is a trade-off. OSPF and RIPv2 do not have this trade-off, but care must still be taken when assigning network masks to a network number. This is shown completely in the next section on advanced IP addressing concepts.

This restriction becomes readily noticeable when assigning an IP address to a serial line (two routers using a leased phone line to connect). There have been circumstances that some router vendors have come up with that allow for the no IP address assignment for a serial line. However, if the serial link needs an address assignment and you are not using RIP version 2 or OSPF, a whole subnet number is wasted on this point-to-point link. A serial link will consume a network number and associated host IDs. Therefore, a unique network number will be assigned and, instead of being able to use all available host IDs, it will be possible to use only two host IDs (there will be only two addressable points on that network).

The rest of the host IDs will be lost for that network number and will be assigned and used for that serial link; therefore they will not be able to be assigned to any other links. If you have a large site that will encompass many serial links and you do not have the ability to assign a large number of network numbers, use subnet addressing and the routing protocol of OSPF. OSPF supports variable-length subnet masks, which will collapse that serial link into two hosts within a network number; therefore, no host numbers are wasted on serial links. Variable-length subnet masks allow a single network number to use multiple masks (unlike RIP version 1, RIP version 2 allows VLSM). This allows more bits to be assigned back to the network, allowing a more efficient use of the address.

A few more things you need to consider: If the network station moves to a new network, does the IP address for that station change? Like the current telephone system, IP addresses must change when the network station is moved to a new network that employs a different network number. If the network station is moved on the same logical network, the IP address may remain the same. For example, if a network station is moved to a different part of the same subnet, the whole IP address may stay the same. If the network station is moved to a different subnet (different subnet number), the IP address of the network station must change.

This subject will be picked up again in the section "Advanced IP Addressing."

Assigning More Than One Address to an Interface

Have a network with 275 hosts but you were assigned all Class C addresses? What can you do here? TCP/IP fully supports the ability to assign more than one subnet or network number to the same segment. Actually the router vendors implemented this as an ability of TCP/IP. This means that one network may employ more than one network number on the same physical cable plant. In order to accomplish this, a router must be used. Network stations continue to believe they are communicating with a remote network station, but the router is simply providing the address translation. The packet goes in one port and then right back out the same port. The two nodes actually reside on the same network segment. A router will take the steps necessary to allow network stations to converse on the network. Implementations are different, so the amount of network numbers that may be assigned to the same cable plant varies.

For example, as shown in the slide, multiple Class C network numbers may be assigned to the same cable plant. Class C addresses allow only for 254 host IDs per network number. This is a rather low number, and some sites will have more than 254 network stations attached to a cable plant. This means that multiple stations on the same cable plant may have different network addresses. A router must be used to translate between two stations that are located on the same cable plant with different network addresses. This is called *multinetting* an interface.

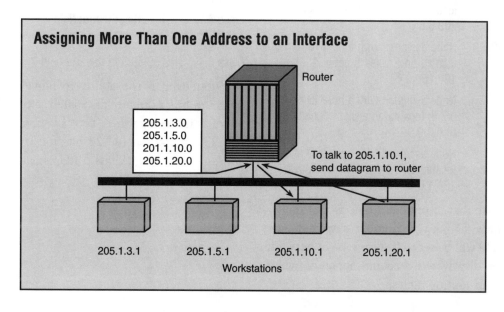

Assigning More Than One Address to an Interface

Router

205.1.3.0
205.1.5.0
201.1.10.0
205.1.20.0

To talk to 205.1.10.1,
send datagram to router

205.1.3.1   205.1.5.1   205.1.10.1   205.1.20.1

Workstations

70

Classful IP Address Review

Let's review. All IPv4 addresses are 32 bits in length and are the grouping of 4 bytes that represents both a network number and host number. This number is usually represented in decimal. With the first bit reserved (set to 0xxxxxxx) in a Class A address, the network numbers can range from 1 to 126. Number 127 is reserved as a local loopback IP address and must not be assigned to a network number and transmitted onto the network. With the first 2 bits reserved in a Class B (10xxxxxx) or 3 bits in a Class C (110xxxxx) address, the network numbers for Class B range from 128.1.0.0 to 191.255.0.0, and for Class C they range from 192.1.1.0 to 223.255.255.0.

Examples:

192.1.1.1	Node assigned with a host ID of 1, located on a Class C network of network 192.1.1.0
200.6.5.4	Node assigned with a host ID of 4, located on a Class C network of 200.6.5.0
150.150.5.6	Node assigned with a host ID of 5.6, located on a Class B network of 150.150.0.0
9.6.7.8	Node assigned with a host ID of 6.7.8, located on a Class A network of 9.0.0.0
128.1.0.1	Node assigned with a host ID of 0.1, located on a Class B network of 128.1.0.0

Notice that to represent a network number only, only the network number is written. The host field will be set to 0. This type of network number display will become apparent when looking at routing tables.

Classful IP Address Review

- In the first field:
  - Class A has the range of 1–126
  - Class B has the range of 128–191
  - Class C has the range of 192–223
  - Class D has the range of 224–239
- Subnetting is the ability to place a mask over the host portion of the address to yield subnets.
  - Allows for another level of hierarchy; efficient for routing
- RIP version 1 has problems with variable subnet masks.

For those not familiar with binary, you need to memorize the starting and stopping points of the first byte of an IP address:

Class A	1–126 in the first field
Class B	128–191 in the first field
Class C	192–223 in the first field

Subnetting is the ability to move a mask over the bits normally associated with a host address and reclaim these bits as a subnet number. The mask can use 22 bits for a Class A address, 14 bits for a Class B address, and 6 bits for a Class C address.

IP Address Restrictions

- Address cannot have the first four bits set to 1.
- Class A address of 127.x.x.x is reserved for loopback.
- The host portion of the address cannot be set to all 0s or all 1s.
- All 0s and all 1s are allowed in the subnet.
- Any address with all 0s in the network portion of the address space is meant to be this network.
- Old form of broadcasting (all 0s in the address) is no longer used.
- IP addresses may be configured without registration.
- Addresses cannot be out of the 255 range for each byte.

1. Addresses cannot have the first four highest bits (in the first field) set to 1111. This is reserved for Class E networks only (a reserved network classification).

2. The Class A address of 127.x is for a special function known as the *loop-back function*. It should never be visible on the network.

3. The bits that define the host portion of the address cannot be set to all 1s or all 0s to indicate an individual address. These are reserved addresses. All 1s indicate a local subnet all hosts broadcast and all 0s indicate a network number.

4. All 0s and all 1s are allowed in the subnet portion of an address as valid subnet addresses. Placing a 0 in the subnet is called *subnet 0* (how clever) and most

routers must be told that subnet 0 is supported. However, you must be careful when assigning all 1s to the subnet portion of the address. This is allowed (according to RFC 1812), but it can wreak havoc on those networks that use all subnets broadcast. If the subnet portion of the address is set to all 1s, this can be used as a *directed broadcast*. Routers will forward this type of datagram, if told to do so (they have to be configured).

5. Any address with all 0s in the network portion of the address is meant to represent "this" network. For example, 0.0.0.120 is meant as host number 120 on "this" network (the network from which it originated).

6. There is an old form of broadcasting known as the *all-0s broadcast*. This will take the form of 0.0.0.0. This form should not be used. 0.0.0.0 is used to indicate a default router (explained later).

7. You can assign your own IP network numbers if you will *never* have access to the Internet or if you plan on using something like a Network Address Translator (NAT, RFC 1631). RFC 1918 allows three IP addresses to be used for private networks.

8. Addresses cannot be out of the 255 (decimal) range for any of the 4 bytes. Therefore, an address of 128.6.200.655 is not a valid address. Likewise, an address of 420.6.7.900 is not a valid address assignment.

72 Address Allocation (The Internet Registry)

RFC 2050 describes the registry system for the distribution of globally unique Internet address space and registry options. This RFC is different from most others. Look in the upper-left corner and notice that the category is "Best Current Practice." It represents an accurate representation of the current practice of the IP address registries.

The Internet Registry hierarchy was established in order to achieve address uniqueness, distribution of hierarchical distribution of global Internet addresses, and, most of all, produce a conservation of IPv4 Internet addressees. It consists of IANA, Regional IRs, and Local IRs.

The IANA is the Internet Assigned Numbers Authority, and it has overall authority for the number space used in the Internet. This number space includes port number, address, IP version numbers, and many other significant number assignments. Read RFC 1700 for a full description of the IANA.

The Regional IRs operate under the authority of IANA. They operate in large geographical areas such as continents. Currently, there are three defined: InterNIC, which serves North America; RIPE, which serves Europe; and APNIC, which serves the Asian Pacific region.

These IRs do not cover all areas. It is expected that each IR covers any area not specifically specified, but within its immediate area. Local IRs are established under the authority of the regional IR and IANA. They cover national dimensions.

Addresses are allocated to ISPs by regional registries, which in turn assign them to their customer base. ISPs that exchange routing

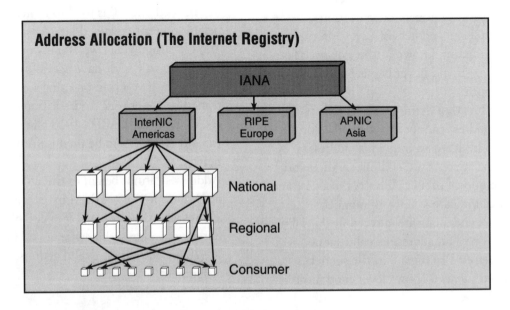

Address Allocation (The Internet Registry)

information directly with other ISPs get their address allocation from their geographic IR. Other ISPs are referred to these ISPs for address assignment. In other words, if your address block has a reasonable chance of being propagated through the global Internet routing tables, then your address allocation will come from the IR. Otherwise, you will get your address assignment from your upstream ISP. Customers (commercial corporations) need not worry about this. They will get their address assignments from the ISP they sign up with. This is just a basic introduction to the IP addressing scheme.

Part Two

The Protocol Suite
of TCP/IP

73 Address Resolution Protocol (ARP)

The Internet, but not the TCP/IP protocol, grew up with high-speed local networks such as Ethernet, Token Ring, and FDDI. Before the Internet, there was the ARPAnet and this too ran the TCP/IP protocol. The ARPAnet started on serial lines to communicate between the sites and Ethernet, or any LAN for that matter, was not a consideration. IP addressing worked just fine in this environment. Routing was accomplished between message processors known as IMPs (Interface Message Processors). The hosts connected to the IMP and the IMP connected to the phone lines, which interconnected all ARPAnet sites. The IP address identified the host (and later the network and subnetwork). There was not a need for physically identifying a host for there was only one host per physical connection to the IMP. Multiple hosts could connect to an IMP, but each had an IP address to which the IMP forwarded the information.

Ethernet was commercially available in 1980 and started to gain more recognition when version 2.0 was released in 1982. Since multiple stations were to connect to a network (single cable segment) like Ethernet, each station had to be physically identified on the Ethernet. The designers of Local Area Networks (LANs) allotted 48 bits to identify a network attachment. This is known as a *physical address* or MAC *address*. Physical addresses identify stations at their datalink level. IP is an addressing scheme used at the network level. On a LAN (Ethernet, Token Ring, etc.), two communicating stations can set up a session

---

> ## Address Resolution Protocol (ARP)
>
> - RFC 826.
>
> - TCP/IP addresses are 32 bits and represent a network, subnet, and host ID.
>
> - Addresses on LANs are represented by physical (MAC) layer addresses and they are 48 bits in length.
>
> - ARP provides the mapping between a host's 32-bit IP address and its 48-bit MAC address.
>
> - ARP works only on the local subnet (it cannot traverse routers).
>
> - ARP builds a table of IP/MAC addresses to properly format a source and destination address field in a packet.

---

only if they know each other's physical address. Think of a MAC address as the number on your house. Lots of houses on your street and each uniquely identified by the number. This is a MAC address.

Since the MAC address is 48 bits and IP is 32 bits, a problem existed and an RFC resolved this problem. The resolution was simple and it did not affect the already established IP addressing scheme. It is known as *Address Resolution Protocol*, or ARP. This is an IP-address-to-physical-station-address resolution (actual name is *binding*).

If you are trying to communicate to a host on the same network number as the one on which you are currently residing, the TCP/IP protocol will use ARP to find the physical address of the destination station. If the network number of the destination station is remote, a router must be used to forward the datagram to the destination. The ARP process is used here as well, but only to find the physical address of the router.

There have been enhancements to this protocol although not through an RFC. Some stations listen to all ARP packets since the originator sends them in broadcast mode. All stations receive these packets and will glean the information that they need. The information in the packets includes the senders' hardware and IP address mapping. In some instances, this information is used by other stations to build their ARP cache. Many ARP tables (cache) empty their tables periodically to reduce the cycles needed to refresh the cache, to conserve memory, and to keep the table up to date. If a station moves from one subnet to another and stations on the subnet do not empty their tables, they will continue to have an entry for that hardware address. ARP is defined in RFC 826.

ARP Packet Format   74

The ARP packet format is shown. It contains just a few fields, but notice one thing: It does not reside on top of IP. It has its own Ethernet Type field (0806), which identifies the protocol ownership of the packet and allows it to uniquely identify itself. It never leaves its local segment, so why use IP?

There are five main fields: the operation (ARP request or ARP reply), the source and destination IP addresses, and the source and destination hardware addresses (more commonly known as MAC addresses).

The type of hardware identifies the LAN (10-Mbps Ethernet, for example), the type of protocol identifies the protocol being used. This makes ARP versatile. It can be used with other types of protocols as well. The most famous one is AppleTalk through the AppleTalk ARP protocol.

The ARP process is shown next.

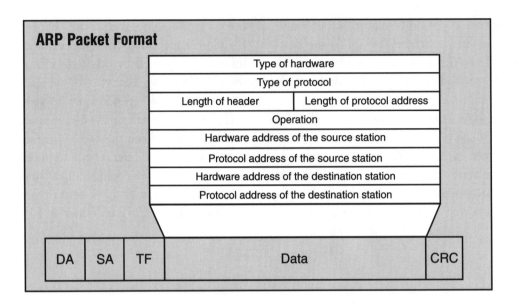

ARP Packet Format

Type of hardware	
Type of protocol	
Length of header	Length of protocol address
Operation	
Hardware address of the source station	
Protocol address of the source station	
Hardware address of the destination station	
Protocol address of the destination station	

| DA | SA | TF | Data | CRC |

75   ARP Operation

As shown in the slide, in order to attach to another station on a TCP/IP network, the source station must know the designation station's IP address. This can be accomplished in many ways; for example, typing the address in directly using a TCP/IP based program, or using a name server. In this example, Station 129.1.1.1 wants a connection with 129.1.1.4 (no subnet addressing is used here). Therefore, the network address of this Class B address is 129.1.0.0 and the personal computer's host address is 1.1; hence, the address is 129.1.1.1.

With ARP, it is assumed that the IP address of the destination station is already known either through a name service (a central service or file on a network station that maps IP addresses to host names, explained in more detail later), or by using the IP address itself. To reduce overhead on the network, most TCP network stations will maintain a LAN physical-address-to-IP-address table on their host machines. The ARP table is nothing more than a section of RAM memory that will contain datalink physical (or MAC addresses) to

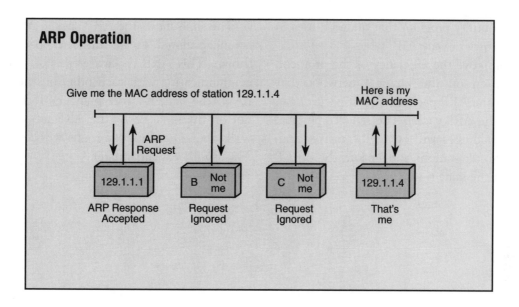

IP address mappings that it has learned from the network.

Once the IP address is known for the destination station, IP on the source station will first look into its ARP table to find the physical address for that destination IP address. If a mapping is found, no ARP request packet will be transmitted onto the network. IP can bind (place the physical addresses on the datalink headers of the packet) the IP address with the physical address and send the IP datagram to the datalink for transmission to the network.

If the address is not in the ARP table, the ARP protocol will build an ARP request packet and send it physically addressed in broadcast mode (destination address FF-FF-FF-FF-FF-FF). All stations on the physical network will receive the packet, but only the host with that IP address will reply. Host 129.1.1.4 will reply to the request packet with

an ARP response packet physically addressed to station 129.1.1.1.

When the host whose IP address is in the request packet responds, it will respond with an ARP reply packet with the source address set to its address (physically and inside the ARP reply packet), and the destination address as the originator. Once the originator of the request receives the response, it will extract the physical address from the source address in the packet and update its ARP table. Now that it has the mapping, it will try to submit its IP datagram to the destination station using the proper addresses (IP and physical address).

This process is automatic. The user will typically be using one of TCP's applications (TEL-NET for terminal service, SMTP for mail service, or FTP for file transfer service) when attempting a connection. Most TCP vendors supply a utility program that allows a user to see the entries in the ARP table.

To improve the efficiency of the protocol, any station on the physical network that receives the ARP packet (request packet) can update the ARP cache. The sender's physical and IP addresses will be in the packet and, therefore, all stations can update their ARP tables at the same time.

The slide shows the ARP packet format. It is encapsulated in an Ethernet packet as shown. This ARP process works for stations communicating with each other on the same LAN (the same network number). If they are not on the same LAN, the ARP process still works, but an address of a router will be found. This is fully explained later.

76   Rules for ARP

1. ARP is not a part of the IP protocol and therefore does not contain IP headers. ARP works directly on top of the datalink layer.
2. ARP requests and responses are transmitted with a destination physical broadcast address (all Fs) and therefore never leave their logical subnet. Plus, with Rule 1, these packets cannot be routed
3. Since ARP is not part of the IP protocol, a new EtherType (the field in the Ethernet packet that identifies the protocol used by the packet) is assigned to

Rules for ARP

- ARP does not run on top of IP and therefore has no IP headers.
- ARP requests are transmitted in broadcast so that all stations receive the packet.
- New EtherType defined 0x0806 for both the ARP request and reply.
- ARP replies are sent directly to the requesting station (unicast, not broadcast).
- ARP tables should age out their entries.
- An attachment should answer an ARP sent to itself.

identify this type of packet. 0806 is an ARP request and 0806 is an ARP reply. Some ARP implementations can be assigned the 0800 EtherType, for IP will be able identify the packet as an ARP request or ARP reply packet. Not all implementers of IP use these types. Some still use the EtherTypes of 0800 for ARP.

4. Some implementations have an ARP aging capability. This allows ARP to delete entries that have not been used for a period of time, reducing the ARP lookup time and saving memory.
5. If a machine submits an ARP request for itself, it must reply to the request.

Reverse Address Resolution Protocol (RARP)

77

This protocol is used when a network station knows its MAC address but does not know its IP address. When would this happen? Diskless workstations are a good example. Notice that RARP uses the ARP packet format and does not involve IP; therefore, this packet cannot be routed. This protocol has been in use for some time, but there are other protocols that do a better job. This is one of the reasons that we use BOOTP and DHCP for address assignment because they can be forwarded over a router (with a little assis-tance from the router). One problem with RARP is that like its cousin ARP, it does not use IP. Therefore, RARP is generally used only on a LAN.

The requesting client machine will send out a RARP request to a server located on the local segment that has the RARP server ser-vice running on it. This RARP server will respond to the request with that particular sta-tion's IP address. Although the RARP server does not need to be located on the same cable segment or extended LAN, it is preferred.

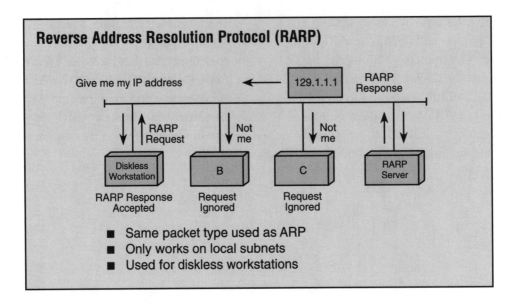

Some router vendors have enabled their routers to forward these requests and responses to other networks.

The packet format for a RARP packet is the same as for ARP. The only difference is that the field that will be filled in will be the sender's physical address. The IP address fields will be empty. A RARP server will receive this packet, fill in the IP address fields, and reply to the sender—the opposite of the ARP process.

Other protocol similar to this are BOOTP and Dynamic Host Configuration Protocol (DHCP). DHCP is more powerful than RARP, but it does supply one of the same functions as RARP: resolving an IP address. Besides being less functional than DHCP, RARP only works on single subnets. RARP works at the datalink layer and therefore cannot span subnets gracefully. DHCP can span subnets.

Proxy ARP protocol is not used much anymore, but it is still worth mentioning. IP was pretty well established when ARP came along, and some TCP/IP implementations did not support ARP. However, TCP/IP over LANs with subnets was being implemented and an interim solution was needed. This was the purpose of Proxy ARP (also known as ARP Hack). Proxy ARP is the ability of a router to be able to respond to an endstation (host) ARP request for a host that thinks the destination IP address is on the local LAN. Therefore, if a host does not support subnet addressing, it could incorrectly mistake an IP subnet number for a host number. The router tricks the transmitting station into believing that the source station is on the local LAN.

Endstation A thinks host B is on the local LAN. Host B supports subnet addressing and endstation A does not. Deciphering the IP address, the first two fields (containing the network ID) are the same. Therefore, endstation A will send out a local ARP request packet when it should be submitting the packet to the router so that it can deliver the packet to the endstation. If the router has proxy ARP enabled, the router will answer for host B. The router, which supports subnetting, will look up the ARP request and then notice that the subnetwork address is in its routing table. The router responds for endstation B. Endstation A will receive this response and think it is from host B—there is nothing in the physical address of a packet to indicate where it came from. The

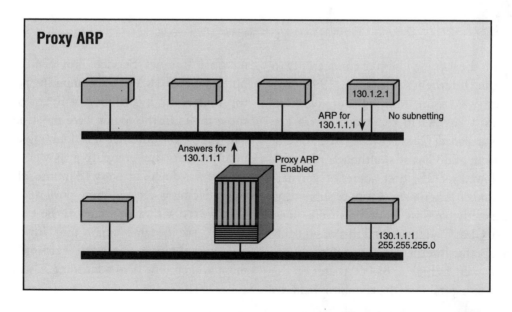

host will then submit all packets to the router and the router will deliver them to endstation A. This communication will continue until one end terminates the session.

Proxy ARP is a very useful protocol for those networks that have been using bridges to implement their IP network and are moving to a router environment. There are other situation for which proxy ARP is appropriate, but its use is waning. Today, most hosts on a TCP/IP internet support subnet masking and most IP networks are using routers.

A potential problem in using proxy ARP is for those networks that implement the mechanism to ensure single IP addresses are on each

network. Most TCP/IP implementations allow users easy access to their network number (that is, they can change it with a text editor). This allows any hacker to change his or her number to another in order to receive datagrams destined for another host. Some implementations of TCP/IP will detect for this. Routers that implement proxy ARP will get caught, for they will answer for any station on a different network, thereby giving the impression that there is one physical address to multiple IP addresses. There is a trust on any IP network that IP addresses will not be arbitrarily assigned. There should be one IP address for each physical address on an internet.

79   What's Wrong with the Address?

With the vast explosion of connectivity to the Internet starting in 1994, the Internet was soon running out of IPv4 addresses. Class As in the range of 64–126 were not assigned; Class Bs were at the point of exhaustion; and Class Cs, although plentiful, only allowed for 254 host addresses per network number assignment. Class C subnetting is not exactly painless. Most sites were given multiple Class C addresses and this was quickly filling up the Internet routing tables, Some estimates were as high as 85,000 routes on the global routing tables (those tables held by

national Internet Service Providers such as Sprint and MCI). Yet, the computing power of the router and availability of RAM to hold those tables in the router were not ready yet. The size of the Internet was doubling every 9 months, yet the computing power of the routers was doubling every 18 months. Instead of producing faster and more powerful routers (like we did with mainframes in the 1970s and 1980s), we became smart and invented a holdover solution using the existing equipment and current IPv4 addressing scheme.

> ## What's Wrong with the Address?
>
> - IP address is 32 bits in length.
>   - Allows for 4,294,967,296 unique addresses
>
> - A problem occurs because the addresses are grouped in a class address.
>   - A range of bits is applied to an address, most of which are wasted
>
> - Addresses were arbitrarily handed out without regard to geographic location.
>
> - Class C addresses were overtaxing the Internet routing tables.
>
> - Class A stopped being handed out and Class B was exhausted.
>
> - RFC 1338 introduced supernetting as a three-year fix.
>
> - It turned into Classless Inter-Domain Routing (CIDR).

Now we hear about the exhaustion of IP address space. Can this be true, with over 4 billion addresses? But wait. We have 32 bits of address space. Ignoring the rules of class addressing this, 2^n32 allows for 4,294,967,296 unicast addresses to be assigned (in some formation of networks and hosts). Seems like a lot of addresses, but remember, IP lived in a class environment, wasting much of the available address space. Subnetting along with protocols such as RIPv2 and OSPF allowed for variable-length subnet masks which allowed for more efficiency of the address bits, but there is still a shortage of IPaddresses.

The original problems were three types of classful addresses and address allocation without a plan. It used to be that anyone who

wanted an address was given one arbitrarily, and addresses were allocated without knowledge of their location or fully understanding their network requirements leading to the proper assignment of an address. In 1992, a study was performed and the conclusion was that not only was the address space near depletion (Classes A and B), assigning the remaining 2 million Class C addresses would cause the Internet's router array to melt down. The Internet backbone routers were already congested and slow with the current routing tables of less than 30,000 routes.

Some organizations and network providers had multiple contiguous networks assigned. Yet, as we learned in the previous section on addressing, each address is a network and holds one record slot in the routing database. The idea of supernetting was introduced in RFC 1338 as a means of summarizing multiple network numbers (one entry details multiple network IDs), further reducing the number of routes reported. This was a 1992 RFC intended as a three-year fix, which matured into CIDR.

80 Extending the Life of the IPv4 Address Space

The following was taken from RFC 760:

Addresses are fixed length of four octets (32 bits). An address begins with a one-octet network number, followed by a three-octet local address. This three-octet field is called the rest field.

Taken from RFC 791, page 6:

Addresses are fixed length of four octets (32 bits). An address begins with a network number, followed by a local address (called the rest field). There are three formats or classes of internet addresses: In Class A, the high-order bit is 0, the next 7 bits are the network, and the last 24 bits are the local address; in Class B, the high-order 2 bits are 1–0, the next 14 bits are the network, and the last 16 bits are the local address; In Class C, the high-order 3 bits are 1–1–0, the next 21 bits are the network, and the last 8 bits are the local address.

RFC 950 introduced us to subnetting:

While this view has proved simple and powerful (two-level model, assigning a network number per network), a number of organizations have found it inadequate, and have added a third level to the interpretation of Internet addresses. In this view, a given Internet network is divided into a collection of subnets.

RFCs 1517–1520 introduced us to Classless Inter-Domain Routing (CIDR):

It has become clear that the first two of these problems (routing information overload and Class B exhaustion) are likely to become critical in the near term. Classless Inter-Domain Routing (CIDR) attempts to deal with these problems by defining a mechanism with which to slow the growth of routing tables and reduce the need to allocate new IP network numbers.

Extending the Life of the IPv4 Address Space

- Original RFC for IP was RFC 760.
  - No concept of classes; address was 8-bit network ID
- RFC 791 introduced a segmentation of the address into Classes.
- RFC 950 introduced subnetting.
  - Allowed for efficiency to exist with Class addresses
- RFCs 1517–1520 introduced CIDR.
  - Used on the Internet routing tables

This section deals primarily with the IPv4 address extensions. Included in this are subnetting (an IP address review, variable-length subnet masks, route aggregation, and CIDR). IPv6 should be included in this as well with the 128-bit address. However, this discussion is held off until after the IPv4 discussion. The CIDR discussion fully reveals the address problem and what was done about it.

IP Address Assignment (The Old Method)

> ### IP Address Assignment (The Old Method)
>
> - Three methods of assigning addresses in the old days:
>   - Acquire a distinct network number for each cable segment separated by a router
>   - Use a single network number for the entire operation, but assign host number in coordination with their communication requirements
>   - Use a single network number and partition the host address space by assigning subnet number to the LANs ("explicit subnets")

Originally, using RFC 791 without subnetting, an organization with a complex (more than one) network topology had three choices for assigning Internet addresses:

1. Acquire a distinct Internet network number for each cable; subnets are not used at all.

2. Use a single network number for the entire organization, but assign host numbers in coordination with their communication requirements (flat networks segmented using bridges).

3. Use a single network number and partition the host address space by assigning subnet numbers to the LANs (explicit subnets). Create your own but don't advertise them to the ARPAnet. This is the most popular method.

Employing the first choice caused routing tables to grow. RFC 950 allowed for subnet addressing to take place within an autonomous system, which allowed for a site to continue to subnet its AS, but the subnets were never propagated to the Internet routing tables. Subnetting and VLSM (variable-length subnet masks, explained later) allowed for the global routing tables to stop growing exponentially and allowed sites to control their own networks as well. However, network numbers were plentiful and subnets slowed the expansion of the Internet routing tables. This was before the commercialization of the Internet in 1994.

The adverse effects of bridges in complex networks are well known. Since the bridge revolution, routers have become the mainstay of the corporate backbone. This worked well for shared environments, but technology was changing: Network attachments were becoming faster and more powerful. The bridging revolution came back as switches in that each desktop could now have its own 10-Mbps pipe. The switches build a small flat network and should be used to front end routers, thus allowing for *microsegmenting* but not *microsubnetting*.

Subnetting one network number caused the Internet routing tables to slow their growth. This worked well with Class B addresses. Class C networks forced the Internet routing tables to grow, and Class A addresses were not handed out. Also, since more than 50 percent of the businesses were small- and medium-sized businesses. Class C addresses were needed. Again, we were in a predicament. We needed a solution.

82   IP Addressing (The Old Method)

Refer to slide 82.

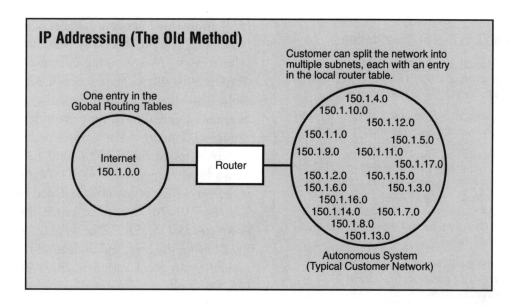

IP Addressing (The Old Method)

One entry in the Global Routing Tables

Internet 150.1.0.0

Router

Customer can split the network into multiple subnets, each with an entry in the local router table.

150.1.4.0
150.1.10.0
150.1.12.0
150.1.1.0
150.1.5.0
150.1.9.0   150.1.11.0
150.1.17.0
150.1.2.0   150.1.15.0
150.1.6.0   150.1.3.0
150.1.16.0
150.1.14.0   150.1.7.0
150.1.8.0
1501.13.0

Autonomous System (Typical Customer Network)

Address Terms and Definitions

83

There are four terms used in this section:

Variable Length Subnet Masks (VLSM). The ability to place a variable-length subnet mask on a single IP network address. Refer to RFC 1817. VLSMs are explained in detail in the OSPF section.

Supernetting. A mask that is shorter than the IP network address natural mask.

Classless Inter-Domain Routing (CIDR). An advertisement mechanism that allows for advertising routes without regard to class assignment. The route could be identified by a supernet or by an extended subnet mask.

Address aggregation. The ability to summarize contiguous blocks of IP addresses as one advertisement.

The ability to manipulate IP addresses is affected not only on customer sites but within the global Internet as well. Class-oriented IP addresses are still used in the customer environment, whereas Classless IP addressing is used in the Internet itself. Customers are free

Address Terms and Definitions

- Varible Length Subnet Masks (VLSM)—
  The ability to place a variable-length subnet
  mask on a single IP network number.

- Supernetting—The ability to apply a mask
  to an IP address that is shorter than its
  natural mask.

- Classless Inter-Domain Routing (CIDR)—
  An advertisement mechanism that allows
  for advertising routes without regard to
  Class assignment. The route could be
  identified by a supernet or by an extended
  subnet mask.

- Address aggregation—The ability to
  summarize contiguous blocks of IP
  addresses as one advertisement.

to use whichever mechanism efficiently uses the address that is assigned to them. No longer are they restricted to use only one subnet mask for their assigned network number. OSPF and RIP2 gave us more flexibility when using the subnet mask. These routing update protocols distribute the subnet mask for each entry in its table. The allowed us great flexibility in mask assignment and allowed for more efficiency of the network address. For a single network ID, we could move the mask around to various masks for the single network ID. A site could make very efficient use of its assigned network ID using VLSM. We could move the mask down to 255.255.255.252 for serial lines allowing 2 bits for the host, and then move the mask around again for a various number of hosts. OSPF also allowed for summaries in the routing updates, which allowed routers to send out one network number with a mask as an update indicating all bits in the mask handled by that router. This is very efficient.

Making the Address Efficient

Making the Address Efficient

- All methods provide for extending the life of IPv4.

- CIDR is very similar to VLSM.

- Addresses allocated in blocks.
  - Example: 205.24.0.0/16 means that the address range of 205.24.0.0 through 205.24.255.0 (256 Class Cs) is assigned to one ISP or consumer, etc.

- Block assignment allows for one route to be placed in the Internet routing tables.

- It allows the ISP to break up the addresses and efficiently hand them out to its customers.

- Consumers must detail their addressing requirements to the ISP.

- Address assignments are still conservative.

The rapid expansion for connectivity and the exploding corporate infrastructure initially caused problems on the Internet. IP addresses were assigned sequentially to requesting organizations without regard to the requester's location or method of Internet connection. What this means is that a requesting company simply called in for an IP address assignment and was assigned an IP address from a list of sequentially listed numbers. For example, a company in California could be assigned 150.1.0.0 and a company in Virginia would be assigned 151.1.0.0 and maybe 40 Class C addresses. Then a company in Texas could apply for 160.1.0.0 and 50 Class C addresses. They could then sign up for any ISP they desired with their newly assigned IP addresses. Very inefficient, but at the time, who knew? The routing system filled up with smaller IP addresses across multiple, long hops of routers, instead of large contiguous addresses. Supernetting, CIDR, and address aggregation provided address flexibility and efficiency to the ISP and the Internet. CIDR is very similar to VLSM. Today, blocks of addresses (as indicated toward the end of this section) are handed out to Internet Service Providers (ISPs) in blocks (or a range) through the Internet Registry (RFC 2050 fully explains this). For example, an ISP may be assigned the address block of 205.24.0.0/16, which allows the ISP to hand out addresses in the range of 205.24.0.0 through 205.24.255.255. In this way, the global routing tables only know that addresses 205.24.0.0 through 205.24.255.255 go in one direction to an ISP. All of these addresses are summarized into one routing table entry, which, using the old method, would have been 255 entries. The entry in the global routing tables would have been 205.24.0.0/16 instead of listing all 255 addresses—the global routing tables do not care about the individual network assignments.

The ISP subdivides this block to hand out individual addresses to its customers as Classful addresses, but how an ISP cuts up the addresses and assigns these blocks is affected using the protocols previously mentioned. One whole block would not be assigned to one company, but multiple companies.

A company requiring Internet connection calls its ISP, detailing its topology and requesting address space. The ISP (knowing it has to assign network numbers sparingly) will then assign the correct number and network range to its downstream customers. The range is then entered into the ISP's routing table, perhaps as one address even though multiple Classes were given to the customer.

85   Masks and Prefixes

Prefix routing has been around a long time. In fact, it is defined in RFC 1338. Prefix routing is the method used on the backbone of the Internet—an IP address is looked at simply as a 32-bit number and a prefix. The prefix is a mask that slides over the IP address to determine its network number. A routing entry in the Internet routing table may simply be 150.0.0.0/8 and a next hop address to the next in-line router to that destination. The router does not care about anything else in the address except that all 150.x.x.x networks are in the indicated direction.

Masks and Prefixes

- The addresses 210.10.40.0/24 and 210.10.40.0/255.255.255.0 mean the exact same thing.

IP Network Address	Prefix	Subnet Mask
128.1.0.0	/16	255.255.0.0
190.1.8.0	/21	255.255.248.0
207.16.16.128	/25	255.255.255.128

A subnet mask and a prefix can be intermixed. In fact, on Cisco routers, you will see the /prefix commonly used throughout their configuration interface.

Throughout this text, I will use both the decimal subnet mask and the prefix; a mask and a prefix are essentially the same thing. For example, a subnet of 255.255.255.0 and a prefix of /24 are the same. To illustrate, you could see an address written as 150.1.0.0/24, which means address 150.1.0.0 subnet 255.255.0.0.

Let's look at a few subnet examples, starting with address assignment at a company site.

Another Try   86

A customer has the base network address of 150.1.0.0 with a subnet mask of 255.255.0.0, or /16 prefix.

This time we are not interested in a requirement of subnets. All we know is that we must be able to have 100 hosts on each subnet. Each subnet will not have that many, but the largest one will, and without multinetting, we must use a mask small enough to accommodate that number. In order to support 100 hosts, 7 bits are needed, which allows for 126 addresses ($2^7 - 2$). This will allow for future growth. The next-lowest mask yields 62 addresses ($2^6 - 2$), so we must allow for 7 bits. Always assign a mask that allows for future growth.

Next we must determine the subnet mask for the network number. Since we will be reserving 7 bits for host assignment, this will leave 25 bits left for the network mask (32 bits − 7 bits = 25 bits). This gives a subnet mask of 255.255.255.128, or /25 prefix. The natural mask for Class B is 255.255.0.0. This mask is 255.255.255.128, which allows for 9 bits to be assigned to the subnet mask, thereby allowing for 512 subnets to be defined. The subnet numbers range from 0 to 521. This gives the range of subnets of 150.1.0.0 (providing for the zero subnet) through 150.1.255.128 (using all 9 bits including the all-1s subnet).

Now that we have separated the subnets from the hosts, we should list them:

Subnets

150.1.0.0 through 150.1.255.128

150.1.1.0 (x – host reserved bits)

10010110 . 00000001 . 00000001 . 0xxxxxxx

150.1.1.0

10010110 . 00000001 . 00000001 . 0xxxxxxx

Host Range

1 through 125 ($2^7 - 2$)

Host 1 (x = network/subnet reserved bits)

xxxxxxxx.xxxxxxxx.xxxxxxxx.x0000001

Host 127

xxxxxxxx.xxxxxxxx.xxxxxxxx.x1111111

Another Try

- Let's first review breaking a network number down with a subnet requirement:

- Requirement: A site has been assigned the network number 150.1.0.0. It requires 100 hosts per subnet. Future growth indicates 120 hosts per subnet. It was determined that expansion was more likely in the case of remote sites than hosts.

- Step 1: Determine the bits required to support at least 100 hosts and future expansion to 120 hosts per subnet.
  7 bits are required for 100–126 hosts.
  Start from the right and move left.

- Step 2: Determine how subnets are defined by 9 bits.
  9 bits support 512 subnets.
  Start from the left and move right.

- Step 3: Determine the mask.
  150.1.0.0/25, or 255.255.255.128

Variable-Length Subnet Masks

We know about the restriction of RIPv1. RIPv2 and OSPF do not have this restriction and can more efficiently use the address. The preceding examples show how to split up a network for subnets assuming one mask per network ID (discussed extensively previously in the book). A concept known as Variable-Length Subnet Mask (VLSM, detailed under the RIP and OSPF sections of this book), allows us to assign variable masks per network ID. We can move the mask around the single network ID. These protocols transmit the subnet mask along with the network ID in the routing update message.

VLSM can be very, very confusing. One rule you should follow: Do not make it overly complicated. As a general rule, do not VLSM more than three times. Yes, efficiency is important, but you must sit down with your team or customer and determine the network topology. For example, if you use the address 150.1.0.0 with a /16 prefix (255.255.0.0), a very effective method of using VLSM is /24 (for subnets with lots of networks), /27 (for subnets with fewer hosts or maybe higher-powered network-hogging apps), and /30 (mask for the serial lines). This is shown next. You can go wild and try to develop a mask for every subnet, but having a few leftover bits is fine. Also, using this method is not efficient as you will be spreading different subnets through the network in a noncontiguous fashion, which can become burdensome on the route tables. However, it does explain the variable-length subnet feature.

First, your base address is 150.1.0.0/16. This goes at the top of the chart. From here we will create 256 subnets using the /24 subnet mask. No hosts have been assigned yet. We currently

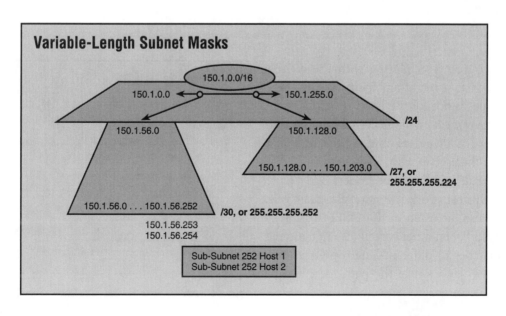

have 50 serial (point-to-point) lines to work with and predict a growth of 100 more remote sites over the next two years. Therefore, we need 150 subnets for the serial lines and there are only two host addresses needed per serial line. We have reserved the 150.1.56.0, 150.1.57.0, and the 150.1.58.0 subnets for serial lines. The 150.1.56.0 network is further subdivided (sub-subnetted) using the first 6 bits of the fourth octet (255.255.255.252 or /30), yielding 64 subnets for serial lines. With each subnet (56, 57, and 58) supporting 64 subnets we now have 192 subnets allotted for serial lines. We leave 2 bits, which allows for two host addresses to be assigned (all 0s and all 1s are not allowed as host addresses). Seventy-five of the subnets will be assigned a another mask (/27) to allow for sub-subnets (subnets of subnets) with a smaller number of hosts per subnet.

88 Longest Match Rule

As you can see, playing with the address leads to a lot of ambiguity. Using these techniques is not for the faint of heart. It can become very, very complicated. Usually, company network manages do not have to overly concern themselves with this schema.

One rule that must be understood before any of this can work is the *longest match rule*. This is also discussed in the OSPF section of the book. When a network ID is encountered that matches to different-length prefixes, the router will always take the path indicated by

Longest Match Rule

- Allows a router to determine the best route based on granularity of the masked address.

- Used when a network ID is found to match more than one subnet mask.

- Example:
  - Received datagram of 200.40.1.1
  - Route table lookup found two entries:
    - 200.40.1.0/24
    - 200.40.0.0/16
  - Route would use the 200.40.1.0/24

- Must be careful when assigning addresses.

the longest mask. For example, if a router receives an IP datagram with the destination address of 200.40.1.1 and a route table lookup found 200.40.1.0/24 and 200.40.0.0/16, the router will forward the datagram out the path indicated by the longest mask: 200.40.1.0. Therefore, you must make sure there are no hosts assigned to 200.40.0.0/16.

The longest match rule is implemented because the longer the mask found, the better granularity the router has in exactly defining the correct route.

Therefore, you must be wary of the fact that the router will route to the route determined by the longest mask match. If there are two entries for the same route, the longest mask wins.

Example One: An ISP Address Assignment 89

Let's look at another example, this time using a better example of address assignment: the Internet Service Provider. The ISP block is 200.24.0.0/16. Hmmmmm. Looks a little strange. This is a Class C address, but there is a 0 in the third octet and the prefix (subnet mask) is only 16-bits wide. The natural mask is 24 bits (255.255.255.0). This is known as *supernetting*, and will be shown in the next pages, so bear with me here.

A customer of the ISP needs three subnets, each supporting 60 hosts. Remember, we assign the mask contiguous starting from the left. Since subnets are divided evenly (due to the binary nature of the address), we cannot have three subnets without dividing the address to provide for four subnets. The address assigned to the customer is 200.24.255.0/24. Therefore:

1. How many bits are needed in the subnet mask to support three subnets?
2. $2^2 = 4$, therefore 2 bits are required in the subnet mask. This leaves one left over but masks must be contiguous.

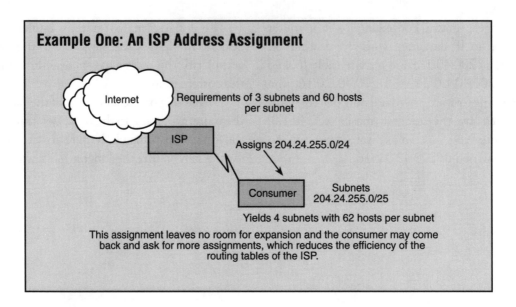

Example One: An ISP Address Assignment

Internet

Requirements of 3 subnets and 60 hosts per subnet

ISP

Assigns 204.24.255.0/24

Consumer

Subnets
204.24.255.0/25

Yields 4 subnets with 62 hosts per subnet

This assignment leaves no room for expansion and the consumer may come back and ask for more assignments, which reduces the efficiency of the routing tables of the ISP.

3. This leaves 6 bits left for host assignment. 2^6 leaves 62 ($2^6 = 64$ and we subtract 2 because we cannot have all 0s or all 1s in the host portion of the address) address assignments for hosts, and therefore we can use this single network address assignment for our company.

This should make you a little nervous. There are only two hosts per subnet left for expansion and there is only one subnet left. The ISP should make very sure that this company will not grow anytime soon.

Example Two: Relaxing the Assignment

The previous assignment works, but is it really good? Although we were able to be very stringent with the address assignment, this is not a good way of assigning or masking the address. It does not leave much room for growth on the host side or on the network side. For example, what if the company expands to 100 hosts per subnet and requires two more subnets? It could call its ISP back and request another address assignment. But by now, the ISP has handed out a few more addresses and the next available address for the customer is 200.24.64.0/24. This is not contiguous with the original assignment and the ISP has to add another entry in the ISP's table when this could have been avoided. To anticipate for this expansion, the customer could have been assigned four Class Cs. The ISP block assigned to the customer could be

200.1.252.0/22 (one entry in the ISP routing table), which yields the Class C addresses of 200.1.252.0, 200.1.253.0, 200.1.254.0, and 200.1.255.0. The customer is free to assign any subnet mask he or she wishes to the addresses without notifying the ISP.

From here the customer could assign 1 bit of subnet mask on the address of 200.1.252.0, which allows for 7 bits of address space yielding 125 ($2^7 - 2$) hosts per subnet. The other address could remain intact or be split with 1 bit subnet mask. The customer could also have simply used all the bits in the fourth octet, using no subnet mask. Yes, 1 bit subnet mask is allowed on a Class C: a 0 subnet and a 1 subnet. Review RFC 1812. The only time this will lead to problems is if the site is using all subnets broadcast. However, check with your router vendor. Cisco does not support 1-bit

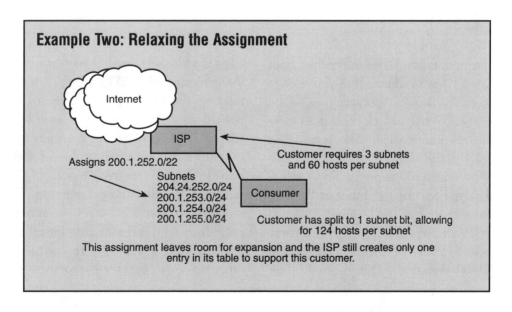

Example Two: Relaxing the Assignment

Internet

ISP

Assigns 200.1.252.0/22

Subnets
204.24.252.0/24
200.1.253.0/24
200.1.254.0/24
200.1.255.0/24

Consumer

Customer requires 3 subnets
and 60 hosts per subnet

Customer has split to 1 subnet bit, allowing
for 124 hosts per subnet

This assignment leaves room for expansion and the ISP still creates only one
entry in its table to support this customer.

subnet masks. In this case, you will have to use the Class C assignment with subnets. With VLSM, the consumer would have to devise a plan to determine which subnets will only have 60 hosts and which require more.

This is a simple example of how you must think about your network design before calling an ISP. You need to know how many hosts and what the traffic patterns are on the network. IP addresses are in short supply and ISPs do not hand them out haphazardly. They must take into consideration their routing tables as well.

91 Supernetting Exposed

In the previous example, we showed a subnet mask for a Class C address that was shorter than the natural mask. Applying this to the example, the ISP has a block of addresses. As far as the ISP is concerned, there is no Class associated with the address; it is simply a block of addresses defined by the prefix. This block is assigned to the ISP by the Internet Registry under the authority of the Internet Assigned Numbers Authority (IANA, yes, the same group, actually only one person who handles the top-level domains). This is small (four

Class C addresses), but it shows up as one entry in the routing table 200.1.252.0/22. Notice the mask at the ISP is pushed back to the left beyond the natural subnet mask of a Class address. This is known as *supernetting*.

The current approach (in lieu of IPv6) is to provide large contiguous blocks of Class C (and possibly other classes) addresses. They are provided by more local levels in an hierarchical fashion. For example, a national backbone provider (call it ISP-1) with connections to other national backbone providers through

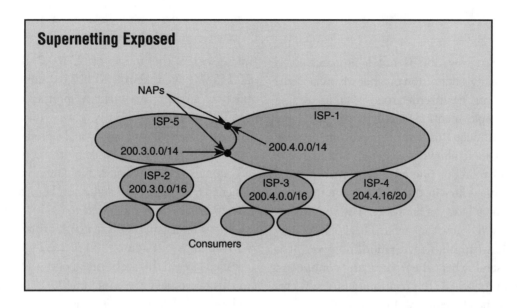

Network Access Points (NAPs) will be assigned a large block (one that will last two years) of Class C addresses. In turn, other regional service providers (call them ISP-2) who utilize ISP-1 will be assigned a block of addresses from ISP-1's address block assign-ment. In turn, ISP-2 will provide address assignment to its customers from the block it was assigned. This allows for very efficient and manageable global routing tables (those routing tables on the top-level providers).

Route Aggregation

Route aggregation is not a protocol. It is actually a definition of what we are accomplishing on the Internet routing tables. Using the example mentioned previously, you have been introduced to a concept known as *route aggregation*. It allows a router to summarize a group of routes as one advertisement. Imagine having one entry in the routing table to represent a large group of addresses. The router simply needs to know the prefix. This is completely possible with route aggregation, however, it is only useful when the routes are contiguous. Punching holes in the continuity of the routes reduces the efficiency of this concept.

To show this benefit clearly, I have chosen a Class A example. The network address is 20.0.0.0. The natural mask for this is /8. or 255.0.0.0. We first subnet the address using a /16 prefix, or 255.255.0.0. This allows for addresses in the range of 20.0.0.0 through 20.255.0.0. We take the 20.127.0.0 subnet and further subnet it with a prefix of /24 (255.255.255.0). Finally, we take the 20.127.1.0 subnet and apply a /27 prefix.

Route aggregation is based on the concept of a common prefix. What is the common prefix assigned to a group of IP addresses? For example, the 20.127.1.0 was subnetted to /27. However, all the subnets that are created by this can be advertised as one route: 20.127.1.0/24. This is detailed later in this section. All of the addresses in this range have the same prefix. This would indicate to all other routers that any network in the range of 20.127.1.0 should be forwarded to that router. The other routers do not care about any of the particular subnets beyond that address. The router that receives the datagram to be forwarded to any subnet below 20.127.1.0

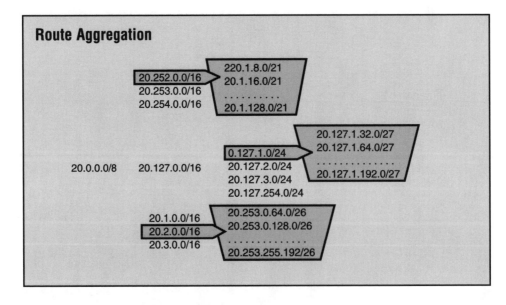

will be identified by the router and it will forward it to the correct network.

The rules are simple:

1. Write down the addresses in the range.
2. Convert each address to binary, one below the other.
3. Check for a contiguous, common prefix.

4. Move the prefix to the last bit of the contiguous binary digit.
5. Write the address starting the first address and apply the step 4 prefix.

Remember, do not make this complicated. It is confusing enough. Three variable subnet masks are enough to work with for most networks (business networks and ISPs excluded).

Determining a Common Prefix 93

The /27 prefix allows for an address range of:

20.127.1.32

20.127.1.64

20.127.1.96

20.127.1.128

20.127.1.160

20.127.1.192

20.127.1.224

Convert this to binary:

000010100.01111111.00000001.00100000 = 20.127.1.32

000010100.01111111.00000001.01000000 = 20.127.1.64

000010100.01111111.00000001.01100000 = 20.127.1.96

000010100.01111111.00000001.10000000 = 20.127.1.128

000010100.01111111.00000001.10100000 = 20.127.1.160

000010100.01111111.00000001.11000000 = 20.127.1.192

Determining a Common Prefix

```
000010100.01111111.00000000|.00100000  -20.127.1.32
000010100.01111111.00000000|.01000000  - 20.127.1.64
000010100.01111111.00000000|.01100000  - 20.127.1.96
000010100.01111111.00000000|.10000000  - 20.127.1.128
000010100.01111111.00000000|.10100000  - 20.127.1.160
000010100.01111111.00000000|.11000000  - 20.127.1.192
000010100.01111111.00000000|.11100000  - 20.127.1.224
000010100.01111111.00000000|.00000000  - Common prefix to all of the above addresses
```

Applying rules 4 and 5, we have 20.127.1.0/24, which represents all of the addresses.

000010100.01111111.00000001.11100000 =
20.127.1.224

000010100.01111111.00000001.00000000 =
Common prefix to all of the preceding
addresses

Therefore, applying rules 4 and 5, we have
20.127.1.0/24, which represents all of the
addresses.

In this example, aggregation is somewhat less efficient, but you would not know it from the address. The following addresses appear to be contiguous:

155.1.140.0

155.1.141.0

155.1.142.0

155.1.143.0

155.1.144.0

But when we translate it to binary to find the common prefix to all of the addresses, we find a noncontiguous bit pattern:

10011011.00000001.***10001100***.00000000 = 155.1.140.0/24

10011011.00000001.***10001101***.00000000 = 155.1.141.0/24

10011011.00000001.***10001110***.00000000 = 155.1.142.0/24

10011011.00000001.***10001111***.00000000 = 155.1.143.0/24

10011011.00000001.***10010000***.00000000 = 155.1.144.0/24

10011011.00000001.***100011xx***.00000000 = Common prefix

The common prefix is 100011xx in the third octet. Why? Because we do not know where 145 or higher is? We have to see which ones have the same prefix and then use that. Any other numbers must be separate entries in the table. This would give us a route aggregation of 155.1.140.0/22, but this leaves out the 155.1.144.0 subnet. Depending on the range that this address is in, it could be listed in

---

Another Look at Route Aggregation

155.1.140.0
155.1.141.0
155.1.142.0
155.1.143.0
155.1.144.0

When we translate it to binary to find the common prefix to all of the addresses, we find a non-contiguous bit pattern:

10011011.00000001.**10001100**.00000000 -155.1.140.0/24
10011011.00000001.**10001101**.00000000 - 155.1.141.0/24
10011011.00000001.**10001110**.00000000 - 155.1.142.0/24
10011011.00000001.**10001111**.00000000 - 155.1.143.0/24
10011011.00000001.**10010000**.00000000 - 155.1.144.0/24
10011011.00000001.**100011xx**.00000000 - Common Prefix

another route aggregation prefix. Since this is all the information we were given, however, 155.1.144.0 must be listed as a separate route: 155.1.144.0/24 (subnet mask of 255.255.255.0). This is due to this address not being within the range of the common prefix of the other addresses even though the decimal address is contiguous. Networks do not calculate routes in decimal!!! Humans do, and this is why we make mistakes.

You should also notice that this allows us to have one route entry instead of four. This may not seem like much, but when this concept is applied to a larger range of addresses (such as those on the Internet routing tables), one route entry is used to aggregate thousands of individual addresses.

The common prefix is 100011, which allows us to aggregate those routes to 155.1.140.0/14.

95 Classless Inter-Domain Routing (CIDR)

There is a lot more to CIDR than what is presented here, but for our purposes, this will do. With CIDR, network numbers and classes of networks are no longer valid for routing purposes. This is where the network IP address format changes to <IP Address, prefix length>. Mind you, this is for the Internet routing tables (ISPs); Class addressing is continuing to be used in customer environments. Classless could operate in a customer environment, but most hosts would not understand this type of implementation. The millions and millions of hosts that are attached to the Internet are still operating in a Class environment; therefore, we simply have created a hierarchical routing environment that does not affect the customer environment whatsoever. Let's start out this discussion by assigning a prefix to the well-known Class addresses. CIDR could operate in a customer environment, but that would require upgrading all routers and hosts to understand CIDR. This is not going to happen. CIDR is primarily used on the Internet routers.

Class A networks have a /8 prefix

Class B networks have a /16 prefix

Class C networks have a /24 prefix

/8? /16? /24? Hopefully, something clicked here! What we have changed to is the network prefix. A network number is basically a network prefix. Nodes on a classless network simply determine the address by finding the prefix value. This value indicates the number of bits, starting from the left, which will be used for the network. The remaining bits are left for host assignment. The prefix can range anywhere from /0 to /32, which allows us to move the network portion of the address anywhere on the 32-bit number.

Imagine then, an address of 198.1.192.0/20. This looks like a Class C address, but the natural mask for a Class C is 24 bits or /24 prefix. This one allows for only 20 bits as the network assignment. But this prefix could be assigned to any address regardless of class. It could be assigned to 15.1.192.0 or 128.1.128.0. The prefix does not care about Class. This is the capability of CIDR. The following section assumes that you can convert binary to decimal and vice versa. If not, please refer to the appendix at the end of this book for an explanation on binary.

Classless Inter-Domain Routing (CIDR)

- Network numbers according to classes of addresses are no longer valid.

- IP address format changes to <IP Address, Prefix>.

- Primarily used in ISP routing tables.
  - The global Internet routing tables
  - Most hosts on a network would not understand this

- Easy examples are changing the class address.
  - Class A has a /8 prefix
  - Class B has a /16 prefix
  - Class C has a /24 prefix

- What about 198.1.192.0/20?
  - Supernetted Class C address that provides for route aggregation using a concept similar to VLSM

You know that I must be leading up to something. It is the next step in understanding IP addresses and Internet routing. It is called CIDR (pronounced cider). CIDR is explained in RFCs 1517–1520, so I am not detailing the CIDR spec here. Just the concept. The concept is simple: Implement a generalization of Variable Length Subnet Masks and move from the traditional Class A, B, C address toward the idea of a 32-bit IP address and a prefix (without the concept of a Class). In CIDR, there are 32 bits and a prefix. To understand CIDR, you must place the concept not on your local network but on the Internet routers. You can employ CIDR on your network, but there is really no reason to (since your hosts would have to be configured to understand supernets). The Internet routing tables were expanding at a exponential rate (without CIDR, they would have passed over 80,000 routes today). The Internet routers are simply those devices that move data towards a destination indicated by its IP address, and therefore do not have large subnets off of them with which to support hosts. CIDR works on the notion that we are routing arbitrarily sized (a range) network address space instead of routing on Class A, B, and C. CIDR routes based on routing information that has the prefix attached to it. For example, the address of 200.15.0.0/16 could be an entry in the Internet routing table—one entry indicating a range of addresses. Any IP datagrams received by that router with the first 16 bits indicating 200.15 would be forwarded out the port indicated in

the routing table. This prefix could be assigned to any range of addresses because CIDR does not associate a prefix with a Class.

Classless Inter-Domain Routing (continued)

- Pronounced "cider."
- Explained in RFCs 1517–1520.
- Uses a generalization of the VLSM.
- Move from traditional Class to a prefix.
- Allows for route aggregation in the Internet routing tables.
  - Reduces the size and therefore increases the speed
- Works on the notion that we are routing arbitrarily sized network address space.
- One entry in a routing table could possibly match millions of addresses.

Prefix	Dotted-Decimal	Number of Addresses	Number of Class Addresses
/13	255.248.0.0	512k	8 Class B or 2048 Class C
/14	255.252.0.0	256k	4 Class B or 1024 Class C
/15	255.254.0.0.	128k	2 Class B or 512 Class C
/16	255.255.0.0	64k	1 Class B or 256 Class C
/17	255.255.128.0	32k	128 Class C
/18	255.255.192.0	16k	64 Class C
/19	255.255.224.0	8k	32 Class C
/20	255.255.240.0	4k	16 Class C
/21	255.255.248.0	2k	8 Class C
/22	255.255.252.0	1k	4 Class C
/23	255.255.254.0	512	2 Class C
/24	255.255.255.0	256	1 Class C
/25	255.255.255.128	128	_ Class C
/26	255.255.255.192	64	_ Class C
/27	255.255.255.224	32	1/8 Class C

We must look at this concept through the ISP networks. ISPs give us the ability to communicate over the Internet. You cannot simply attach to the Internet unless you connect with an ISP. ISPs come is a variety of flavors: some are large and provide access to other ISPs and individuals, and some are small and only provide Internet connectivity to individuals and businesses. ISPs are allocated blocks of addresses that are contiguous in range. The concept first used Class C addresses since Class B addresses were exhausted and Class A addresses were not handed out (they are being handed out today). The basic idea of the plan is to allocate blocks of Class C (first, other Class A and B addresses to follow) net-work numbers to each network service provider. (It is very helpful here to read RFC 2050 before continuing this section). The customers of these providers are then allocated bit mask-oriented subnets of the service provider's address. The assignment blocks to the IR can be found at the end of this section.

Prefix Assignments

Prefix	Dotted-Decimal	Number of Addresses	Number of Class Addresses
/13	255.248.0.0	512k	8 Class B or 2048 Class C
/14	255.252.0.0	256k	4 Class B or 1024 Class C
/15	255.254.0.0.	128k	2 Class B or 512 Class C
/16	255.255.0.0	64k	1 Class B or 256 Class C
/17	255.255.128.0	32k	128 Class C
/18	255.255.192.0	16k	64 Class C
/19	255.255.224.0	8k	32 Class C
/20	255.255.240.0	4k	16 Class C
/21	255.255.248.0	2k	8 Class C
/22	255.255.252.0	1k	4 Class C
/23	255.255.254.0	512	2 Class C
/24	255.255.255.0	256	1 Class C
/25	255.255.255.128	128	_ Class C
/26	255.255.255.192	64	_ Class C
/27	255.255.255.224	32	1/8 Class C

An ISP has been assigned this block from the InterNIC:

209.16.0.0/16.

At first glance, this address looks like a Class C, but the prefix does not match a Class C. It is a Class B prefix. Again, this is known as *supernetting* and shows that CIDR does not care about Classes. With a prefix of /16, this would represent 256 Class C addresses. However, in CIDR, the ISP is free to choose any method of segmenting this address and handing it out to its customers. The ISP also knows that IANA and the InterNIC do not just hand out lots of addresses; therefore, the ISP is very careful about carving up the addresses.

The ISP pulls off a portion of the address space using a /20 prefix: 209.16.16.0/20. This represents a small portion of the addresses, or 16 Class C addresses. The ISP leaves the upper 4 bits of the address reserved for future use. 209.16.16.0/20 is the address space that we will work with. Based on some surveys with its customers, the ISP cuts the address into two pieces yielding 209.16.16.0/21 and 209.16.24.0/21. (For those not familiar with binary, shifting right 1 bit divides the number by 2. Shifting left 1 bit multiplies the number by 2). 209.16.16.0/21 (eight Class Cs) is assigned to a single customer. The other half of the address, 209.16.24.0, is cut up again into three pieces:

A Look at the Addresses of an ISP

- ISP is allocated a block of addresses: 209.16.0.0/16.
  - It must now find an efficient breakup of the address

ISP segments off 16 addresses of the original address	209.16.0.0/16 becomes 209.16.16.0/20	11010001.00010000.00000000.00000000 11010001.00010000.0001 I 0000.00000000
ISP splits this new address in half, yielding two address ranges	209.16.16.0/21 209.16.24.0/21	11010001.00010000.00010 I 000.00000000 11010001.00010000.00011 I 000.00000000
Based on a customer survey, 209.16.16.0/21 is given to a single customer	Yields 8 Class C addresses	
209.16.24.0/21 is split up again	209.16.24.0/22 209.16.28.0/23 209.16.30.0/23	11010001.00010000.000110 I 00.00000000 11010001.00010000.0001110 I 0.00000000 11010001.00010000.0001111 I 0.00000000

209.16.24.0/22 representing _ of the address (four Class Cs)

209.16.28/23 representing 1/8 of the address (two Class Cs)

209.16.30.0/23 representing 1/8 of the address (two Class Cs)

How is this done?

Action	Address Space	Binary Equivalent
ISP segments off 16 addresses of the original address	209.16.0.0/16 becomes 209.16.16.0/20	11010001.00010000.00000000.00000000 11010001.00010000.0001 | 0000.00000000
ISP splits this new address in half, yielding two address ranges	209.16.16.0/21 209.16.24.0/21	11010001.00010000.00010 | 000.00000000 11010001.00010000.00011 | 000.00000000
Based on a customer survey, 209.16.16.0/21 is given to a single customer	Yields eight Class C addresses	
209.16.24.0/21 is split again	209.16.24.0/22 209.16.28.0/23 209.16.30.0/23	11010001.00010000.000110 | 00.00000000 11010001.00010000.0001110 | 0.00000000 11010001.00010000.0001111 | 0.00000000

Therefore, customer A gets the Class C address range of 209.16.16.0 through 209.16.23.0.
  Customer B gets the Class C address range of 209.16.24.0 through 209.16.27.0.
  Customer C gets the Class C address range of 209.16.28.0 through 209.16.29.0.
  Customer D gets the Class C address range of 209.16.30.0 through 209.16.31.0.

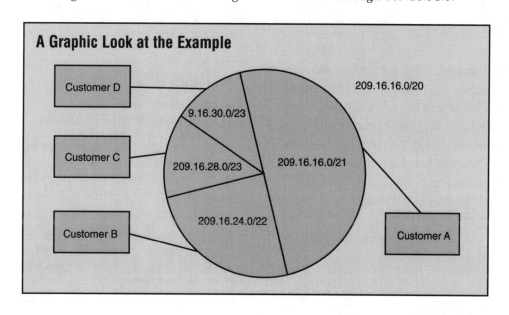

A Graphic Look at the Example

Use the preceding addresses and count up in binary using the table and you will get a better picture of how this operates.

So CIDR is at the ISP and Class addressing is at the customer site. What does this buy us? Not necessarily anything (except a faster network with the ISP), but it does great things for the ISP's routing tables and, therefore, the Internet routing tables. Whereas the ISP would have had 16 entries in the routing table, it now has 4. Whereas the Internet routing tables would have had 256 entries in the global routing table, they now have 1. Now multiply this by the number of ISPs worldwide and I think you begin to see the efficiencies of this protocol, and without it the explosion of the Internet routing tables.

100 CIDR and VLSM Comparison

CIDR and VLSM seem similar; in essence, they are. Why not use VLSM instead of CIDR? The difference is that CIDR allows for the efficient routing mechanism to take place by the recursive allocation of an address block. Routing is then based on this address block allocation and not on an individual Class address. This block is handed down by the IANA to the IR, to the upper-level ISP down through the ranks of downstream ISPs, and, finally, to the customer.

CIDR and VLSM Comparison

- CIDR and VLSM are similar.
- CIDR allows for the efficient routing mechanism to take place by the ability of the recursive allocation of an address block.
- Routing is based on the address block allocation and not the individual Class address.
- VLSM permits recursion at will but more so on an individual address space in use by the customer.
- VLSM allows for variable lengths based on a Class address assigned by an ISP.

VLSM permits recursion as well, but more so on an individual address space in use by the customer. A customer division of an address space is not visible by the Internet. VLSM still operates with Class addresses.

Variable-length masks allow for variable-length subnets per network ID based on an address assignment by an ISP. This allows one network number to contain different masks and is a better use of an IP address. With VLSM, a lot of the bits in an address space are wasted. The example is assigning an IP address to a point-to-point WAN link, which wastes 252 address bits.

This allows for greater flexibility when dividing up a network ID into subnets and hosts. Without VLSM, you have to choose between having enough networks, with close to the right amount of hosts, or having the right amount of hosts with close to the right amount of networks.

Special Subnet Considerations   101

RFC 950 (page 5) states that we should preserve the all 0s and all 1s in the subnet field, for they have special meaning in the certain fields indicated by IANA-assigned RFC numbers. For example, the address 130.1.255.255 could be interpreted as meaning all hosts on the network 130.1, or the address 0.0.0.1 could be interpreted as meaning host 1 on this network.

It is useful to preserve and extend the interpretation of these special addresses in subnetted networks. This means the values of all 0s and all 1s in the subnet field should not be assigned to actual (physical) subnets.

Due to increasing demand to make full use of all of the bits in the 32-bit wide address, subnet 0s and 1s are allowed. However, you must exercise caution when doing so. RFC 1812 (Requirements for IPv4 Routers) states:

All-subnets broadcasts (called multisubnet broadcasts) have been deprecated. . . . In a CIDR routing domain, wherein classical IP network numbers are meaningless, the concept of an all-subnets-directed-broadcast is also meaningless.

Basically, there are not subnets in CIDR.

Now, while the preceding extract was talking about the CIDR router domain, it could be misread by any routed domain. Many router vendors interpret RFCs different ways. For example, 3Com has the ability to turn ASB (All Subnets Broadcast) routing on or off, thereby allowing all 1s subnetwork number free to be assigned.

You may think, why would you want to place an ASB? This can come in handy when multicasting. As of this writing, the multicast protocols are not being used on customer networks, mainly due to inexperience and nervousness of the router support staff and its management. Routed networks are tricky enough without thoroughly understanding multicasting. Therefore, multicast application software vendors support ASB to route their information in a nonmulticast network. Unruly, yes, but it works.

This thinking may be propagated down to the lowest levels of routing in the Internet: the customer AS. If the customer AS has "deprecated" ASB, then you will be implementing all 0s and all 1s subnets. However, if a customer network has implemented it (all 1s subnets), then a packet addressed to an ASB will be routed to the subnet represented by the all 1s.

Special Subnet Considerations

- RFC 950 originally indicated that 0s and 1s should not be used in either host or subnet assignments.
  - Special meaning in that 0.0.0.1 means host 1 on this subnet.

- Increasing pressure forced the use of all available bits for subnetting.

- CIDR has no concept of subnets, therefore it has no concept of 0s or 1s being reserved.

- You should be careful in using all 0s or 1s in a subnet. An all 1s subnet could be misinterpreted as an all-subnets broadcast.
  - All 1s in the subnet field could direct a router to forward the packet to all subnets under the indicated network ID.

Internet Assigned Numbers Authority

- The owner of all number assignments for the TCP/IP protocol, including many other number assignments from other protocols that are asociated with TCP/IP.
    - This includes port numbers, multicast address, IP addresses, etc.
- IANA chartered by the Internet Society (ISOC) and the Federal Network Council (FNC).
- Current RFC number is RFC 1700.
- Updates are available through: ftp://ftp.isi.edu/in-notes/iana/assignments

The Internet protocol suite, as defined by the Internet Engineering Task Force (IETF) and its steering group (the IESG), contains numerous parameters, such as internet addresses, domain names, autonomous system numbers (used in some routing protocols), protocol numbers, port numbers, management information-based object identifiers (including private enterprise numbers), and many others.

The Internet Assigned Numbers Authority (IANA) is the central coordinator for the assignment of unique parameter values for Internet protocols. The IANA is chartered by the Internet Society (ISOC) and the Federal Network Council (FNC) to act as the clearinghouse to assign and coordinate the use of numerous Internet protocol parameters.

Certain fields within IP and TCP are required to be unique. Imagine a port number that is arbitrarily assigned for FTP, or an IP address that is allowed to be assigned by any site and then wants to connect to the Internet. It is the task of the IANA to make those unique assignments as requested and to maintain a registry of the currently assigned values.

As of this writing, RFC 1700 contains the compilation of assigned numbers. However, an up-to-date FTP site is available at:

ftp://ftp.isi.edu/in-notes/iana/assignments

Requests for parameter assignments (protocols, ports, etc.) should be sent to:

<iana@isi.edu>

Requests for SNMP network management private enterprise number assignments should be sent to:

<iana-mib@isi.edu>

The IANA is located at and operated by the Information Sciences Institute (ISI) of the University of Southern California (USC). If you are developing a protocol or application that will require the use of a link, socket, port, protocol, and so forth, please contact the IANA to receive a number assignment (refer to RFC 1700).

Current IANA Address Block Assignments

Address Block	Registry - Purpose	Date
000–063/8	IANA	Sep 81
064–095/8	IANA—Reserved	Sep 81
096–126/8	IANA—Reserved	Sep 81
127/8	IANA	Sep 81
128–191/8	Various Registries	May 93
192–193/8	Various Registries—MultiRegional	May 93
194–195/8	RIPE NCC—Europe	May 93
196–197/8	Internic—Others	May 93
198–199/8	Internic—North America	May 93
200–201/8	Internic—Central and South America	May 93
202–203/8	APNIC—Pacific Rim	May 93
204–205/8	Internic—North America	Mar 94
206/8	Internic—North America	Apr 95
207/8	Internic—North America	Nov 95
208/8	Internic—North America	Apr 96
209/8	Internic—North America	Jun 96
210/8	APNIC—Pacific Rim	Jun 96
211/8	APNIC—Pacific Rim	Jun 96
212–223/8	IANA—Reserved	Sep 81
224–239/8	IANA—Multicast (Class D)	Sep 81
240–255/8	IANA—Reserved (Class E)	Sep 81

Current IANA Address Block Assignments

Address Block	Registry - Purpose	Date
000–063/8	IANA	Sep 81
064–095/8	IANA—Reserved	Sep 81
096–126/8	IANA—Reserved	Sep 81
127/8	IANA	Sep 81
128–191/8	Various Registries	May 93
192–193/8	Various Registries—MultiRegional	May 93
194–195/8	RIPE NCC—Europe	May 93
196–197/8	Internic—Others	May 93
198–199/8	Internic—North America	May 93
200–201/8	Internic—Central and South America	May 93
202–203/8	APNIC—Pacific Rim	May 93
204–205/8	Internic—North America	Mar 94
206/8	Internic—North America	Apr 95
207/8	Internic—North America	Nov 95
208/8	Internic—North America	Apr 96
209/8	Internic—North America	Jun 96
210/8	APNIC—Pacific Rim	Jun 96
211/8	APNIC—Pacific Rim	Jun 96
212–223/8	IANA—Reserved	Sep 81
224–239/8	IANA—Multicast (Class D)	Sep 81
240–255/8	IANA—Reserved (Class E)	Sep 81

IP Routing

We had to go through the IP addressing section in order to understand routing. Hopefully, this section will be a lot more comprehensible. Packets are routed based on the address that is in the packet. Routers read this information and determine the best path known as the next hop. A packet switched network (compared to a circuit switched network) is based on a unit of information (known as a *datagram*) and its ability to make its way through the network to the destination. The datagram may be routed locally (the destination is on the same subnet as the originator) which is known as *direct routing*, or it may invoke the use of a forwarding device such as a router if the destination is remote (on a different subnet than the originator). The latter is known as *indirect routing*, which infers hierarchical routing. A datagram that is sent may invoke both direct and indirect routing.

Why not just have one large flat network? Place everyone on the same network. ATM tried to do this as well as switches and bridges. Eliminate indirect routing completely. Flat networks do have their place: in small networks or WAN protocols or to extend a subnet through switches or bridges. With the current suite of network protocols, a large flat network is inefficient (it does not scale well), especially when you estimate the millions of addressable stations that are attached to it. And the protocols that currently run on networks are broadcast oriented. This means the network allows for multiple stations to be attached and grouped to a single network, and these stations

---

IP Routing

- Two types: direct and indirect.
- Routing provides for efficient network topologies.
- Flat networks cannot scale.
- Protocols used today are the same ones that were used back in the shared network environment.
- Two types of routing protocols: IGP and EGP.
    - IGP provides for routing within a single AS
    - EGP provides for routing between ASs

---

see all data on their network no matter who sent it and who it is for. The protocols were built for shared environments. These networks were invented before the advent of switches and routers. Also, when stations need to communicate, the initial communication could be sent in broadcast mode. Communication between certain devices (routers) is always done in broadcast or multicast. This is a special type of packet that enables all stations to receive the packet and hand it to their upper-layer software to filter or process. As you scale for growth, a network cannot remain flat. There must be some sort of hierarchy to allow for efficiency.

Not all stations need to see each other. As a network scales, it must maintain its manageability. To make any network more manageable, it will be split into many networks called *subnets* (virtually any network today, whether split or not, is called a *subnet*). To make these subnet networks manageable they will in turn be split further into sub-subnets. The interconnection of these subnets is accomplished by forwarding devices known as *routers*. Routers enable data to be forwarded to other networks in a very efficient manner. It will always be easier to manage many smaller networks than it will be to manage one large network. Also, broadcast data stays on its network or subnet. It is not forwarded by routers (exceptions occur and they will be noted in those sections, such as DHCP or all subnets broadcast).

In order for routers to forward data to other networks, they use special protocols (known as *routing* protocols) to enable them to internally draw a map of the entire internet for the purposes of routing. To accomplish this, there are two types of protocols used: Interior Gateway Protocols (IGPs) and Exterior Gateway Protocols (EGPs). The Exterior Gateway Protocol used with IP is known as Border Gateway Protocol (BGP). The IGPs that I will explain are known as the Routing Information Protocol (RIP and RIP2) and Open Shortest Path First (OSPF).

Direct Routing   105

As stated before there are two type of routing: direct and indirect. This section gives you a brief introduction to direct routing. Throughout this section, different network numbers will be used. The examples will not employ the use of subnets. Subnets effectively act like network numbers. Subnets are also separated by a router. For example, in the slide, the network numbers could be 140.1.1.1 on the network with endstation B, and 140.1.2.1 on the network containing host A. Using a subnet mask of 255.255.255.0 would yield two different networks: 140.1.1.0 and 140.1.2.0. For simplicity in explaining routers, I have chosen to use completely different network numbers.

How does a network station know whether the packet has to be directly (local) or indirectly (remote) routed? For the network station, it is a relatively simple process. The whole basis for routing is in the IP network number assigned to the network station.

Remember from the previous section on Addressing that an IP address contains the network number as well as the host number.

With the first 1, 2, 3, or 4 bits of the 32-bit IP network address identifying the class of the address, this allows for any network station (workstation or router) to quickly extract the network portion out of the class of IP address. In other words, by reading up to the first 4 bits of the IP address, a network station can quickly determine how much of the IP address to read to determine the network number of the address. The sending station will compare the packet's destination network number to that of its own network number. If the network number portion of the destination IP address matches it own, the packet can be routed directly on the local LAN, without the use of a router. The packet is simply transmitted to the station (using ARP if necessary).

Once this determination is made, and the packet is destined for a local route, the net-work station would check its ARP table to find the IP-to-physical-address mapping. If one is found, the packet is physically addressed and transmitted onto the network. The physical destination address (located in the datalink header) will be that of the receiving station. If the station's address is not in the ARP cache, the ARP request process is invoked.

Referring to the slide, endstation B and host A are located on the same network.

Again, a point needs to be brought up here: There is a difference between a routing protocol and a routable protocol. A routable protocol is one that allows for routing such as NetWare (IPX) and TCP/IP. NetBIOS and LAT (a DEC terminal/printer protocol) are not routable protocols. RIP and OSPF, are routing protocols whichenable the routing functions to work properly.

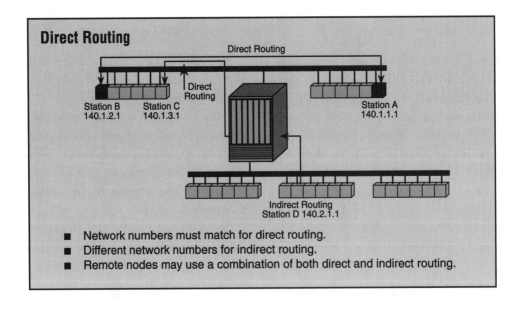

Indirect Routing

> ## Indirect Routing
>
> - Occurs when the source and destination network or subnet do not match.
> - Source will ARP for a router and send the datagram to the router.
> - The router will either forward the packet directly to the destination or it will forward it to another router in the path to the destination.
> - Routers decrement the TTL field.
> - Routers forward the packet based on the IP address and not the MAC address.

If the source and destination stations are on different networks, they must use the indirect routing services of a router. The transmitting station will address the physical destination address of the packet to that of the router (using ARP, if necessary, to find the physical address of the router) and submit the packet to the router. Each workstation may be able to determine the address of its closest router, or it can be preconfigured with the address of its default router. The router has two choices:

1. If the destination network indicated by the address in the IP header is directly attached to the router, it will forward the packet directly to the destination station.
2. If the destination network indicated by the address in the IP header is not directly attached to the router, it must use the services of another router to forward the packet and let that router determine the next hop path.

Notice here, the destination physical address is that of the router and not the final destination station. This type of routing is indirect routing. The final destination IP address is embedded in the IP header.

Sending a packet to its final destination might be accomplished by using both direct and indirect routing. For example, when a packet is to be delivered across an internet, the originating station will address it to the router for delivery to its final network. This is indirect routing. The originator and destination may be separated by more than one router. No matter whether the final destination network ID is directly connected to that router or whether the packet must traverse a few routers to reach its final destination, the last router in the path must use *direct routing* to deliver the packet to its destination host.

Depending on the Options field settings, it should be noted that the original IP datagram, will not be altered with two primary exceptions: the TTL (Time to Live) field and the Cyclic Redundancy Check field. If an IP datagram is received by a router and it has not arrived at its final destination, the router will decrement the TTL field. If TTL > 0, it will forward the packet based on routing table information. The IP datagram's header contents will remain the same (with the exception of an error-detection field known as the Cyclic Redundancy Check, or CRC). Since the TTL field changed, the

CRC must be recalculated throughout all the networks and routers that the datagram traverses. Otherwise, the only alterations that are made are to the datalink headers and trailers. The IP addresses in the IP header will remain the same, as the datagram traverses any routers in the path to its destination.

IP routers forward datagrams on a connectionless basis and therefore do not guarantee delivery of any packet. They operate at the network layer, which provides best-effort or connectionless data transfer. Routers do not establish sessions with other routers on the internet. In fact, IP routers do not know of any workstations (nonrouters) on their subnets.

These routers forward packets based on the network address of the packet (in the IP header) and *not* on the physical address (the 48-bit address for broadcast networks) of the final destination (the receiver). When the router receives the packet, it will look at the final network address (embedded in the IP header of the packet) and determine how to route the packet. Routers only route packets that are directly addressed to them. They do not operate in promiscuous mode (watching all LAN traffic) for forwarding datagrams.

107 A Flowchart

The slide shows the flowchart of the routing process.

Before complete confusion takes over here, there are some entities that need to be explained about the IP layer that allow the internet to operate. In other words, when a router receives a packet, how does it know where and how to send these packets? In order for a packet to be delivered through a router, the router must know which path to deliver the packet to in order for the packet to reach its final destination. This is accomplished through IP routing algorithms, which involves two steps: maintaining a table of known routes (network numbers), and learning new routes (network numbers) when they become available.

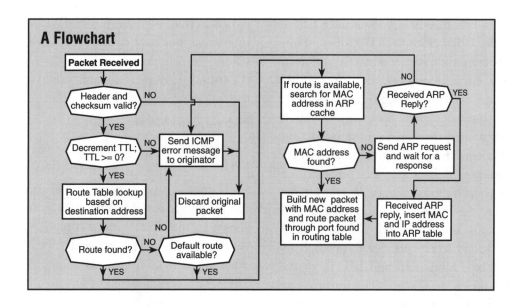

A Flowchart

Packet Received

Header and checksum valid? — NO

YES

Decrement TTL; TTL >= 0? — NO

Send ICMP error message to originator

YES

Route Table lookup based on destination address

Discard original packet

Route found? — NO

NO — Default route available?

YES

YES

If route is available, search for MAC address in ARP cache

Received ARP Reply? — NO

YES

MAC address found? — NO

Send ARP request and wait for a response

YES

Build new packet with MAC address and route packet through port found in routing table

Received ARP reply, insert MAC and IP address into ARP table

Routing Protocols— Distance Vector   108

Information is kept in the router that allows to it to know all the networks or subnets in its domain and the path to get to those networks. The information is about networks and their paths. This information is grouped together into a table—a table is the same thing as a table in Microsoft Word. It contains a grouping of like information to be use as a whole. There are two standard methods for building these tables: distance vector and link state. Link state will be covered later. Distance vector means that the information sent from router to router is based on an entry in a table consisting of <vector, distance>. *Vector* means the network number and *distance* means what it costs to get there. The routers exchange this network reachability information with each other by broadcasting their routing table information consisting of these distance-vector entries. This broadcast is local and each router is dependent on other routers for correct calculation of the distance.

Each entry in the table is a network number (the vector) and the amount of routers (distance) that are between it (the router) and the final network (indicated by the network number). This distance is sometimes referred to as a *metric*. For example, if the source station wants to transmit a packet to a destination station that is four hops away, there are probably four routers separating the two networks.

Any time a datagram must traverse a router (thereby passing through a new network number) it is considered a hop (metric). For RIP, the maximum diameter of the internet is 15 routers (hops). A distance of 16 is an indication that the network is not reachable. In other words, if the network is more than 15 routers away, it is considered unreachable. Remember: This is RIP and RIP is an IGP, which is under one domain. The Internet itself encompasses many domains and the diameter of the Internet is much larger than 15 hops.

As shown in the slide, each router will contain a table with starting entries of those networks that are directly attached to it. For a router that has only two network connections (there are no other routers on the internet), the initial entries in the table would look like the following:

Network	Metric	Port	Age
134.4.0.0	1	1	XXX
134.3.0.0	1	2	XXX

There are actually more header entries in a routing table, but the significant portions are shown in the slide. From this table, we know that networks 134.4.0.0 and 134.3.0.0 are directly connected to this router. Network 134.4.0.0 is assigned to port 1 of the router and 134.3.0.0 is directly attached to port 2. It is running the RIP protocol, and xxx indicates how long the route has before it is deleted from the table.

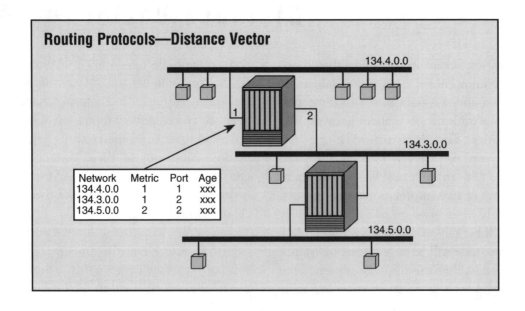

Updating Other Routers (Distance Vectors) 109

Updating Other Routers (Distance Vectors)

- Upon initialization, each router reads its preconfigured IP address and metric (cost in hops) of all its active ports.

- Each router transmits a portion of its routing table (network ID, metric) to each "neighbor" router.

- Each router uses the most recent updates from each neighbor.

- Each router uses the update information to calculate its own "shortest path" (distance in hops) to a network.

- Tables are updated only:
  - If the received information indicates a shorter path to the destination network.
  - If the received update information indicates a network is no longer reachable.
  - If a new network is found.

Some but not all the entries of the router's route table are sent out the ports to update other routers as to the networks that this router knows about. There are a few exceptions, which will be explained in a moment. These updates are not forwarded by any router, meaning the updates stay on the network on which they originated. Any router that is located on the same network will receive the packet, read the routing table data, and update its table if needed. All participating routers will accomplish this. In other words, all routers forward their tables out each active port. As each table is received, the routers are building a picture of the network. As each broadcast is transmitted, more and more information is being propagated throughout the network. Eventually, all routers will know of all networks on their internet.

There are three possibilities that can cause a router to update its existing table based on just-received information:

1. If the received table contains an entry to a network with a lower hop count, it will *replace its entry* with the new entry containing the lower hop count.

2. If a network exists in the just-received table that does not exist in its own table, it will *add the new entry*.

3. If the router forwards packets to a particular network through a specified router (indicated by the next-hop router address) and that router's hop count to a network destination changes, it will change its entry. In other words, if router A normally routes data for a network X through router B, and router B's hop-count entry to that network changes, router A changes its entry.

A Bigger Update

This slide shows what happens when router A submits its routing table out of its port connected to network 2. This slide assumes all routers are newly initialized. (For simplicity, the slide shows the updating through one port only. In reality, routing tables are submitted out all ports of a router, with a few restrictions on which entries of the table get transmitted.)

Router A transmits its table containing two networks: Z and Y. Each of these networks is one hop away (they are directly connected). Router B will receive this packet and will add 1 to each hop-count entry in the received table. (This is accomplished assuming the RIP cost assigned to that port of router B is 1. The configured hop count could be set to something else.)

Router B examines its table and notices that it does not have an entry for network Z. It

will add this entry to its table as: network 1, available through port 1, two hops away. It will then check the next entry. Network Y will not be added, for router B already has network 2 in its table with a cost of 1. Since the incoming table reports network Y has a cost of 2, router B will ignore this entry. (There are rules that will prevent router A from sending out information about network 2, which will be discussed later.)

Once its table is updated, router B will transmit its table out its ports every 30 seconds (again, for simplicity only one router update is being shown). Router C will receive this table from router B and will perform the same steps as router B. Eventually, all information about all networks on the internet will be propagated to all routers.

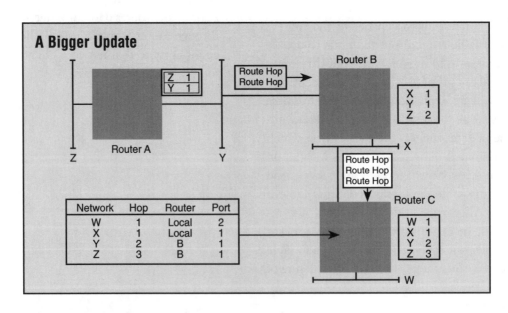

The slide shows an example of what is in a routing table. This is a distance-vector routing table, not a link-state routing table. OSPF would have a different kind of table. In this table, it is important to note the network number, hops to that network number, and the next router in the path to that network.

Routing table fields vary, depending on the update mechanism used. The following table is a sample of a routing table used by the routing information protocol (RIP) for the IP protocol.

The route table entries on the slide are defined as follows:

Network number. A known network ID.

Next router to deliver to. The next router that the packet should be delivered to if the destination network is not directly connected. A directly connected network is one that is physically connected to the router, since most routers today have more than two connected networks.

Hops. This is the metric count of how many routers the packet must traverse before reaching the final destination. A 1 indicates a local route.

Learned from. Since many routing algorithms may exist in a router (i.e., RIP, OSPF, and EGP may exist in the same router), there is usually an entry in the table to explain how the route was acquired.

Time left to delete. The amount of time left before the route will be deleted from the table.

Port. The physical port on the router from which the router received information about this network.

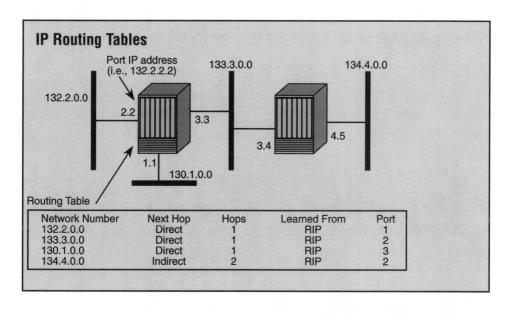

IP Routing Tables

Network Number	Next Hop	Hops	Learned From	Port
132.2.0.0	Direct	1	RIP	1
133.3.0.0	Direct	1	RIP	2
130.1.0.0	Direct	1	RIP	3
134.4.0.0	Indirect	2	RIP	2

112 The Routing Information Protocol (Version 1)

Routing tables allow routers to determine the next hop path for a received datagram. But what builds those tables? Dynamic updating is the process by which routers update each other with reachability information. Before the advent of dynamic updates of routing tables, most commercial vendors supported manual updates for their router tables. This meant manually entering network numbers, their associated distances, and the port numbers into the router table. The Internet was then known as the ARPAnet and it employed a routing update scheme known as the Gateway Information Protocol and later the Gateway to Gateway Protocol (GGP). This is beyond the scope of this book and is not used anymore. Independent router vendors did not have that many routers and subnets to update, so placing a manual entry in the routers was not all that bad. As networks grew larger, this became a cumbersome way of building tables. Commercially, RIP was the protocol that enabled automatic updates of router tables.

The RIP algorithm is based on the distance-vector algorithms just described. RIP placed the fundamentals of distance-vector in a simple routing algorithm. Implementations of these protocols were first found on the ARPAnet in 1969 using the Gateway Information Protocol. However, it was first devised by Xerox Corporation as the routing algorithm used by Internet Datagram Protocol of XNS.

RFC 1058 first defined RIP for TCP/IP, and it was formally adopted by the IAB in 1988. Although it was not primarily intended as *the* routing algorithm for TCP, it gained widespread acceptance when it became embedded

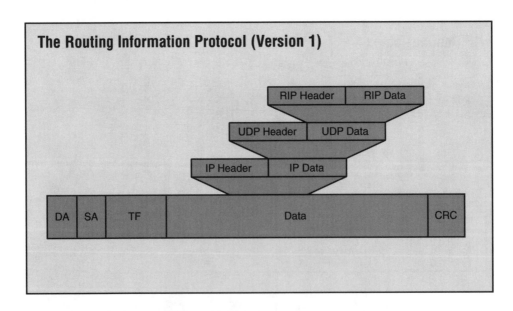

The Routing Information Protocol (Version 1)

into the Berkeley 4BSD Unix operating system through a service known as routed (pronounced "route d"—d is for the daemon process that runs the protocol in Unix). Placing the functions of RIP into an RFC allowed for interoperability and detailed certain functions.

With RIP information, any router knows the length of the shortest path (not necessarily the best) from each of its neighbor routers (routers located on the same network) to any other destination. There are many deficiencies in this protocol and they are discussed at the end of this section.

The RIP packet is quite simple. The slide shows the RIP header and data encapsulated in an Ethernet packet. The RIP data is the table information one router shares with another.

RIP Operational Types 113

RIP Operational Types

- RIP can operate in either ACTIVE or PASSIVE mode.

- Active means that it builds routing tables and responds to RIP requests.

- Passive means that it can build a routing table for its own use, but it does not respond to any RIP requests.

- Most workstations (PCs) use a default gateway (i.e., router) and not a routing update protocol like RIP.

There are two types of RIP packets that traverse a network (indicated by the command field, shown next): one to request information and the other to give information (a response packet). A response packet is generated for a request packet and is used for periodic RIP updates. Most RIP packets that traverse a local network will be the periodic RIP table updates. Does RIP operate in a workstation? The answer is, "yes and no." Some workstations implement RIP. Windows NT and Unix both use RIP; however, most simple workstations such as Windows 95 do not (they have a default gateway). If a workstation does implement RIP, it is usually in what is known as *passive mode*, which means it can receive and process updates, but cannot respond to RIP requests or broadcast its table.

In passive mode, RIP listens only for RIP updates. (It may build its own tables or it may not. If it does, it will not broadcast these tables.) It will build a table so that it will not have to request information from other routers on the network. Passive end is used for non-routing network stations. These devices have no reason to broadcast updates, but have every reason to listen for them. Today, most DOS PC computers will use a concept of a default gateway, explained later. Even Windows 95 uses a default gateway if prompted. It can build a routing table, but Windows 95 is not RIP-enabled.

The RIP passive protocol allows the host to maintain a table of the shortest routes to a network and designates which router to send the packets to. This consumes a considerable amount of RAM for both the table and the algorithm. Without it, TCP/IP requires a default gateway entry, which specifies that when a packet is destined for a remote network, the host must submit the packet to a specified gateway for processing, even if this gateway is not the shortest path to that network. Passive implementations add no overhead to the network, for they listen only to routing table updates that are on the network. Without passive RIP, these devices have to maintain their own tables or implement a default route.

Most workstations do not invoke active versions of the RIP protocol They do not build tables and keep track of networks. To communicate with a router, workstations generally use their default gateway parameter. This is for simplicity. Higher-powered workstations, such as Sun SPARC workstations, can build and maintain routing tables. However the early implementations of ICP/IP were not powerful and required a simple method.Remember, RIP packets do not leave their local network. All participants in the RIP protocol (for example, routers) will receive the packet, update their tables if necessary, and then discard the packet. They will compute the reachability of networks based on adding a cost (usually 1) to the just-received tables or count entry, and then broadcast their tables out their ports (usually being mindful of a protocol named *split horizon*, which is explained a little later).

The fields in the RIP packets are:

Command	Description
1	Request for partial or full routing table information
2	Response packet containing a routing table
3–4	Turn on (3) or off (4) trace mode (obsolete)
5	Sun Microsystems' internal use

Version. Used to indicate the version of RIP. Currently set to 1 for RIP version 1.

Family of net x. Used to show the diversity of the RIP protocol and to indicate the protocol that owns the packet. It will be set to 2 for IP. Since XNS could possibly be running on the same network as IP, the RIP frames would be similar. This shows that the same RIP frame can be used for multiple protocol suites. AppleTalk, Novell NetWare's IPX, XNS, and TCP/IP all use the RIP packet. Each packet is changed a little for each protocol.

IP address. Indicates the IP address of a specific destination network. This would be filled in by the requesting station. An address of 0.0.0.0 indicates the default route (explained later). The address field needs only 4 bytes of the available 14 bytes, so all other bytes must be set to 0. This will be explained in RIP Version 2.

If this is a request packet and there is only one entry, with the address family ID of 0 and a metric of 1, then this is a request for the entire routing table.

As for the distance-to-network field, only the integers of 1 to 16 are allowed. An entry of

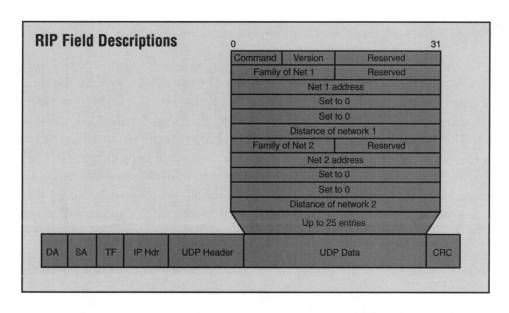

RIP Field Descriptions

16 in this field indicates that the network is unreachable.

The next entry in the field would start with the IP address field through the metric field. This would be repeated for each table entry of the router to be broadcast. The maximum size of this packet is 512 bytes.

The RIP protocol relies on the transport-layer protocol of the User Datagram Protocol (UDP, discussed in the next section on transport-layer protocols). In this will be the specification for the length of the RIP packet. Also, for those interested, RIP operates on UDP port number 520 (port numbers are discussed in the UDP section).

115 Default Router and Gateways

On a TCP/IP network, there is a concept known as the *default route*. Except for proprietary implementations, this is not part of any other network protocol (XNS, AppleTalk, IPX, etc.). The default route can be maintained in two places: the router and the endstation.

For an endstation that does not support the active or passive functions of the RIP protocol, thereby allowing it to find a route dynamically, the default router (commonly called a *default gateway*) is assigned to it. This is the 32-bit address of the router the workstation should route to if remote routing is necessary. The IP layer in the endstation would determine that the destination network is not local and that the services of a router must be used. Instead of implementing the RIP protocol, the endstation may submit the packet to the default router as assigned by the default route number. The router will take care of ensuring the packet will reach its final destination. If that router does not have the best route, it will send a message (using the ICMP protocol) to the endstation to inform it of a better route. This will be explained later.

A router may also be assigned a default route. It is indicated as 0.0.0.0 in its routing table. There is no subnet mask associated with it. This is implemented for when a router receives a packet and does not have the network number in its table. The router will forward the packet to another router for which it has an assigned default route. This means that when a router has received a packet to route, and its table does not contain the network number indicated in the received packet, it will forward the packet to its default router, hoping that the default router will have the network number in its table and will be able to properly forward the packet. The default router will receive the packet and, if the network number is in its table, it will forward the

packet. If the network number is not in its table with the best route, it, too, may have a default router, and it will forward the packet to that router. If there is no route and there is not another default route, the last router will send a control message (through ICMP) back to the originating station indicating it could not forward the packet.

The problem with default routes in workstations is that a workstation's default router may go down and the workstation will not know if there is another router on the network. The network number may change or there may be a better path for the workstation to take. The default gateway allows for the elimination of routing tables in the network station and routers by allowing groups of networks to become available through the default route.

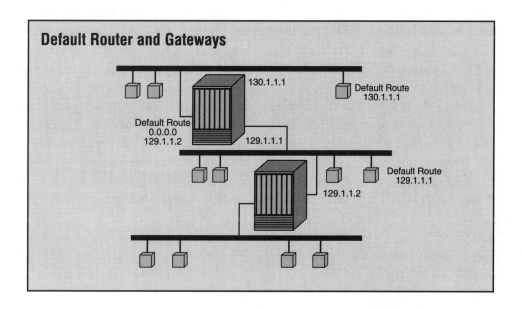

Default Router and Gateways

116 Disadvantages of the RIPv1 Protocol

As noted earlier, the acceptance of RIP in the Internet community was based on its implementation into the popular Berkeley 4BSD Unix operating system through a process known as *routed* (Pronounced Route - d, two words). Unfortunately, it was implemented before the rapid growth of TCP/IP. RIP had many disadvantages that were not considered limiting at the time it became accepted. Before RIP was implemented, some router tables had to be constructed manually. RIP allowed these tables to be updated dynamically, which was a real advantage. The disadvantages follow.

RIP, based on a simple hop count, understands only the shortest route to a destination, which may not be the fastest route. RIP understands only hop counts. For example, there may be two paths to a destination: one that traverses two T1 lines (three hops) and another that has two hops, but is a 9600 baud serial line. RIP would pick the 9600 baud line, because its shorter (two hops). There are variations of RIP that allow the network administrator to assign an arbitrary RIP hop count or cost to a route to disallow for this. This solves one problem, but creates another. This incremented RIP number adds to the upper limit of a 15-hop diameter in RIP, which creates another problem. The number of hops that a network may be distanced from any network station is limited to 15—a hop count of 16 is considered unreachable. If you add additional hops to a path, you decrease the total number of routers allowed in a path.

Disadvantages of the RIPv1 Protocol

- RIPv1 only understands the shortest route to a destination, based on a simple count of router hops.

- It depends on other routers for computed routing updates.

- Routing tables can get large and these are broadcasted every 30 seconds.

- Distances are based on hops, not on real costs (such as the speed of a link).

- Patched with split horizon, poison reverse, hold-down timers, triggered updates.
  - It continues to be a router-to-router configuration. One router is fully dependent on the next router to implement the same options.

- Fix one problem and others appear.

With RIP, routing table updates are only as accurate as the router that submitted them. If any router made a computational error in updating its routing table, this error will be received and processed by all other routers.

What may also be apparent is the fact that the routing tables could get very large. If the network consisted of 300 different networks (not uncommon in larger corporations), each routing table of every router would have 300 entries. Since RIP works with UDP (connectionless transport-layer service), the maximum datagram size of a RIP packet is 512 bytes (576 bytes, including all media headers). This allows for a maximum of 25 <network number, distance> combinations in each packet. Therefore, it would take 13 packets from each router to broadcast its routing table to all other routers on all the local networks in the internet. This would be broadcast every 30 seconds by each of the 300 routers. All this, and the possibility that nothing had changed from the previous update! This is an unnecessary consumption of bandwidth, especially over slow-speed serial lines.

This leads to the second disadvantage. RIPv1 normally broadcasts (datalink physical address of all FFs) to the network every 30 seconds, even across slower-speed serial links. This makes the datalink pass the packet up to the upper-layer protocols on all stations on the network, even if the stations do not support RIP.

Every time we solved one problem, another popped up.

Scaling with RIP 117

Here is where RIP really shows off the limitations. Try and build a large network based on RIP. RIP was designed for small stable networks. It states this in the Xerox documentation. RIP does not handle growth very well. This problem is twofold. The first limitation is that a destination network may be no more than 15 hops away in diameter (a distance of 16 in any routing table indicates the network is unreachable). Careful planning is needed to implement large-scale networks based on the RIP protocol.

The other scaling problem is the propagation of routing information. Four terms need to be understood here, for they are used quite frequently: *split horizon, hold-down timer, poisoned reverse,* and *triggered updates.*

Refer to the slide. With router A directly attached to network z, it advertises that route through *all* its ports as a distance of 1 (whatever the RIP-assigned cost of the port that attaches to that network is). Router B receives this and updates its table as network z1 with a distance of 2. Router B then broadcasts its table (at the 30-second update timer) and router C receives this and updates its table as network n with a distance of 3. Notice that all routers broadcast all the information in their tables through all ports (even the ports from which they received the update).

Why would router B broadcast a reachability of network z when router A already has a direct attachment to it? Wouldn't this confuse router A if network z is located? Normally it would, but remember that the only changes that a router will make to its tables is when the hop-count distance is lower, is a new entry, or if the next hop router path taken to a network changes its hop count. Since that hop count is higher, router A will simply ignore that particular entry in the update table.

Using the original algorithm, a serious problem occurs when router A loses it reachability to network z. It will update its table entry for that network with a distance of 16 (16 indi-cates not reachable), but will wait to broadcast this information until the next scheduled RIP update. So far, so good, but if router B broadcasts its routing table before router A (notice that not all routers broadcast their tables at the same time), router A will then see that router B has a shorter path to network z than it does (a distance of 2 for router B versus a distance of 16 for router A). Router A will change its entry for network z. Now, router A, on its next RIP update broadcast, will announce that it has a path to network z with a distance of 3 (2 from the table entry received from router B plus 1 to reach router B). There is now a loop between routers A and B. A packet destined for network z will be passed between routers A and B until the TTL counter is 0. When router B receives a packet destined for network z, it will forward the packet to router A; router A will forward it back to router B; and this will continue until the TTL field reaches 0. This is

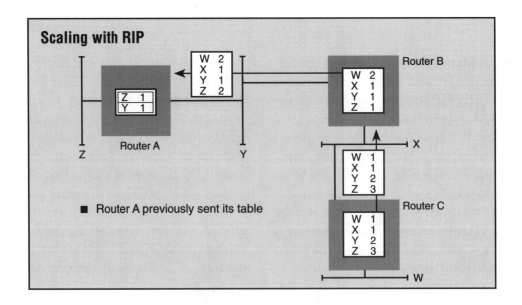

known as *looping*. The RIP protocol works extremely well in a stable environment (an environment where routers and their networks rarely change). The process of clearing out dead routes and providing alternate paths is known as *convergence*.

Even future RIP updates will not quickly fix the convergence in this case. Each update (every 30-second default) will add 1 to the table entry, and it will take a few updates to outdate the entry in these routers. This is known as *slow convergence*, and it causes errors in routing tables and routing loops to occur. What if you had a network diameter of 15 routers and each was exactly opposite on the timer to broadcast its update? In other words, when one router broadcasts its table, the receiving router just finished its broadcast. The lost route could take many minutes to update those routers at the end of the network.

Routers and Subnet Masks

118

From the previous discussion on choosing a subnet mask, a routing protocol known as RIP version 1, or RIP1, requires that a subnet mask be uniform across an entire network ID. An address assignment of 150.1.0.0 must contain one network mask. The fault here is the inability of RIP1 to supply a subnetmask entry in its routing updates to be consumed by other routers. Therefore, RIP1 is forced to make assumptions. It assumes that the mask is the same for the learned subnet of the same network ID as its configured ports. This means

that if a subnet route is learned on a port that has the same network ID as the port, RIP will apply the assigned mask to that learned route as the port. If the learned subnet route has a different network ID than the port it learned the subnet route from, it assumes the learned subnet route is not subnetted and falls back to applying the natural mask for that class.

Here's an example: A router has two ports. Port 1 is assigned an address of 150.1.1.1 with a subnet mask of 255.255.255.0. Port 2 has an address of 160.1.1.1 with a subnet mask of

255.255.255.0. If the router learns of a route 150.1.3.0, then it will apply the 24-bit subnet mask because it has the same network ID as its port. However, if the router learns a subnet route of 175.1.6.0, this network ID is not on either one of its ports and it will apply a natural subnet mask of 255.255.0.0 to that address before updating its table. That is for learned routes.

How about routing updates? When does a router apply the subnet mask to a route and then include it in the routing update? The same rule applies. Using the network numbers from the preceding example, when the router would like to broadcast its table, it will apply the subnet mask of 255.255.255.0 to the learned route of 150.1.3.0 when it sends its update out Port 1. However, it will send the address of 150.1.0.0 when sending the update out Port 2. Port 2 has a different network ID associated with that port and, therefore, the natural mask is applied before sending out the table.

This is why RIP1 supports only one subnet mask for network ID.

The next section gives more examples of address assignment and Variable-Length Subnet Masks (VLSM).

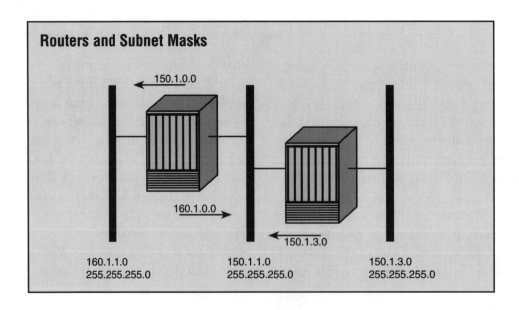

Routers and Subnet Masks

150.1.0.0

160.1.0.0

150.1.3.0

| 160.1.1.0 | 150.1.1.0 | 150.1.3.0 |
| 255.255.255.0 | 255.255.255.0 | 255.255.255.0 |

RIP Fixes

- **Split Horizon**—Rule states that a router will not rebroadcast a learned route back over the interface from which the route was learned.

- **Hold-Down Timer**—Rule states that when a router receives information about a network that is unreachable, the router must ignore all subsequent information about that network for a configurable amount of time.

- **Poisoned Reverse and triggered updates**—Rule states that a router is allowed to rebroadcast a learned route over the interface from which it learned it, but the metric is set to 16. A triggered update allows a router to broadcast its table when a network is found to be down.

To overcome the limitations, a few rules were added to the IP RIP algorithm:

Split horizon. Implemented by every protocol that uses a variation of RIP (AppleTalk, IPX, XNS, and IP), this states that a router will not broadcast a learned route back through a port from which it was received. Therefore, router B will not broadcast the entry of network z back to router A. This keeps router B from broadcasting the reachability of network z back to router A, thereby eliminating the possibility of a lower hop count being introduced when network z becomes disabled. The entry in router B's update to router A would not include an entry for network z.

Hold-down timer. This rule states that once a router receives information about a network that claims a known network is unreachable, it must ignore all future updates that include an entry (a path) to that network (typically, for 60 seconds). Not all vendors support this in their routers. If one vendor does support it and another does not, routing loops may occur.

Poison reverse and triggered updates. These are the last two rules that help to eliminate the slow convergence problem. They state that once the router detects a disabled network connection, the router should keep the present entry in its routing table and then broadcast "network unreachable" (metric of 16) in its updates. These rules become efficient when all routers in the internet participate using *triggered updates*, which allow a router to broadcast its routing table immediately following receipt of this "network down" information. The two most common are *split horizon* and *poison reverse*.

Split Horizon Demonstrated

In the slide, there are three routers, labeled A, B, C, and four subnets, labeled W, X, Y, Z. Upon startup, the routers learn of their immediate subnets. Router A learns about subnets Y and Z. Router B learns about subnets X and Y. Router C learns about subnets W and X. The routers may or may not automatically broadcast their tables out after initialization (this is vender independent). Router C transmits its table containing subnets W and X. It will transmit this information out the ports connecting to subnets W and X. Router B will transmit its table containing subnet X and Y out both of its ports, and router A will transmit its table containing subnets Y and Z out both of its ports. All of the costs in these tables are set to 1. So far, so good.

Router C picks up the information that router B transmitted out and makes some decisions. It will add to each entry the cost associated with the port on which it received the information. In this case, that port was assigned a cost of 1. Therefore, it now has two entries in the received table, each with a cost of 2. It then compares it to its table. It already has a entry for subnet X and it has a cost of 1, so it discards that information. The next entry is for subnet Y with a cost of 2. It does not have that entry, so it will add this entry to its table with a cost of 2. Router C figures it is now complete. Eventually, router C will update its table with the entry for subnet Z (propagated by router B after router B received this information). Router C now has the entries in its table of subnet Z, cost 3; subnet Y, cost 2; subnet X, cost 1; and subnet W, cost 1).

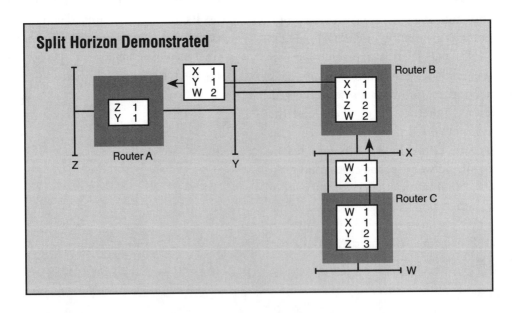

Split Horizon Demonstrated

The periodic timer has expired (every 30 seconds) and router C is ready to broadcast its table. Out the port associated with subnet W, it will list the entries for subnets W, X, Y, and Z. However, on the port associated with subnet X, it will only include those entries for subnet X (some routers do not include this entry if they know of another router on this segment) and subnet W. It will not include the entries for subnets Y and Z. This is known as *spilt horizon*. The rule for split horizon is not to rebroadcast a known route back over the port that the router learned it on. *Poisoned reverse* allows for the network number to be rebroadcast out, but it will include a 16 in the hop count so no other router can update its tables. This is used to avoid routing loops in oddly looped networks.

RIP Version 2   121

In November, 1994, RIP was modified with some additions (extensions) to overcome some of its shortcomings. RIP version 1 continues to exist on many routers and as of this writing, continues to outnumber OSPF networks. However, there is no reason not to implement version 2 of the protocol. Version 2 is backward compatible with version 1 and contains all of the capabilities of the version 1 protocol.

RIP version 2 implemented the following features:

- Authentication—simple text password
- Subnet masking
- Next host
- Multicast—to allow for variable-length subnet masks to be implemented
- Route tag—to provide a method of separating RIP routes from externally learned routes
- Compatibility switch—to allow for interoperability with version 1 routers

Notice that the same format is used for RIPv1 and RIPv2. Apparently, there was some

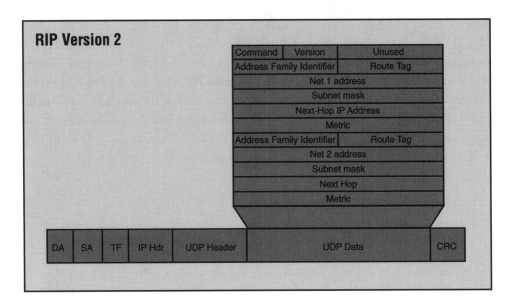

thought when building RIPv1 that future protocols of RIP may be different and that more information is to be carried in the packet. The original packet indicated that the field must be set to 0, and not reserved. Now you can see why. If not, we will revisit this in the subnet mask topic of this section.

There really is not room in the RIP update datagram for authentication. But since this has become commonplace (OSPF), room was made for it. The address family identifier (AFI) is used for authentication. If the AFI contains a 0xFFFF, then the first entry in the route entry list is the password to be used for authentication. The header of the RIP datagram changes as shown in the slide. The authentication type is type 2 (simple password) and the next 16 bytes contain this password (any amount of characters up to 16 bytes). RIPv1 will ignore this entry (the first entry), for the AFI is not set to an address family of IP.

If a RIPv2 router is configured with no authentication, it will accept and process both RIPv1 and v2 unauthenticated messages and discard authenticated messages.. If the RIPv2 router is configured for authentication, it will accept RIPv1 and v2 messages that pass authentication. Remember, not all v1 implementations follow the RFC. They may play with the fields and still be able to be processed by RIPv1 routers! This is not recommended. Unauthenticated RIPv2 messages will be discarded.

Authentication

0		31
Command	Version	Unused
0xFFFF		Authentication Type
Password		
Password		
Password		
Password		
Address Family Identifier		Route Tag
Net 2 address		
Subnet mask		
Next Hop		
Metric		

Subnet Mask Field

This is what is making RIP stick around a little longer. Yes, it still has problems with scaling and still needs split horizon and poisoned reverse to operate properly. But to use the address scheme more efficiently, RIP version 2 now has the ability to support multiple subnet masks per network address. As we learned in other sections of this book, one of the biggest problems with RIP was its inability to support a subnet mask in the routing update. This led to the shortcoming of one subnet mask per network ID. Subnet masking really extends the life of RIP. RIP v1 does not indicate a subnet mask on a route entry. This can create many problems, two of which are learning and updating. How does RIPv1 know how to apply a subnet mask for a learned IP address? How does RIP provide a mask for its updates? Good questions! The answer is not real good

though. RIP assumed that the IP address uses the same subnet mask as it does providing the IP network ID portion of the address is the same as its own and there is a subnet mask applied to its interface.

For example, a router has two interfaces: Interface 1 has an IP address of 130.1.1.1 and a subnet mask of 255.255.255.0. Interface 2 has an IP address of 205.1.1.1 and a subnet mask of 255.255.255.0. When interface 1 receives a routing update, any entry that has the same network ID as its own, 130.1.x.x, will apply the subnet mask that is configured to its port to those entries. You will see an entry in the routing table for that learned address. So, if a RIPv1 update was received on interface 1 and the update contained the entry 130.1.4.0, then the interface will record 130.1.4.0 in its routing table. However, if interface 1 received

Subnet Mask Field

Command	Version	Unused	
0xFFFF		Authentication Type	
Password			
Password			
Password			
Password			
Address Family Identifier		Route Tag	
Net 2 address			
Subnet mask			
Next Hop			
Metric			

0 ... 31

155.1.1.0 on that interface, it would only place 155.1.0.0 into its table because it does not know the subnet mask for the address of 155.1.0.0. You must be safe when you assume.

When the router must transmit its table, how does it know to apply a mask to any of the entries in the table? It will depend on the interface from which it is transmitted. On interface 1, the router will transmit two entries: 150.1.1.0 and 200.1.1.0.

So, RIPv1 and subnet masks did not understand each other. RIPv2 fixes that. Notice in the slide that the format of the RIP datagram is preserved. The two fields in RIPv1 that stated "must be 0" are not used for the subnet mask and next-hop entries. Each route entry in the datagram will have an associated subnet mask with it. If the field contains a 0, there is not a subnet mask associated for the route entry. Also, in coordination with RIPv1 routers, a mask that is shorter than the Class's natural mask should never be advertised.

Route Tag and Next-Hop Fields 124

The route tag entry is used to advertise routes that were learned externally (not in this IGP). OSPF has this capability and allows the OSPF IGP to learn about routes external to the IGP. For example, if the routes were learned via BGP-4 (a routing protocol used between autonomous systems), the route tag entry could be used for setting the autonomous system from which the routes were learned.

The next-hop field allows the router to learn where the next hop is for the specific route entry. If the entry is 0.0.0.0, then the source address of the update should be used for the route. Over a point-to-point link (to routers connected by a serial line) there is not much use for this entry (the next hop could be extracted from the source IP address in the IP header of the packet). This field does have considerable use in instances where there are multiple routers on a single LAN segment using different IGPs to communicate to multiple LANs.

Route Tag and Next-Hop Fields

0			31
Command	Version	Unused	
0xFFFF		Authentication Type	
Password			
Password			
Password			
Password			
Address Family Identifier		Route Tag	
Net 2 address			
Subnet mask			
Next Hop			
Metric			

125   Multicast Support

A key improvement for the RIP protocol is the ability to use a multicast address for its packets and for its datagram IP header. The multicast address for RIPv2 is 224.0.0.9 with a MAC address of 01-00-5E-00-00-09. Of course, this must be mapped to an Ethernet multicast address (for more information on this, please refer to Part Six, BOOTP, DHCP, RSVP, and SNMP in this book, or RFC 1700).

Multicast Support

- RIPv2 uses the multicast address of 224.0.0.9 to multicast, does not broadcast its table.

- MAC address of 01-00-5E-00-00-09.
  - Details of this conversion are covered in RFC 1700 and the multicast section of this book.

- RIPv1 uses a broadcast address in both the IP header and the MAC header.

- IGMP is not used for this multicast support.

If you read the section on multicasting, you know that the benefits of multicast are great. RIPv1 uses a broadcast address that not only interrupts the NIC but the IP service layer as well, even if the packet is not destined for that host. Why interrupt the host when the packet/datagram is destined for some other host? All broadcast packets must be received and processed. Not a problem when RIPv1 was introduced to the IP community (there were not many hosts to contend with).

Multicast allows only those hosts that have specified their NICs to receive and process multicast packets. All other multicast packets will be ignored.

Even though multicast is used, it is not IGMP (Internet Group Management Protocol) and is not to be used for the address in a local multicast address. This means the packet will never leave the network it was transmitted on (i.e., it will not be forwarded by routers).

RIPv2 Compatibility with RIPv1   126

RIPv2 Compatibility with RIPv1

- Configuration parameters on the router for:
  - RIPv1 only—Version 1 messages will be sent
  - RIPv1 compatibility—RIP 2 messages as broadcast
  - RIPv2—Messages are multicast
  - None—No RIP messages are sent

So, if all of these new "features" are used, how do we communicate with version 1 RIP routers? There are two sides to this story. Some simple rules apply:

- If a RIPv2 router receives a RIPv1 update, it will process it as a v1 update and does not try to convert any of the information received into RIP features.
- If a RIPv1 request is received by a RIPv2, the RIPv2 router should respond with a version 1 response.

Now, there are many changes (multicast, broadcast, etc.) to which a v2 router could respond. Therefore, during the configuration of a v2 router, there will be configuration parameters that allow for the v2 router to act in many different ways:

- RIP-1—only version 1 messages will be sent
- RIP-1 compatibility—RIP 2 messages are sent with broadcast addresses (IP header and MAC)
- RIP-2—messages are multicast
- None—no RIP messages are sent

Although not required, some routers have implemented a receive parameter listing which allows for RIP-1 only, RIP-2 only, or both.

Also, for compatibility, RFC 1058 stated that the version field should be used in the following format:

- Any version field of 0—discard the entire packet.
- Any version field of 1 and MBZ fields that are not 0 are discarded.
- Any version greater than 1 should not be discarded simply because the MBZ fields contains a value other than 0.

Therefore, routers that strictly adhere to RFC 1058 may be able to process RIPv2 updates and build routing tables based on that information. RIPv1 routers will ignore the subnet mask and next-hop field. They will also ignore the route tag field (it is a reserved field in RIPv1). RIPv1 will ignore any AFI that is set to FFFF (for RIPv2 authentication) and the route that applies to the AFI. (For RIPv2, it will be the first entry of a RIPv2 datagram. All other entries will be valid RIP route entries).

Open Shortest Path First (OSPF, RFC 2178)

- Shortest-path routes based on true metrics, not just a hop count.
- Computes the routes only when triggered to or every 30 minutes (whichever is less).
- Pairs a network address entry with a subnet mask.
- Allows for routing across equal paths.
- Supports ToS.
- Permits the injection of external routes (other ASs).
- Authenticates route exchanges.
- Quick convergence.
- Direct support for multicast in both the IP header and the MAC header.

The major shortcomings of the RIP protocol are:

- The maximum distance between two stations (the metric, measured in router hops) is 15 hops. A destination (network ID) whose hop count is 16 is considered unreachable.
- The cost to a destination network is measured in hops. RIP determines a route based on a hop count that does not take into consideration any other measurements except for the number of routers between the source and destination networks. A two-hop high-speed network will be bypassed for a one-hop low-speed link.

A router can be tricked into taking a better path by adjusting the hop-count metric on the router port, but this reduces the available diameter.

- RIP updates it entire table on a periodic basis consuming bandwidth using the broadcast address. (RIPv1; RIPv2 uses multicast or broadcast).
- RIP sends its update in a 576-byte datagram. If there are more entries than 512 bytes, multiple datagrams must be sent. For example, 300 entries require 12 back-to-back 512-byte datagrams.
- RIP suffers from slow convergence. In the worse case, a RIP update can take over 15 minutes end to end. This can cause black-holes, loops, etc.
- RIPv1 does not support VLSM.

The first shortest-path-first routing protocol was developed and used in the ARPAnet packet switching network all the way back in 1978. This research work was developed and used in many other routing protocol types and prototypes. One of those is OSPF.

OSPF Features

- Shortest-path routes are based on true metrics, not just a hop count.
- The routing tables are updated only when needed, or every 30 minutes using a multicast address.
- A network address entry is paired with a subnet mask.
- Routing across equal paths is allowed, performing load balancing.
- Type of Service (ToS) routing is supported.

- The injection of external routes is permitted (routes from other autonomous systems).
- Route exchanges are authenticated.

- Quick convergence is realized.
- Multicast is directly supported.

128 An OSPF Network

The following diagram is a picture on OSPF topology. OSPF introduces many new concepts. OSPF has areas, and runs metrics based on true costs. OSPF does not broadcast its table out; only link information is sent to a specific router.

The metrics assigned are based on a number set by the network administrator. It should be based on the speed of the line—a lower cost for higher-speed lines. For example, if workstation A wants to converse with workstation Z, OSPF will produce a routing table that routes the datagram over the two T1 lines instead of the 56k line.

The name for this routing protocol is elusive. Shortest path first? Shouldn't any routing protocol try the shortest path first? This protocol evolved after many years of research on the Internet and was the aggregate of many routing protocols. It was a Xerox Network Systems protocol and was widely distributed through the Berkeley Unix system. RIP was not invented on the Internet; however, OSPF was.

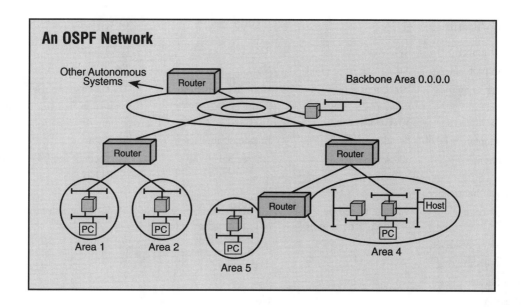

A Routing Protocol Comparison

129

When reading through the following sections on the OSPF protocol, keep one main goal in mind: network design. OSPF allows us to build very efficient networks through segmenting of an autonomous system into small groups called *areas*, variable-length subnet masks, Type of Service routing, and a host of other betterments compared to the RIP protocol. It was mentioned at the beginning of this section that there are two types of routing methods: IGP and EGP. The table compares RIP with OSPF.

Function/Feature	RIPv1	RIPv2	OSPF
Standard number	RFC 1058	RFC 1723	RFC 2178
Link-state protocol	No	No	Yes
Large range of metrics	Hop count (16=Infinity)	Hop count (16=Infinity)	Yes, based on 1–65535
Update policy	Route table every 30 seconds	Route table every 30 seconds	Link-state changes, or every 30 minutes
Update address	Broadcast	Broadcast, multicast	Multicast
Dead interval	300 seconds total	300 seconds total	300 seconds total, but usually much less
Supports authentication	No	Yes	Yes
Convergence time	Variable (based on number of routers × dead interval)	Variable (based on number of routers × dead interval)	Media delay + dead interval
Variable-length subnets	No	Yes	Yes
Supports supernetting	No	Yes	Yes
Type of Service (TOS)	No	No	Yes
Multipath routing	No	No	Yes
Network diameter	15 hops	15 hops	65535 possible
Easy to use	Yes	Yes	No

A Routing Protocol Comparison

Function/Feature	RIPv1	RIPv2	OSPF
Standard number	RFC 1058	RFC 1723	RFC 2178
Link-state Protocol	No	No	Yes
Large range of metrics	Hop count (16=Infinity)	Hop count (16=Infinity)	Yes, based on 1–65535
Update policy	Route table every 30 seconds	Route table every 30 seconds	Link state changes or every 30 minutes
Update address	Broadcast	Broadcast, multicast	Multicast
Dead interval	300 seconds total	300 seconds total	Up to 300 seconds total; Usually shorter
Supports authentication	No	Yes	Yes
Convergence time	Variable based on (number of routers × dead interval)	Variable based on (number of routers × dead interval)	Media delay + dead interval
Variable-length subnets	No	Yes	Yes
Supports supernetting	No	Yes	Yes
Type of Service (TOS)	No	No	Yes
Multipath routing	No	No	Yes
Network diameter	15 hops	15 hops	N/A but up to 65535
Easy to use	Yes	Yes	No

There are two types of standardized IGPs: RIP (versions 1 or 2) and OSPF. Like RIP, OSPF is an IGP, which means that it is designed to run internally to a single autonomous system (AS). (An AS is described as those networks and routers grouped into a single domain under one authority.) It exchanges routing information within a single autonomous system. It can be used in small, medium, or large internetworks, but the most dramatic effects will be readily noticed on large IP networks. As opposed to RIP (a distance vector protocol), OSPF is a link-state protocol. It maintains the state of every link in the domain.

The following is a simple algorithm for OSPF:

- Upon initialization, each router records information about all its interfaces.

- Each router builds a packet known as the Link State Advertisement (LSA).
- The packet contains a listing of all recently seen routers and their costs.
- LSAs are restricted to being forwarded only in the originated area.
- Received LSAs are flooded to all other routers.
- Each router makes a copy of the most recently "seen" LSA.
- Each router has complete knowledge of the topology of the area to which it belongs.
- Adjacencies are formed between a designated router (and backup DR) and other routers on a network.
- Shortest-path trees are constructed after routers exchange their databases.

OSPF Overview

- Upon initialization, each router records information about all its interfaces.

- Each router builds a packet known as the Link State Advertisement (LSA).
  - Contains a listing of all recently seen routers and their cost
  - LSAs are restricted to being forwarded only in the orginated area

- Received LSAs are flooded to all other routers.
  - Each router makes a copy of the most recently "seen" LSA

- Each router has complete knowledge of the topology of the area to which it belongs.

- Adjacencies are formed between a Designated Router (and Backup DR) and other routers on a network.

- Shortest Path Trees are constructed after routers exchange their databases.

- Router algorithm only when changes occur (or every 30 minutes, whichever is shorter).

- Router algorithm updates only when changes occur (or every 30 minutes, whichever is shorter).

This information is "flooded" to all routers in the domain. *Flooding* is the process of receiving the information on one port and transmitting it to all other active ports on the router. In this way, all routers receive the same information and can compute their own routes. This information is stored in a database called the *link-state database*, which is identical on very router in the AS (or every area if the domain in split into multiple areas). Based on information in the link-state database, an algorithm known as the Dykstra algorithm runs and produces a shortest-path tree based on the metrics, using itself as the root of the tree. The information this produces is used to build the routing table.

131   OSPF Media Support

OSPF supports broadcast and nonbroadcast multiaccess (NBMA), and point-to-point networks. Broadcast networks, like Ethernet, Token Ring, and FDDI, can support one, or more network attachments together with the ability to address a single message to all those attachments; a broadcast network. Alternatively, non-broadcast networks, like X.25, ATM or Frame Relay, support one, or many hosts but do not possess a method for broadcasting. Point-to-point is exactly that, a link that has two connection points. Two routers

---

OSPF Media Support

- Broadcast—Networks such as Ethernet, Token Ring, and FDDI.

- Non-broadcast Multiaccess (NBMA)—access that does not support broadcast but allows for multiple station access such as ATM, Frame Relay, and X.25.

- Point-to-Point—Links that only have two network attachments, such as two routers connected by a serial line.

connected together through a serial line (56k through T1) is an example of a point-to-point link. There can be no other connections in between these two points.

Router Types   132

When there is only one area, there is basically only one specialized type of router: the ones that deal with external routes. When an OSPF environment is split into multiple areas, multiple routers are required. There are six types of routers in an OSPF environment:

Backbone Router (BR): A router that has an interface to the backbone.

Area Border Router (ABR): A router that has interfaces to multiple areas.

Autonomous System Boundary Router (ASBR): A router that exchanges routing information with routers that are attached to different autonomous systems.

Internal Router (IR): A router whose attachments all belong to the same area.

Designated Router (DR): One router on a subnet that is selected as the designated router. All other routers on the subnet form an adjacency (a logical point-to-point connection on a subnet) to this router. Information about networks to and from

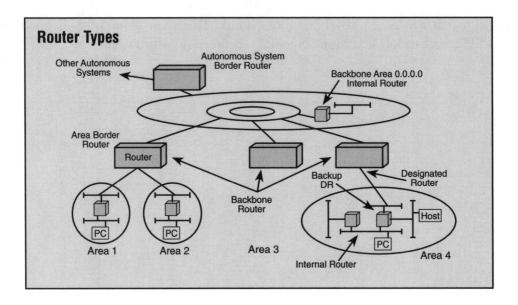

the subnet is transferred over the DR. The DR generates network LSA on behalf of its subnet and floods this information throughout its area. This advertisement in the DR identifies all routers adjacent to this DR and records the link-states of all the routers currently attached to the network.

Backup Designator Router (BDR): Backs up the DR in case the DR fails.

Some of these router types have overlapping roles. For example, an ABR can also be a backbone router.

Router Names and Routing Methods

- Three types of routing in an OSPF network:
  - Intra-Area routing—Routing within a single area
  - Inter-Area routing—Routing within two areas of the same AS
  - Inter-AS routing—Routing between AS systems

There are three types of routing in an OSPF network:

Intra-area routing. Routing within a single area.

Inter-area routing. Routing between two areas.

Inter-AS routing. Routing between autonomous systems.

OSPF routers pass messages to each other in the form of Link-State Advertisements (LSAs). Each link-state advertisement describes a piece of the OSPF routing domain. All link-state advertisements are then flooded throughout the OSPF routing domain, but within a single area. A single area can be an entire OSPF domain. The flooding algorithm is reliable, ensuring that all routers have the same collection of link-state advertisements.

Type 1—Router Links Advertisement: This message is flooded within an area and contains information about neighbors' router links (basically the IP address of an interface and the cost associated with that interface). Every router originates a router links advertisement.

Type 2—Network Links Advertisement: This message is flooded within an area. It is generated by the designated router (DR) and includes information on all routers on this multiaccess network. Whenever the router is elected the DR, it originates a network links advertisement.

Type 3—Summary Links Advertisement: Flooded into an area by an Area Border Router (ABR). This message describes reachable networks from outside the area (in other areas of the OSPF domain).

Type 4—AS Boundary Router Summary Link Advertisement: This message is flooded into an area by an ABR. The message describes the cost from this router to an AS Boundary Router.

Message Types

- OSPF routers communicate by sending Link State Advertisements (LSAs) to each other.
  - Type 1—Router Links Advertisement
  - Type 2—Network Links Advertisement
  - Type 3—Summary Links Advertisement
  - Type 4—AS Boundary Router Summary Link Advertisement
  - Type 5—AS External Link Advertisement
  - Type 6—Multicast Group Membership LSA
- LSAs contain sequence numbers to detect old and duplicate LSAs.

Type 5—AS External Link Advertisement: This message is flooded to all areas except stub areas (explained later). It describes an external network reachable via the AS Boundary Router that generated it.

Type 6—Multicast Group Membership LSAs: Allows multicast-enabled OSPF router to distribute IGMP (multicast group information).

One last thing about LSAs: They contain 32-bit sequence numbers. This number is used to detect old and duplicate LSA packets. Each new LSA uses an incremented sequence number; therefore, OSPF routers keep their LSA databases current by updating them with an LSA of a higher sequence number. This also allows the OSPF router to flush out old entries.

Another method employed by OSPF on its LSA database is the age field. Each LSA entry has an expiration timer that can expire, allowing the database to purge old entries.

Metrics (Cost) 135

Metrics (Cost)

- Reference RFC 1253

- Metric = 10^8 / interface speed

- Examples:
  - => 100 Mbps   1
  - 10 Mbps   10
  - E1   48
  - T1   65
  - 64 kbps   1562
  - 19.2 kbps   5208
  - 9.6 kbps   10416

A cost is associated with the output side of each router interface. This cost is a configurable parameter on the router. When LSAs are transferred between routers, the cost of the individual links is added as well. The cost of a link is the cost associated on the outbound link and this information is added up in a router (receiving LSAs) before Dykstra runs. Multiple paths can be found to a destination and the path with the lowest cost will be placed in the routing table. Simply stated, the lower the cost of a router port, the more likely the interface is to be used to forward data traffic.

According to RFC 1253 (OSPF Version 2 MIB), the following is a recommendation for assigning costs to links in an OSPF environment:

Speed	Cost
>= 100 Mbps	1
Ethernet/802.3	10
E1 (2.048 Mbps)	48
T1 (ESF or 1.544 Mbps)	65
64 kbps	1562
56 kbps	1785
19.2 kbps	5208
9.6 kbps	10416

For costing a link, there is a default value that can be used. It is only a recommendation and any number can be used. For example, if you are using a higher-speed link (such as those available with the ATM protocol) room should be left to compensate for this. This yields a number having the following typical values:

Metric = 10^8 /interface speed

Network type/bit rate—Metric

136 Generic Packet Format

As of this writing, there are seven types of advertisements. All OSPF packets have the same header, but the body of the packet is different and this is noted by the LSA specific field.

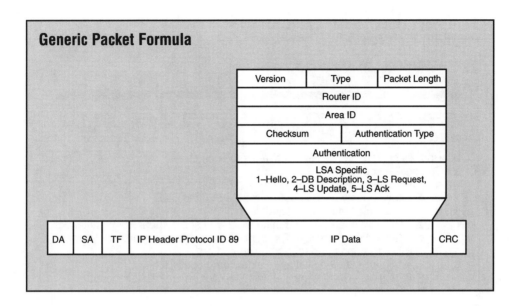

Generic Packet Formula

Version	Type	Packet Length
Router ID		
Area ID		
Checksum	Authentication Type	
Authentication		
LSA Specific 1–Hello, 2–DB Description, 3–LS Request, 4–LS Update, 5–LS Ack		

DA	SA	TF	IP Header Protocol ID 89	IP Data	CRC

The Hello Protocol 137

Routers periodically transmit Hello packets to not only find other OSPF routers on their subnet but also to transmit and make sure that certain parameters are set to the same values within all the routers on that subnet. The Hello packet format is shown here. The Hello packet stays on the local subnet; it is not forwarded by the router. The Hello packet contains:

- The router's selection of the DR (designated router) and BDR (backup designated router)

- The router's priority used to determine the DR and BDR
- Configurable timers that include the Hello Interval (time a router expects to hear hellos) and the RouterDeadInterval (the time period before a router is declared down)
- A list of neighboring routers that this router has received hellos from

The most basic exchange between routers is called the Hello protocol. This protocol allows OSPF routers to discover one another

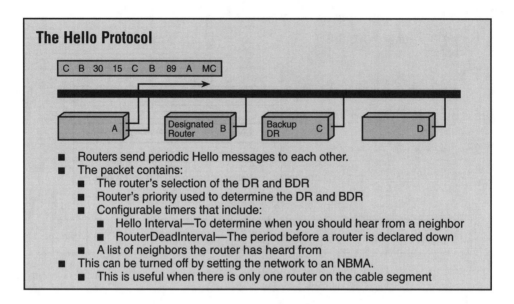

The Hello Protocol

| C | B | 30 | 15 | C | B | 89 | A | MC |

- Routers send periodic Hello messages to each other.
- The packet contains:
  - The router's selection of the DR and BDR
  - Router's priority used to determine the DR and BDR
  - Configurable timers that include:
    - Hello Interval—To determine when you should hear from a neighbor
    - RouterDeadInterval—The period before a router is declared down
  - A list of neighbors the router has heard from
- This can be turned off by setting the network to an NBMA.
  - This is useful when there is only one router on the cable segment

(in a single area) and allows for the building of relationships between routers. This is the protocol that allows for the DR and BDR to be selected. Once the DR is selected, adjacencies are formed (discussed next).

For multiaccess networks, when a router transmits a Hello packet it is sent using the ALL-SPF-Routers (which means all OSPF routers) multicast address of 224.0.0.5

OSPF routers build and maintain their relationships by periodic exchanges of Hello packets. Included in the transmitted Hello packets is a list of all the routers a router has heard from (i.e., received Hello packets from). When a router sees its address in a received Hello packet, it knows that the router that transmitted that packet has seen it. Once this is accomplished, the DR and the BDR are selected. Any DR with a priority of 0 counts itself out of the selection. There is one DR and DBR per subnet or LAN segment.

These packets are continually sent every Hello period specified in the packet. This is how a router can detect that another router is down (DeadInterval), which it uses to wait and build a new database with the Dykstra algorithm.

After the Hello discovery process has allowed for the DR and BDR to be selected, routers on a single LAN segment determine whether to form an adjacency with one another. An adjacency is important because it enables two routers to allow the exchange of routing information through link-state advertisements. The following are the requirements for establishing an adjacency:

- The link is a point-to-point link or a virtual link (discussed later).
- The router is the DR or BDR.
- The neighbor is the DR or BDR.

So, you can see that if the router is the DR or BDR, an adjacency is formed between the DR/BDR and an attached router. If these conditions are not met, then an adjacency is not formed. That is, not all routers form adjacencies with each other, only with the DR and BDR or a point-to-point link.

As the adjacency is formed, the "adjacent" routers' databases must become "synchronized." That is, each must contain the exact same information. There is a series of steps before full adjacency. The reason for this is to synchronize the link-state database. The adjacent routers transmit to adjacent neighbors a summary list of LSAs using the *database description packet*. The router takes this information, compares it to its own LSA database, and then builds a request list of LSAs that are in the received summary list but not in its LSA database, and LSAs that are in the database but not in the received information from its adjacent neighbor.

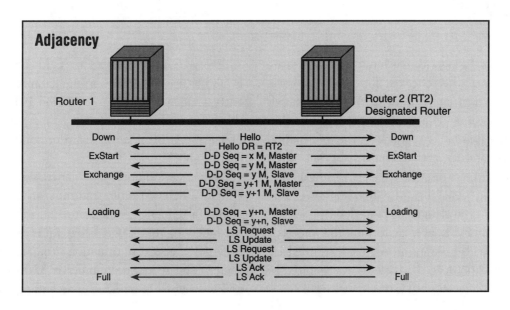

This newly build request list is then transmitted to its neighbor using the Link State request packet. Each router that receives this request list responds to each requested record in the list. The router that received the request packet responds with a Link State Update packet. Neighbors are considered to be *fully adjacent* when they have received all responses to the requests and become fully adjacent on a one-on-one basis with each router that has formed an adjacency. After the routers become fully adjacent, each will run the SPF algorithm using the information supplied in the database. The outcome of the algorithm is OSPF routes, which are added to the routing table.

139 Maintaining the Database

After the algorithm is run, the databases are continually checked for synchronization between adjacencies using LSAs and the flooding procedure. The flooding procedure is simple: Receive an LSA, check for the information in the database, and determine whether or not to forward it to another adjacency using a LSA. To ensure reliability, the flooding procedure uses an acknowledgment procedure.

Reliability is also built into the protocol. When an LSA is transmitted, it is acknowledged. An unacknowledged packet is retransmitted by the issuing router until it is acknowledged.

Every LSA contains an age field. This field is used to age old entries in the database. If an entry is aged out, this information is flooded throughout the domain (a single area) and the Dykstra algorithm is run again to build a new router table.

Sequence numbers are generated for all LSAs. When a router transmits an LSA, it applies a sequence number to it. In this way, the receiving router will know if it is receiving the most recent information from another-router. The sequence number is 32 bits long and is assigned to an LSA in ascending order.

Maintaining the Database

■ After Dykstra runs, the database is checked for consistency.

■ Uses the flooding procedure:
  ■ Receive an LSA
  ■ Check for the information in the database
  ■ Determine whether or not to forward this LSA to an adjacency

■ Reliability checked using an acknowledgment procedure.

■ Each LSA contains an age entry.

■ Sequence numbers are generated for every LSA.

Changes in the LSA database require a rerunning of the SPF algorithm and an update of the routing table depending on the outcome of the algorithm.

OSPF Areas   140

OSPF uses a concept known as an *area*. Refer to Slide 140.0. An area is a grouping of contiguous networks and its associated routers that have interfaces belonging to those networks and hosts. An OSPF autonomous system can simply be one area (in this case, it must be the backbone area) or it can consist of many areas. Each area runs its own copy of the link-state routing algorithm, allowing for each area to build its own topological database. It is important to note that an area limits the flooding of an LSA. LSAs do not leave the area from which they originated. Furthermore, splitting a domain into areas allows for routing traffic bandwidth savings as well.

Each area is identified with a 32-bit number known as the *area ID*. This number is formatted in the same manner as an IP address; however, it has nothing to do with the IP addressing scheme of your network. It simply identifies an area. Common area IDs are 0.0.0.0 (a single area must be configured with the area ID of 0.0.0.0, or a multiple area must have one of its areas labeled 0.0.0.0, known as

Area 0). Other area IDs are 1.1.1.1 to identify area 1, or 0.0.0.1 to identify area 1. There is no strict method to accomplish area ID numbering except for area 0.0.0.0.

Furthermore, each router in an area is assigned an router ID regardless of its area ID assignment . This number is a 32-bit number that uniquely identifies that router in the autonomous system. Typically, the router ID is chosen from the IP address assignments of one of the router interfaces.

The topology of an area in not known to any other area. This means that the internal routers of an area do not contain any information about the OSPF topology outside their area, giving the benefit of reduced routing overhead. A single area that is spread over sparse environments (WAN links) must contain the same topology database for the entire area no matter how large it has become. So how does an area determine routes that are not

within its area? This is accomplished via the backbone area and the summary links advertisement.

ABRs play an important role in an OSPF network. Since areas do not know the topology in areas other than their own, some mechanism must be provided to allow network reachability information to traverse different areas. After all, it wouldn't do much good to be able to dynamically route in your own area and then have to statically point to networks in other areas. ABRs compact the topological information for an area and transmit it to the backbone area. Routers in the backbone area make sure that it is forwarded to the areas that are attached to it. In order to accomplish this, ABRs run multiple copies of the OSPF algorithm, one for each area (including the backbone area). Areas also allow for the advantages of hierarchical topologies to be built.

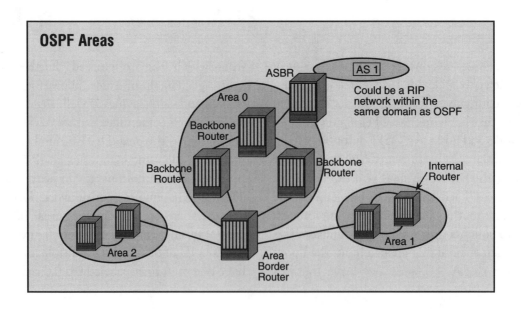

The Backbone Area

- There must be at least one area in an OSPF network.
  - It is called the backbone area
- Designated by area ID of 0.0.0.0.
- Primary responsibility to propagate information between areas.
- Has the same attributes as any other area.
- Any network topology can make up the backbone.
- It can be used as a real network with attachments.

The backbone area has all the attributes of any typical area. This includes the fact that its topology is not known to any other area attached to it. The topologies of the areas that attach to the backbone are not known to any backbone router as well. It looks like any other area except for its area number assignment 0.0.0.0.

One of the areas is a specialized area. It is known as the *backbone* area and is labeled as 0.0.0.0 or Area 0. When a domain is split into areas, the areas communicate with one another through the backbone area. This area contains those routers and networks not contained in any other area and routers that connect to multiple areas (An ABR, explained next). Its primary responsibility is to distribute routing information between areas. The backbone area contains all the properties of its area, its topology is not known by any other area, and it does not know the topology of any other area. Okay, now that we have the distribution area (if you will), what causes the information to be in the backbone area? The ABR accomplishes this.

142 The Area Border Router (ABR)

There is a special router type known as the Area Border Router. Its job is to connect an area to the backbone and to summarize its area topology information (for all areas that it connects to) to the backbone area, where it is received by other ABRs to be included in their tables. ABRs also receive other area summaries from the backbone and propagate this to their areas. ABRs are part of the backbone area; therefore, ABRs belong to a minimum of two areas: their own and the backbone area. If there is only one area in the AS (the backbone area), there are no ABRs.

Since an ABR belongs to two or more areas, it has a separate database for each area to which it belongs. It also executes a single copy of the routing algorithm for each area to which it belongs. For a typical ABR, it maintains connections to its area and to the backbone area. For its area, it receives flooded LSAs that are within its area and maintains a synchronized database for the area. The other copy of the algorithm runs for the attachment to the backbone. ABRs do not flood learned information about its area to the backbone. It summarizes this information using summary link advertisements. These advertisements are pushed to other ABRs on the backbone, allowing those areas to learn about each other without directly participating in the backbone's routing advertisements (remember, the backbone is a real area, too!).

Since, area reachability information is propagated only over the backbone area, every area must touch the backbone through the use

---

The Area Border Router (ABR)

- Connects an area (or areas) to the backbone.

- Summarizes its area topology to the backbone.

- Propagates summarized information from the backbone into its area.

- Final router that receives an area's LSA.
  - ABRs do not flood LSA information into the backbone
  - Only produces summaries to the backbone for the backbone to propagate to other areas

- Uses the network summary LSA.

- Summarized information is propagated in an area by the DR and its adjacencies.

---

of an ABR. An area is not allowed to be segmented from the backbone. A special condition does exist to allow an area to be extended off an area that is not the backbone through a concept known as a *virtual link*.

A virtual link is shown in the slide. The backbone must be contiguous. This means that an ABR must connect directly to the backbone and not to another area. Area-to-area communication is not allowed directly, only through the backbone. However, there will be designs that force the creation of an area that will not have direct connectivity to the backbone. This makes the backbone is no longer contiguous. Backbone connectivity is restored through a virtual link.

Virtual links can be configured between any two ABR routers that have an common interface to a nonbackbone area. The virtual link is configured on each ABR and acts like a point-to-point link. Virtual links belong to the backbone. The routing protocol traffic that flows along the virtual link uses intra-area routing only.

As shown in the slide, the two endpoints of the link are ABRs and the link is configured in both routers. The two ABRs used in the virtual link also must belong to a common area, not the backbone area.

Simply stated, a virtual link is like a point-to-point link between two fully adjacent ABRs that allows an area to receive and transmit summary information (learn routes within the AS) when it is not directly connected to the backbone area. That's simply stated?

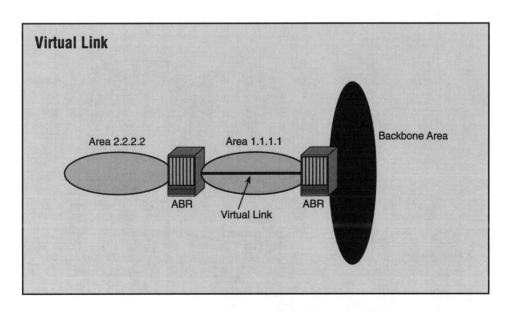

Virtual Link

Area 2.2.2.2   Area 1.1.1.1   Backbone Area

ABR   Virtual Link   ABR

144 Inter-Area Routing

Routing a packet between areas involves transmitting a packet from its source, through its internal area to the ABR. The ABR transmits the packet over the backbone area to another ABR, where it is transmitted internally on the area to the destination host. Areas cannot route directly to other areas!

Again, the backbone area is a special area. Its main function is to distribute information from areas to other areas. It consists of networks that are not contained in any other defined area, and routers that are attached to an area or areas.

Why do areas? Breaking the AS into routable areas greatly reduces the amount of overhead in the form of routing information updates that need to be distributed throughout the AS. While this may not seem like much, remember, that each area can be unique. One area can have a majority of WAN links, while others are mostly networks, and others are a combination of multiple network types. Why make the update process very complex, and why bother other areas with your information? Remember, when the routing algorithm runs, every router in an area must run it. If one router in an area runs the algorithm, the routers in other areas may not have to run it. Dykstra runs in one area only. ABR will have a minimum of two copies of the Dykstra, one for each area it connects to.

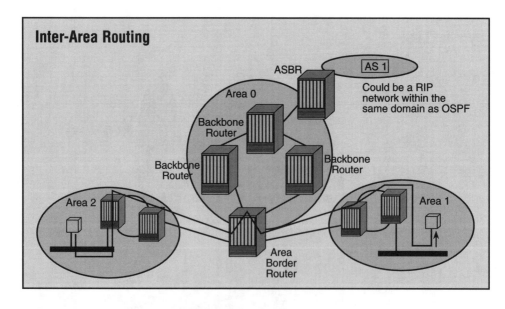

Inter-Area Routing

Information from other Autonomous Systems

- Uses the ASBR.

- Other ASs according to OSPF may simply be a RIP network within the same OSPF domain.

- External LSA used.

- Type 1—The preferred route and used when considering the internal cost of the AS.

- Type 2—Advertising the same metric as was advertised by the ASBR.

- These are used to calculate the shortest path to the ASBR.

Now, what about talking to other autonomous systems (outside of the OSPF domain)? Through the use of a special router type—the Autonomous System Boundary Router (ASBR)—OSPF networks can communicate with other ASs. This adds another level of hierarchy to the OSPF routing. The first is the intra-area routing. The second level is area-to-area routing through the backbone. The third level is external autonomous systems.

ASBRs run the OSPF protocol and some type of Exterior Gateway Protocol (such as Border Gateway Protocol defined in RFC 1403, BGP, or even RIP). RIP is seen as an external network and its routes are imported into a Link State Database as such. An external AS need not be another AS in the sense of a BGP. OSPF treats any routing protocol unlike itself as an external AS. This type of protocol allows for information to be exchanged between ASs. The EGP type of protocol only runs on the interfaces that are between the ASs. OSPF runs on the interfaces internal to the AS. An ASBR does not have to directly attach to the backbone.

To allow for this, another type of advertisement is used, known as the External Links Advertisement. Each ASBR in the AS generates one of the advertisements. This is the only advertisement that is flooded into every area in the AS. These advertisements describe routes that are external to the AS. There is one entry for every external route. As you can see, this could quickly fill up a routing table with external routes.

The external route uses one of two available types of metrics: Type 1 or Type 2. Type 1 metrics are the preferred route and are used when considering the internal cost of the AS. This means that Type 1 metrics include the Link State Metric as well as the metric that was assigned to it. Therefore, any router that receives this type of update for an external route must use the internal (AS) metrics to reach the ASBR advertising that external route. So, the computation for cost to reach that route uses metrics that are internal to the AS and the AS that was supplied in the advertisement.

Type 2 metrics are the same metrics that were advertised by the ASBR. Internal AS metrics are not added to the ASBR metric for the route when computing a path (based on cost) for that external route. (that is, to reach the ASBR advertising that external route).

146

Stub Areas

External link advertisements could quickly fill up a routing table. In some instances, a majority of the entries in the routing table will simply be routes external to the OSPF domain. There is one entry for every external route. As you can see, this could quickly fill up a routing table with external routes.

Stub areas were created to reduce these entries. If an area has a single entry or exit point to or from that area that is used for all external traffic, it can be configured as a stub area. A stub area blocks the importation of the AS External Link Advertisements into the area, thereby reducing the number of entries in the stub area's database.

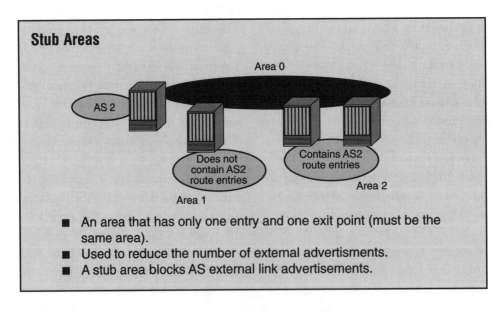

Stub Areas

- An area that has only one entry and one exit point (must be the same area).
- Used to reduce the number of external advertisments.
- A stub area blocks AS external link advertisements.

2178 DS: J. Moy, "OSPF Version 2," 07/22/97 (211 pages) (.txt format) (obsoletes RFC 1583).

2154 ES: M. Murphy, B. Badger, A. Wellington, "OSPF with Digital Signatures," 06/16/97 (29 pages) (.txt format).

1850 DS: F. Baker, R. Coltun, "OSPF Version 2 Management Information Base," 11/03/95. (80 pages) (.txt format) (Obsoletes RFC 1253).

1793 PS: J. Moy, "Extending OSPF to Support Demand Circuits," 04/19/95 (31 pages) (.txt format).

1765 E: J. Moy, "OSPF Database Overflow," 03/02/95 (9 pages) (.txt format).

1745 PS: K. Varadhan, S. Hares, Y. Rekhter, "BGP4/IDRP for IP—OSPF Interaction," 12/27/94 (19 pages) (.txt format).

1587 PS: R. Coltun, V. Fuller, "The OSPF NSSA Option," 03/24/94 (17 pages) (.txt format).

1586 I: O. deSouza, M. Rodrigues, "Guidelines for Running OSPF Over Frame Relay Networks," 03/24/94 (6 pages) (.txt format).

1585 I: J. Moy, "MOSPF: Analysis and Experience," 03/24/94 (13 pages) (.txt format).

1584 PS: J. Moy, "Multicast Extensions to OSPF," 03/24/94 (102 pages) (.txt, .ps formats).

1403 PS: K. Varadhan, "BGP OSPF Interaction," 01/14/93 (17 pages) (.txt format) (obsoletes RFC 1364).

1370 PS: Internet Architecture Board, "Applicability Statement for OSPF," 10/23/92 (2 pages) (.txt format).

148 Static versus Dynamic Routing

The last topic of discussion is the ability of routing protocols to accept information for their tables from two sources: the network or a user.

Although the RIP protocol allows for automatic updates for routing tables, manual entries are still allowed and are known as *static entries*. These entries must be entered manually. A default route is a static entry. An endstation that is configured with a default router is said to have a static route entry. Static routes can be configured to be included or not included in a dynamic update. Static routes refer to the process of manually placing an entry in the table. For any given router, the network administrator may update that table with a static route. Static routes override dynamic routes.

Static tables have many disadvantages. First, as discussed earlier, static tables are not meant for large networks that incur many changes such as growth. As the topology changes, all the tables must be manually reconfigured. Second, in the case of router failure, the tables have no way of updating themselves. The route will be disabled, but no alternative route is put in place. Cisco employs a concept called a *floating static route* that allows for this. Dynamic tables overcome the disadvantages of static entries.

The primary advantage that a static entry may have is for security, for static tables can be configured *not* to broadcast their routes to other routers. In this way, users can customize their routers to become participants on the network without their network identity being broadcast to other routers on the network. Static routes

Static versus Dynamic Routing

- Entries in a routing table can be static (manually entered by the network administrator) or dynamic (learned through a routing protocol such as RIP).

- Static entries:
    - In the workstation for either:
        - Default Gateway (router)—used by indirect routing
        - Place a static route in for one that is not learned through RIP, etc.

- In the router:
    - Entered as 0.0.0.0 and the next hop (no subnet) to indicate a default route
    - Routers can broadcast this information to their networks to let all know which is the default router
        - A default router is one that all others look to for networks that are not in their tables
    - Static routes can be used to increase security on the network
    - Any IP network address can be manually entered into the routing table
    - The router administrator supplies:
        - IP Network address
        - Subnet mask
        - Next hop interface (the IP address of the next routers interface to get to that network)

also allow a user to update a routing table with a network entry that will be used in endstations with the dynamic function turned off. This allows the user to maintain the routing table.

Static entries are also used in various IP topologies. For example, in a hub-and-spoke topology where a business has a centralized corporate office and many remote offices (such as a bank), there really is no reason to fully enable RIP at the branch offices. Why not turn RIP supply (the ability to broadcast routes but not listen for any) at the remote branch and add a default route, in the remote branch router, pointing to the upstream router located at the corporate office. In this way, the upstream router dynamically learns about all the remote offices (and learns when they go away) and the branch office

has one simple entry in its table (besides its attached subnets): a default route to the upstream router. Since there is no other path besides that one link to the upstream router, the router simply passes on any packets that it receives from its attached workstation on the network. This reduces the amount of memory and processor power needed at the remote branch, enabling a cheaper router to be placed out there.

This is also an example of why OSPF need not be turned on for a complete network. There is no reason whatsoever to run OSPF out at the branch offices; there are plenty of reasons to run it at the corporate offices. OSPF will simply pull in the RIP networks as external networks (but this could possibly build large routing tables).

149 Remote Networks

There are times when networks must be connected when they are geographically separated. This means that networks cannot be connected by the conventional means of a LAN interconnect. Imagine trying to cable a network together with one subnet in California and another in Virginia. Ethernet cannot stretch that far. The only feasible way of doing this is by using some type of WAN service from the telephone company. AT&T, MCI, and Sprint all provide WAN services for data networks. They come in many forms, but again, for simplicity, this book will explain point-to-point serial lines. The choices available are Frame Relay, Switched Multimegabit Data Service (SMDS, primarily used in metropolitan areas and not cross country), Integrated Service Digital Network (ISDN), or leased lines. For simplicity reasons, leased lines will be explained here. The slide shows networks connected via serial lines.

Just as the router has physical connectors to connect to a LAN, the router has a connection that enables this type of connection. Instead of the LAN interface on the router, the router will have a serial line interface. The connector for this is usually a V.35, EIA-232 (formerly RS-232-D), or an RS-449 connector. The connection will then be connected to a device known as a Data Service Unit/Customer Service Unit (DSU/CSU). This is a box that receives the serial signal from the router and repeats it to the telephone switching office.

The leased line is a specially conditioned line that is provided by the phone company. This line has been conditioned to handle high-speed digital traffic. It is not the normal line that is used with voice switching. This line is permanently switched to provide a connection between two points. Therefore, it is sometimes called a *point-to-point* link. It is analogous to

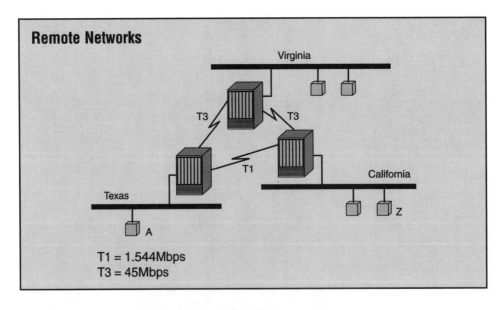

dialing a number, receiving a connection, and never hanging up.

The router at the remote end will also be attached to a DSU/CSU. It will be able to receive the signals generated at the remote end. The typical speeds at which these lines run vary. The most common are 56 Kbps and T1 (1 .544 Mbps) lines, called *leased lines* because the customer does not own the line. It is leased from the phone company and the rates vary depending on the length of the line. Rates are usually cheaper for short runs (the other point of the network is a few miles away)

and more expensive for longer runs. Rates also vary depending on the speed of the line.

The serial line provides a simple interconnect between two routers that cannot be connected directly by a LAN. The real problem in using them in an IP internet is that they consume a full network number or a subnet number. There have been methods to overcome this using variable-length subnet masking, which is available with the routing algorithms of OSPF and RIPv2. Otherwise, they generally act as a full network even when there are only two points connected.

Datagram Routing 150

Now that routing fundamentals, the RIP and OSPF protocols, and routing tables have been discussed, the slide shows a routed packet using direct and indirect routing. This is regardless of the routing protocol. In this slide, we can see that a PC (endstation A) is trying to pass a datagram to a host machine, called host D. The host machine is one hop (one router) away. The IP layer of the PC (endstation A) knows that it must use a router (the source and destination network addresses are different), and will use RIP or the default

gateway to determine the IP address of the router to use. Upon determining the router's physical address, it will physically (MAC layer) address the packet to the router at port B. The source and destination IP addresses in the IP header of this datagram will be the PC as the source, and the destination IP address as the host. The source (PC) and final destination (the host) IP addresses will be embedded into the IP header and will not change throughout the routing of this datagram.

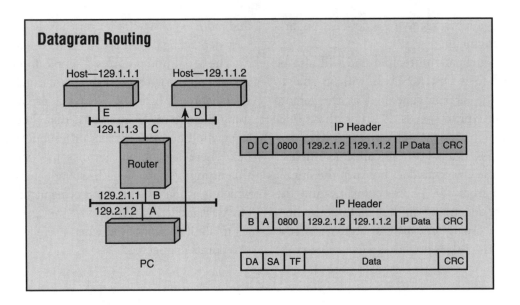

The router will receive this packet and extract the network number from the final destination IP address in the received IP header. The physical address headers will be stripped. The extracted network number will be compared to the router's internal routing table.

The router will determine that the destination network can be reached directly through one of its ports (the destination network is directly attached). The router will determine the destination station's physical address through its ARP table (or it may request it through the ARP process). The router will then build a packet with the original datagram sent by endstation A to submit to host D. The physical source address will be the router's, the physical destination address will be host D's. The packet is then transmitted to host D.

Notice throughout this that only the MAC addresses changed; the IP addresses in the IP header stayed the same. The router will change the TTL and the CRC in the IP header, but that is the only thing that changes in the IP header.

Part Three

Internet Protocol
Version 6 (IPv6)

151 Introduction

"The next IP." "Version 6." "Completely redone IPv4." If you hear statements like this, ignore or correct them. IPv6 is *not* a new network layer protocol. Remember this, if anything, about IPv6: It is an evolutionary step for IP. Calmer heads prevailed during the two years of IPng working group and IPv6 has become an efficient IPv4 that is extensible.

IPv4 has proven to be a robust network layer protocol and there have been very few changes to it over the last 20 years. The biggest problem with IPv4 was the addressing, and these are the changes that were made. The addressing has not changed, but the methods of employing the 32-bit addressing have. IPv6 is a direct result of the shortages of the address space of IPv4. IPv6 is not revolutionary. It is the next step in the datagram delivery protocol known as IP. It is not a replacement for IPv4 per se, but there are many new and some revised functions of the protocol that improve upon it. Currently, there are enough fixes and extensions to the IPv4 protocol (not that there are many problems with the protocol) to make it last well into the year 2000. I have heard over the years, why implement a new version of IP when this one is working just fine? IPv4 simply put a Band-Aid a problem within a time period of need to further enhance the Internet to reach more people and business requirements.

As you read through this section, you should start to understand that the timing of this upgrade to IP is about right. The capabilities of IPv6 require a much more sophisticated

Introduction
■ An evolution of IPv4.
■ Builds on IPv4.
■ Most notable change is address changes to 128 bits.
■ Dynamic environment.
■ Requires a much more sophisticated operating environment.
■ Over 58 other protocols have changed with it.
■ Will run as islands using IPv4 as the backbone.
■ Cannot simply "flip a switch" to convert.

computer than was required with IPv4. Generally, IPv4 could run on low-powered routers and endstations. The versatility of IPv6 will make use of the higher-powered routers and workstations.

When we changed IP, we did not change the function of any other protocol—again, the advantage of modular protocols. TCP and UDP stayed the same. Yes, the software calls to the IP interface are different: the socket interface known as Berkeley sockets (Unix), or for PCs the Winsock interface. But the basic functions of TCP/UDP and the applications that use them are the same. The other protocols that have to change are those that directly interface with IP. These are Domain Name Server, DHCP, OSPF, RIP, ICMP, and others.

You will hear a lot about IPv6 over the next few years, and IPv6 implementations will continue to remain as islands in the IPv4 Internet. This is the correct approach for IPv6. You cannot "flip the switch" as we did in January 1983 with IPv4. The Internet of today is extremely large and very commercial. There are still quite a few studies in progress to determine IPv6 addressing allocation, effects of IPv6 on IPv4 networks, tunneling, and so on. Slow-but-sure implementation. Test before implementing. Apply applications that have a need in the marketplace to IPv6. Work out the kinks before commercialization.

IPv6 (continued) 152

Whatever happened to IPv5? Well, it exists and is known as the Internet Stream Protocol (ST2) and is defined in RFC 1819. ST2 is an experimental resource reservation protocol intended to provide end-to-end real-time guarantees over an internet. It allows applications to build multidestination simplex data streams with a desired quality of service. The revised version of ST2 specified in RFC 1819 is called ST2+.

ST2 operates at the same layer as connectionless IP. It has been developed to support the efficient delivery of data streams to single or multiple destinations in applications that require guaranteed quality of service. ST2 is part of the IP protocol family and serves as an adjunct to, not a replacement for, IP. The revised version of ST2 specified in RFC 1819 is called ST2+. The main application areas of the protocol are the real-time transport of multimedia data (e.g., digital audio and video packet streams, distributed simulation/gaming) across internets. ST2 can be used to reserve bandwidth for real-time streams across network routes.

IPv6 (continued)

- IPv5 exists and is known as the Streams 2 (ST2) Protocol:
  - RFC 1819
  - Operates at the same layer as IP
  - Developed as an IP layer for real-time applications
  - Includes QoS capabilities

- IPv6 truly works on the finer aspects of IPv4.

- Requires a dynamic environment:
  - Many discovery options, including:
    - Autoconfiguration
    - Finding the maximum path MTU
    - Finding other workstations without ARP
    - Finding routers

IPv6 nodes and IPv6 routers will enable an IPv6 network to be established immediately via dynamics. Neighbor discovery protocols initiate and find the nodes on the network, nodes can autoconfigure their addresses, and routers simply have to have their interfaces configured and enabled, and off we go. IPv4 networks prevail, however; probably about 99.99 percent of all networks are IPv4. Therefore, we must make IPv6 work within the bounds of the existing IPv4 network.

The foundation of IPv6 is IPv4. Like most great things in life, you build upon a foundation, something that you know works. Cars, over the years, are still built in the same fashion and still have tires, transmissions, engines, and bodies. But after many years, the extensions of those basics have led to more than just basic transportation. Many efficiencies and add-ons have been applied to the basic car to make it safer, better for the environment, and so forth.

The biggest change that you will notice throughout this text is the word *dynamic*. Routers and hosts discovery each other dynamically, hosts can configure themselves dynamically. There is even a replacement for the DHCP protocol that enforces (and efficiently uses) IP addressing. And, of course, the biggest change of all for IP: the address! Placing IPv6-capable nodes on a network with other

IPv6 Features

- Extended addressing capabilities.
- Header format simplication.
- Improved support for extensions and options.
- Flow label capability.
- Authentication and privacy capabilities.
- IPv6 routing similar to IPv4 routing using CIDR.
  - OSPF, RIP, IDRP, and IS-IS can be used with minor modifications

Widespread implementation of IPv6 will be phased in for the next couple of years. IPv6 is up and running today, however, through a series of islands that run autonomously and also use part of the current IPv4 Internet. It is known as the 6Bone and complete information can be found at:

www.6bone.net.

IPv6 can be grouped into the following categories:

Expanded addressing capabilities. IPv6 increases the IP address size from 32 bits to 128 bits to support more levels of addressing hierarchy, a much greater number of addressable nodes, and simpler autoconfiguration of addresses. There are three types of addresses: unicast, anycast, and multicast. The scalability of multicast routing is improved by adding a "scope" field to multicast addresses. There is no broadcast address defined.

Header format simplification. To make IPv6 more efficient, some of the header fields have been dropped and the header is a static 40 bytes.

Improved support for extensions and options. Since the IP header is a static 40 bytes and changes in the header cannot be made, the concept of header extensions is in. This provides greater flexibility for introducing new options in the future.

Flow labeling capability. A new capability is added to enable the labeling of packets belonging to particular traffic "flows" for which the sender requests special handling, such as nondefault quality of service or "real-time" service.

Authentication and privacy capabilities. Added support for authentication, data integrity, and optional data confidentiality through the extensions.

IPv6 routing uses the concept of prefix routing. Every address has an associated prefix which is simply a mask identifier to indicate how many of the bits, starting from the left are used for routing and how many bits are used to identify a host. The routers will use the prefix in order to build routing tables. End stations make the prefix similar to today's subnet mask.

The existing routing protocols can employ IPv6 addresses as well. There is no need to specifically upgrade your network to employ Interdomain Routing Protocol to use IPv6. The existing routing protocols mostly have to change to understand 128-bit addressing.

From IPv4 to IPv6

IPv6 was not the result of one meeting. Many proposals were developed and algorithms were experimented with before being presented.

One proposal that had a lot of support wanted to replace IP with the ISO (International Organization for Standardization) OSI CLNP Protocol. ISO CLNP (Connectionless Protocol), which was demonstrated as TUBA (TCP and UDP over Bigger Addresses. RFCs 1247, 1526, and 1561).

With many changes to the TCP and IP layers, IP version 7 (also known as TP/IX. RFC 1475) eventually evolved into the CATNIP (RFC 1707).

IP in IP evolved into IPAE (IP Address Encapsulation). It proposed running two layers of the IP protocol, one for the worldwide backbone and one for the regional IP networks. This eventually evolved into Simple IP, or SIP. This moved the address to 64 bits and did away with some of the unused features of ICMP.

During 1992 and 1993, the Pip internet protocol, developed at Bleacher, was one of the candidate replacements for IP. It had many improvements in routing strategies and in mid-1993, Pip was merged with the Simple Internet Protocol (SIP), creating SIPP (SIP Plus).

SIPP (RFC 1710) is a new version of IP designed to be an evolutionary step from IPv4. It can be installed as a normal soft-

---

From IPv4 to IPv6

- Built up to the IPv6 specification that we have today using various proposal submissions such as:
  - ISO CLNP—demonstrated as TUBA (TCP and UDP over Bigger Addresses)
  - IP version 7 (aka TP/IX, RFC 1475)
  - IP in IP—evolved to IP address encapsulation
  - PIP—merged into SIP creating SIPP (RFC 1710)

---

ware upgrade in internet devices and is interoperable with the current IPv4.

While it is true that IPv6 solves the addressing problem, as you can see from the preceding list, it has a few other properties that improved upon the IPv4 protocol.

The following table identifies the IP version numbers. There are more than you probably thought!

IP Version Numbers According to RFC 1700			
Decimal	**Keyword**	**Version**	**References**
0	Reserved		
1–3	Unassigned		
4	IP	Internet Protocol	RFC 791
5	ST	ST Datagram Mode	RFC 1190, JWF
6	IPv6	RFC 1883	
7	TP/IX	TP/IX: The Next Internet	
8	PIP	The P Internet Protocol	
9	TUBA	TCP and UDP over Bigger Addresses	
10–14	Unassigned		
15	Reserved		

IPv6 Header

Notice the differences between IPv4 and IPv6 headers. IPv6 seems to be missing a few options, but they are there; they just cannot be seen (yet!). In fact, the only field that seems to not have changed or moved positions is the VERS field. This field was to play a great role. It was going to be used as the delineating factor to determine if a received IP packet was based on IPv4 or IPv6. In other words, the EtherType field of an Ethernet packet would remain as 0800(h) and the version field of the header would determine the processing of a received IP datagram. This changed and IPv6 has its own Type (for Ethernet packets) field: 86DD(h) (and SAP in IEEE 802 networks).

The internet protocol (version 4) uses four key mechanisms to provide its service: Type of Service (TOS), Time to Live (TTL), Options, Fragmentation, Protocol and Header Checksum. However, in looking at the slide, these fields are missing.

These mechanisms were previously discussed, but the options field is further described here. The Options provide for control functions needed or useful in some situations but unnecessary for the most common communications. The options include provisions for timestamps, security, and special routing (strict and loose source route—nothing to do with Token Ring). However, over the years, it was noticed that these options fields were not being used by the majority of Internet hosts for various reasons. First, IP datagrams that contain options cannot be simply forwarded; they require special attention. They are placed in another queue and the router operates on this queue separately from the received datagram queue. Second, if the

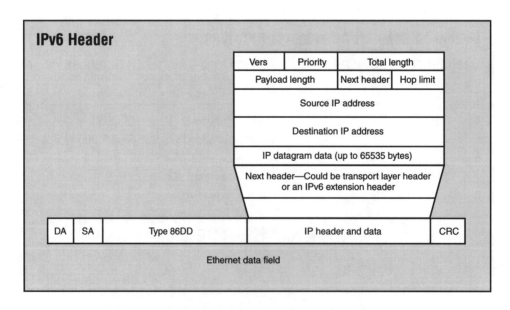

options fields were not used very often, many implementers of routers did not optimize their software to operate on datagrams that included special options. This generally resulted in a performance penalty on the router.

So, why have them? Well, their functions *are* used in some cases. IP multicasting, for example, uses the loose source route option when incorporating the tunneling mechanism for DVMRP (refer to Part V, "Multicasting," to understand more IPv6 decided to allow for it to be extensible, so IPv6 implements the concept of an *extension header*.

IPv4 Options — A Review   157

IPv4 Options — A Review

- Security
- Loose source routing
- Strict source routing
- Record route
- Stream ID
- Internet timestamp

With the IP header becoming fixed, all of the options fields in the header were not eliminated completely, they merely changed forms. Basically, IPv4 options are now IP header extensions. The following are the IPv4 options:

Security. Used to carry security, compartmentation, user group (TCC), and handling restriction codes compatible with DOD requirements.

Loose source routing. Variable in length and used to route the internet datagram based on information supplied by the source. Not all the routing hops will be in this field. This option allows some flexibility in providing a path.

Strict source routing. Variable in length and used to route the internet datagram based on information supplied by the source. The routing information provided in this field must be explicitly followed.

Record route. Variable in length and used to trace the route an internet datagram takes.

Stream ID. Used to carry the stream identifier.

Internet timestamp. The timestamp is a right-justified, 32-bit field that indicates a time in milliseconds since midnight UT (Universal Time). There are placeholders for multiple timestamps and a flags field to indicate timestamps only. A timestamp is preceded with the internet address of the registering entity, the internet address fields are prespecified, or an IP module only registers its timestamp if it matches its own address with the next specified internet address. This can be used for measurements of the transport layer protocols and other utilities.

158 IPv4 and IPv6 Header Differences

The first thing to notice about the IPv6 header is that it is a static 40 bytes in length. The length of the packet header is not variable in length. The checksum was removed. IP first ran over copper serial lines that tended to be noisy (static in voice speak). Checksums are all over the TCP/IP protocol suite and all over the access methods of FDDI, Ethernet, and Token Ring. The removal of the checksum also allowed for all systems that forwarded IP datagrams to speed up because they do not have to compute the checksum at every hop.

Ipv4 and Ipv6 Header Differences

- IPv6 header is a static 40 bytes in length.
- Total length field is replaced with payload length.
- IPv6 allows for jumbograms (larger than 64k).
- Extension headers.
- TTL field is replaced with the hop limit.
- Many IPv4 options were moved to independent protocols.

IPv4's total-length field is replaced with a payload length. No significant changes here except that IPv6 is a static 40 bytes, so the payload length is truly a measurement of the payload and the IPv6 header is not included as part of the sum. This field is 16 bits in length, which allows for a maximum of 65,355 byte payload. However, IPv6 allows for a new concept known as *jumbo datagrams* (jumbograms), which allows for various network attachments such as I/O connections between high-speed computers that can process data segments higher than 64k (see RFC 2146).

One of the more interesting changes to IP with version 6 is the concept of *concatenated headers*. This is accomplished using the next header field on the IPv6 header. In IPv6, the protocol type field is set and that header would immediately follow. For example, if the payload was UDP then the protocol type is set to 17(decimal) and the UDP header would immediately follow.

The Time to Live (TTL) field is one of the more versatile fields in IP. It is used to prevent datagrams from constantly looping, keep packets on a local network, used in multicast datagrams to indicate scope (hearing range), and probably has many other private uses as well. In IPv6, this field is renamed to Hop Limit, because it is really used as a count-down-by-1 counter. The original intention of the field was to indicate a time (in seconds). It could be used, for example, by a router. If the router cannot forward the packet within the amount of time indicated in the TTL field, it should discard the datagram and generate an ICMP message. However, over time, most router delays were measured in milliseconds, not seconds. The accepted decrement of the field was set to 1, and therefore became a hop count and not an indication of time.

IPv6 Extension Headers

Since the fields on the preceeding slide were deleted from use in the IPv6 header how do we continue their use? For example, how do we indicate the protocol of the next header?

The IPv6 header is straightforward. Some of the options for IPv4 were better served by other TCP/IP protocols and some were kept as a part of IPv6 and are now known as IPv6 extension headers. These extension headers allow for IPv6 to become extensible beyond a specified (and limited) options field. It can be modified at later dates to include other options. The current IPv6 specification calls for the following headers (in the order they should appear in the datagram):

IPv6 header (not directly part of the extensions but shown here to show header order).

Hop-by-Hop Options (RFC 1883). The Hop-by-Hop Options header is used to carry optional information that must be examined by every node along a packet's delivery path. One of the options is the jumbo datagram option.

Destination Options (RFC 1883). The Destination Options header is used to carry optional information that needs be examined only by a packet's destination node(s).

Routing (Type 0) (RFC 1883). The Routing header is used by an IPv6 source to list one or more intermediate nodes to be "visited" on the way to a packet's destination. This function is very similar to IPv4's Source Route options.

Fragment (RFC 1883). The Fragment header is used by an IPv6 source to send packets larger than would fit in the path MTU to their destinations.

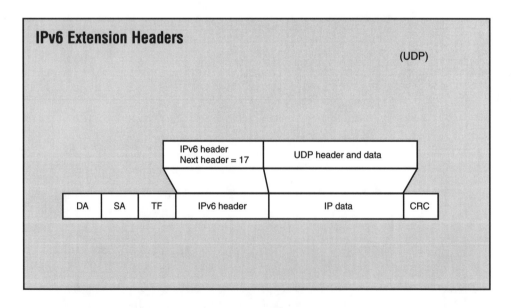

Authentication (RFC 1826).

Encapsulating Security Payload (RFC 1827).

Upper-layer header. (not part of the extension header, but shown here to show order).

From end-to-end communication, these fields should be ignored by all stations that may receive it. These fields are generally built and consumed by the source and destination stations only. The exception is the hop-by-hop options field, which may be reviewed by routers in the path to the destination.

Fragmentation 160

Another missing field deals with fragmentation was discouraged in IPv4. It continues to be discouraged in IPv6, but the onus of protocol was passed to the source node instead of the router, like in IPv4. In order to send a packet that is too large to fit in the MTU of the path to its destination, a source node may divide the packet into fragments and send each fragment as a separate packet, to be reassembled at the destination.

Fragmentation causes problems mainly due to efficiency of the routers and endstations.

Any missing fragment causes the whole TCP segment to be retransmitted (RFC 1122, page 58). This creates bandwidth problems, memory problems, and CPU cycles. In IPv4 it consumes considerable resources on the router (fragmentation) and host (reassembly). IPv6 encourages implementing RFC 1191. This is the specification for dynamic *path MTU discovery*, or having the host dynamically find out maximum packet sizes for the path to the destination (that is, determine the networks that the datagram will transit). MTU is the

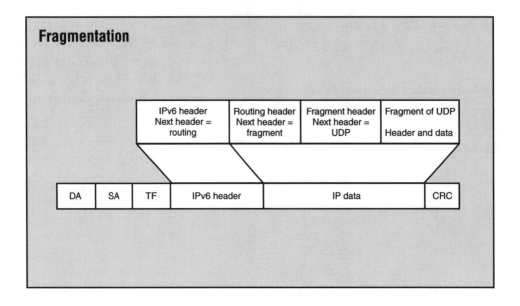

Fragmentation

| IPv6 header Next header = routing | Routing header Next header = fragment | Fragment header Next header = UDP | Fragment of UDP Header and data |

| DA | SA | TF | IPv6 header | IP data | CRC |

acronym for *maximum transmit unit,* or "how large a datagram can I transmit to the destination station." By enabling this, we eliminate the packet identification, the control flags, and the fragment offset. Any lost fragment means all the fragments in the segment must be retransmitted (RFC 1122, page 58).

Most hosts simply avoid the problem of discovering the maximum size of a packet on the destination path (if not local) and set the packet size to 576 bytes (the accepted minimum packet size for most IP networks), even though RFC 1191 presents a simple way to determine this. Some implementations transmit a large packet and wait to see if an ICMP "datagram too big" message is returned. The originating host will return to using 576-byte packets. Picking the right size is a very complex matter and most hosts stick to 576 bytes for nonlocal destination hosts.

This eliminates fragmentation and associated problems. However, this also creates an inefficiency in that some networks allow for large packet sizes. Imagine transferring information between Token Ring networks separated by an FDDI backbone. Not all networks are Ethernet. Why move the size down to 512 bytes just because the data traverses routers? There can be considerable consequences if the file is 100 Mbytes in length. Therefore, MTU discovery is more efficient than fragmentation by spreading the responsibility around to multiple entities.

Path MTU discovery is discussed in RFC 1191. It changed part of the ICMP RFC 793 in that it recommends using one of the previously unused header fields as the next-hop MTU-size indicator. This is an interesting aspect of ICMP for IPv6 in that it really does improve upon previous experience and knowledge and does not intend to replace.

Priority and Flow Label

Priority and Flow Label

- Still under much study.

- Priority field distinguishes the datagram among other datagrams.

- Two types of controlled traffic:
  - Congestion
  - Noncongestion

- Flow labels allow the router to identify a flow and place this label in the routing table for quick lookup.

4	Attended bulk transfer (i.e., file transfer)
5	Reserved
6	Interactive traffic
7	Control traffic (i.e., routing protocols and network management)

The second type of flows, noncongestion-controlled, doesn't care about congestion on the network. This can include delay-sensitive applications such as real-time audio and video. This is still under study and further clarifications based on case studies will soon come about.

As experimental as priorities are, so are flow labels. A flow distinguishes a traffic pattern. Flows are traffic streams from one sender to one or more receivers.

The two new fields in the IPv6 header are the *flow label* and *priority*.

These fields are still under much study, but a brief explanation is provided here. More information is available in the RFC 1809 and 1883.

The Priority field distinguishes the datagram among other datagrams on the network. It provides priorities for two types of traffic: congestion- and noncongestion-controlled traffic.

The following table lists the seven specific priorities for congestion-controlled traffic:

0	No specific priority
1	Background traffic (i.e., news)
2	Unattended data transfer (mail)
3	Reserved

162 IPv6 Addressing

The addressing of IPv6 is probably the best-known feature of IPv6. Ask anyone about the differences between IPv4 and IPv6, and the first response will be the change from 32-bit to 128-bit addressing. While it is true that the addressing was changed to 128 bits, there are many more features about the address space and its allocation that were carefully crafted. The first expansion of the address space was to 64 bits. It was later increased to 128 bits. It was proven that 64 bits was easily adequate but 128 bits was the final outcome. IPv6 addresses provide the same function as IPv4: identifiers for interfaces and sets of interfaces. Even though 128 bits are written for use, currently only 15 percent of the available address space is allocated for use. There are three types of addresses:

Unicast. An identifier for a single interface. A unique address delivered to a single destination.

Anycast. New for IP (version 6), an anycast address is an identifier for a set of interfaces (typically belonging to different nodes). This is similar to a multicast, but a packet sent to an anycast address is delivered to one of the interfaces identified by that address (the "nearest" one, according to the routing protocols' measure of distance).

> ### IPv6 Addressing
>
> - **Unicast**—identifies a single interface.
> - **Anycast**—new for IPv6, it identifies a set of interfaces usually belonging to different nodes. Used to deliver datagrams to the "nearest" of the interfaces.
> - **Multicast**—an identifier belonging to a group of interfaces. IPv6 extensively uses the multicast interface.
> - There is no broadcast address in IPv6.

Multicast. An identifier for a set of interfaces (typically belonging to different nodes). A packet sent to a multicast address is delivered to all interfaces identified by that address.

In IPv6, a broadcast address is not defined. It was superseded by multicast addresses.

In IPv4, we identified addresses by their 32-bit value, normally, written in a form known as *dotted-decimal notation*; for example, 132.1.8.10. An IPv6 address is written in hexadecimal and consists of groupings of 8 containing 4 hexadecimal digits or 8 groups of 16 bits each. This takes the form:

xxxx : xxxx : xxxx : xxxx : xxxx : xxxx : xxxx : xxxx

FEDC:BA98:7654:3210:FEDC:BA98:7654:3210 is an example of an IPv6 address. Another example is the following unicast address:
1080:0000:0000:0000:0008:0800:200C:417A
Since writing an IPv6 address has become unwieldy (DNS becomes very important here), there are provisions allowed to condense the address into its smallest available form.

Therefore, the preceding unicast address can be compressed into:
1080:0:0:0:8:800:200C:417A
or even
1080::8:800:200C:417A

The double colon has special significance. It is a demarcation point for compressing leading 0s. Notice here that only leading 0s can be compressed and the :: symbol can be used only once during the compression.

Therefore if you had the address of:
1080:0:0:5698:0:0:9887:1234
you cannot write it as:
1080::5698::9887:1234
The algorithm that runs the expansion for the address would get confused. How many 0s go in each of the colon-compressed slots? The

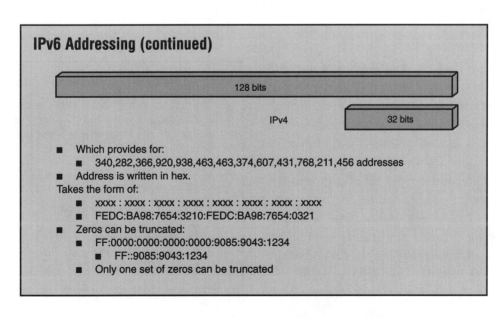

IPv6 Addressing (continued)

128 bits

IPv4   32 bits

- Which provides for:
  - 340,282,366,920,938,463,463,374,607,431,768,211,456 addresses
- Address is written in hex.
- Takes the form of:
  - xxxx : xxxx : xxxx : xxxx : xxxx : xxxx : xxxx : xxxx
  - FEDC:BA98:7654:3210:FEDC:BA98:7654:0321
- Zeros can be truncated:
  - FF:0000:0000:0000:9085:9043:1234
    - FF::9085:9043:1234
  - Only one set of zeros can be truncated

correct way to compress this address would be to compress one or the other sides.

1080::5698:0:0:9887:1234 or 1080:0:0:5698:: 9887:1234

164   IPv6 Addressing (continued)

As with IPv4, the first few bits of the IPv6 address tells something about the address (this has nothing to do with Class addressing). The table in Section 165 shows this. This time we are not dealing with classes or addresses, more so where the address has been assigned an address type and is known as the format prefix.

To get the amount of space used is simple. The formula is $1 / 2^n X$, where x is the number of bits used. For example, if the first 8 bits are 0000 0000, then this is $1 / 2^n 8$, or 1/256.

IPv6 Addressing (continued)

- The first few bits are indicators (as shown in a moment).
  - They do not register as a Class of address as in IPv4.

- Similar to CIDR, prefixes are used to indicate the routing.

- Special addresses are reserved:
  - Unspecified address
  - Loopback address
  - Embedded IPv4 address
  - Multicast address

Prefixes are also used in this environment just like in the CIDR environment. A /30 indicates the first 30 bits are used for routing. Also notice that fields in certain types of addresses are given names to further identify the subaddress portions. Refer to slide 165 for an example.

There are three address types that are assigned out of the 0000 0000 format prefix space. These are the "unspecified address," the loopback address, and the IPv6 addresses with embedded IPv4 addresses. This allocation supports the direct allocation of provider addresses, local use addresses, and multicast addresses. Space is reserved for NSAP addresses, IPX addresses, and geographic addresses. The remainder of the address space is unassigned for future use. This can be used for expansion of existing use (e.g., additional provider addresses, etc.) or new uses (e.g., separate locators and identifiers).

A value of FF (11111111) identifies an address as a multicast address; any other value identifies an address as a unicast address. Multicast addresses are used extensively throughout autoconfiguration of addresses and neighbor discovery. Anycast addresses are taken from the unicast address space, and are not syntactically distinguishable from unicast addresses.

IPv6 Addressing Prefix

Refer to slide 165.

IPv6 Addressing Prefix

Allocation	Prefix (binary)	Fraction of Address Space
Reserved	0000 0000	1/256
Unassigned	0000 0001	1/256
Reserved for NSAP Allocation	0000 001	1/128
Reserved for IPX Allocation	0000 010	1/128
Unassigned	0000 011	1/128
Unassigned	0000 1	1/32
Unassigned	0001	1/16
Unassigned	001	1/8
Provider-based Unicast address	010	1/8
Unassigned	011	1/8
Reserved for geographic-based unicast addresses	100	1/8
Unassigned	101	1/8
Unassigned	110	1/8
Unassigned	1110	1/16
Unassigned	1111 0	1/32
Unassigned	1111 10	1/64
Unassigned	1111 110	1/128
Unassigned	1111 1110 0	1/512
Link local use Addresses	1111 1110 10	1/1024
Site Local Use Addresses	1111 1110 11	1/1024
Multicast Addresses	1111 1111	1/256

There is an address that is reserved for testing IPv6 on the IPv6 Backbone (6Bone). The following slide shows the IPv6 (6Bone) test addressing as assigned by IANA.

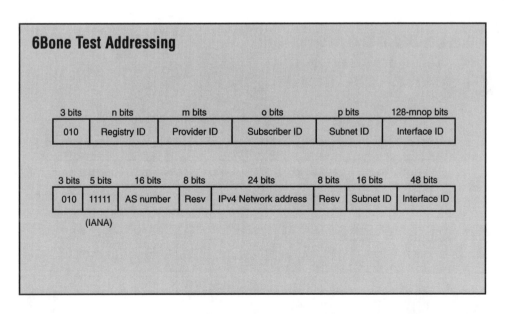

Like today's internet, IP addresses will be handed out by an internet service provider (an ISP such as MindSpring™, MCI™, AT&T™, Concentric Networks™, and any of the other thousands of internet connectivity providers out there). Connection of a commercial entity directly to the Internet will not be allowed, unless that entity is an ISP. The address shown on this slide was extracted from the previous slide for it is the most common address format that will be used (except for the multicast addresses).

The first 3 bits identify the address as a provider-oriented unicast address. The *registry ID* identifies the internet address registry (currently InterNIC [for the Americas], APNIC [for Asia-Pacific], and RIPE [for Europe] which assigns provider identifiers, indicated by the *provider ID* field, to internet service providers, which then assigns portions of the address space to subscribers. This is a process similar to the address assignment policy used with CIDR and described in RFC 2050. The *subscriber ID* distinguishes among multiple subscribers attached to the internet service provider identified by the provider ID. This is like a customer number. The *subnet ID* identifies a specific physical link. There can be multiple subnets on the same physical link; however, a specific subnet cannot span multiple physical links. The *interface ID* identifies a single interface among the group of interfaces identified by the subnet prefix.

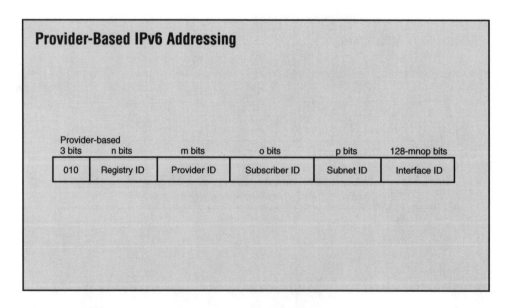

Provider-Based IPv6 Addressing

Provider-based 3 bits	n bits	m bits	o bits	p bits	128-mnop bits
010	Registry ID	Provider ID	Subscriber ID	Subnet ID	Interface ID

This addressing is used exactly as the name implies: locally. This can be subnet local or subscriber local, which gives the two names *link local* and *site local*. The slide shows the format of these two addressing types. Notice that both addressing types use the reserved prefix format of FE.

This is an indicator, if you will, such that the internet will not attempt to route packets that are designated as local. You can think of these addresses as the private addresses used in IPv4.

Stations that are not configured using a provider based address or a site local address use the link local address. This is an address that can be used between two stations on a single link or network. This type of address will not be processed by a router, so it cannot span subnets. It can be used by a station that is starting up and does not know its location on the network. Basically, it is the concatenation of its 48-bit MAC address and the well-known link local prefix of FE80::48-bit MAC address. When the make address cannot be used, a serial number or some other unique identification of the card can be used.

A site local address is used to allow a site to configure its network without being connected to the Internet. Unlike IPv4, a site can devise and implement a complete addressed Internet network. This will allow that site to communicate with all interfaces at the site (it may span globally); however, none of these stations may communicate over the Internet. There may be many reasons for this; for example, some companies may not want connection to the Internet until a specified time in the future. I witnessed this at a bank that set up its complete internet based on private addressing

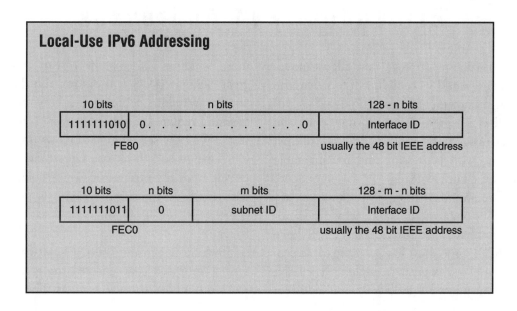

(IPv4, that is). Problem is it did not use the RFC 1918 private address space allocation to accomplish this. The site was up and operational for two years without a hitch (well, not too many!). When connection to the Internet was desired, the bank had a choice of providing for Network Address Translation (NAT, RFC 1631) or readdressing its network. A lot of thought went into it and based on many factors—scalability, peer-to-peer communication, and others—the bank readdressed its site.

This would not have occurred with IPv6 site local addressing. The addressing allows for any entity to pick any number out of the blue and configure its site (in this case, all of its company locations). If, at some later time, the bank is assigned a global provider address prefix, its network will not have to be completely renumbered.

Site local addresses may not be routed over the Internet, without having a different prefix assigned, such as a global-provider-based prefix. The subnet ID is what you are suspecting. It is an ID assigned to a subnet.

169 IPv6 Addresses with Embedded IPv4 Addresses

A transitioning strategy that allows movement from IPv4 to IPv6 will be key to the successful implementation of IPv6—IPv6 will never be accepted if a one-time complete cutover needs to be applied. IPv4 is working, stumbling with addressing and routing table explosion, but working. It is embedded. Therefore, installations must be allowed to "try before they buy" into it. This is why other protocols that have tried to overtake TCP/IP have failed (OSI). You must have a compatible procedure in place. A great example, is Microsoft when it introduced Windows 95. It allowed for most Windows 3.x programs to run. Another great example is OS/2. It did not run the very popular Windows 3.1 programs very well and basically required a major cutover to make it work. We now see where Windows 95 is and OS/2 is not, so I think you know how important it is for IPv6 to be backwards compatible with IPv4. A transition scheme is provided courtesy of RFC 1933 and is not that difficult to read.

IPv6 hosts can use the IPv4 network as a virtual interface that enables these hosts to reach other hosts through tunnels. The address

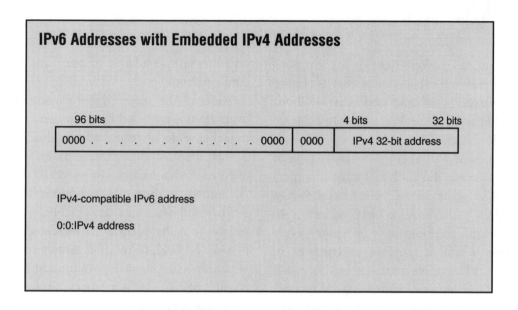

that is used to allow for this is a special type of link local address called the IPv4-compatible address, shown in Slide 169. Also needed for the transition is for hosts to become dual stack (supporting both IPv4 and IPv6 IP stacks) and tunneling. To allow for this, a mechanism is provided in the IPv6 addressing structure.

IPv4-compatible IPv6 address-0::0:IPv4 address.

There was another address method known as the IPv4 mapped address that would allow for translation, but this is out of favor and the method today is the preceding stated address scheme.

170 Unicast Addresses

The unicast address space is a contiguous bit-wise, maskable address that is similar to the addressing scheme used in IPv4 CIDR. The address types for unicast addressing are shown in the slide.

An expected to be very common type of address is where the IEEE 802.x (or Ethernet) LAN MAC addresses will be used as shown in the slide. The IEEE 802.x MAC address is 48 bits in length and because of its registry, every card has a unique number assigned to it. However, where these addresses are not available, E.164 (telephone) addresses could be used.

An interested point is that by using the IEEE 802.x MAC address, an IPv6 node could simply listen to the cable plant for router advertisements, which would yield the subnet ID for itself. Putting the two together would give it a unique address to use. This is auto-configuration.

Refer to the slide. Global communication using IPv6 is provided by the unicast addressing scheme of a global-based provider. The first 3 bits identify the address as a provider-oriented unicast address. The *registry ID* identifies the internet address registry (currently IANA, RIPE, APNIC, and INTERNIC), which assigns provider identifiers, indicated by the *provider ID* field, to internet service providers, which then assign portions of the address space to subscribers. This is a process similar to the address assignment policy used with CIDR and described in RFC 2050. The *subscriber ID* distinguishes among multiple subscribers attached to the internet service provider identified by the provider ID. This is like a customer number.

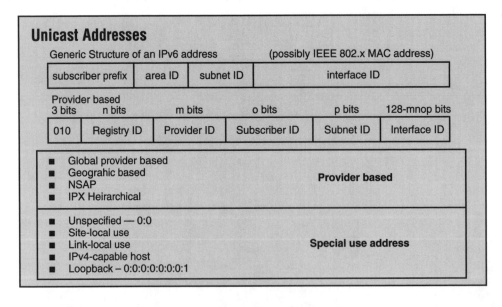

The *subnet ID* identifies a specific physical link. There can be multiple subnets on the same physical link; however, a specific subnet cannot span multiple physical links. The *interface ID* identifies a single interface among the group of interfaces identified by the subnet prefix.

Autoconfiguration 171

Autoconfiguration is the ability of an IPv6 node to start up and dynamically attain its node and network addresses. There are two types of autoconfiguration:

Stateful. Some external device assists the node at startup to determine its network address (prefix), node address, and perhaps some router addresses. A consideration of this is for DHCP to enable the configuring of an initializing node.

Stateless. This means that the node will configure itself and find its resources on the network through the use of multicast addresses. This allows the node to start up and send out request messages to which other nodes will respond. The node can then determine its network address and prefix and node address based on these responses. IPv6 nodes start this behavior by joining the all-nodes multicast group upon startup. This is accomplished by initializing the interface to the all-nodes multicast address of FF02::1. These nodes can solicit information from routers using the all-

Autoconfiguration

- Stateless autoconfiguration.
    - Initializing hosts join the all-nodes multicast address of FE02::1

- Stateless autoconfiguration allows for a node to start up using the link-local prefix and some sort of token.
    - This will probably be the 48-bit Ethernet address
    - Address would be FE80::48-bit address (multicast)

- Hosts send a solicitation message to all-routers using the all-routers multicast address of FF02::2.
    - Used to determine the node's routing prefix and other routing parameters

- Stateful autoconfiguration uses.

routers multicast address of FF02::2 as the destination and their own link local addresses as the source.

Stateless autoconfiguration has its advantages in that it is really automatic and very simple to use. However, this type of configuration is vulnerable to hackers who could simply place their network station on the subnet and immediately gain access to the resources on that subnet. Stateful autoconfiguration was developed to combat such a threat.

Neighbor Discovery

- RFC 1970.

- Very extensive and best to read RFC.

- Nodes used Neighbor Discovery to determine link-layer addresses for neighbors.

- Finds link-local hosts and routers.

- Detects which neighbors are reachable and detects link-layer address changes.

- ARP is *not* used with IPv6.
  - This is the robust replacement for ARP (IPv4)

Neighbor Discovery is presented in RFC 1970. Although it uses ICMP, do not expect to find its listing in ICMPv6 RFC (RFC 1885).

The Address Resolution Protocol is not used with IPv6. It is part of the Neighbor Discovery protocol. Nodes (hosts and routers) use Neighbor Discovery to determine the link-layer addresses for neighbors known to reside on attached links and to quickly purge cached values that become invalid. Hosts also use Neighbor Discovery to find neighboring routers that are willing to forward packets on their behalf.

Nodes use the protocol to actively keep track of which neighbors are reachable and which are not, and to detect changed link-layer addresses. When a router or the path to a router fails, a host actively searches for functioning alternates.

This sounds like a happy medium between ARP for IPv4 and the methods employed by ES-IS procedures of the CLNP (Connectionless Network Protocol) from the OSI suite. In ES-IS (part of the routing update protocol for the OSI protocol suite), the active endstations send Hello packets to which the active routers on a network listen and build a database of. In this database is a listing of all the endstations that the OSI router has heard from. The OSI router also transmits a packet to allow itself to be known on the network as well. The workstations record the router's address so that it can send packets to it, either the first packet transmitted locally or all off-network forwarding. The OSI router will inform the node about the location of the destination station. It was once recommended that CLNP replace IPv4. However, CLNP was actually a clone of IP, basically outdated by the time the IPng group formed in 1992, and pushed aside. Anyway, the IPv6 Neighbor Discovery protocol corresponds to a combination of the IPv4 protocols ARP (RFC 826), ICMP Router Discovery (RFC 1256), and ICMP Redirect (RFC 791).

173 Neighbor Discovery (continued)

A question that may be asked here is: With all the dependency on dynamically discovering link-layer addresses between hosts and routers, how can an ICMP message be sent, if the media (link-layer) address is not yet known (i.e., the Neighbor Discovery procedures have not yet determined the link-layer addresses for all dependencies on a node local link)? This is easily solved by using a well-known IPv6 multicast address. ICMP cannot work without the media address being known.

However, a special multicast address at the MAC layer has been invented. All stations should be listening to their special MAC multicast address. This is formed by placing 3333 and the last 32 bits of their IPv6 address as one of the addresses to listen for on the NIC card. Therefore, if an address of 3333 is received by the NIC, it will process the last 32 bits as well. If this matches its address, it will pass it on to the IPv6 IP layer of its upper-layer software.

With the exception of Non-Broadcast Multiaccess (NBMA) networks (ATM Frame Relay, + X.25) or if a link-layer interaction is specified in another document, RFC 1970 applies to all link-layer types. However, because ND uses link-layer multicast for some of its services, it is possible that on some link types (e.g., NBMA links), alternative protocols or mechanisms to implement those services will be specified (in the appropriate document covering the operation of IP over a particular link type). The services described in this document that are not directly dependent on multicast (e.g., Redirects, Next-Hop

determination, Neighbor Unreachability Detection, etc.) are expected to be provided as specified in this document. The details of how one uses ND on NBMA links is an area for further study.

Neighbor Discovery (continued)

- In IPv6, Discovery messages use the various multicast address assignments for router discovery, neighbor discovery, etc.
- The media (MAC) address is a multicast address as well:
  - 33-33-last 32 bits of the IPv6 address
- RFC 1970 applies to all link-layer types except NBMA and various proprietary interfaces.

Neighbor Discovery Types

> **Neighbor Discovery Types**
>
> - Router Discovery
> - Prefix Discovery
> - Parameter Discovery
> - Address Autoconfiguration
> - Address Resolution
> - Next-Hop determination
> - Neighbor Unreachability Detection
> - Duplicate Address Detection
> - Redirect

This protocol solves a set of problems related to the interaction between nodes attached to the same link. It defines mechanisms for solving each of the following problems:

Router Discovery. This protocol allows hosts to locate and identify routers on their local link.

Prefix Discovery. How hosts discover the set of address prefixes that define which destinations are on-link for an attached link. (Nodes use prefixes to distinguish destinations that reside on-link from those only reachable through a router.)

Parameter Discovery. How a node learns such link parameters as the link MTU or such Internet parameters as the hop-limit value to place in outgoing packets.

Address Autoconfiguration. How nodes automatically configure an address for an interface.

Address Resolution. How nodes determine the link-layer address of an on-link destination (e.g., a neighbor) given only the destination's IP address.

Next-Hop Determination. The algorithm for mapping an IP destination address into the IP address of the neighbor to which traffic for the destination should be sent. The next-hop can be a router or the destination itself.

Neighbor Unreachability Detection. How nodes determine that a neighbor is no longer reachable. For neighbors used as routers, alternate default routers can be tried. For both routers and hosts, address resolution can be performed again.

Duplicate Address Detection. How a node determines that an address it wishes to use is not already in use by another node.

Redirect. How a router informs a host of a better first-hop node to reach a particular destination.

Also contained in RFC 792 is the original ICMP redirect message in which a router sends to a host stating, "I will forward the packet that you sent to me to my next hop port. However, there is a better path to the destination that you indicated and it is through Router X."

175 Neighbor Discovery and IPv4

The IPv6 Neighbor Discovery protocol corresponds to a combination of the IPv4 protocols ARP, ICMP Router Discovery, and ICMP Redirect. In IPv4 there is no generally agreed upon protocol or mechanism for Neighbor Unreachability Detection, although Hosts Requirements RFC 1122 and 1123 does specify some possible algorithms for Dead Gateway Detection (a subset of the problems that Neighbor Unreachability Detection tackles). Router Discovery is part of the base protocol set; there is no need for hosts to "snoop" the routing protocols. Router advertisements carry link-layer addresses; no additional packet exchange is needed to resolve the router's link-layer address. Router advertisements carry prefixes for a link; there is no need to have a separate mechanism to configure the "netmask." Router advertisements enable Address Autoconfiguration. Routers can advertise an MTU for hosts to use on the link, ensuring that all nodes use the same MTU value on links lacking a well-defined MTU.

Address resolution multicasts are "spread" over 4 billion ($2^{n}32$) multicast addresses, greatly reducing address resolution-related interrupts on nodes other than the target. Moreover, non-IPv6 machines should not be interrupted at all. Redirects contain the link-layer address of the new first hop; separate address resolution is not needed upon receiving a redirect.

Multiple prefixes can be associated with the same link. By default, hosts learn all on-link prefixes from Router Advertisements.

However, routers may be configured to omit some or all prefixes from Router Advertisements. In such cases, hosts assume that destinations are off-link and send traffic to routers. A router can then issue redirects as appropriate.

Neighbor Discovery and IPv4

- IPv6 Neighbor Discovery combines IPv4 protocols of ARP, ICMP Router Discovery, and ICMP Redirect.

- IPv4 has no agreed-upon method for Dead Gateway Detection and Neighbor Unreachability detection.

Neighbor Discovery and IPv4 (continued)

- IPv6 assumes a redirect next hop is on-link—on the same link that it resides.

- IPv6 detects half link failures (neighbors that are suspect or that have gone away).

- IPv6 Router advertisements do not contain a Preference field.

- Using link-local addresses to identify routers means that this relationship is maintained even if the provider address changes.

- Address resolution is accomplished at the ICMP layer.

Unlike IPv4, the recipient of an IPv6 redirect assumes that the new next hop is on-link (the same subnet as itself). In IPv4, a host ignores redirects specifying a next-hop that is not on-link according to the link's network mask. The IPv6 redirect mechanism is analogous to the redirect facility. It is expected to be useful on nonbroadcast and shared media links in which it is undesirable or impossible for nodes to know all prefixes for on-link destinations.

Neighbor Unreachability Detection is part of the base significantly improving the robustness of packet delivery in the presence of failing routers, partially failing or partitioned links and nodes that change their link-layer addresses. For instance, mobile nodes can move off-link without losing any connectivity due to stale ARP caches.

Unlike ARP, Neighbor Discovery detects half-link failures (using Neighbor Unreach-ability Detection) and avoids sending traffic to neighbors with which two-way connectivity is absent. Unlike in IPv4 Router Discovery the Router Advertisement messages do not contain a preference field. The preference field is not needed to handle routers of different "stability"; the Neighbor Unreachability Detec-tion will detect dead routers and switch to a working one. The use of link-local addresses to uniquely iden-tify routers (for Router Advertisement and Redirect messages) makes it possible for hosts to maintain the router associations in the event of the site renumbering to use new global prefixes.

Using the Hop-Limit-equal-to-255 trick, Neighbor Discovery is immune to off-link senders that accidentally or intentionally send ND messages. In IPv4, off-link senders can send both ICMP Redirects and Router Advertisement messages. Placing address resolution at the ICMP layer makes the protocol more media independent than ARP and makes it possible to use standard IP authentication and security mechanisms as appropriate.

177 Address Resolution

The purpose of address resolution is to determine the link-level address of a destination given only its IP address. This is performed only for those IP addresses that are local (hop count set to 1 for these messages). When a multicastable interface starts, it must join both the all-nodes multicast group and the solicited-node multicast group. This enables the node to receive and process packets without having all of its addressing established. In fact, a node must keep the multicast addresses until all addressing has been resolved. Address resolution consists of sending a Neighbor Solicitation message and waiting for a Neighbor Advertisement using multicast addressing. The solicitation is sent to the solicited-node multicast address corresponding to the target address. The solicited-node multicast address is a link-local scope multicast address that is computed as a function of the solicited target's address. The solicited-node multicast address is formed by taking the low-order 32 bits of the target IP address and appending those bits to the 96-bit prefix FF02:0:0:0:0:1 to produce a multicast address within the range of FF02::1:0:0 to FF02::1:FFFF:FFFF. For example, the solicited node multicast address corresponding to the IP address 4037::01:800:200E:8C6C is FF02::1:200E:8C6C. IP addresses that differ only in the high-order bits (e.g., due to multiple high-order prefixes associated with different providers) will map to the same solicited-node address, thereby reducing the number of multicast addresses a node must join. In response to this request (the sender may send it multiple times if no response

> ## Address Resolution
>
> - Purpose is to determine the link level-address of a destination given only its IP address.
> - Consists of sending a Neighbor Solicitation message and waiting for a reply.
>   - All nodes start up by joining the all-nodes multicast address and the solicited node multicast address
>   - Solicited node address is taking the 96 bit prefix FF02:0:0:0:0:1 and placing the low order 32 bits of the destination IP address to this
>   - This allows for a range of FF02::1:0:0 through FF02::1:FFFF:FFFF
>   - The full target address is embedded in the ICMP packet

is found within a certain period of time), a Neighbor Advertisement should be generated by the remote node. The originating node should receive this packet and update its Neighbor cache with the information in the received Neighbor Advertisement (the link-layer information). The MAC address is set as previously indicated by taking the low-order 32 bits of the target IPv6 address and prepending 3333 to that address, which is the IPv6 all-nodes MAC multicast address.

One more check is accomplished each time a Neighbor cache (link-layer information) entry is accessed while transmitting a unicast packet: The sender checks Neighbor Unreachability Detection-related information according to the Neighbor Unreachability Detection algorithm. This is not so much a protocol as keeping an eye on the progression of the upper-layer protocols with this address. This unreachability check might result in the sender transmitting a unicast Neighbor Solicitation to verify that the neighbor is still reachable.

If at some point communication ceases to proceed, as determined by the Neighbor Unreachability Detection algorithm, next-hop determination may need to be performed again. For example, traffic through a failed router should be switched to a working router. Likewise, it may be possible to reroute traffic destined for a mobile node to a "mobility agent."

Note that when a node redoes next-hop determination, there is no need to discard the complete Destination cache entry. In fact, it is generally beneficial to retain such cached information as the PMTU and round-trip timer values that may also be kept in the Destination cache entry.

Next-hop determination is done the first time traffic is sent to a destination. As long as subsequent communication to that destination proceeds successfully, the Destination cache entry continues to be used. All of this is detailed further later in the book.

Methods of Deploying IPv6 178

Methods of Deploying IPv6

- Dual IP layer—a node that is running both the IPv4 and IPv6 TCP/IP protocol stacks.

- IPv6 over IPv4 tunnel—the process of taking an IPv6 datagram and wrapping an IPv4 header on it for transit across IPv4 routers.
  - Configured tunnel—IPv4 tunnel endpoint address is determined by the encapsulating node
  - Automatic tunnel—IPv4 tunnel endpoint is determined from the IPv4 address of the IPv6 packet

- Transition consists of:
  - IPv4-only node

IPv6 will not be cut over in an hour's time. A period of transition will take place. In order to effect the transition some suggested methods are provided:

Dual IP layer. IPv4 and IPv6 running at the network layer in both hosts and/or routers. These nodes have the ability to send and receive both IPv4 and IPv6 datagrams. This requires that a node be configured with both an IPv4 and IPv6 address that may or may not be related. In this way, IPv4-only hosts can access services that exist on an IPv6 host.

IPv6 over IPv4 tunneling. This is the process of taking an IPv6 datagram and wrapping an IPv4 header on it for transit across IPv4 hosts or routers. Two methods are available: *configured* and *automatic*. These nodes are configured with an IPv4-compatible IPv6 address. This is that special unicast address that has a 96-bit prefix of all 0s. The next 32 bits is an IPv4 address.

Configured tunneling is when the IPv4 tunnel endpoint address is determined by the encapsulating node.

Automatic tunneling is when the IPv4 tunnel endpoint is determined from the IPv4 address of the IPv6 packet. A node may be capable of automatic and/or configured tunneling. Automatic tunneling uses the IPv4-compatible address scheme as shown in the slide. A node does not have to support dual stack IP to support tunneling.

The transition will also have special nodes:

IPv4-only node. A node that only understands IPv4.
IPv4/IPv6 node. A node that is running dual IP stacks and understands both IPv4 and IPv6.
IPv6-only node. A node that understands IPv6 only.

IPv6 Tunneling Introduction

IPv6 Tunneling Introduction
■ Host to Router
■ Router to Router
■ Router to Host
■ Host to Host

Tunneling is very simply the method of transporting IPv6 packets over IPv4 routing topologies. It is being used today with the 6Bone (www/6Bone.com). Two scenarios occur here. The first one is the following two tunneling methods:

Host to Router: Dual-stack IP hosts can tunnel IPv6 packets to an intermediary dual-stack IP router that is reachable via an IPv4 infrastructure.

Router to Router: A router that is running the dual-stack IP interconnected by an IPv4 infrastructure can tunnel IPv6 datagrams between routers.

With these types of tunnels, the tunnel endpoint is an intermediary router that must decapsulate the IPv6 packet and forward it to its final destination. The endpoint of the tunnel is different from the destination of the packet being tunneled. Therefore, the address in the IPv6 packet being tunneled does not provide the IPv4 address of the tunnel endpoint. The tunnel endpoint address must be determined from information that is configured on the node performing the tunneling. This is the configured tunnel approach. The endpoint is explicitly configured.

Tunnels are characterized by two endpoint IPv4 addresses. The IPv4 protocol identifier is 41, the assigned payload type number for IPv6.

Router to Host: Dual-stack IP routers can tunnel IPv6 packets to their final destination dual-stack IP host.

Host to Host: Dual-stack IP hosts can tunnel IPv6 packets between themselves over an IPv6 infrastructure (without the use of a router).

These two types provide for tunneling all the way to a final destination. In these cases, the tunnel endpoint is the node to which the IPv6 packet is addressed. This is automatic tunneling and it simply allows for IPv6 packets that are to be sent to IPv6 destinations using the IPv4-compatible address and located remotely (off-link) to be encapsulated in IPv4 headers and sent through the IPv4 infrastructure.

180 IPv6 Tunnel Addressing

Now, which type of tunneling is used where, and how does this thing work? Well, it depends on the address of the destination. If the address is an IPv6 address and the destination is local (on-link), then it simply sends the packet. If the address of the end node is an IPv4 address and it resides on a different subnet, then an IPv4 router must be used.

The key to all of this is the special address 0:0:0:0:0:0:<IPv4 32-bit address>. IPv4-compatible router.

Dual IP stack hosts will recognize the special address and immediately encapsulate the packet with an IPv4 header. This is called an *end-to-end* tunnel. The receiving station will decapsulate the datagram (strip off the IPv4 header) and read it as an IPv6 datagram.

IPv6-only hosts can also use the IPv4 Internet through the use of dual-stack IP routers. The IPv6-only host will transmit the IP datagram as an IPv6 datagram. The dual-stack IP router will recognize the special address and wrap it in an IPv4 header (using the last 32 bits of the special address in the IPv4 destination IP address).

Finally, if the address is an IPv6 address but not of the special address, a configured tunnel can be used instead of an automatic tunnel (which recognizes the special address). This requires configuration in the IPv6 host to allow for this. This is a more or less manual configuration and tells the IPv6 host where to send the packet.

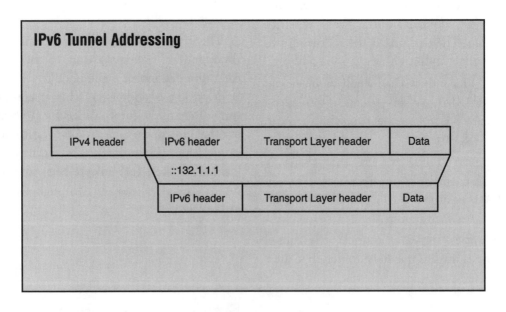

IPv6 Tunnel Addressing

| IPv4 header | IPv6 header | Transport Layer header | Data |

::132.1.1.1

| IPv6 header | Transport Layer header | Data |

The following slide shows the IPv6 and IPv4 dual-stack capability of a host. Based on the EtherType field of the received packet, the NIC software can hand off the decapsulated packet to either of the TCP/IP software stacks.

Since the Ethernet type field has a new number for IPv6, this method is very easy to implement. When a packet is received, the type field is checked. If the type field contains 0800 (in hex) the packet is handed off to the IPv4 protocol stack, otherwise the type field contains 86DD, then the packet is handed off to the IPv6 stack.

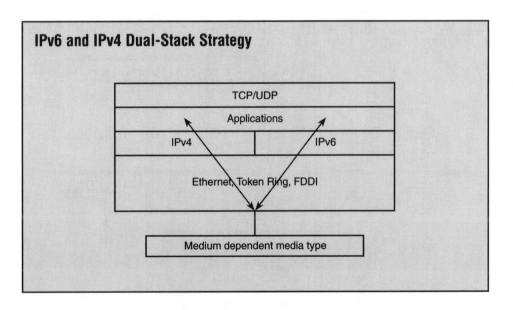

IPv6 and IPv4 Dual-Stack Strategy

TCP/UDP

Applications

IPv4   IPv6

Ethernet, Token Ring, FDDI

Medium dependent media type

IPv6 Tunneling

The slide shows an IPv6 tunneling strategy. IPv6 and IPv4 nodes can peacefully coexist on a network using tunneling. This slide shows an IPv4/IPv6 router that can attach to an IPv4 router. Notice here that IPv4 and IPv6 hosts can exist with the IPv6/IPv4 routers. However, an IPv6-only host cannot make use of the IPv4 router. This is shown on the right side in the middle of the slide. An IPv6 host is situated behind an IPv4 router. These two devices have no method of communicating.

The flowcharts in the following section give full descriptions for examples that can be used with this slide.

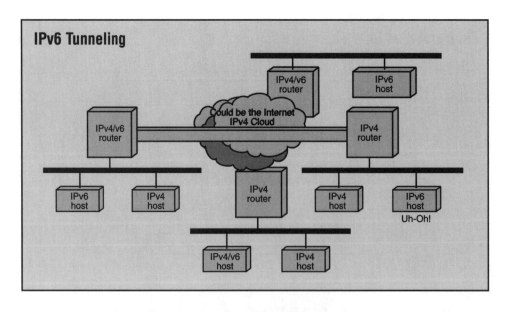

This slide shows four possible methods of IPv6 tunneling data flow.

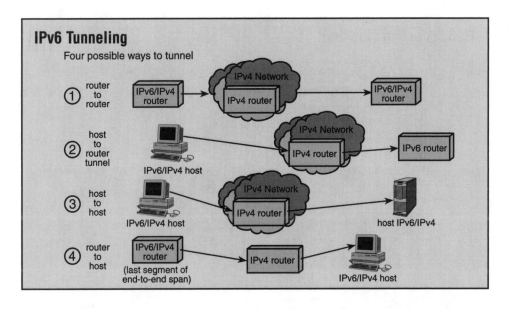

IPv6 Tunneling

Four possible ways to tunnel

(1) router to router

IPv6/IPv4 router → IPv4 Network (IPv4 router) → IPv6/IPv4 router

(2) host to router tunnel

IPv6/IPv4 host → IPv4 Network (IPv4 router) → IPv6 router

(3) host to host

IPv6/IPv4 host → IPv4 Network (IPv4 router) → host IPv6/IPv4

(4) router to host

IPv6/IPv4 router (last segment of end-to-end span) → IPv4 router → IPv6/IPv4 host

IPv6 Tunneling Flowchart 1

This slide shows IPv6 tunneling when the end node address is an IPv4-compatible IPv6 address.

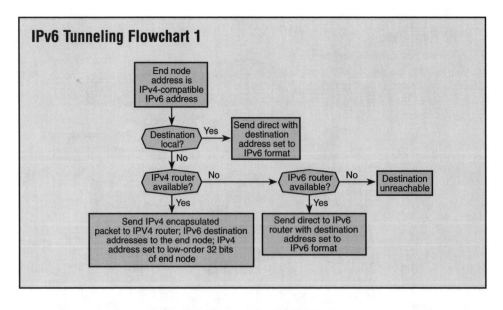

IPv6 Tunneling Flowchart 1

This slide shows IPv6 tunneling when the end node is an IPv6-only address.

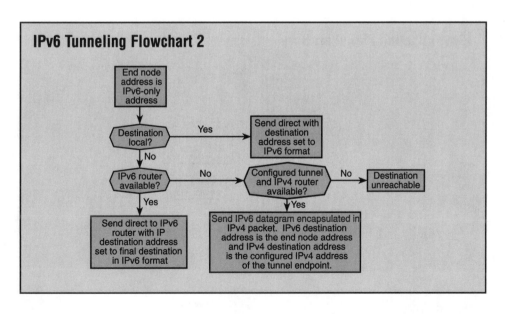

This slide shows tunneling IPv6 when the end node address is an IPv4 address.

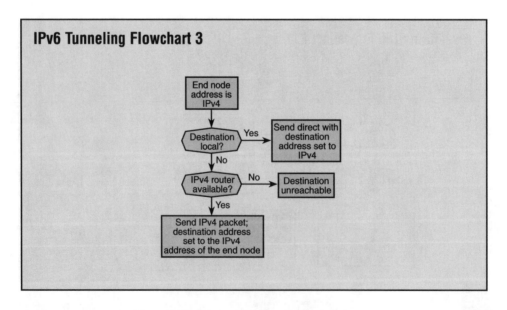

IPv6 Tunneling Flowchart 3

Anycast Addressing

> **Anycast Addressing**
>
> - Similar to a multicast address.
>
> - Address is sent to a group address (anycast) but the router delivers the datagram to the nearest member of the group.
>
> - Provides for applications such as file and print servers, time servers, name servers, DHCP, etc.
>
> - Similar to the NetWare protocol of "Get Nearest Server" request.

An anycast address is similar to a multicast address. The exception here is that a packet sent to an anycast address is routed to the "nearest" interface having that address, using distance as a factor.

A source node sends a datagram addressed as an anycast address. This address will be recognized by all destinations of a given type. The routing system is key here; it is the routing system that delivers the datagram to the nearest server. This has applications to find servers of type file/print, timer, name, DHCP, and so forth.

This concept may sound familiar to those who know the Novell NetWare protocol. Functionally, it is implemented differently, but the concept is the same.

Multicasting for IPv6

Multicasting for IP started in 1988 with IGMP. IANA also assigned a new class of addressing known as Class D addressing. Multicasting is carried over to IPv6 and its addressing allows for more granularity. Multicasting is used extensively with IPv6. The format of the address is shown in the slide. The first 8 bits must be set to FF. The next 4 bits are called the *flag* bits, of which only one is defined. The T bit is the transient bit. Setting this to 1 indicates the multicast address is not permanently assigned by the IANA. A 0 indicates it is permanently assigned.

The scope is 4 bits in length and controls the "hearing range" of the multicast address. It performs the same function as the TTL field in an IPv4 multicast packet. The following table indicates what scopes are currently assigned.

Scope	Range
0	Reserved
1	Node local scope
2	Link local scope
3	Unassigned
4	Unassigned
5	Site local scope
6	Unassigned
7	Unassigned
8	Organization local scope
9	Unassigned
A	Unassigned
B	Unassigned
C	Unassigned
D	Unassigned
E	Global scope
F	Reserved

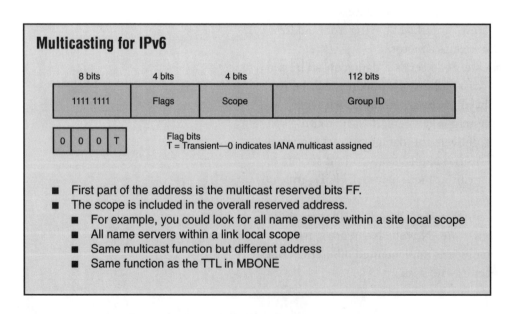

Multicasting for IPv6

8 bits	4 bits	4 bits	112 bits
1111 1111	Flags	Scope	Group ID

| 0 | 0 | 0 | T |

Flag bits
T = Transient—0 indicates IANA multicast assigned

- First part of the address is the multicast reserved bits FF.
- The scope is included in the overall reserved address.
    - For example, you could look for all name servers within a site local scope
    - All name servers within a link local scope
    - Same multicast function but different address
    - Same function as the TTL in MBONE

Notice that in IPv6 multicast addresses, weaving the scope in as part of the address makes it possible to have multiple multicast addresses for the same function. The first part of the address is the multicast address identifier, but the scope is included in the overall address. This allows for multiple multicast addresses to be assigned to the same function. For example, there is one multicast address looking for all DHCP servers in a radius of 3 hops. Another would allow for a radius of 10 hops, but it is still the same multicast function.

IPv6 Routing   189

IPv6 Routing

- Existing routing protocols (OSPF, RIP, IDRD, etc.) are straightforward extensions of IPv4 routing.

- IPv6 includes new routing extensions such as:
    - Provider selection
    - Host mobility
    - Auto-readdressing

- OSPF:
    - Creates a separate link-state database
    - Makes room for the 128-bit address
    - Cannot interoperate with IPv4

Routing in IPv6 is almost identical to IPv4 routing under CIDR except that the addresses are 128-bit IPv6 addresses instead of 32-bit IPv4 addresses. With very straightforward extensions, all of IPv4's routing algorithms (OSPF, RIP, IDRP, ISIS, etc.) can used to route IPv6.

IPv6 also includes simple routing extensions that support powerful new routing functionality. These capabilities include:

- Provider selection (based on policy, performance, cost, etc.)

- Host mobility (route to current location)
- Auto-readdressing (route to new address)

The new routing functionality is obtained by creating sequences of IPv6 addresses using the IPv6 Routing option. The Routing option is used by an IPv6 source to list one or more intermediate nodes (or topological group) to be "visited" on the way to a packet's destination. This function is very similar in function to IPv4's Loose Source and Record Route option.

OSPFv6 for IPv6, like IPv4, will run directly on top of IPv6. OSPFv6 will run as a separate protocol just like any other "ships in the night" type of protocol in a multiprotocol router. It will have a separate link-state database than OSPFv4. In short, nothing will be shared between OSPFv4 and OSPFv6 (in the router, that is). Each will not know the other exists.

However, in order to make IPv6 operate with OSPFv6, some changes are necessary. Most notably will be the 128-bit address. Router IDs, links, and areas will be associated with an 128-bit number.

RIP made it through as well. How could we forget good old RIP? Hey, it's still a good, decent protocol for small networks and is very easy to implement. And, with the advent of RIP2, RIP is alive and well. As with the advantage of VLSM with RIP2, the dominance of RIP continues and extensions for 128 bit addressing have been provided.

The packet format is shown in the slide and it is represented by RFC 2080. Notice that the same amount of space is taken up for the route table entries as IPv4 (160 bits per entry). One feature that was added extended the packet size to beyond the limit of 576 bytes as in RIPv1 and v2. It was noted that these update packets will never traverse a router, and therefore the limit on the Route Table Entries (RTE) is simply limited by the MTU of the medium over which the protocol is being used.

The formula is:

# of RTE = (MTU - sizeof(IPv6_hdrs) - UDP_hdrlen - RIPng_hdrlen)) / RTE_Size

The 8-bit subnet mask is used to identify the number of bits in the prefix. Since there are 8 bits, this gives us the capability of a 256-bit prefix, which is more than enough for the 128 bits of IPv6.

Legend

- hdrs – headers
- hdrlen – header length

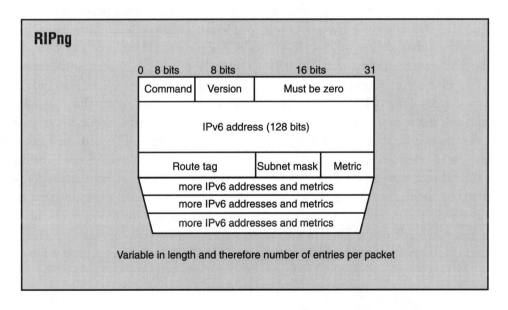

191 ICMP

Like IPv4, IPv6 does not provide error detection. This is a function of ICMP. ICMP for IPv6 has been addressed as well.

Internet Control Message Protocol (ICMP) for IPv6 is found in RFCs 1885 and 1970. ICMP for IPv6 is explained in RFC 1885, but the individual functions of ICMP for IPv6 (for example, path MTU discovery) are detailed in existing RFCs such as RFC 1191. Hopefully, you are not too confused? If you are, welcome to the world of RFCs. IPv6 and its extension protocols used previous RFCs if they were found relevant to the protocol.

ICMPv6 is an IPv4 extension. It is originally documented in RFC 792 and is an integral part of the IP. Along the years, other functions that utilize ICMP were added, such as router discovery (RFC 1256). ICMPv6 is a version of ICMP for IPv6 (seeing a "v6" after a protocol name is a very common way of specifying which version of IP you are representing when explaining the protocol). There are currently two RFCs that define all the ICMP functions for IPv6: RFC 1885 and RFC 1970. RFC 1885 provides for information on new functions and names the older functions that made it through the review process. RFC 1970 includes the discovery protocols of RFC 1256 and a few other discovery protocols. It also includes the redirect message.

ICMPv6, as defined in RFCs 1885 and 1970, is currently using control and information messages previously defined in RFCs 791, 1112, and 1191. Therefore, the procedures for certain ICMP functions continue to be defined

ICMP

- Found in RFC 1885 and originally found in RFC 792.
  - The functions of ICMP are explained in 1885, but many other RFCs are referenced:
    - 1970 for Neighbor Discovery
    - 1191 for Path MTU Discovery
- IPv4 extension.
- Continues to provide some maintenance for an unreliable IPv6.
- No ICMPv6 messages are sent for ICMPv6 errors.

in their respective RFCs. You must read the original RFCs to fully explain the procedures used.

As indicated in the previous text on IP, the Internet Protocol is an "unreliable" protocol. ICMP is an add-on protocol that does not make IP reliable, but is a control message protocol, the purpose of which is to provide feedback about problems in the communication environment. There are still no guarantees that a datagram will be delivered or a control message will be returned. Some datagrams may still be undelivered without any report of their loss. The higher-level protocols that use IPv6 must still implement their own reliability procedures if reliable communication is required.

The ICMP messages typically report errors in the processing of datagrams. To avoid the problem of ICMP messages about ICMP messages, none are sent.

ICMPv6 is used by IPv6 nodes to report errors encountered in processing packets, and to perform other internet-layer functions, such as diagnostics (ICMPv6 "ping") and multicast membership reporting. ICMPv6 is an integral part of IPv6 and *must* be fully implemented by every IPv6 node.

ICMPv6 Encapsulation
192

The following slide shows the encapsulation of ICMP in IPv6.

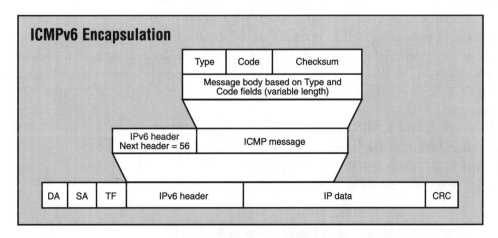

ICMPv6 and ICMPv4

ICMPv6 cleaned up ICMPv4, mainly any control messages that were not used (gone from being specifically identified as ICMP messages are timestamp, timestamp reply, source quench, information request and reply). Most of these procedures are incorporated into other protocols. For example, source quench is not used anymore, for other mechanisms, such as TCP "slow start and congestion control," were found to be more useful. Why put the onus on the routers when a mechanism is better defined and more useful elsewhere? Also, certain codes for a specific type have been moved or eliminated (for example, source route failed code for the Destination Unreachable Type). The address fields, obviously, had to be extended to handle ICMPv6 128-bit addressing. The multicast control functions of IGMP were also included in ICMPv6 to allow for the group membership Query, Report, and Termination. With all of the changes just discussed, ICMPv6 is not backwards compatible with ICMPv4. It uses the next-header function of IP and the next-header type of 56. One last change is that ICMPv4 messages copied the original IP header and 64 bits of data in the returned message. The exception to this is Echo Request or Echo Reply. ICMPv6 allows for a maximum of 576 bytes of data to be copied from the offending datagram.

The format of the ICMPv6 header is shown in the slide. It is the same format as ICMPv4. The type field indicates the type of the message. Its value determines the format of the

---

ICMPv6 and ICMPv4

- Cleaned up ICMPv4.
  - Timestamp, source quench, and information request and reply were deleted (picked up by other protocols)
- Eliminated unused codes and types.
- IGMP is moved into ICMPv6.
  - ICMPv6 is not compatible with ICMPv4; however, it is the same format
- ICMPv6 does copy more of the offending datagram when sending an error message.
- Error messages have types from 0–127 and informational messages have types from 128–255.

---

remaining data. Error messages are identified as such by 0 a 0 in the high-order bit of their message Type field values. Thus, error messages have message Types from 0 to 127; informational messages have message Types from 128 to 255. The code field depends on the message type and further identifies the ICMP message. The checksum field is used to detect data corruption in the ICMPv6 message and parts of the IPv6 header. For the most part, the destination address is set to the source address of the previously received offending packet.

ICMPv6 Error Messages

- Destination Unreachable:
  - No route to destination
  - Communication with destination administratively prohibited
  - Not a neighbor
  - Address Unreachable
  - Port Unreachable

- Packet Too Big:
  - Returns the largest packet size available for the forwarded port

- **Destination Unreachable**

  Type: 1

  Code:

  0 No Route to Destination. There was no corresponding route in the router's forwarding table (only for routers that do not possess a default route entry).

  1 Communication with Destination Administratively Prohibited. For example, a firewall or other restrictive administrative command.

  2 Not a Neighbor. There was an attempt to deliver the datagram to a neighbor that was indicated in the strict source routing entries, but the next hop indicated is not a neighbor of this router.

  3 Address Unreachable. The router could not resolve the link-layer address for the indicated network address.

  4 Port Unreachable. The destination does not have a service port available (not a hardware port!). For example, the datagram is intended for TCP, but all available resources are taken for TCP (there are no listener ports available). Or, the datagram was sent to a service port that the destination does not support; for example, whois, or finger, or the route daemon.

  The first 32 bits after the ICMP header are unused and must be initialized to 0 by the sender and ignored by the receiver. Destination Unreachable messages generally originate from a router, but can also be generated by the originated node. They are generated for any reason except congestion. There are no ICMP messages to indicate congestion (other protocols monitor and report this condition).

- **Packet Too Big**

  Type: 2

  Code: 0

  The first 32 bits after the ICMP header indicate the maximum transmission unit (MTU) for the selected forwarded (next hop) port. This error message is important, for datagrams do not necessarily have to be 576 bytes in size. FDDI-to-Token-Ring topologies, for example, do very well with streaming large packets. This is an indicator of the size of a packet to be forwarded along the path from source to destination. This is the path MTU discovery procedure, which is outlined in RFC 1191. This error message also provides an exception to the rules: It can be sent in response to a packet received with an IPv6 multicast destination address, or a link-layer multicast or link-layer broadcast address.

195   ICMPv6 Error Messages (continued)

- **Time Exceeded**

  Type: 3

  Code:

  0   Hop limit exceeded in transit

  1   Fragment reassembly time exceeded

  The first 32 bits of the ICMP message are specified as unused for all code values and must be initialized to 0 by the sender and ignored by the receiver. This can be sent if a router receives a packet with a hop limit of 0, or a

---

ICMPv6 Error Messages (continued)

- Time Exceeded.
  - Hop limit exceeded in transit
  - Fragment reassembly time exceeded

- Parameter Problem.
  - Erroneous header field encountered
  - Unrecognized nest header type encountered
  - Unrecognized IPv6 option

router decrements a packet's hop limit to 0. The packet then must be discarded, and an ICMPv6 Time Exceeded message with Code 0 must be sent to the source of the packet. This indicates either a routing loop or too small an initial hop limit value.

- **Parameter Problem**

Type: 4

Code:

0   Erroneous header field encountered

1   Unrecognized Next Header type encountered

2   Unrecognized IPv6 option encountered

The first 32 bits of the ICMP message comprise a pointer that identifies the octet offset within the invoking packet where the error was detected. It points beyond the end of the ICMPv6 packet if the field in error is larger than the 576-byte limit of an ICMPv6 error message.

If an IPv6 node cannot process the datagram due to some error in the headers, it must discard the packet and should send an ICMPv6 Parameter Problem message to the packet's source, indicating the type and location of the problem. A pointer field is provided to indicate the type of problem. The pointer field indicates the point in the originating header where the error was detected. For example, an ICMPv6 message with Type field = 4, Code field = 1, and Pointer field = 40, would indicate that the IPv6 extension header following the IPv6 header of the original packet holds an unrecognized Next Header field value.

ICMP Informational Messages

- **Echo Request**

  Type: 128

  Code: 0

  The first 16 bits of the ICMP message are an identifier to aid in the construction of an Echo Reply to an Echo Request. It may contain a 0. The next 16 bits are a sequence number to aid in matching specifically multiple echo requests from the same source. It, too, may contain a 0.

  The remaining message is option data that may have been typed in on the request and is echoed on the reply.

  This is the PING command that you may have typed in. For example, PING 192.1.1.1 is an echo request to an echo server residing on host 192.1.1.1.

- **Echo Reply**

  Type: 129

  Code: 0

  The first 16 bits (after the ICMP header) comprise an identifier field from the previously received Echo Request message, which is used to match replies with requests. The next 16 bits comprise a sequence number from the node that sent the echo request number message. This is useful to match multiple requests from the same host.

  The rest of the message contains echoed data copied from the received echo request.

ICMP Informational Messages

- Echo Request
- Echo Reply
- Good ol' PING

ICMP and Neighbor Discovery

ICMP and Neighbor Discovery

- Router Solicitation
- Router Advertisement
- Neighbor Solicitation
- Neighbor Advertisement
- Redirect

Address resolution is accomplished via Neighbor Discovery messages, which are generated and processed by ICMP. The following are those messages:

Router Solicitation. Hosts send Router Solicitations in order to prompt routers to generate Router Advertisements quickly.

Router Advertisement. Routers send out Router Advertisement messages periodically, or in response to Router Solicitations. These messages contain information related to the local prefixes and if the router can act as a default router.

Neighbor Solicitation. Nodes send Neighbor Solicitations to request the link-layer address of a target node while also providing their own link-layer address to the target.

Neighbor Solicitations are multicast when the node needs to resolve an address and unicast when the node seeks to verify the reachability of a neighbor.

Neighbor Advertisement. A node sends Neighbor Advertisements in response to Neighbor Solicitations, and sends unsolicited Neighbor Advertisements in order to (unreliably) propagate new information quickly. For example, if a node has determined some changes, such a link-level address change, it can quickly relay this information to its neighbors.

Redirect. Routers send Redirect packets to inform a host of a better first-hop node on the path to a destination. Hosts can be redirected to a better first-hop router, but can also be informed by a redirect that the destination is in fact a neighbor. The latter is accomplished by setting the ICMP Target Address equal to the ICMP Destination Address.

- **Group Membership messages**

    The functions of IGMP were moved into ICMPv6. The ICMPv6 Group Membership messages are used to convey information about multicast group membership from nodes to their neighboring routers. Please refer to Part Six for more information on the IGMP functions. This function of ICMPv6 allows for IGMP messages to be sent. These are Group Membership messages for Query, Reports, and Reduction (or leaving a group with a termination message). Due to the dynamic nature of the IPv6 and its Neighbor Discovery protocols (routers and hosts), IGMP functions were moved into the ICMP protocol suite. For example, when a node initializes (in an IPv6 environment), it must immediately join the all-nodes multicast address on that interface, as well as the solicited-node multicast address corresponding to each of the IP addresses assigned to the interface.

    In the IPv6 header the Destination Address is set as follows: In a Group Membership Query message, the multicast address of the group being queried, or the Link-Local All-Nodes multicast address. In a Group Membership Report or a Group Membership Reduction message, the multicast address of the group being reported or terminated.

> **ICMPv6 and Multicast**
> - Group Membership messages
>   - Group Membership Query
>   - Group Membership Report
>   - Group Membership Reduction (Leave Group)

The hop limit is set to 1 to ensure this message does not leave the local subnetwork. The ICMPv6 fields are set as follows:

Type:

130—Group Membership Query

131—Group Membership Report

132—Group Membership Reduction

Code: 0

The first 16 bits after the ICMP header are used for the Maximum Response Delay. In Query messages, it is the maximum time that responding Report messages may be delayed, in milliseconds. In Report and Reduction messages, this field is initialized to 0 by the sender and ignored by receivers. The next 16 bits are unused and they are initialized to 0 by the sender and ignored by receivers. The rest of the message is filled with the Multicast Address, which is the address of the multicast group to which the message is being sent. In Query messages, the Multicast Address field may be 0, implying a query for all groups.

IPv6 Cache Entries   199

IPv6 Cache Entries

- Destination cache—contains link layer information about destinations to which data has been recently sent.

- Neighbor cache—contains link-layer information about a neighbor.

- Prefix List cache—created from router advertisements, this is a listing of local prefixes.

- Router List cache—contains information about those routers to which packets may be sent.

All of the following caches are built in part by the Neighbor Discovery process. Instead of the simplex ARP cache used with IPv4, IPv6 maintains four caches. (Actually, four caches may not be maintained. Implementers can integrate this information any way they wish, including simply using one large table or four linked tables in one database, but all the required information must be gathered and maintained. The entries are shown here separately for simplicity reasons.)

Destination cache. This cache contains information about destinations to which traffic has been recently sent. It includes both local and remote destinations and associates an IPv6 address of a destination with that of the neighbor toward which the packets are sent. This cache is updated with information learned from ICMP Redirect messages. Other information such as the Path MTU (PMTU) and round-trip timers maintained by transport protocols can be in this cache. Entries are created by the next-hop determination procedure.

Neighbor cache. A record that contains information about individual neighbors (host or a router may be an entry) to which traffic has been recently sent. It contains such information as the neighbor's link-layer address, an indication of whether the neighbor is a host or a router, and a pointer to any queued packets waiting for address resolution to complete. This information is also used by the Neighbor Unreachability protocol.

Prefix List cache. Created from information received in Router Advertisements, this is a listing of the local prefixes and an individual expiration timer that defines a set of addresses that are on-link. Nodes receive and store this information that is transmitted from a router in this cache. This enables a node to determine a remote destination. A special "infinity" timer value specifies that a prefix remains valid forever, unless a new (finite) value is received in a subsequent advertisement. For example, the prefix of the local link to which a node is attached is considered to be on the prefix list with an infinite invalidation timer, regardless of whether routers are advertising a prefix for it. Received router advertisements cannot change this value.

Router List cache. Built from received router advertisements, this list contain information about those routers to which packets may be sent. Router List entries point to entries in the Neighbor cache; the algorithm for selecting a default router favors routers known to be reachable over those whose reachability is suspect. Each entry is mated with an associated expiration timer value (extracted from Router Advertisements). This timer is used to delete entries that the node has not received advertisements from.

IPv6 Algorithm

- Easier if you understand RFC 1970.

- To transmit a datagram, the source must consult the destination cache, prefix list, and the default router.
  - It needs to determine the "next hop"

- A source first looks in the destination cache for a matching entry to the destination IP address.
  - If one is not found here, consult the prefix list cache
  - Local address, the next hop is simply that of the destination IP address

If you are looking for more information on how IPv6 routes datagrams, you must first read RFC 1970. This is a very important RFC for your understanding of the IPv6 routing algorithm. It contains the Neighbor Discovery mechanism and includes everything on IPv6 subnets, such as hosts and routers. IPv6 does not use ARP; it uses Neighbor Discovery.

IPv6 needs the previously listed cache entries to assist in routing a datagram. If an IPv6 node needs to transmit a datagram, it must first find out the next hop towards the destination (known as *next-hop determination*). In other words, it must determine if the destination station is local or remote, and therefore sends the packet directly to the destination or utilizes a router. This process uses the Prefix List cache and the Destination cache. Once the next hop is known, it must determine the next hop's link-layer address.

To route a datagram in IPv6, we consult the Destination cache, the Prefix List, and the Default Router List to determine the IP address of the appropriate next hop. The next-hop determination is invoked to create a Destination Cache entry. The results of next-hop determination computations are saved in the Destination cache (which also contains updates learned from Redirect messages).

Therefore, a sending node first looks in the Destination cache for a matching entry to the destination IP address. If one is not found, the Prefix List cache is consulted. The sending node compares the destination prefix mask with the entries in the Prefix List cache. If a match is found, it is then determined whether the destination is local or remote. If it is local, then the next-hop address is simply the destination address of the datagram; otherwise, the destination is remote and the node must select a router from the default router list. If there are no entries in the default router list, then the destination is assumed to be local. The results of this next-hop determination lookup are stored in the Destination cache (along with received ICMP redirects).

Once the next hop has been determined, the corresponding entry is added to the Destination cache and the Neighbor cache is used to determine the media address of that next-hop neighbor.

Once the IP address of the next-hop node is known, the sender examines the Neighbor cache for link-layer information about that neighbor. If no entry exists, the sender creates one, and then starts the address resolution procedure to complete the entry. The datagram to

be transmitted must wait for this to complete. Once the neighbor entry is complete, this entry will be used for subsequent transfers to that destination station. No other procedures are needed.

201   RFCs Related to IPv6

1883: Describes the IPv6 protocol (RFC 2147 updates [does not replace] RFC 1883).

2147 PS: D. Borman, "TCP and UDP over IPv6 Jumbograms," 05/23/97, (3 pages) (.txt format) (updates RFC 1883).

2133 I: R. Gilligan, S. Thomson, J. Bound, W. Stevens, "Basic Socket Interface Extensions for IPv6," 04/21/97 (32 pages).

2080 PS: G. Malkin, R. Minnear, "RIPng for IPv6," 01/10/97 (19 pages).

2073 PS: Y. Rekhter, P. Lothberg, R. Hinden, S. Deering, J. Postel, "An IPv6 Provider-Based Unicast Address Format," 01/08/97 (7 pages).

2030 I: D. Mills, "Simple Network Time Protocol (SNTP) Version 4 for IPv4, IPv6, and OSI," 10/30/96 (18 pages).

2019 PS: M. Crawford, "Transmission of IPv6 Packets Over FDDI," 10/17/96 (6 pages).

1972 PS: M. Crawford, "A Method for the Transmission of IPv6 Packets Over Ethernet Networks," 08/16/96 (4 pages).

1971 PS: S. Thomson, T. Narten, "IPv6 Stateless Address Autoconfiguration," 08/16/96 (23 pages).

1970 PS: T. Narten, E. Nordmark, W. Simpson, "Neighbor Discovery for IP Version 6 (IPv6)," 08/16/96 (82 pages).

1933 PS: R. Gilligan, E. Nordmark, "Transition Mechanisms for IPv6 Hosts and Routers," 04/08/96 (22 pages).

1924 I: R. Elz, "A Compact Representation of IPv6 Addresses," 04/01/96 (6 pages).

1897 E: R. Hinden, J. Postel, "IPv6 Testing Address Allocation," 01/25/96 (4 pages).

1888 E: J. Bound, B. Carpenter, D. Harrington, J. Houldsworth, A. Lloyd, "OSI NSAPs and IPv6," 08/16/96 (16 pages).

1887 I: Y. Rekhter, T. Li, "An Architecture for IPv6 Unicast Address Allocation," 01/04/96 (25 pages).

1885 PS: A. Conta, S. Deering, "Internet Control Message Protocol (ICMPv6) for the Internet Protocol Version 6 (IPv6)," 01/04/96 (20 pages).

1884 PS: R. Hinden, S. Deering, "IP Version 6 Addressing Architecture," 01/04/96 (18 pages) (.txt format).

1883 PS: S. Deering, R. Hinden, "Internet Protocol, Version 6 (IPv6) Specification," 01/04/96 (37 pages) (updated by RFC 2147).

1881 I: I. IESG, "IPv6 Address Allocation Management," 12/26/95 (2 pages).

1809 I: C. Partridge, "Using the Flow Label Field in IPv6," 06/14/95 (6 pages).

Part Four

Beyond the IP Layer

The job of IP is to address and route (local or remote) a datagram. That's it. Once transmitted, IP looks for the next packet to transmit or receive. Since IP is a connectionless, unreliable delivery service, allowing routers and hosts on an internet to operate independently, there are certain instances when errors will occur. Some of these errors could be: a packet is not routed to the destination network, the router is too congested to handle any more packets, or a host may not be found on the internet. There is no provision in IP to generate error messages or control messages; ICMP is the protocol that handles these instances for IP. The purpose of these control messages is to provide feedback about problems in the communication environment, not to make IP reliable.

ICMP does not use a transport layer and runs directly on top of IP. Therefore, ICMP is an "unreliable" function and no ICMP error message is sent for an ICMP message.

For example, when a transmitting station transmits a packet using indirect routing to a remote destination, what happens if a final router cannot find the endstation (the endstation is not in the router's ARP cache and it does not respond to the router's ARP request)? This is one of the reasons for the ICMP service. The router sends an ICMP message back to the originator of the datagram, endstation A, that the destination node cannot be found. This error message is then transmitted to the user.

Notice that each ICMP message has a Type field and a Code field. The Type field identifies the ICMP datagram and the Code field provides

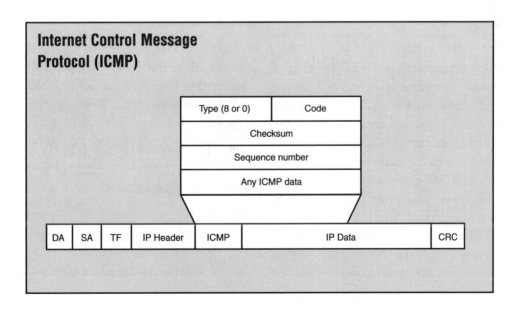

Internet Control Message Protocol (ICMP)

further granularity. For example, Type Code 3 indicates that the destination is unreachable, but a Code field of 1 gives us a further clue that the destination host (and not the port or network) is unreachable. This could mean the network was found but no station responded to an ARP request when transmitted by the sending router. The receiver of that ICMP datagram would then post a message either to a screen or to a log file interpreting the ICMP message. Try this on your own. Try pinging a device that you know does not exist.

ICMP will also copy the first 64 bits (IPv6 increases this to 512 bytes) of data from the original datagram into its own. This provides some information about the offending datagram and can be used in troubleshooting. ICMPv6 provides more of the original data.

The slide shows the format for ICMP and the encapsulation inside of IP. ICMP reports on many entities on an internet. As the table in the slide shows, there are many functions of ICMP as indicated by the use of a Code field. ICMP datagrams are routable since they use IP to deliver their messages. IP resides on top of IP and does not use TCP or UDP for its transport. ICMP is a separate protocol from IP, but it is an integral part of IP's operation.

ICMP is extensible beyond control mechanisms as you will see next.

203   ICMP PING

Ask anyone involved in troubleshooting an IP network and he or she will tell you the most-used application is the PING application—one of the most common uses for ICMP is the PING program. PING (not originally named, but commonly called Packet Internet Groper) is an ICMP message that tries to locate other stations on the internet to see if they are active or to see if a path is up. PING is an echo program. The originator of a datagram sends a PING request and the destination station should echo this request. Information can be contained in the PING datagram, which the destination station should echo. PING has the following format (using Windows 95):

Usage

ping [-t] [-a] [-n count] [-l size] [-f] [-i TTL] [-v TOS]
[-r count] [-s count] [[-j host-list] | [-k host-list]]
[-w timeout] destination-list

Options

-t	Ping the specified host until interrupted
-a	Resolve addresses to hostnames

Options (continued)

-n count	Number of echo requests to send
-l size	Send buffer size
-f	Set Don't Fragment flag in packet
-i TTL	Time to Live
-v TOS	Type of Service
-r count	Record route for count hops
-s count	Timestamp for count hops
-j host-list	Loose source route along host-list
-k host-list	Strict source route along host-list
-w timeout	Timeout in milliseconds to wait for each reply

Notice that you can test many things along the path to a destination using the PING command; for example, timing, source route, route recording, and data. Another use of the PING command is to check for network delays along a path. The response to a PING request can report the response delay (usually measured in milliseconds).

A lot of network management software uses this command to determine the status of a given station. Network management software will build maps to show the topology and placement of network stations. Using colors (green for active, yellow for possible errors, and red for not responding), a network manager can trace problems on the network. A lot of the work is done through the use of the PING utility.

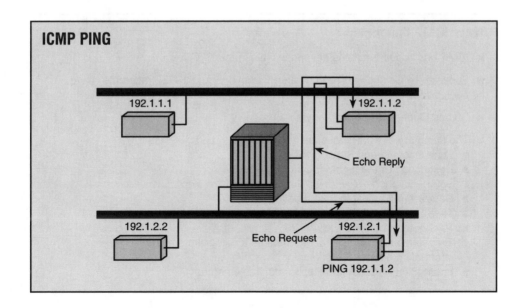

ICMP has added functions over the years as indicated by RFCs 1256 (Router Discovery) and 1393 (ICMP Traceroute). ICMP running in a router can respond to a host's request to find the subnet address mask for its network. A host, upon startup, can request of a router the subnet mask assigned to the network.

Although not really used anymore (there are better methods for controlling traffic, such as the Slow Start algorithm discussed in a moment). *Source quench* is the endstation's ability to indicate to the originator of a message that the host cannot accept the rate at which the sender is submitting the packets. A source quench packet is continually generated to the originator until the rate of data flow slows down. The intended recipient of a source quench will continue to slow down its data rate until it receives no more source quench packets. The station that was requested to slow down will then start to increase the data rate again. This is similar to a flow control, except that it is more like throttle control—the data is not stopped, merely slowed down and then increased again. It is generated by any network station on the internet to indicate that the node cannot handle the rate of the incoming data. This ICMP type was not included in ICMPv6. It was found that other protocols handle congestion better than forcing the routers to handle it.

There are many other uses of the ICMP protocol. When a router receives a datagram, it may determine a better router that can provide a shorter route to the destination network. This is an ICMP Redirect, and this message informs the

---

More ICMP Functions

- ICMP has added functions beyond what is in the RFC.

- Separate RFCs such as 1256 (Router Discovery) and 1393 (traceroute) have been added as separate RFCs.

- Source Quench is not used anymore.

- The summary of ICMP message types are:
    - Echo Request and Reply (PING)
    - Destination Unreachable (host or network)
    - Source Quench—slow down the rate of transmission
    - Redirect (tell a host to take a better path)
    - Time Exceeded (TTL decremented to 0)
    - Parameter problem
    - Timestamp and Reply—record the time a datagram arrived/send the information back to the originator
    - Information Request and Reply—not implemented

sender of a better route. If the TTL field is 0, a router will inform the originator of this through an ICMP message (Time Exceeded). A user's workstation can request a timestamp from a router, asking it to repeat the time when it received a packet. This is used for measuring delay to a destination.

Summary of Message Types

0	Echo Reply
3	Destination Unreachable
4	Source Quench
5	Redirect (there is a better route message)
8	Echo
11	Time Exceeded (TTL)
12	Parameter Problem
13	Timestamp
14	Timestamp Reply
15	Information Request
16	Information Reply

User Datagram Protocol (UDP) 205

A transport layer allows communication to exist between network stations. Data is handed down to this layer from an upper-level application. The transport layer then envelopes the data with its headers and gives it to the IP layer for transmission onto the network. There are two transport-layer protocols in TCP/IP: UDP and TCP.

The functionality of UDP should sound familiar. It is a connectionless, unreliable transport service. It does not issue an acknowledgment to the sender upon the receipt of data. It does not provide order to the incoming packets, and may lose packets or duplicate them without issuing an error message to the sender. This should sound like the IP protocol. The only offering that UDP has is the assignment and management of port numbers to uniquely identify the individual applications that run on a network station and a checksum for simplex error detection. UDP tends to run faster than TCP, for it has low overhead (8 bytes in its header compared to TCP's typical 40 bytes). It is used for applications that do not need a reliable transport. Some examples are network management, name server, or applications that have built-in reliability.

Any application program that incorporates the use of UDP as its transport-level service must provide an acknowledgment and sequence system to ensure that packets arrive, and that they arrive in the same order as they were sent.

As shown in the slide, an application's data is encapsulated in a UDP header. The transport layer has its own header, independent of all other layers, that it prefaces to the data handed to it from its upper-layer protocol. The UDP header and its data are then encapsulated in an IP header. The IP protocol would then send the datagram to the data-link layer, which would then encapsulate the datagram with its headers (and/or trailers) and send the data to the physical layer for actual transmission.

Upon receipt of the packet, the datalink would interpret the address as its own, strip off its header (and/or trailers), and submit the packet to the IP layer. IP would accept the packet based on the correct IP address in the IP header, strip off its header, and submit the packet to the UDP-layer software. The UDP layer accepts the packet and now has to demultiplex the packet based on the port number in the UDP header.

Looking at the slide, the packet header for UDP is small (the minimum packet size is 8 bytes), but functional. The message length indicates the size of the UDP header and its data in bytes. The checksum is used to check for the validity of the UDP header and data. It does not have to be implemented and would be set to 0 if not implemented. UDP is primarily used by applications to simply provide for an application MUX at the transport layer. This is described next.

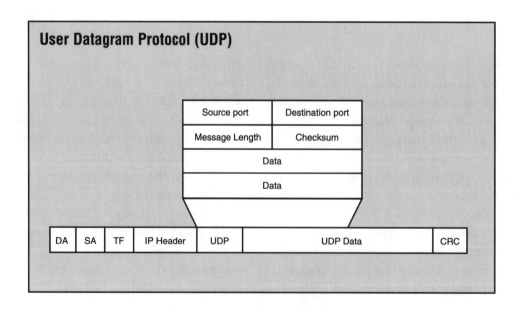

UDP accepts data from the application layer, formats it (UDP header) with its information, and presents it to the IP layer for network delivery. UDP will also accept data from the IP layer and, depending on the port value, present it to the appropriate application. As shown in the slide, UDP is responsible for directing the rest of the packet (after stripping off its headers) to the correct process according to the port number assigned in the UDP header. This process is called *demultiplexing*. There are many different types of port numbers to indicate any application running on the network station. UDP reads the Destination Port field of the UDP header (demultiplex) and gives the data to the application. When the application (identified by the port number) initializes, the station's operating system works in conjunction with it and provides a buffer area in which information may be stored. UDP will place the data in this area for retrieval by the application. UDP does provide one error mechanism for ports that are not valid. It can generate an ICMP Port Unreachable message to be sent to the originator of the packet.

Since the TCP/IP protocol suite includes applications that are specifically written to it (TFTP, Domain Name Service, etc.), there are statically assigned port numbers that identify these applications. Certain port numbers are reserved and cannot be used by any unknown application. The reserved port numbers are specified in RFC 1700.

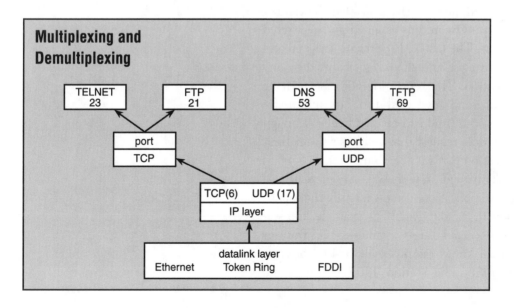

207 Port Numbers

Review RFC 814. Since many network applications may be running on the same machine, a method is needed to allow access to these applications, even though they reside on the same machine and the machine contains one IP address. One IP address and many applications? How do we decide which datagram belongs to which application?

It would not be advantageous to assign each process an IP address, nor to change the IP addressing scheme to include a marker to identify a unique application in the machine. Instead, both the TCP and UDP protocols provide a concept known as *ports* (sometimes mistakenly called *sockets*, which is not correct). Ports, along with an IP address, allow any application in any machine on an internet to be uniquely identified.

There are three different types of port numbers: *assigned*, *registered*, and *dynamic*. The RFC of assigned numbers (RFC 1700 at the time of this writing) contains assigned and registered numbers. The first 1024 ports are assigned and in specific use and should not be used by any application. The remaining addresses can be dynamic and registered (16 bits allows for 65,535 ports) and can be used freely, although IANA does request that vendors register their application port numbers with them.

When a station wishes to communicate to a remote application, it must identify that application in the datagram. For example, if a station needed to use a simple file transfer protocol known as *trivial file transfer program* (TFTP) on the station 130.1.1.1, it would

address the datagram to station 130.1.1.1 and insert *destination port* number 69 in the UDP header. The *source port* number identifies the application on the local station that requested the file transfer, and all response packets generated by the destination station would be addressed to that port number on the source station. Generally, the source port is randomly generated by the source station. If the source port is not used (broadcast RIP update tables), it should be set to 0. So, when the IP layer demultiplexes the packet and hands it to UDP, UDP will pass the data to the locally assigned port number for it to process the data.

Assigned, Registered, and Dynamic Port Numbers

Assigned, Registered, and Dynamic Port Numbers

- RFC 1700.

- FTP site: ftp://ftp.isi.edu/in-notes/iana/ assignments.
  - Up-to-date assignments of numbers

- Assigned numbers range from 0–1023.
  - Assigned are reserved by IANA and cannot be used
  - Used for TCP, IP, UDP, and various applications such as TELNET

- Registered numbers range from 1024–65535, and these are companies that have registered their application.

- Dynamic port numbers also range from 1024–65535.

Reference RFC 1700 and the FTP site ftp://ftp.isi.edu/in-notes/iana/assignments (point your URL to this address on your browser). In the TCP/IP protocol, UDP port numbers come in three flavors: *assigned*, *registered*, and *dynamic*. Assigned numbers come in the range of 0–1023 and are fully controlled by the Internet Assigned Numbers Authority (refer to RFC 1700). These are numbers that deal with protocols such as TELNET, FTP, Network Time Protocol (NTP), and so on. No matter which implementation of TCP/IP (i.e., which vendor's TCP) is in use, those applications listed beside the port number will always be the same (they are known as *well-known port numbers*). These are assigned by a central authority. In this case, RFC 1700 spells out which processes are assigned to which port numbers. Assigned port numbers (those formally reserved through Internet Address Numbers Authority) range from 0–1023 for TCP/UDP port numbers. After that, any application may use any port number beyond 1023 but less than 65,535. Some companies have registered their port numbers with IANA and other companies respect this by not using the same port number.

Here's an example of an assigned port number: If station A wants to access the TFTP process on station B, it calls it in the UDP header with a destination port number of 69 (decimal). The source station requesting TFTP services also has a port number that is dynamically assigned by its TCP/IP stack. RFC 1700 suggests methods for assistance in assigning a dynamic port number. In this way, the server and client can communicate with one another using the port numbers to uniquely identify the service for that datagram.

Dynamic Port Numbers

TCP/IP also implements dynamic port numbers. Since the Port Number field in the UDP header is 16 bits long, 65,535 ports (minus the assigned port assignments) are available for individual use. This range can be used for registered and dynamic ports. One use for a dynamic port is as a source station that is requesting the services of TFTP on a remote station. The source station dynamically assigns itself an available port number (usually above 1024 to use so that the remote station knows what port to access when it transfers the file). In other words, if a user initiates a trivial file transfer (TFTP), the TFTP request packet sent to the TFTP server includes in its UDP header a dynamic port number of the requesting network station that wanted the

TFTP, called the source port. Let's say it is assigned port 2000. The destination port number would be 69. In this way, the server will accept the packet, give it to the TFTP process in the host and, when the host responds, it will know how to address the port number in the response packet. In the response packet, the server would fill out the UDP header with a destination port of 2000, source port of 69, and send the packet back to the requesting station.

Another use is when network vendors implement proprietary schemes on their devices; for example, a proprietary scheme for a network station to boot or a proprietary scheme to allow network management statistics to be gathered. All these applications are

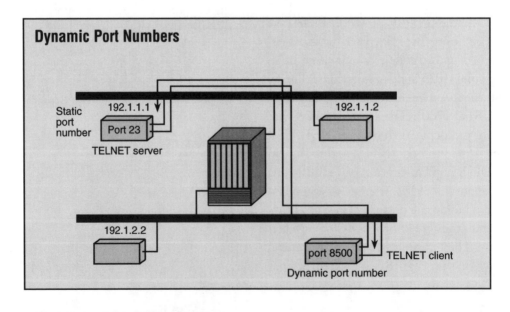

Dynamic Port Numbers

Static port number — 192.1.1.1 — Port 23 — TELNET server

192.1.1.2

192.1.2.2

port 8500 — TELNET client
Dynamic port number

valid and may run on any TCP environment using a dynamic port assignment.

The disadvantage of dynamic ports occurs when a broadcast IP datagram is transmitted to the network using a dynamic port. This port could be used by another vendor on the network, and another network station may invoke a process to accommodate that request. This is rare, but has been known to happen.

Dynamic port numbers are assigned by the TCP/IP software at the local workstation, and can be duplicated from workstation to workstation without respect to the application. This is because an application on any network station is uniquely identified by the IP address (network number, host number) and the port number. When taken as a whole number, it is called the *socket number*, and cannot be duplicated on an IP network except by negligence.

Final note: Some people like to use the terms *port* and *socket* interchangeably. You can, but proper IP semantics state that a port number and a socket number are not the same thing, as indicated in the preceding paragraph.

Transmission Control Protocol (TCP) 210

Transmission Control Protocol (TCP)

- The protocol responsible for the reliable transmission and reception of data.

- Unreliable service is provided by UDP.

- Transport layer protocol.

- Can run multiple applications using the same transport.
  - Multiplex through port numbers

TCP is also a transport-layer protocol. Unlike the UDP protocol, the purpose of the transport-layer software TCP is to allow data to be reliably exchanged with another station on the network. It, too, provides the demultiplexes of port numbers to identify an application in the host, but also provides reliable transport of data, including many different options that may or may not be sent by the originating station. A communications facility needs to be able to reliably transfer data between two points. Imagine setting up a communications system that only allowed for unreliable data transfer—the post office transfers most of its mail in this manner. When you mail a letter, you have no idea if it really reached its destination unless you make the effort to check. Should make you a little nervous on that critical data. This is further exemplified by a packet switch network in which the same communication channel is used by multiple entities all vying for the same path, and each header contains its own directional information.

TCP/IP hosts originally were connected via telephone lines (commonly known as *serial* lines). This mode of communication was not the same in the early 1970s as it is today. The lines were noisy and were not conditioned to handle high-speed data. Therefore, the TCP protocol has strict error-detection algorithms built in to ensure the integrity of the data. The following paragraphs explain the TCP protocol and show how its strictness in its structure ensures the integrity of the data.

211   TCP Details

Not all networks use a separate transport-layer software to converse on a network. The best example of this is Novell with its LAN workgroup operating system of NetWare. NetWare relies on the network-layer software to transport data and the NetWare Core Protocol (as an application) to provide the sequence numbering of the packets. There is nothing wrong with this, and it generally speeds up the communication process between two stations on the network. The overhead of the role of transport layer is diminished, but those types of protocols were developed on high-speed, low-error-rate media such as Ethernet. TCP was not, and is much more robust in its transport-layer protocol. TCP is actually a protocol and not a separate piece of software.

The protocol of TCP uses sequence numbers and acknowledgments to reliably converse with other stations on the network. Sequence numbers are used to determine the ordering of the data in the packets and to find missing packets. Since packets on an internet may not arrive in the same sequence in which they were sent (for example, a single packet in a series of packets being transmitted was discarded by a router), sequencing the data in the packets ensures that the packets are read in the same order in which they were sent. Also, a receiving station may receive two of the same packets. The sequence number with acknowledgments is used to allow a reliable type of communication. This process is called *full duplex*, for each side of a connection maintains its own sequence number for the other side.

TCP is a byte-oriented sequencing protocol. Other protocols such as Novell NetWare are packet-oriented sequencing protocols. This applies a sequence number to each packet transmitted and not to each data byte in the packet. Byte oriented means that every byte in each packet is assigned a sequence number. This does not mean that TCP transmits a packet containing only 1 byte. TCP will transmit data (many bytes) and assign the packet one sequence number. Assigning one sequence number per byte in the packet may sound repetitious, but remember that TCP/IP was first implemented over noisy serial lines and not reliable high-speed LANs.

The slide shows two datagrams that have been transmitted. Normally, each TCP segment is 512 or 536 bytes in length (but can be larger). The short number of bytes in this picture is shown for clarity only. Each datagram is assigned one sequence number according to the number of bytes in the TCP Data field. Notice how the sequence number jumps by the same amount of bytes that are in each packet. The receiver of these datagrams will count the amount of bytes received and increment its sequence number of received packets. The first packet received has a sequence number of 40 and contains 4 bytes. The receiver expects the next sequence number to be 44. It is, and that packet contains 7 bytes of data. The receiver expects the next packet to be sequence number of 51. It is. This is how the byte sequencing of TCP works.

The sliding window scheme is discussed later. First, the TCP header definitions.

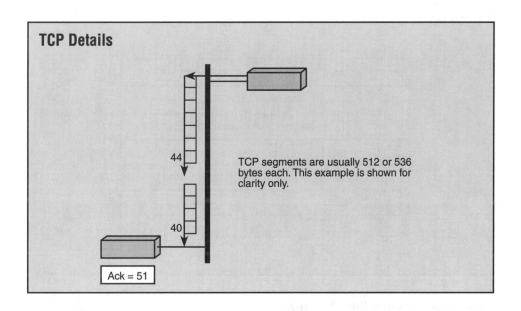

TCP Details

44

40

Ack = 51

TCP segments are usually 512 or 536 bytes each. This example is shown for clarity only.

TCP Fields

The slide shows the TCP header fields as encapsulated in a IP datagram.

Source port. The port number (application) of the originating station.

Destination port. The port number (application) for the receiving station.

Sequence number. A number assigned to a TCP datagram to indicate the beginning byte number of a packet unless the SYN bit is set. If this bit is set, the sequence number is the initial sequence number (ISN) and the first data byte is ISN + 1.

Acknowledgment number. A Number sent by the destination station to the source station, acknowledging receipt of a previously received packet or packets. This number indicates the next sequence number the destination station expects to receive. Once a connection is established, this field is always set.

Data offset. Indicates how long the TCP header is (i.e., the number of 32-bit words in the TCP header). It indicates where the TCP header ends and the data begins.

Reserved. Reserved for future use. Must be set to 0.

Control bits:

URG Urgent pointer: Used to send a message to the destination that urgent data is waiting to be sent to it. This could be sent to a destination station, when the destination station has closed the Receive window to the sender. However, the receiver will still accept packets with this bit set.

TCP Fields

Source port							Destination port
Sequence number							
Acknowledgment number							
data offset	Reserved	U R G	A C K	P S H	R S T	S Y N	F I N	Window
Checksum							Urgent pointer
Options							Padding
TCP data							

ACK   If set, this packet contains an acknowledgment to a previously sent datagram(s).

PSH   Push function: Immediately sends data when read the segment.

RST   Reset the connection. One function for this is to not accept a connection request.

SYN   Used at startup and to establish sequence number.

FIN   No more data is coming from the sender of the connection.

Window. The number of data octets beginning with the one indicated in the Acknowledgment field that the sender of this segment is willing to accept. It indicates the available buffers (memory) on the receiver.

Checksum. An error-detection number.

Urgent pointer. The urgent pointer points to the sequence number of the byte following the urgent data. This field is interpreted only in segments with the URG bit set.

Options. Variable in length, it allows for TCP options to be presented. These are:

End of Option List, No Operation, and Maximum Segment Size (MSS).

TCP Services   213

TCP Services

- Basic data transfer
- Reliability
- Flow control
- Multiplexing
- Connections
- Precedence and security

As noted earlier, the primary purpose of TCP is to provide reliable, securable logical circuit or connection service between pairs of processes. Providing this service on top of a less-reliable internet communications system requires facilities in the following areas, which are fully described in the next few sections:

- Basic data transfer
- Reliability
- Flow control
- Multiplexing
- Connections
- Precedence and security

214 TCP Connection Establishment

Unlike its brother UDP, TCP provides for reliable connections. A TCP connection between two stations on a network must be established before any data is allowed to pass between the two. Applications such as TELNET and FTP communicate using TCP through a series of function calls. This may seem a little confusing now, but the functions are very simple. These calls include OPEN and CLOSE a connection, SEND and RECEIVE (information) to that connection, and STATUS to receive information for a connection.

When a connection to a remote station is needed, an application will request TCP to place an OPEN call. There are two types of OPEN call: *passive* and *active*. A passive OPEN is a call to allow connections to be accepted from a remote station. This usually occurs

when an application starts on a network station (such as TELNET, FTP), and it will indicate to TCP that it is willing to accept connections from other stations on the network. TCP will note the application through its port assignment and will allow connections to come in. The number of connections allowed depends on the number of passive OPENs issued. This passive end of the TCP actions is known as the *responder* TCP. It will open up connection slots to accept any incoming connection request. This may be thought of as the server end of TCP. These passive OPEN calls do not wait for any particular station request.

An active OPEN is made when a connection attempt to a remote network station is needed. Referring to the slide, station A wishes to connect to station B. Station A issues an

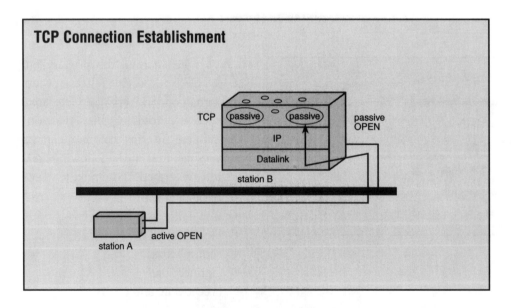

TCP Connection Establishment

active OPEN call to station B. In order for the connection to be made, station B must already have issued a passive OPEN request to allow incoming connections to be established. In the connection attempt packet is the port number that station A wishes to use on station B. Station B's operating system will spawn a sepa-

rate process on its system to maintain that connection. This process will act as if it is running locally on that station. TCP will then await another incoming connection request. This process is similar to the way a multitasking operating system handles multiple applications.

The Three-Way Handshake   215

A connection will only be active after the sender and receiver exchange a few control packets to establish the connection. This is known as the *three-way handshake*. Its purpose to synchronize each endpoint at the start of a TCP connection with a sequence number and acknowledgment number.

Refer to slide 215. Station A will place an active OPEN call to TCP to request connection to a remote network station's application. Station A will build a TCP header with the SYN (the sync bit shown was shown previously in the TCP Header fields) bit set and

then assign an initial sequence number (it does not always start at 0 and can start at any number; I have chosen 100) and place it in the Sequence Number field. Other fields will be set in the TCP header (not pertinent to us at this time) and the packet will be given to IP for transmission to station B.

Station B will receive this packet and notice it is a connection attempt. If station B can accept a new connection it will acknowledge station A by building a new packet. Station B will set the SYN and the ACK bits in the TCP header shown in the slide, place its own initial sequence number (200) in the Sequence field of the packet, and the Acknowledgment field will be set to 101 (the station A sequence number plus 1, indicating the next expected sequence number).

Station A will receive this response packet and notice it is an acknowledgment to its connection request. Station A will build a new packet, set the ACK bit, fill in the sequence number to 101, fill in the acknowledgment number to 200 + 1, and send the packet to station B. Once this has been established, the connection is active and data and commands from the application (such as TELNET) may pass over the connection. As data and commands pass over the connection, each side of the connection will maintain its own sequence number tables for data being sent and received across the connection. They will always be in ascending order.

Sequence numbers do not have to and probably will not start at 0. However, it is fundamentally important to note that they will wrap to 0.

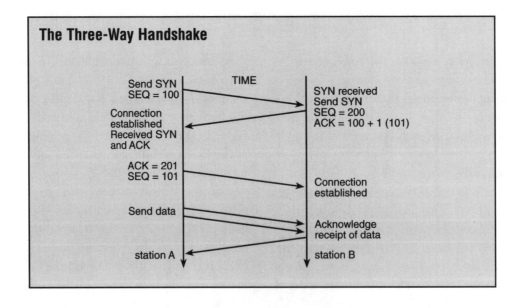

The Three-Way Handshake

Send SYN
SEQ = 100

TIME

SYN received
Send SYN
SEQ = 200
ACK = 100 + 1 (101)

Connection established
Received SYN and ACK

ACK = 201
SEQ = 101

Connection established

Send data

Acknowledge receipt of data

station A

station B

Everything that TCP sends is called a *segment*. This informational unit can be control data or user data. Segments are used to establish a connection, send and receive data and acknowledgments, advertise window sizes, and close a connection. A TCP segment will contain the TCP header (shown in Slide 216) and its data. The data handed to TCP for transmission is known as a *stream*; more specifically, an *unstructured stream*. A stream is a flow of bytes of data and an unstructured stream is an unknown type of data flow of bytes. This means that TCP has no way of marking the data to indicate the ending of a record or the type of data that is in the stream. When TCP receives a datastream from the application, it will divide the data into segments for transmission to the remote network station. A segment can have control or data information—it is simply an unstructured stream of data bytes sent to a destination.

A TCP segment may be as long as 65,535 bytes (or longer, known as jumbograms in IPv6), but is usually much less than that. Ethernet can only handle 1500 bytes of data in the Data field of the Ethernet packet (Ethernet v2.0, 1496 bytes for IEEE 802.3 using IEEE 802.2). FDDI can handle a maximum of 4472 bytes of data in a packet, and Token Ring packet size varies depending on the speed. For 4 Mbps, the maximum size is 4472 bytes. For 16 Mbps, the maximum size of the packet is 17,800 bytes, but is usually set to 4472 bytes. To negotiate a segment size, TCP uses one of

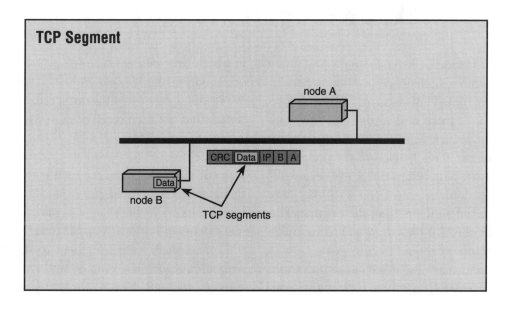

TCP Segment

node A

CRC Data IP B A

Data

node B

TCP segments

the Options (MSS) fields located in the TCP header to indicate the largest segment size it can receive, and submits this packet to the remote network station.

TCP does not care what the data is; data in a TCP segment is considered a stream. This stream is constructed at the sender and sent to the receiver. The receiver reconstructs this stream from the variable segments that it receives. Once the connection is established,

TCP's main job is to maintain the connection(s). This is accomplished through the sequence numbers, acknowledgments and retransmissions, flow control, and window management.

Since the connection between stations A and B is now established (by way of a successful three-way handshake), TCP must now manage the connection. The first of the management techniques to be discussed is *sequence numbers*.

217 Sequence Numbers and Acknowledgments

A point should be made right up front. Acknowledgments do not simply refer to a datagram or a TCP segment. TCP's job is to reconstruct a piece of data that was transmitted by the sender. Therefore, the acknowledgment number actually refers to the position in the stream of data being sent. Why? Because IP is connectionless and retransmissions may contain a different size from the original. The receiver collects information and reconstructs an exact copy of the data being sent.

Segments may also arrive out of order, and it is TCP's job to place them back in the order

in which they were sent. However, errors may occur during this process and TCP will only ACK the longest contiguous prefix of the stream that has been received correctly.

Refer back to Slide 211. TCP calculates a sequence number for each byte of data in the segment taken as a sum. For each byte of data that is to be transmitted, the sequence number increments by 1. Let's say a connection was made between stations A and B (refer to Slide 217). Station A sends a segment to station B with a sequence number of 40 and knows the segment contains 4 bytes; therefore, it incre-

Sequence Numbers and Acknowledgments

- Sequence numbers are used to reassemble data in the order in which it was sent.

- Sequence numbers increment based on the number of bytes in the TCP data field.
  - Known as a Byte Sequencing Protocol

- Each segment transmitted must be acknowledged.
  - Multiple segments can be acknowledged

- The ACK (Acknowledgement) field indicates the next byte (sequence) number the receiver expects to receive.

- The sender, no matter how many tranmitted segments, expects to receive an ACK that is one more than the number of the last transmitted byte.

ments its sequence number to 44. Upon acknowledgment from station B (containing the ACK number of 44), station A then transmits the second segment to station B, which contains 7 bytes. Station A's sequence number increments to 51, and it waits for an acknowledgment from station B. Note here that station A may not necessarily wait for an ACK from station B.

Each transmission window will contain as many bytes as indicated by the destination (windows are discussed in a moment). The sequence number is set to the number of the first byte in the datagram being sent—the last received ACK number from the destination. The TCP segment (the data) is then given to IP for delivery to the network.

Multiple datagrams may be sent with one acknowledgment to all received good segments. This is called an *inclusive* or *cumulative* ACK. TCP accomplishes this bidirectionally across the same connection. Each datagram transmitted will have the TCP header ACK bit set. With the ACK bit set, TCP will read the Acknowledgment field to find the next byte number of the segment that the other end of the connection expects. In other words, the number in the ACK field equals the sequence number of the original segment transmitted plus the number of the bytes successfully received in that segment plus 1. The ACK number is stuffed into a datagram to make TCP more efficient. There is usually not a separate datagram on the network used just for ACK packets. All data bytes up to but not including the ACK number are considered good and accepted by the receiver.

Since TCP is a byte-oriented transport protocol, sequencing and acknowledgments are accomplished for each byte of TCP data to ensure the integrity of the data and successful delivery to the destination. LAN protocols such as Novell NetWare and Xerox XNS were developed to work on high-reliability mediums (shielded copper cable in controlled environments). Their sequence numbers are based not on bytes in their data segment but on the number of packets. TCP ACKs TCP bytes of data not packets, datagrams, or segments.

Sequence and Acknowledgment Example

As shown in the slide, the connection was established using an initial sequence number from the sender and an initial sequence number supplied by the receiver (the destination). Each side will maintain its own sequence number, which may be in the range of 0 to 2,147,483,647. Each side of a TCP connection knows the upper and lower limits of the sequence numbers, and once the limit has been reached, it will roll over to 0 (each side knows to include 0). The initialization sequence numbers are selected at random. Each side must ACK each other's received datagrams.

ACK No. = sequence number + good bytes read in the segment + 1

This is a clean, fast, efficient way of determining which bytes were successfully received and which were not. The sender must retain a copy of transmitted data until it receives an acknowledgment for those bytes from the remote network station of a connection.

Acknowledgment packets are not necessarily separate packets with only the acknowledgment number in the packet. This would be inefficient. For example, if station A opens a connection to station B, and station A and station B are sending data to each other, the ACK datagram can be combined with the response data packet. In other words, one datagram transmitted contains three things: the data from station B to station A, the acknowledgment from station B of the data previously sent from station A, and the sequence number for the data B is sending to A.

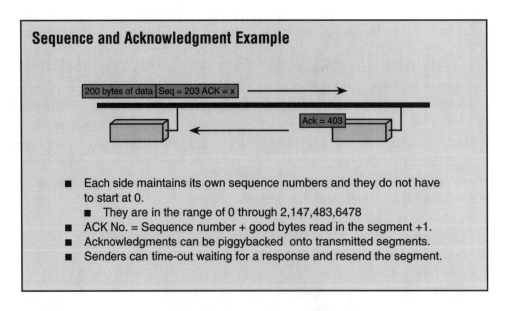

Sequence and Acknowledgment Example

- Each side maintains its own sequence numbers and they do not have to start at 0.
  - They are in the range of 0 through 2,147,483,6478
- ACK No. = Sequence number + good bytes read in the segment +1.
- Acknowledgments can be piggybacked onto transmitted segments.
- Senders can time-out waiting for a response and resend the segment.

If the sender does not receive an acknowledgment within a specified time, it will resend the data starting from the first unacknowledged byte. TCP will time-out after a number of unsuccessful retransmissions. The retransmission of a datagram is accomplished using the Go-back-to-N routine. Any number of outstanding bytes may not be acknowledged. When the destination station does acknowledge the receipt of a series of bytes, the source will look at the ACK number. All sequence numbers up to but not including the ACK number are considered received in good condi-

tion. This means that a source station can start the sequence number with 3 and then send two datagrams containing 100 TCP segment bytes each. When it receives an ACK from the destination of 203 (3 to 102, and then 102 to 202, leaving the ACK at 203 as the next expected byte), it will know that the data in both datagrams previously sent are considered received in good condition.

The number of outstanding packets allowed is the next topic of discussion.

TCP Flow and Window Management 219

Two functions are required of TCP in order for the protocol to manage the data over a connection: *flow control* and *transmission control*. Do not confuse these functions with the ICMP source quench mechanism. Source quench is for a host to inform the source of transmissions that the host is full and the host would like the sender to slow its rate of transmission.

For those readers who do not understand flow control, it is a mechanism used to control the flow of data. For example, if data is being received at a destination station faster than that station can accept it, it needs to tell the source

station to slow down or to stop completely until it can clear out some space (replenish buffers).

How many segments may be outstanding at any one time? Data management using a "window" is accomplished as shown in the following slide. Data for TCP to transmit to the remote network station will be accepted by TCP from an application. This data will be placed sequentially in memory where it will wait to be sent across a connection to a remote station (for IP to send the packet). TCP places a "window" over this data in which to structure the data: data sent and acknowledged, data sent but not acknowledged, and data waiting to be sent. This is called a *sliding window*, for the window will slide up the data segment as each data packet is sent and acknowledged.

Refer to slide 219. Sequence numbers 100–104 have been transmitted to the destination station and the destination station has acknowledged receipt of these segments. Packets containing sequence numbers 105–108 have been transmitted by the source station, but it has not received an acknowledgment. Segments containing sequence numbers 109–114 are still in the source station and are waiting to be sent. Packets containing 115–118 are not yet in the window.

The important thing to notice is the black box covering the segments. This is the window. It will constantly move in ascending sequence order upon receipt of acknowledgments from the destination station.

This window size is variable through the use of the Window Size field in the TCP header of an acknowledgment. When the receiving station (the destination station) is running low on buffer space (an area of memory in which to store incoming data), it can inform the sender to slow its transmission rate to the amount of data it can accept. This is accomplished through the Window field in the TCP header packet. This field will contain the number of bytes (by indicating the range of sequence numbers) that the destination station is willing to accept. Slide 212 shows the TCP header, specifically, the Window field in the TCP header.

When the remote network station cannot accept any more data, it may set this Window field to a 0. It will continue to submit these 0

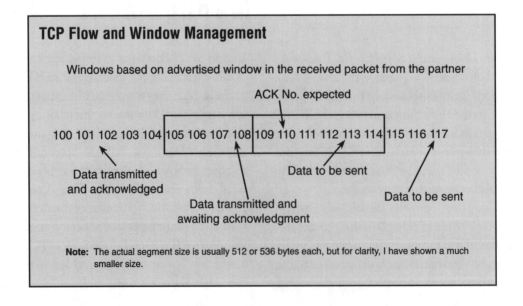

TCP Flow and Window Management

Windows based on advertised window in the received packet from the partner

ACK No. expected

100 101 102 103 104 | 105 106 107 108 | 109 110 111 112 113 114 | 115 116 117

Data transmitted and acknowledged

Data transmitted and awaiting acknowledgment

Data to be sent

Data to be sent

Note: The actual segment size is usually 512 or 536 bytes each, but for clarity, I have shown a much smaller size.

packets until it can again accept data (that is, the sender can send data to a host, and this host should respond with the ACK set to the previous ACK sent and a window set to 0). When buffer space is freed up, it can again submit a packet with the window size set to a number other than 0 to indicate it can again accept data. However, if the urgent bit is set, this indicates to the receiver that the sender has urgent data waiting to send.

This connection management technique allows TCP to maintain control of the data transfer by informing TCP on the sending side how much data the receiver is willing to accept. This enables both a sender and receiver of data to maintain consistent data flow over the connection.

TCP Retransmission

220

One last function to discuss is TCP's capability to know when to send a retransmission of a packet. This is a fairly complex subject that will only be briefly discussed here. Since data runs on an Internet that has varying delays caused by routers and low- or high-speed networks, it is nearly impossible to determine an exact timer delay for an acknowledgment. The acknowledgment could show up one time in a matter of milliseconds, or it could show up in a matter of seconds. The time is variable is due to the heterogeneous nature of the Internet. TCP accommodates

this varying delay by using an adaptive retransmission algorithm. This allotted time is dynamic (not held to one number) and is accomplished as follows: When TCP submits a packet to be sent, TCP records the time of the transmission and the sequence number of the segment. When TCP receives an acknowledgment to that segment, it will again record the time. Using this delta, TCP builds a sample round-trip delay time. TCP uses this time to build an average time for a packet to be sent and an acknowledgment to be received. When it calculates a new value from another sample, it will slowly change its timer delay for the waiting of the ACK packet.

TCP Retransmission

- TCP will retransmit a segment upon expiration of an adaptive transmission timer.

- The timer is variable.

- When TCP transmits a segment, it records the time of transmission and the sequence number of the segment.

- When TCP receives an acknowledgment, it records the time.

- This allows TCP to build a sample round-trip delay time.

- TCP will build an average delay time for a packet to be sent and received.

- The timer is slowly changed to allow for the varying differences in the Internet.

---

221 Slow Start and Congestion Avoidance

Other features of TCP are the *slow start* and *congestion avoidance* mechanisms. Original versions of TCP would start a connection with the sender transmitting multiple segments into the network, up to the window size advertised by the receiver (set up during the three-way handshake). Local subnets were not affected as much as communication between subnets. If there are routers and slower links between the sender and the receiver, problems can arise. A huge amount of data could possibly be sent at startup. The method to avoid this is called the *slow start*. When congestion occurs, TCP must

slow its transmission rate of packets into the network, and then invoke slow start and/or congestion control to get things going again. In practice, they are implemented together.

Slow start operates by observing that the rate at which new packets should be transmitted on the network is the rate at which the acknowledgments are returned. Slow start adds another window to the sender's TCP: the *Congestion* window. This is not advertised in the TCP header; it is assumed. When a new connection is established with a local or remote host, the congestion window is initial-

Slow Start and Congestion Avoidance

- Before this, TCP would start to transmit as much data as was allowed in the advertised window.

- A new window was added called the congestion window.
  - It is not negotiated, it is assumed. It starts out with one segment
  - Segment size is variable, but usually set to 512 or 536 bytes

- Multiply this by the millions of hosts that are conversing on the Internet and you can see that immediate congestion follows.

- Slow start initializes a congestion window of 1 segment.
  - Each subsequent ACK increments this window expotentially (1, 2, 4, 8, etc.) eventually to the advertised window size

- As long as there are no time-outs or duplicate ACKs during the transmission between two stations, it stays at the advertised window size.

ized to one segment. Segment sizes are variable depending on the computer or LAN type used, but the default, typically 536 (yes, 536 for it the segment size [TCP layer] that we are working with) or 512, could be used. Each time an ACK is received, the Congestion window is increased by one segment. The sender can transmit up to the minimum of the Congestion window and the advertised window. The distinction here is that the congestion window is flow control imposed *by the sender*, while the Advertised window is flow control imposed *by the receiver*.

The sender starts by transmitting one segment and waiting for its ACK. When that ACK is received, the Congestion window is incremented from 1 to 2, and 2 segments can be sent. When each of those 2 segments is acknowledged, the Congestion window is increased to 4. This rate continues to increase exponentially until the TCP Advertised window size is met. Once the Congestion window size equals the Advertised window size, segments are continually transferred between stations using the window size for congestion control on the workstations (just as if slow start had never been invoked).

However, upon congestion (as indicated by duplicate ACKs or time-outs), the algorithm kicks back in but starts up another algorithm as well (known as *congestion control*). When congestion occurs, a comparison is made between the congestion window size and the TCP advertised window size. Whichever is smaller, this number is then halved and saved in a variable known as the *slow-start threshold*. This value must be at least 2 segments unless the congestion was a time-out and then the congestion window is set to 1 (slow start). The TCP sender then can either start up slow start or congestion avoidance. Once ACKs are received, the congestion window is increased. Once the congestion window matches the value saved in the slow-start threshold, the slow-start algorithm stops and the congestion avoidance algorithm starts. This algorithm allows for more controlled (linear, not exponential like the slow-start algorithm) growth in transmission in that it multiples the segment size by 2, divides this value by the congestion window size, and then continually increases the rate based on this algorithm each time an ACK is received. This allows for growth on the TCP connection but at a more controlled rate

The effects of these algorithms were dramatic on the Internet. All versions of TCP/IP software now include these algorithms and their effects are not only based on remote connections. These algorithms are placed into action between two stations on a local subnet as well.

Slow Start and Congestion Avoidance (continued)

- Upon congestion (duplicate ACKs or time-out), the algorithm kicks back in.
  - A comparison is made between the congestion window size and the advertised window size
  - Whichever is smaller, is halved and saved as the slow-start threshold
  - The value must be at least 2 segments unless the congestion was a time-out, and then the congestion window is set to 1 (slow start)
  - The TCP sender can start up in slow start or congestion avoidance

- If the congestion value matches (or is greater than) the value of slow-start threshold, the congestion avoidance algorithm starts; otherwise, slow start is brought up.

- Upon receipt of ACKs, the congestion window is increased.

- Allows for a more linear growth in transmission rate.

Finally, TCP must be able to gracefully terminate a connection. This is accomplished using the FIN bit in the TCP header. Since TCP offers a full-duplex connection, each side of the connection must close the connection. Refer to slide 225 for two communicating devices, endstation A and host station B. The application running on endstation A indicates to host B that it wishes to close a connection by sending a packet to host station B with the FIN bit set. Host station B acknowledges that packet and no longer accepts data from end-

station A. However, host station B does accept data from its application to send to endstation A. Endstation A continues to accept data from host station B. This way, station A can, at a minimum, accept a FIN packet from host station B to completely close the connection. To finalize the closing of this connection, host station B sends a packet to endstation A with the FIN bit set. Endstation A ACKs this packet and the connection is closed. If no ACK is received, FINs are retransmitted and will eventually time-out if there is no response.

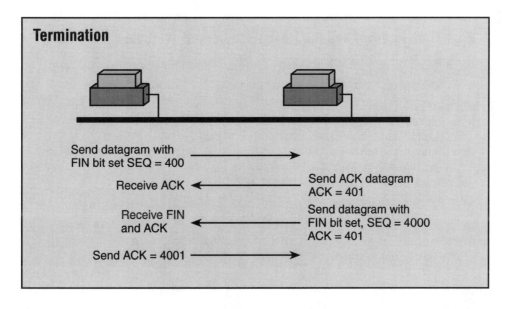

Termination

Send datagram with FIN bit set SEQ = 400

Receive ACK

Send ACK datagram ACK = 401

Receive FIN and ACK

Send datagram with FIN bit set, SEQ = 4000 ACK = 401

Send ACK = 4001

224 Real-Time Protocol and the Real-Time Control Protocol

Multimedia over the Internet. It used to be that data was simply moved over the Internet in order for people to communicate with one another. Moving data such as a file or an email is relatively simple and very forgiving. Other applications, such as viewing a video clip as it is being downloaded to your network station, require special attention. This type of data movement is not very forgiving. Dropped packets cause faded pictures and jerky or intermittent audio.

Some examples of multimedia are the transmission of corporate messages to employees, video- and audio-conferencing for remote meetings and telecommuting, live transmission of multimedia training, communication of stock quotes to brokers, updates on the latest election results, collaborative computing with

times such as electronic whiteboarding, transmission over networks of live TV or radio news and entertainment programs, and many others. All of this is generally grouped into one category known as *multimedia*.

Data transfer, whether it is text or voice and video can be classified as real-time and nonreal-time. Multimedia can be both real-time and non-real time data. Real time is the ability to see and hear "data" as it is happening. For example, viewing a video clip as it is being downloaded to your network station is classified as real time. A camera that is capturing a speech and, in conjunction with IP video servers, is distributing the captured data to thousands of desktops for immediate viewing is another example. Voice and video require special considerations. Let me be more specific: Real-time

---

Real-Time Protocol and the Real-Time Control Protocol

- Multimedia data is becoming commonplace on the Internet.

- A communication platform is needed to support this new type of data.

- Classified as real- and nonreal-time.
    - Real time is the ability to use the information as it is being transferred (e.g., electronic whiteboards, videoconferencing, etc.)
    - Nonreal-time is known as store-and-forward, which means the entire data file is transferred to be used at a later time
        - Examples are CBT, video playback, etc.

- RTP provides end-to-end delivery service for real-time applications.
    - The RFC consists of RTP and its control protocol RTCP

- Services are provided through payload type identification, sequence numbering, timestamping, and delivery monitoring.

applications have specific requirements, as you will see in a moment.

Nonreal-time is the ability to transfer data and view it at a later date. Relatively speaking, time is not a consideration. You can download a multimedia file and view it at your leisure. Another nonreal-time example is Web browsers. It make take a few seconds or minutes to view the Web page, but once all the data is received, the Web page is accurate, not fuzzy or incomplete.

RTP provides end-to-end data delivery for real-time (time-sensitive) applications such as those required by transporting voice and video. It accomplishes this through payload type identification, sequence numbering, time-stamping, and delivery monitoring. It does not provide any quality-of-service guarantees.

Real-Time Protocol (continued) 225

Real-time data requires special treatment, and protocols have been developed to handle it. An early attempt to move real-time data across IP networks was adopted as Streams 2 (ST2) protocol (RFC 1819). It was known as IP version 5 and was the IP replacement for streaming data. IPv4 handled delivery of non-real-time data and ST2 was the IP protocol to handle real-time streaming. It included the ability to do multicast, transport, and quality of service in one protocol. However, the ability of ST2 to scale was limited due to its requirement of static (manual) binding to end node addresses. Besides, the user community wanted the ability to do both bursty data and streaming data over a common IP layer. Therefore, the IETF working groups came out with multiple protocols: RSVP, multicast support, and a new streaming protocol known as the Real-Time Transport Protocol, or RTP.

RTP resides at the same layer as TCP. RTP is more an architecture than a protocol and, as stated in the RFC, "[RTP] is a protocol framework that is deliberately not complete." The RFC includes descriptions of those functions that should be common across applications that develop toward RTP. It provides a framework for a protocol in that it defines the roles, operations, and message formats. Applications written toward RTP usually incorporate the functions of RTP, thereby adding to the RTP.

RTP follows the architecture known as *application layer framing*, which allows for a more cooperative relationship between protocol layers than a strict adherence to them. RTP is considered to be adaptable and is often implemented in the application rather than a separate protocol, such as TCP. RTP replaces the TCP layer for applications and in most cases, RTP works with the UDP layer for socket addresses (multiplexing) and checksum capability. RTP works in conjunction with a control protocol known as the Real-Time Control Protocol (RTCP). Port number 5004 has been registered for RTP and 5005 for RTCP. The source and destination port are the same for the sender and the receiver for RTP.

From the preceding text, your mind has probably wandered and now you are thinking about multimedia and multicast. This is the right way of thinking in that audio and video are generally used in group receivers. RTP is designed for multicast operation. This is obvious in one sender to many receivers but also for the control protocol that is used for feedback of control information.

Feedback is not simply delivered to the sender. If feedback is transmitted in multicast, all participants in the multicast receive this information. Feedback is sent by a receiver of the multicast but the feedback information is sent with an IP multicast destination. This has many advantages. It allows all those involved in the multicast group to receive the feedback information and process it. This also allows any receivers who are experiencing difficulties to determine if the problem is unique to them or more widespread.

Real-Time Protocol (continued)

- An early protocol tied to real-time data was called Streams 2 (RFC 1819).
  - It combined the ability to do multicast, transport, and QoS into one layer-3 protocol
  - Good start but not used much

- Protocols of Streams 2 were developed separately and are now out as RTP, RTCP, RSVP.
  - All can be used over the existing IPv4 infrastructure

- RTP resides at the same layer as TCP (RTP with IPv4 uses UDP).

- RTP is more of a structure or framework than it is a protocol.
  - Deliberately left incomplete

- Follows an architecture called *application layer framing*.

- Designed with multicast in mind.

The RTP protocol is open, which allows for many different encoding schemes to be used. This provides many advantages. Some protocol schemes are better used in different topologies than others. Mixers and translators are used to compensate for differences in encoding schemes, and transmission and reception rates. Translators and mixers reside in the middle of a multimedia network, and are network attachments like any other attachment. Their application makes them reside logically between senders and recipients and they process the RTP information as they receive it and then retransmit the information. The translator functions are the easiest to explain, so we will start there.

As shown in the slide, a translator simply translates from one payload format to another. Take the example of a network station that would like to participate in a stream but is located beyond a WAN link that provides very little bandwidth. The high-speed workstations could simply reduce their capabilities to provide for the low-bandwidth link, but with the translator they do not have to. The translator can simply receive the high-bandwidth signal and translate it to a low-bandwidth signal for the remote network station. In this way, receivers of high-quality links can continue using them, while receivers of low-bandwidth links participate as well.

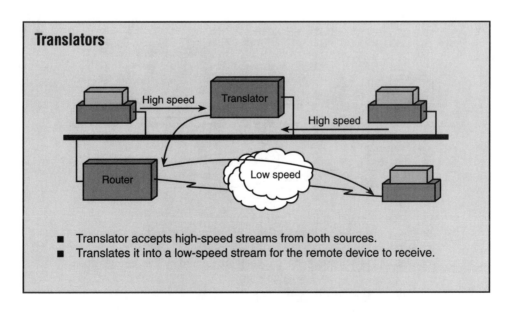

Translators

- Translator accepts high-speed streams from both sources.
- Translates it into a low-speed stream for the remote device to receive.

227 Mixers

Mixers perform a vital service. Mixers do not intake a source stream and translate it to another type of stream. Mixers combine multiple source streams into one single stream and preserve the original format. For example, if you were having a audio conference between four network stations, and another network station over a low-speed link would like to join, the mixer would simply pull the three network stations into one single stream instead of three for communication to the network station over the low-speed link. As shown in the slide, a digital audio conversation is being carried on between four workstations, each consuming 64 kbps for their own personal use.

When the fifth network station wants to join the conversation, but its link is only 64 kbps, the mixer combines all four higher-speed audio signals into one 64 kbps stream. This allows the network station over the low-speed link to join the conversation and the other network stations maintain their high-speed and probably high-quality audio links.

Basically, mixers and translators allow for variances to occur in an multimedia stream. Whether it is translating streams from one format to another, or allowing for the mixing of signals to accommodate for differences, these two types of devices are very much a part of the RTP protocol.

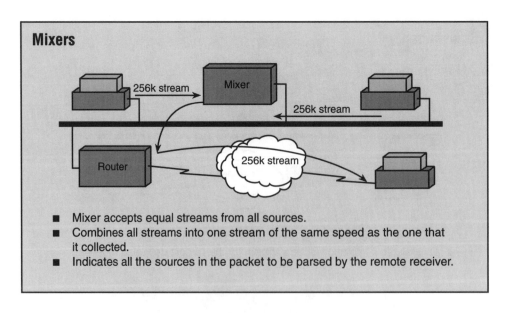

Mixers

- Mixer accepts equal streams from all sources.
- Combines all streams into one stream of the same speed as the one that it collected.
- Indicates all the sources in the packet to be parsed by the remote receiver.

RTP Message Format

Vers indicates the version, which as of this writing is 2 (version 1 was the draft spec and 0 was used for the public domain Visual Audio Tool [VAT]). The P bit indicates that padding is used at the end of the datagram and the last byte indicates how many bytes of padding. The X bit is the extension bit, which indicates that the RTP fixed header is followed by an extension header. This has limited use, but it does allow for extensibility. An extension mechanism is provided to allow individual implementations to experiment with new pay-load-format-independent functions that require additional information to be carried in the RTP data packet header. The sequence number is 16 bits long and increments by 1 for each message sent. The start number is like TCP and can be started anywhere within a 16-bit range. The

timestamp indicates a number reflective of the time of the transmission of the first byte in the RTP data packet and increments sequentially. Timestamps are used to exact the timing as it was sent from the source. Several messages may have the same timestamp, which could indicate they were sent at the same time and belong to the same video frame.

Synchronization Source field is a 32-bit number that indicates the originator of the message that inserted the sequence number and the timestamp for the data so as not to be dependent on the IP address. As shown in the previous slide on mixers, there are two sources of audio data. Each packet will contain their address for the packets that they send. The selection of the identifier is beyond the scope of this book, but there is a random number

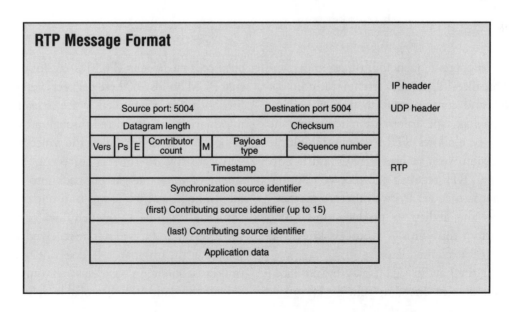

RTP Message Format

		IP header
Source port: 5004	Destination port 5004	UDP header
Datagram length	Checksum	
Vers	Ps	E	Contributor count	M	Payload type	Sequence number	
Timestamp		RTP
Synchronization source identifier		
(first) Contributing source identifier (up to 15)		
(last) Contributing source identifier		
Application data		

generated for this field by the source, thereby allows each source to be unique. If two sources do select the same identifier, RTP does have the mechanisms with which to detect and correct this. This field could indicate an alternate source if the received message was originated by a mixer. If the two packets entered a mixer, the mixer would insert its 32-bit number as the

source and push the previous SSRC numbers into the Contributing Source Identifier.

The Contributing Source Identifier indicates a source or sources (the original IDs of the sources) of a stream of RTP packets that were involved in the combined stream produced by a mixer.

229   Support for Time-Sensitive Apps

RTP supports sequencing, timestamps, synchronizes different streams (audio or video), and contains information describing RTP's payload type. Information describing the payload type allows RTP to support multiple compression types such as MPEG and H.261. In fact, an RTP receiver can receive information that is encoded by two different methods and has the ability to produce one single stream from this. This is a process known as *mixing*. It is explained later.

A digitized audio signal may be produced using an simplex encoding scheme known as

pulse code modulation (PCM). Say, for example, that PCM builds 160 byte packets every 20 milliseconds for a sampled voice stream. This information is transmitted through an Internet using IP. The digitizing of the voice signal is very sensitive to time. The reception of the stream of voice must be put back into the original timing in which it was transmitted; otherwise, there will be an uneven flow for voice at the receiver and it will not be received as it was spoken at the originator. IP does not care about timing, sequencing, or delays. It only has to deliver the data. IP will probably deliver these packets at different times and may deliver them in varying order. Therefore, an RTP application must put the packets back in the original order and reapply the timing between the packets. RTP provides information on this but does not accomplish this directly. Timestamps, which mark the relative beginning of the event, are provided with the packet and this provides enough information to the application to rebuild the original audio stream.

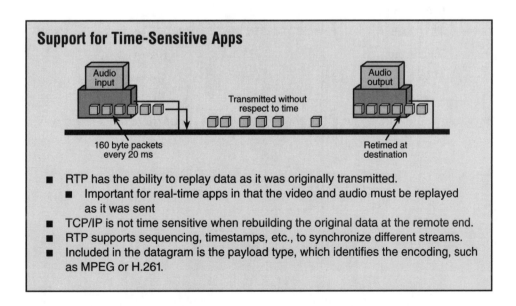

Support for Time-Sensitive Apps

Audio input

Transmitted without respect to time

Audio output

160 byte packets every 20 ms

Retimed at destination

- ■ RTP has the ability to replay data as it was originally transmitted.
  - ■ Important for real-time apps in that the video and audio must be replayed as it was sent
- ■ TCP/IP is not time sensitive when rebuilding the original data at the remote end.
- ■ RTP supports sequencing, timestamps, etc., to synchronize different streams.
- ■ Included in the datagram is the payload type, which identifies the encoding, such as MPEG or H.261.

230

Payload Type

The next field is the payload type. Payload types are listed in the following table:

> **Payload Type**
> - The text page indicates the wide range of support for audio and video payload types for RTP.

0	PCMU audio	16–22	Unassigned audio
1	1016 audio	23	RGB8 video
2	G721 audio	24	HDCC video
3	GSM audio	25	CelB video
4	Unassigned audio	26	JPEG video
5	DVI4 audio (4 kHz)	27	CUSM video
6	DBI4 audio (16 kHz)	28	nv video
7	LPC audio	29	PicW video
8	PCMA audio	30	CPV video
9	G722 audio	31	H261 video
10	L16 audio (stereo)	32	MPV video
11	L16 audio (mono)	33	MP2T video
12	TPS0 audio	34–71	Unassigned video
13	VSC audio	72–76	Reserved
14	MPA audio	77–95	Unassigned
15	G728 audio	96–127	Dynamic

Not that you would care about all of these payload types, but there are a few that you should recognize.

RTCP (Real-Time Control Protocol) is the control mechanism for RTP and it provides information, in the form of feedback, on network conditions and reception quality. Using RTCP allows RTP applications to adapt to variances in the media. For example, a router carrying the stream could become overloaded and slow down the forwarding of packets. Another application on the network is using considerable bandwidth and the receivers of RTP cannot receive as many packets as quickly as they want to. RTCP allows for control information to be distributed to not only the server but also the receivers. This allows for receivers and senders to make their own decisions about the quality. Another feature of RTCP is the gathering of user information. RTCP reports who that are attending a "session."

RTP can work alone, but usually does not. RTP relies on RTCP to control information. The message format that RTP uses is the same format for all of its message.

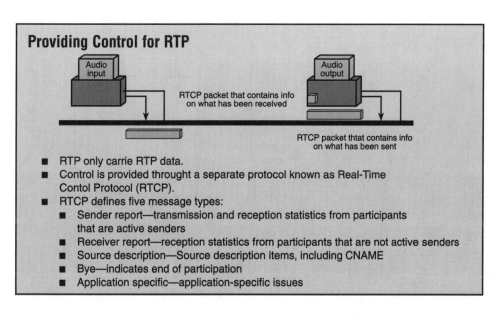

Providing Control for RTP

Audio input

Audio output

RTCP packet that contains info on what has been received

RTCP packet thtat contains info on what has been sent

- RTP only carrie RTP data.
- Control is provided throught a separate protocol known as Real-Time Contol Protocol (RTCP).
- RTCP defines five message types:
    - Sender report—transmission and reception statistics from participants that are active senders
    - Receiver report—reception statistics from participants that are not active senders
    - Source description—Source description items, including CNAME
    - Bye—indicates end of participation
    - Application specific—application-specific issues

Sender Reports

Reports for RTCP allow senders and receivers to communicate with each other for quality reasons. Each sender sends a report giving statistics for its transmissions. Receivers consume this data and also send out reports to indicate how well they are receiving data. The senders use this data to tune their transmissions.

There are two types of reports that RTP receivers may send: Sender and Receiver reports (SR and RR, respectively). The type of report sent depends on whether the receiver is also a sender. RTP receivers provide reception quality feedback using the RTCP reports. The sender report tells receivers what they should have received. The V is for the version number, which should be set to 2. The R Cnt is the receiver block count and contains the number of receiver blocks in the message. The Length field indicates the length of the packet in bytes.

Both types of reports are very similar. The only difference between the two reports, besides the packet type, is the 20-byte sender information section in the Sender report. The Sender report is issued to let the receiver know what should have been received. Both the SR and RR can include from 0 to 31 blocks (notice the blocks are simply replicated); 1 block for each of the synchronization sources from which the receiver has received RTP data packets since its last report.

The SSRC field ties the Sender report to any RTP data packets the source may have sent. The NTP timestamp is the actual time of day. It is used as a control to measure the delta for

Sender Reports

V	P	R	Cnt	PT = 200	Length	Header information
SSRC of sender						Sender information
NTP timestamp						
RTP timestamp						
Sender's packet count						
Sender's byte count						
SSRC of first source						Report block 1 More report blocks could follow this.
% Lost	Cumulative packets lost					
Extended highest seq.num.recv.						
Interarrival jitter						R Cnt, above, is the block count for this message
Time of last sender report						
Time since last sender report						
SSRC of last source						Last report block
Repeat from above (% lost, etc.)						
Application-specific data						

timestamps extracted from reception reports. This allows for an estimate to be made as to the round-trip propagation delay to those receivers. The RTP timestamp allows receivers to put this message in an order relative to the RTP packets. The last fields indicate the number of packets and bytes the sender has transmitted.

The next sections are receiver blocks. In the Sender report, they allow the sender to report its transmitted data but also any RTP data that is has received. Each block represents one remote source. The block indicates the fraction of packets from that source that were lost since the last report and the total number of packets lost since inception. The Extended Highest Sequence Number Received is the highest sequence number from that source. The Interarrival Jitter field allows for the receiver to estimate the variance of the source's interarrival times. A high value indicates that this receiver is receiving a stream of packets irregularly.

The last two fields indicate when the last report from this source arrived.

233

Receiver Reports

The Receiver report is basically the same as the Sender report, with the exception that the sender information is stripped out. The Packet Type field is set to 201.

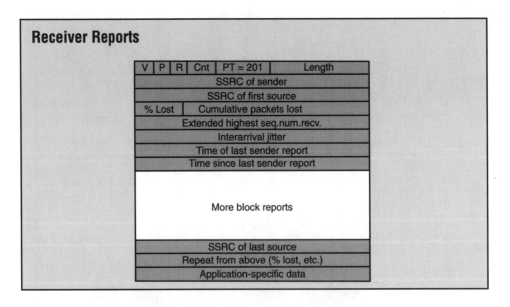

Receiver Reports

V	P	R	Cnt	PT = 201	Length
SSRC of sender						
SSRC of first source						
% Lost	Cumulative packets lost					
Extended highest seq.num.recv.						
Interarrival jitter						
Time of last sender report						
Time since last sender report						
More block reports						
SSRC of last source						
Repeat from above (% lost, etc.)						
Application-specific data						

The SSDP is used to provide more information about the source. The RTP header is used and the packet type is set to 202. The first field contains the SSRC or CSRC identifier of the source. Applications are free to put their own items in as well. The canonical name (CNAME) is the most important field in the packet and the other fields may or may not be filled out. Since SSRC identifiers can be duplicated, the RTP protocol provides mechanisms to detect and correct this duplication. Therefore, the CNAME further identifies a source using the format of user@domain-name.

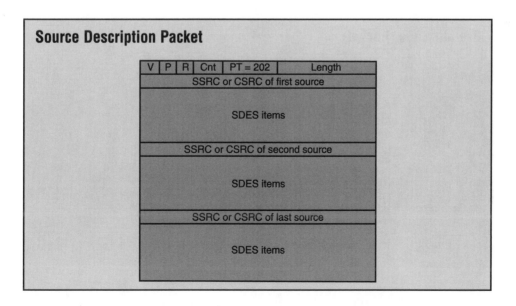

Source Description Packet

| V | P | R | Cnt | PT = 202 | Length |

SSRC or CSRC of first source

SDES items

SSRC or CSRC of second source

SDES items

SSRC or CSRC of last source

SDES items

235

Bye Message (Packet)

In order for a source to leave a conference, it uses the Bye packet. Eventually, all participants in the conference would notice the source is missing, but this message allows this to be quickly learned. Included in the packet is a field that allows the source to identify the reason that it is leaving. This field is optional.

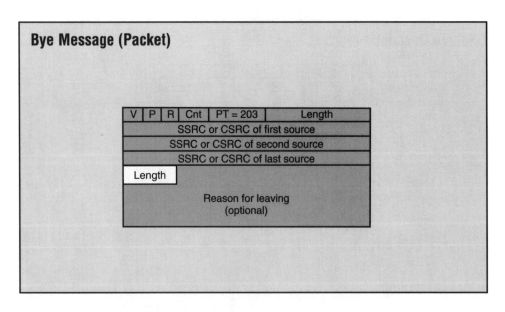

Bye Message (Packet)

V	P	R	Cnt	PT = 203	Length
SSRC or CSRC of first source					
SSRC or CSRC of second source					
SSRC or CSRC of last source					
Length					
Reason for leaving (optional)					

Application-Specific Message

Application-Specific Message

- Used by an application to send and receive its own messages.

- Allows for uniqueness to an application.

- Allows for the RTCP protocol to be extensible.

This type of message allows for experimentation of the RTCP protocol. It allows for application developers to place their own messages in a packet to be used by a receiver or sender of their application. This is another example of how this protocol is really not finished and never will be, which allows for uniqueness and extensibility.

Caveats

Caveats

- RTP does not provide any QoS capabilities.

- RTP does not guarantee delivery or out-of-sequence packets.

- RTP is only a framework.
  - Molded into an application

- RTP is extensible.
  - More information can be added to the packet passed between RTP clients and servers

RTP does not provide for any Quality of Service (QoS) parameters such as those that allow for timely delivery. RTP does not guarantee delivery or in-sequence packets. It provides sequencing, but merely for the transport sequencing of placing the order of packets in operations like decoding; however, the packets can be decoded out of receiving sequence. Like most other TCP/IP protocols, a protocol is a protocol and not two protocols. RTP expects other TCP/IP protocols to provide for QoS services.

238 RFCs

To see what is playing on the MBONE:

www.precept.com/cgi-bin/iptv/iptvmain.pl

or

www.cilea.it/collabora/MBone/agenda.html

RTP and RTCP are contained in RFC 1889.

RFCs

- RFC 1889—The Real-Time Protocol (this includes the RTCP protocol as well).

239 Selected TCP/IP Applications

This section gives you an introduction to TELNET, FTP, TFTP, SMTP (including POP), and DNS.

There can be many applications written for the TCP/IP environment, and many exist today. There are word processing systems, CAD/CAM systems, mail systems, and so on. The seven most common applications (besides Web applications) that run on the TCP/IP network system are:

TELNET (Remote Terminal Emulation)

File Transfer Protocol (FTP)

Selected TCP/IP Applications

- Remote Terminal Emulation (TELNET)

- File Transfer Protocol (FTP)

- Trivial File Transfer Protocol (TFTP)

- Simple Mail Transfer Protocol (SMTP)

- Post Office Protocol (POP)

- Domain Name Service (DNS)

- Simple Network Management Protocol (SNMP)

Trivial File Transfer Protocol (TFTP)

Simple Mail Transfer Protocol (SMTP)

Post Office Protocol (POP)

Domain Name Service (DNS)

Simple Network Management Protocol (SNMP)

These applications are fully documented in the RFCs and almost always are delivered with any TCP/IP protocol suite in the market today. This means that you can switch to almost any type of computer using TCP applications software and the commands and functions of these programs will be the same.

The applications were specifically written for TCP/IP and basically provide almost all the applications that users need to access any network. Database programs, word processing programs, and so forth, are all viable programs, but are not pertinent to the operation of a TCP/IP network. Using the foregoing application, a user can find any other needed application on the Internet. The ones just listed are the bare minimum needed to create a networked user environment in which all users can actively communicate and share data with each other across the network.

One nice thing about these available network applications is that they run on TCP/IP no matter which operating system is being used. The commands, their connection techniques, the commands that control the application, and the interface to the user almost always will be the same. So, if you normally work with Unix and then switch for a day to DOS, the same FTP commands that operated on the Unix machine will be there in the DOS machine. It is hard to say that with most applications today. The discussion starts with the TELNET protocol.

The protocols are covered briefly. Please refer to the TCP/IP books listed at the back of this book for more information about these protocols.

TELNET

The TELNET connection simply allows a terminal service over the TCP/IP network as if the terminal were directly connected. Remember that computers and terminals were connected by a cable and the terminals were directly attached to the host computer. The TELNET service provides a terminal service for the network. It allows for any terminal to attach to any computer over the network. It can emulate many different types of terminals, depending on the manufacturer of the TEL-NET program. There are TELNET programs that emulate DEC VTxxx series of terminals, IBM 3270 and 5250 terminals, and more.

The advantage to the TELNET program is that a user may log on to any host on the TCP/IP internet (provided security options are allowed). Sessions are set up over the TCP/IP network.

The slide shows a typical TELNET connection on a TCP/IP network.

The TELNET protocol uses TCP as its transport. The user starts the TELNET protocol at his or her workstation, usually by typing **TELNET <domain name or IP address>**. The TELNET application may be started with or without an argument. The argument allows a simpler procedure to be invoked so that the TELNET process will automatically try to connect to the host signified by the argument statement. The TELNET application starts and attempts to establish a connection to the remote device (by accessing the services of the Domain Name Server or directly with the IP address; DNS will be discussed later). If an argument is not supplied, the TELNET application waits for the user to issue an OPEN command connection using the DNS or an IP address.

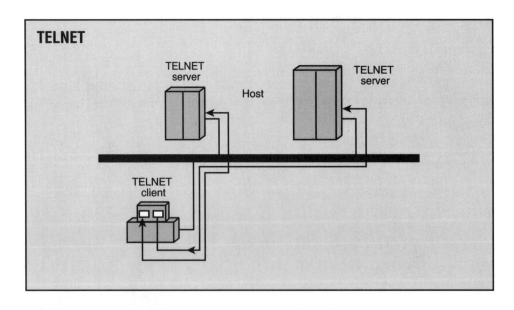

TELNET Options

- Each side of the connection requests or tells its partner the options it wants or can do.

- Options are formatted in:
  - WILL or WON'T <option>
  - DO or DON'T <option>

- Negotiates options such that symmetry can be set up between two stations.

- Options include:
  - Ability to echo
  - Terminal type
  - Setting line mode so that groups of characters can be sent

The TELNET program is extensible through the use of options. Each side of the connection requests or tells the remote end of the connection which of these options it can support and which one the remote end should support. This provides for symmetry. The TELNET protocol was written so that it would work on a variety of operating systems. Therefore, before a connection is made to the remote device, the TELNET protocol has some work to do in order to synchronize the connection with the remote device. For example, the DOS operating system for personal computers requires that a CR-LF (carriage return-line feed) be used to terminate a line of text. Other systems such as Unix require a line of text to be terminated with an LF. Another example is the echoing of characters. Upon

connection attempt, the TELNET protocol will negotiate with the remote device as to who will do the echoing of typed characters to the initiator of a connection. During the connection attempt between a source and destination station, the two stations will communicate options. These options indicate how each end of the connections will respond on the TELNET connection. These options include:

1. The ability to change from 7-bit text to 8-bit binary
2. Allowing one side or the other to echo characters
3. Specifying a terminal type
4. Requesting the status of a TELNET option from the remote connection
5. Setting a timing mark to synchronize two ends of a connection
6. The ability to terminate a record with an EOR code
7. Setting line mode so that strings of characters may be sent instead of a character-at-a-time transmit
8. Stopping the go-ahead signal after data

The options are negotiated between the two network stations in the following manner:

Request	Response
WILL <option>	DO or DON'T <option>

For example, WILL ECHO from station A is requesting that station A provide the echoing of characters. The response will either be DO ECHO, meaning the remote end agrees, or DON'T ECHO, meaning the remote end will not allow station A to echo.

Agreement between the two TELNET ends communicated for a DO <option> will be responded to with a WILL <option> or WON'T <option>. An example of this option negotiation: If the TELNET application is running on a DOS personal computer which is set up for local echo, upon the connection setup the TELNET option from the PC will be WILL ECHO and the response should be DO ECHO. If the PC had been set up without the local echo option and you wish the remote end

to provide echo, the PC should negotiate echo with DO ECHO and the response will be WILL ECHO.

Using WILL, WON'T, DO, and DON'T provides symmetry. Either side of the connection can provide the command or the response. One side provides services in exactly the same manner as the other side.

242   File Transfer Protocol (FTP)

TELNET provides users with the ability to act as a local terminal even though users are not directly attached to the host. One other TCP/IP application that provides network services for users on a network is a *file transfer protocol*. With TCP/IP, there are three popular types of file access protocols in use: FTP, Trivial File Transfer Protocol (TFTP), and Network File System (NFS). This FTP protocol provides for files to be transferred reliably across the network under the complete control of the user. FTP is transaction based. Every command is replied to using a number

scheme similar to the SMTP protocol (discussed in a moment).

FTP is very robust. Remember the previous discussion on ports and sockets and how they are established and used. The FTP protocol actually uses two port assignments (and therefore two connections): 20 and 21. Remember that most connections between two network stations are made via one source port and one destination port. A network station wanting a connection to a remote network station must connect to two ports on the destination station in order for FTP to work.

Port 20 is used for the initial setup of the connection and as the control connection. No data passes over this circuit except for control information. Port 21 is used for user data (the file to be transferred) to pass over the connection.

Similar to the TELNET arguments, simply typing **FTP <domain name or IP address>** will establish the connection. The command line should then read FTP> (this depends on your application). With the advent of Windows and Windows-like operating systems, FTP now has a GUI interface in order to take some of the harshness out of the protocol. After the connection is established, the server process awaits a command from the client. To transfer a file from the server to the client, the user types in **get <a name of a file>**, which is transmitted over to the remote network station. With this, a second connection is established between the server and client FTP process. It is known as the *data connection*. Now we have two connections, but only during the file transfer process. Once the file is transferred, the data connection port is closed.

This is the well-known (or assigned) FTP data port. From a user's standpoint, to establish a connection between itself and a remote station, the command is similar to TELNET: **FTP <domain name or IP address>**. A user could also type in FTP and wait for the FTP prompt. At the prompt, the user would use the OPEN command to establish the connection.

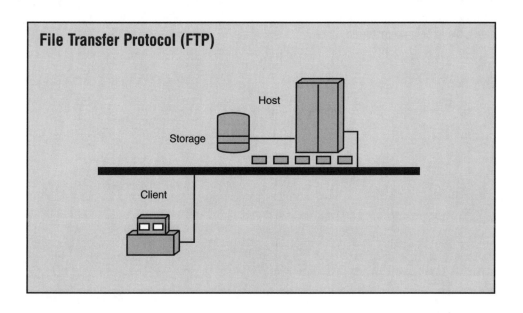

File Transfer Protocol (FTP)

Host

Storage

Client

The following are the available commands in FTP. There are a lot of commands listed but, in reality, only a few are used. They are:

open   Open a connection to a remote resource.

close   Close a connection to a remote resource.

bye   End this FTP session.

binary   Indicate that the file transfer will be a file of binary type (i.e., executable file, Lotus file, etc.).

get   Get a file from the remote resource; get <filename>; mget <multiple files, wildcards included>.

put   Put a file to the remote resource; put <filename>; mput <multiple files, wildcards included>.

cd   Change directory on the remote device; to change the directory on the local end, use lcd.

dir   Get a directory listing on the remote device; to get a directory listing on the local end, use ldir.

hash   Display hash marks on the screen to indicate a file is being transferred.

FTP Commands

- open—creates a connection between two hosts.
- close—closes a connection between two hosts.
- bye—ends the FTP session.
- binary—indicate that the file is binary data.
- get—get the remote file.
- mget—wildcard to get multiple files.
- put—puts a file to the remote resource.
- mput—wildcard to put multiple files.
- cd—change directory on the remote device.
- dir—get a directory listing on the remote device.
- ldir—get a local directory.
- hash—display hash marks during the transfer.

FTP Data Transfer

```
C:\WINDOWS>ftp
ftp> open mnauglepc
Connected to mnauglepc.
220 mnauglepc FTP service (NEWT v4.01)
    ready for new user.
User (mnauglepc:(none)): mnaugle
331 mnaugle, please enter your password.
Password:
230 User mnaugle logged in.
ftp> pwd
257 "c:\" is the current directory.
ftp> lcd
Local directory now C:\WINDOWS
ftp> get autoexec.bat autoexec.002
200 PORT command successful.
150 Opening ASCII mode data connection
    for autoexec.bat.
226 File transfer complete.
1911 bytes received in 0.00 seconds
    (1911000.00 Kbytes/sec)
ftp> bye
221 Goodbye.
```

Refer to the slide. Commands such as the following are sent over the control port. Once the connection is established, file transfer actually occurs over the data port. If a user wants to establish an FTP connection between 148.1.1.2 and an FTP server process on 148.1.1.19, the following sequence of events take place on a DOS PC (for other operating systems, the prompt would change, but the commands are all the same in every FTP implementation):

C> FTP or FTP <domain name or IP address>

If multiple files are needed, the user can use the commands MGET or MPUT, which stands for Multiple GET and Multiple PUT, respectively. If the file we want is a binary file (a spreadsheet and an application are examples of binary files), the user has to type in the keyword **binary** at the FTP prompt. This indicates to the FTP program that the file to be transferred is a binary file. Any of the commands may be entered at the FTP prompt. The protocol is transaction based and the numbers preceding each line are for the node to interpret the next command. The text is for human consumption.

> C:\WINDOWS>ftp
>
> ftp> open mnauglepc
>
> Connected to mnauglepc.
>
> 220 mnauglepc FTP service (NEWT v4.01) ready for new user.
>
> User (mnauglepc:(none)): mnaugle
>
> 331 mnaugle, please enter your password.
>
> Password:
>
> 230 User mnaugle logged in.
>
> ftp> pwd
>
> 257 "c:\" is the current directory.
>
> ftp> lcd
>
> Local directory now C:\WINDOWS
>
> ftp> get autoexec.bat autoexec.002
>
> 200 PORT command successful.
>
> 150 Opening ASCII mode data connection for autoexec.bat.
>
> 226 File transfer complete.
>
> 1911 bytes received in 0.00 seconds (1911000.00 Kbytes/sec)
>
> **ftp> bye**
>
> 221 Goodbye.

245 Trivial File Transfer Program (TFTP)

An alternative to the FTP program is the TFTP program. This is a simplex file transfer program and is primarily used to bootstrap diskless network workstations (the program is small enough to fit in a ROM chip on the diskless workstation to initiate a boot across the network) or even network components (network bridges and routers). The FTP program is an extremely robust and complex program, and situations exist that require file transfer capabilities without complexity. Hence, FTP is also a larger file. TFTP is a small file and provides a more restrictive file transfer (for example, no user authentication); it is also a smaller executable software program.

There are differences between FTP and TFTP. TFTP does not provide a reliable service; therefore, it uses the transport services of UDP instead of TCP. It also restricts its datagram size to 512 bytes, and every datagram must be acknowledged (no multiple-packet windowing). There are no windows for packets to be acknowledged. It could be said that it has a window of 1.

The protocol is very simple. The first packet transmitted from the client process to the server process is a control packet, which specifies the filename and whether it is to be read from or written to the remote workstation (GET or PUT command). Subsequent packets are data packets and file transfer is accomplished with 512 bytes transferred at one time. The initial data packet is specially marked with a number of 1. Each subsequent data is incremented by 1. This is the sequence numbering system for TFTP. The receiving station will acknowledge this packet immediately upon

---

Trivial File Transfer Program (TFTP)

- A simplex file transfer program.
- Uses UDP.
- Transfers 512 bytes at a time.
- Transfers one segment at a time.
- Acknowledged by the application.
- Any datagram less than 512 bytes indicates the last datagram in the transfer.
- Popular for network booting of devices.

---

receipt, using this number. Any packet of less than 512 bytes in length signifies the end of the transfer. Error messages may be transmitted in place of the data in the data field, but any error message will terminate the transmission. Also notice that only one connection is made to the remote resource. FTP has one for data and one for control information. FTP is a very robust protocol, one that can handle many types of transfers over various (not so good) media types. The commands of GET and PUT are used the same as in the FTP program.

The sequencing of the data is accomplished through the TFTP application, not the transport-layer service of UDP. UDP provides only unreliable, connectionless service. TFTP keeps track of the sequencing of the blocks of data and the acknowledgments that should be received. For those readers familiar with NetWare, this is the same type of transaction accomplished between the NetWare Core Protocol (NCP, not using Burst mode) and its underlying delivery system, IPX.

Domain Name Service (DNS)

Read RFCs 1034 and 1035. These contain the bulk of the DNS information and are supplemented by RFCs 1535–1537. DNS has many uses, but its main function continues to be the mapping of IP address to human-usable names.

There are millions of hosts on the Internet today representing even more millions of users. Most users have no idea what the underlying protocols are doing, nor do they care. But most of them would if they had to memorize IP addresses and determine other functions such as mail. Actually, most would be frustrated by the numbering system and the Internet would not be as popular as it is. When the Internet was young, an early method of mapping the 32-bit address to a hostname required downloading a file maintained by (at the time) the Network Information Center (NIC). It was a single file (hosts.txt) that contained a simple mapping of Internet addresses to hostnames. This file was usually contained in the /etc subdirectory on a workstation and various TCP/IP applications could access the information in this file. Not having this file meant that a user had to type in the 32-bit address for connectivity to a remote host. Secondly, population of the Internet was becoming very diverse and more autonomous. In the 1980s the Internet was known as the ARPAnet (now shut down) and the hosts were primarily time shared. More and more connections to the Internet were sites that had LANs installed and connected to these LANs were mainframe and minicomputers or even personal computers. These sites were administering their own names and

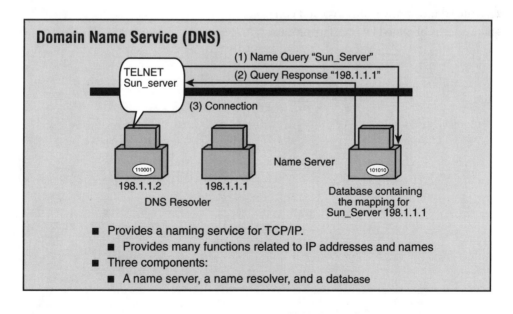

Domain Name Service (DNS)

(1) Name Query "Sun_Server"

TELNET
Sun_server

(2) Query Response "198.1.1.1"

(3) Connection

Name Server

198.1.1.2   198.1.1.1

DNS Resovler

Database containing
the mapping for
Sun_Server 198.1.1.1

- ■ Provides a naming service for TCP/IP.
  - ■ Provides many functions related to IP addresses and names
- ■ Three components:
  - ■ A name server, a name resolver, and a database

addresses in the hosts.txt file, but had to wait for the NIC to change hosts.txt to make changes visible to the Internet at large. Lastly, with the additions of more sites to the Internet, the applications on the Internet were getting more sophisticated and creating a need for a general-purpose name service.

After many experimental RFCs, the global name system for the Internet became known as the Domain Name System (DNS). DNS is comprised of three components: a *name server*, a *database*, and a *name resolver*. Name servers make information available to the resolvers. The information the name servers contain are IP addresses, aliases, mail information, and so forth. The resolvers usually reside on users' workstations and are embedded in the applications of TCP such as TELNET and FTP. They are not separate programs. The name server is a separate program and resides anywhere on a network answering queries from the resolvers. The domain servers each maintain a portion of the hierarchical database under separate administrative authority and control. Redundancy is obtained by transferring data

between cooperating servers (primary masters and secondary masters).

Your site may not require a DNS. You may have just a few hosts and can depend on another DNS to supply the information you need. For the Internet itself, it must have the DNS system. A great example on the dependency of DNS was when a corrupted database (containing "directions" to other hosts) file was posted on the nine root servers (explained in a moment). Millions of on-liners were without the capability of attaching or communicating with other hosts on the network for hours. Without information (the IP address) of a remote system, two nodes cannot communicate. We could look up the information in the InterNIC database, but without prior knowledge on how to query their database manually, one is literally lost on the Internet. DNS provides information about hosts, not users, on the Internet.

The Domain Name Space is very much like a file system on Unix or DOS. It starts with a root and branches attach from this root to give an endless array of paths. Each branch in the file system is given a directory name, whereas in DNS it is called a *label*. Each label can be 63 characters in length, but most are far less than that. This means that each text word between the dots can be 63 characters in length, with the total domain name (all the labels) limited to 255 bytes in overall length assuming a screen line length of 80 characters this is just 3 screen lines.

The IP protocol mandates the use of IP addresses. Any user may use this address to connect to any service on the network; however, for a user to remember the addresses of all the network servers on the network is an impossible task. Users are more likely to remember names than they are to remember numbers.

For those familiar with database environments, the domain name server is simply a database (consisting of information such as names and IP addresses, and much more) to which any station on the network can make queries using the domain name resolver. The domain name system is not necessarily complex, but it is involved. It is based on a hierarchical structure as shown in the slide. The assignment of names is relatively simple and is accomplished via the Internet Registries with the ultimate authority being IANA. The domain name is simply that: a name assigned

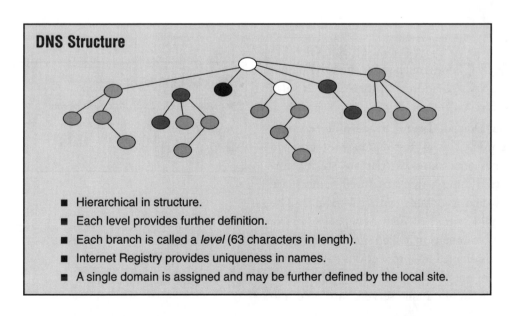

DNS Structure

- Hierarchical in structure.
- Each level provides further definition.
- Each branch is called a *level* (63 characters in length).
- Internet Registry provides uniqueness in names.
- A single domain is assigned and may be further defined by the local site.

to a domain For example, isi.edu, cisco.com, and 3Com.com represent the domain name at those companies or educational institutions. The naming within those domains (naming of the hosts) is left up to those individuals who are assigned those domain names. The InterNIC does not care. The hierarchical structure allows hosts to have the same name as long as they are in different branches of the structure or in different domains.

248 DNS Components

DNS does much more than the name-to-address translation. It also allows for:

The Domain Name Space and resource records. This is the database of grouped names and addresses that are strictly formatted using a tree-structured name space and data associated with the names. The domain system consists of separate sets of local information called *zones*. The database is divided up into sections called *zones*, which are distributed among the name servers. While name servers can have sev-

---

DNS Components
- Domain Name Space and resource records
- Name servers
- Resolvers

eral optional functions and sources of data, the essential task of a name server is to answer queries using data in its zones. Conceptually, each node and leaf of the domain name space tree names a set of information, and query operations are attempts to extract specific types of information from a particular set. A query names the domain name of interest and describes the type of resource information that is desired.

Name servers. These are workstations that contain a database of information about hosts in zones. This information can be about well-known services, mail exchanger, or host information. A name server may cache structure or set information about any part of the domain tree, but in general, a particular name server has complete information about a subset of the domain space, and pointers to other name servers that can be used to lead to information from any part of the domain tree. Name servers know the parts of the domain tree for which they have complete information; a name server is said to be an authority for these parts of the name space. Authoritative information is organized into units called *zones*, and

these zones can be automatically distributed to the name servers that provide redundant service for the data in a zone. The name server must periodically refresh its zones from master copies in local files or foreign name servers.

Resolvers. These are programs that generally reside on users' workstations and send requests over the network to servers on behalf of the users. Resolvers must be able to access at least one name server and use that name server's information to answer a query directly, or pursue the query using referrals to other name servers.

When a DNS server responds to a resolver, the requester attempts a connection to the host using the IP address and not the name. The preceding example could have used only part of a name: host. This is known as a *relative name*. It is part of a larger name known as the *absolute name*. The absolute name for the preceding example could be host.research.Naugle.com. This name would be in the domain name server. Most resolvers will step through a preconfigured list of suffixes (in order of configured input), append it to the name, and attempt a lookup when the full DNS (absolute) name is not specified.

249 Domain Structure

DNS is hierarchical in structure, as shown previously. A domain is a subtree of the domain name space. The advantage of this structure is that at the bottom, the network administrator can assign the names.

From the root, the assigned top-level domains (TLD) are as follows:

GOV   Government body.

EDU   Educational body.

COM   Commercial entity.

MIL   Military.

ORG   Any other organization not previously listed.

CON   Any country using the ISO standard 3166 for names of countries As stated in RFC 1591, "the IANA is not in the business of what is and what is not a country." Therefore, it is up to ISO to determine who is on that list.

Now let's look at the generalized format for a domain name.

Going down the tree, we can pick out a domain name, such as research.Naugle.com. This would signify the Research department (which is a subdomain of domain Naugle.com) at Naugle Enterprises, which is defined as a commercial entity of the Internet. Naugle.com can be a node in the domain acting as a name server, or there may be different name servers for Naugle.com.

A user at workstation 148.1.1.2 types in the TELNET command and the domain name of host1.research.Naugle.com. This workstation must have the domain name resolver installed on it. This program would send out the translation request to a domain name server to resolve the hostname-to-IP address. If the hostname is

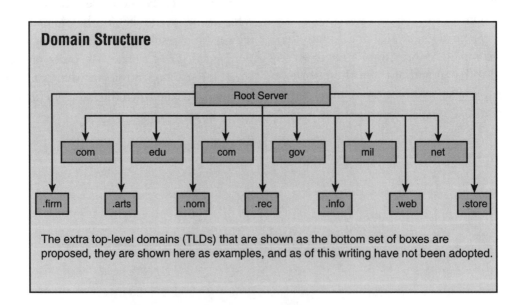

Domain Structure

The extra top-level domains (TLDs) that are shown as the bottom set of boxes are proposed, they are shown here as examples, and as of this writing have not been adopted.

found, the domain name server would return the IP address to the workstation. If the name is not found, the server may search for the name elsewhere and return the information to the requesting workstation, or return the address of a name server that the workstation (if able) can query to get more information. More on that in a moment. A domain contains all hosts whose domain names are within a certain domain. A domain name is a sequence of labels separated by dots. A domain is a subdomain of another domain if it is contained within that domain. This relationship can be tested by seeing if the subdomain's name ends with the containing domain's name. For example, research.Naugle.com is a subdomain of Naugle.com. Naugle.com is a subdomain of .com, and " " (root).

There are special servers on the Internet that provide guidance to all name servers. These are known as root name servers and, as of this writing, there are nine of them. They do not contain all information about every host on the Internet, but they do provide direction as to where domains are located (the IP address of the name server for the uppermost domain a server is requesting). The root name server is the starting point to find any domain on the Internet. If access to the root servers ceased, transmission over the Internet would eventually come to a halt.

Name Servers

The programs that keep information about the domain name space are called *name servers*. The name resolvers do not usually store information, nor are they programmed with information like a name server. All information is kept in the server.

Name servers keep information about some part of the name space, called a *zone*. Name servers can be "authoritative" about one or more zones. Being authoritative means that this server is all-knowing about the zone. A server can be authoritative for more than one zone, and it can be a primary name server for one zone and a secondary name server for another. However, these functions rarely cross; name servers are either primary or secondary for the zones they load.

There are two types of name servers: *primary masters* and *secondary masters*. The primary master builds its database from files that were preconfigured on its hosts, called *zone* or *database* files. The name server reads these files and builds a database for the zone it is authoritative for. Secondary masters can provide information to resolvers just like the primary masters, but they get their information from the primary. Any updates to the database are provided by the primary. This system was set up for ease of use. It is also important to note that there should be more than one name server per zone or domain.

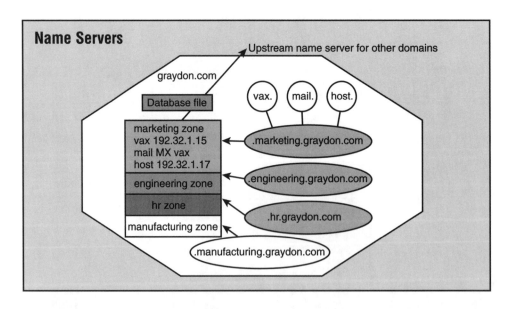

L et's take a simple example. You are a host on domain Naugle.com. Specifically, host1.research.Naugle.com. You are looking for a host named labhost.bnr.ca.us. You type in TELNET labhost.bnr.ca.us. The name server on your network is a primary and is not authoritative for the .us domain. Your name server then sends out a query to the root server that it knows about and that root server refers you to the name server for the .us domain. Your name server will send out a request to that name server for .ca. The .ca name server refers you to another name server authoritative for the domain bnr.ca. Your server then sends one final

request to that server for information on labhost.bnr.ca. That server responds with the IP address, which your server returns to your workstation. The TELNET protocol then uses that IP address to attempt a connection to your requested destination. A point to bring out here is that the information in the name server database is not dynamic in that it does not know of the status of any station (that station may be turned off, not accepting any new connections, etc). The name server function simply responds to requests for information that is contained in its database.

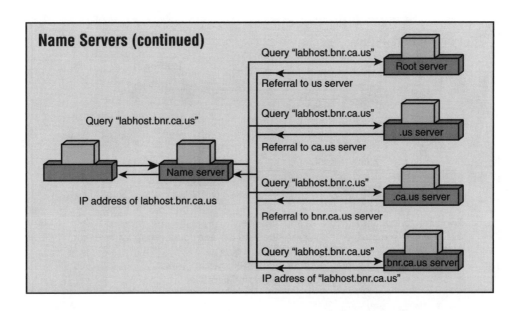

Query Function Types

There are two types of queries issued: *recursive* and *iterative*.

Recursive queries received by a server forces that server to find the information requested or post a message back to the querier that the information cannot be found. Iterative queries allow the server to search for the information and pass back the best information it knows about. This is the type that is used between servers. Clients used the recursive query. This is shown in the slide.

Generally (but not always), a server-to-server query is iterative and a client-resolver-to-server query is recursive.

You should also note that a server can be queried or it can be the person placing a query. Therefore, a server contains both the server and client functions.

A server can transmit either type of query. If it is handed a recursive query from a remote source, it must transmit other queries to find the specified name, or send a message back to the originator of the query that the name could not be found.

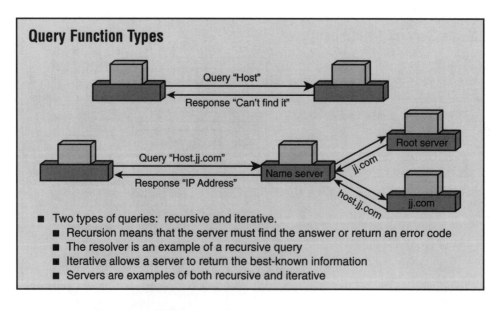

Query Function Types

- Two types of queries: recursive and iterative.
  - Recursion means that the server must find the answer or return an error code
  - The resolver is an example of a recursive query
  - Iterative allows a server to return the best-known information
  - Servers are examples of both recursive and iterative

Example DNS Database

- Records in the database include:
  - A—host's IP address
  - PTR—host's domain name, host identified by its IP address
  - CNAME—host's canonical name, host identified by an alias domain name
  - MX—host's or domain's mail exchanger
  - NS—host's or domain's name server(s)
  - SOA—Indicates authority for the domain
  - TXT—generic text record
  - SRV—service location record
  - RP—text name of the person responsible for the domain DNS

will know exactly what the resolver is requesting; this could be a mail server, an IP address translation, or simply a request for some generic information.

I am not going to explain *all* the records in the database, but some of the more useful ones are discussed next.

A database is made up of records and the DNS is a database. Therefore, common resource record types in the DNS database are:

A	Host's IP address,
PTR	Host's domain name, host identified by its IP address
CNAME	Host's canonical name, host identified by an alias domain name
MX	Host's or domain's mail exchanger
NS	Host's or domain's name server(s)
SOA	Indicates authority for the domain
TXT	Generic text record
SRV	Service location record
RP	Responsible person

When a resolvers requests information from the server, included in the request will be one of the preceding types. In this way, the server

SOA Record

The Start of Authority record is the first entry in the database file. This record indicates that the name server is the best-available source of information for this domain. For example:

```
Naugle.com.          IN        SOA              ns1.Naugle.com     Matt.NT1Server.Naugle.com.(
1567                           ;Serial
18000                          ;Refresh after 5 hours
3600                           ;Retry after 1 hour
604800                         ;Expire after 1 week
86400                          ;Minimum TTL of 1 day
```

The numeric entries above are indicated in seconds.

Notice that anything following a semicolon is ignored. The first entry on the first line indi-

cates the domain this server is authoritative for: Naugle.com. The next field indicates the class of data in Internet (other types are defined, but not used today). The first name after the SOA indi-

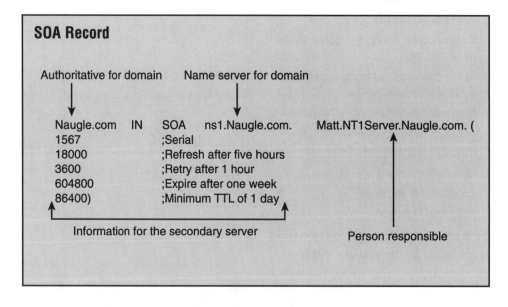

336   **Part Four: Beyond the IP Layer**

cates the primary name server for this domain, and the field after this indicates the person to contact. Replace the first "." with the @ symbol and send an email there for more information. The information contained in the parentheses is for the secondary name server. For example, the serial number on the primary name server should be incremented when new information is placed in the database. In this way, the secondary servers will know they have old information and should be updated by this primary.

Notice that some domain names are written with or without a dot at the end. The ones with a dot on the end are known as *absolute* names and they specify a domain name exactly as it lies in the hierarchy name space starting from the root. Those names that do not end with a dot are domain names that may trail from some other domain. This is again, best exemplified through the directory system. To change directories in DOS or Unix, you use the CD (CHDIR) command. With this you can specify directly from the root which directory you would like to change to, or you can change directories relative to another directory. You do not have to type in the full directory pathname each time you want to change directories.

This is the same for DNS using the dot to signify the full pathname (with the dot) and relative to another pathname (without the dot).

Name Server Records 255

Name Server Records

- Naugle.com. IN NS ns0.Naugle.com.
- Naugle.com. IN NS ns1.Naugle.com.
- Naugle.com. IN NS ns2.Naugle.com.
- Naugle.com. IN NS ns3.Naugle.com.
- Naugle.com. IN NS ns4.Naugle.com.

The next entry in our server database is for name server resource records. If you have five name servers in your domain, you should list them here.

```
Naugle.com.  IN  NS  ns0.Naugle.com.
Naugle.com.  IN  NS  ns1.Naugle.com.
Naugle.com.  IN  NS  ns2.Naugle.com.
Naugle.com.  IN  NS  ns3.Naugle.com.
Naugle.com.  IN  NS  ns4.Naugle.com.
```

The preceding entries indicate that there are five name servers for domain Naugle.com. Name servers can be multihomed (one station connected to more than one subnet).

The following indicates the name-to-IP-address mappings:

Localhost.Naugle.com.	IN	A	127.0.0.1
DatabaseServer.Naugle.com.	IN	A	128.1.1.1
HRServer.Naugle.com.	IN	A	128.1.15.1
EngServer.Naugle.com.	IN	A	128.1.59.150
NS0.Naugle.com.	IN	A	128.1.1.2
NS1.Naugle.com.	IN	A	128.1.15.2
NS2.Naugle.com.	IN	A	128.1.16.190
NS3.Naugle.com.	IN	A	128.1.59.100
NS4.Naugle.com.	IN	A	128.1.59.101

; Aliases

NT1Server.Naugle.com	IN	CNAME	DBServer.Naugle.com.
NT2.Naugle.com	IN	CNAME	HRServer.Naugle.com.
NT3.Naugle.com	IN	CNAME	EngServer.Naugle.com.

Address Records

LocalHost.Naugle.com.	IN	A	127.0.0.1
DatabaseServer.Naugle.com.	IN	A	128.1.1.1
HRServer.Naugle.com.	IN	A	128.1.15.1
EngServer.Naugle.com.	IN	A	128.1.59.150
NS0.Naugle.com.	IN	A	128.1.1.2
NS1.Naugle.com.	IN	A	128.1.15.2
NS2.Naugle.com.	IN	A	128.1.16.190
NS3.Naugle.com.	IN	A	128.1.59.100
NS4.Naugle.com.	IN	A	128.1.59.101

;Aliases

NT1.Naugle.com.	IN	CNAME DBServer.Naugle.com.	
NT2.Naugle.com.	IN	CNAME HRServer.Naugle.com.	

This file has new types: A (address) and CNAME (canonical name). The A record type stands for Address (A for 32-bit address, and AAAA for IPv6 addresses). There can be more than one address for a name, as in the case of a multihomed host (a host with a connection to more than one subnet). This could be stated as:

;multhomed hosts

NT5.Naugle.com	IN	A	128.1.60.5
	IN	A	128.1.61.5

Name servers will return the closest address to the requester, depending on the requester's address. If they are on the same network, the name server will place the closest address first. Since the DNS has no idea of route tables, if the requester and its network address are different, it will return both addresses. With each subsequent address, it will reverse the IP addresses in the response to provide some balance.

Aliases are just that, a name for another name. When a request comes in and the server finds a CNAME record, it replaces the name with the CNAME. It will then do another lookup, find the address, and return this to the requester.

One of the largest uses of the Internet is email, and DNS plays a major role in this as well. It does not send or receive mail, but it does provide information on the mail servers for a given name. In the database is a resource record of MX. DNS uses this single type of resource record for mail routing. It specifies a mail exchanger for a domain name. This mail exchanger is a host that will either process the mail or forward it on. Processing is simply the task of providing for delivery to the addressee or providing a path to another mail transport. It may also forward the mail to its final destination or pass it on to another mail exchanger in closer proximity of the recipient using SMTP (explained next). An example record is:

```
engineering.naugle.com.          IN          MX          5          mail.naugle.com.
```

What the preceding record states is the mail exchanger for the domain engineering.naugle.com is mail.naugle.com. The number (5, in this case) is a precedence value. It can range from 0 to 65535. If there is only one MX for a domain, this field is useless. For example:

```
engineering.naugle.com.          IN          MX          5          mail1.naugle.com.
engineering.naugle.com.          IN          MX          10         mail2.naugle.com.
```

Mail Exchange Records (MX)

engineering.naugle.com.	IN	MX	5	mail.naugle.com.
engineering.naugle.com.	IN	MX	5	mail1.naugle.com.
enginering.naugle.com.	IN	MX	10	mail2.naugle.com.

A mail program (such as SMTP) should use the mail exchanger with the lowest value first. If this fails, the next one associated with that domain is used. If there are no records associated with a domain or host, the mail must be able to deliver the message directly, and some versions of mail senders have this capability. The most common mail transport out there today is called *sendmail*.

Playing with the Database 258

Playing with the Database

- nslookup <domain name> <IP Address>

- Go to Web site:
  ://ds/internic.net/cool/dns.html

- Use this to see if a domain name is already assigned!!

There is a program available (not usually available on Windows 95, but is on all Unix systems) called *nslookup*. This is a program that transmits queries to a specified name server. If you have this program, you can use it and another name server to supply information to you.

nslookup <domain name such as starburst-com.com) 198.49.25.10

With the preceding command and arguments you are asking a name server whose address is 198.49.25.10 (this is one of the

InterNIC's name servers) to supply information about a domain such as starburstcom.com.

If you have access to the Web, then head up to the InterNIC (US, RIPE for Europe, and APNIC for Asia Pacific) Point your browser to: ds.internic.net/cool/dns.html.

All the records for the domains that it is authoritative for (which are all the top-level domains: .com, .net, etc.) are there. Check "any information" plus the ANY radio dial button and see what comes back.

259 WHOIS Command

Another useful utility is WHOIS. This command is included with most Unix systems, but for those who do not have access to their Unix systems or are using Windows, the InterNIC provides this function at:

r s . i n t e r n i c . n e t / c g i - b i n / w h o i s

> Whois ascend.com

Ascend Communications, Inc.
ASCEND-DOM
1275 Harbor Bay Pkwy
Alameda, CA 94502
Domain name: ASCEND.COM

Administrative contact, technical contact, zone contact:

Rochon, Lyle LR88
lrochon@ASCEND.COM (510) 769-6001
Record last updated on 10-Jul-97.
Record created on 05-Dec-90.
Database last updated on 3-Aug-97
04:39:20 EDT.
Domain servers in listed order:
DRAWBRIDGE.ASCEND.COM
198.4.92.1
NS.UU.NET

WHOIS Command

- Enables you to get more information on domain names, networks, etc., on the Web.
- ://ds.internic.net/cgi-bin/whois.
- "whois ascend.com" (without the quotes).
- Details Ascend.com domain such as:
  - Administrative contact (who to call)
  - Domain servers
- Can determine IP address blocks.
  - WHOIS net 192.1
  - BBN Corporation NETBLK-BBN-C NETBLK BBN-NCETBLK 192.1.0.0-192.1.255.255

Let's say you wanted to find out who owned the 192.1 Class C block of addresses. At the whois server you would type in **whois net 192.1** and a listing would follow:

BBN Corporation
NETBLK-BBN-CNETBLK BBN-CNET-BLK   192.1.0.0 - 192.1.255.255

Actually, there was a lot more information listed but it was too much for this page. Try it yourself and see what happens! You can use the InterNIC's whois server as shown previously or TELNET into their server by typing **Telnet whois.internic.net**. After you have a connection, type in the command WHOIS and you should get the WHOIS prompt. From there you can check on person (whois pe robbins), domain (whois dom baynetworks.com), and network numbers (whois net 192.32). Pretty cool stuff and very, very open!

DNS is available through a program known as BIND (Berkeley Internet Name Domain, and not pronounced BIN-DEE). It is available on most Unix and Windows NT systems. It is customizable through example files that are included. Most implementations simply set up for their hosts and point to an upstream root name server for reference to other sites on the Internet.

BIND (DNS) ships with most versions of Unix, but if for some reason it does not, you can download BIND from the following site:

www.isc.org

This site also contains information on DHCP and Windows NT port of BIND (not supported).

There are many sites around the Web to assist you (for a small charge) with DNS. DNS can be a daunting task, especially for large installations. You may want to consult help for your first install. Otherwise, once you get the hang of it and read a few books on DNS, you will see how simplistic it is. One of the best (and only) books about this is *DNS and BIND* by Paul Albitz and Cricket Liu (O'Rielly) ISBN 1-56592-236-0.

More DNS Information

- **2136 PS:** P. Vixie, S. Thomson, Y. Rekhter, J. Bound, "Dynamic Updates in the Domain Name System (DNS UPDATE)", 04/21/97 (26 pages).

- **2137 PS:** D. Eastlake, "Secure Domain Name System Dynamic Update," 04/21/97 (11 pages) (.txt format).

- **1996 PS:** P. Vixie, "A Mechanism for Prompt Notification of Zone Changes (DNS NOTIFY)," 08/28/96 (7 pages) (.txt format).

- **1995 PS:** M. Ohta, "Incremental Zone Transfer in DNS", 08/28/96 (8 pages) (.txt format).

- www.isc.org

- DNS and BIND
  Book by Paul Albitz and Cricket Liu
  ISBN 1-56592-236-0

Simple Mail Transfer Protocol (SMTP)

- Today known as Electronic Mail, or email.

- RFCs 821, 822, 974.

- Email still cannot transport packages and other items.

- Email is very fast and guarantees delivery.

- Three protocols are used for today's email:
  - SMTP—operates over TCP
  - POP—operates over TCP
  - DNS—operates over UDP

- SMTP allows for the sending/receiving of email.

- POP allows us to intermittently retrieve email.

- DNS makes it simple.

RFC 822 defines the structure for the message, and RFC 821 specifies the protocol that is used to exchange the mail between two network stations. It truly is amazing how old the original mail protocol is, and it is still in use today.

So we have email to send to one another, completely bypassing the postal system. There are some who call the postal system "snail mail." True, if stated without emotion; otherwise, I call these people who state that arrogant. Many people today still immensely enjoy receiving a handwritten letter from a family member, friend, or a business correspondence through the postal system. Suffice it to say that the postal system will be here for many years to come.

Also, I have the hardest time sending packages through the email system and some I do

get through (attachments) get banged up along the way. Yes, the postal system is old and cranky, but it works, and in some cases better than email. But this is an electronic discussion and I will keep it at that. Email does have many, many advantages and one of the top advantages is speed. The biggest disadvantage: lack of emotion. Like everything else, email has its place, but it is not 100 percent of the pie; it is merely another form of communication.

In order to send and receive mail between users, there are actually two protocols (possibly three) that are used:

SMTP: Used for the actual transport of mail between two entities (mail servers).

POP (Post Office Protocol): A protocol that allows single users to collect their mail on one server.

DNS: Used to identify the mail hosts for a domain or hostname.

Mail can be sent and received using only SMTP, but the other protocol involvement makes it much easier to use and is more efficient. This section will concentrate on SMTP and POP. The hooks into DNS were already explained in the *Mail Exchanger* section of DNS and are shown again on slide 264. SMTP was created first and then POP, so I will start with the SMTP protocol. This is a protocol that allows users to transmit messages (mail) between other users. It is one of the most widely used applications of the TCP/IP protocol.

262 SMTP Functions

The protocol is relatively simple. A message will be created, properly addressed, and sent from a local application to the SMTP application, which will store the message. The server will then check (at periodic intervals) to see if there are any messages to deliver. If there are, the mail server will try to deliver the message. If the intended recipient is not available at the time of delivery, the mail server will try again later. The mail server will try a few times to deliver the message and, if it cannot, will either delete the message or return it to the sender.

The address has the general format of local-part@domain-name. By this, you should recognize the domain name format. For example, an address at the SMTP header could be matt@engineering.naugle.com. This would indicate that the message is addressed to a user named Matt in the domain of engineering.naugle.com. When DNS is used to look up the mail handler for Matt, it will have some sort of entry like:

engineering.naugle.co IN MX 10 NT1mail_server.engineering.naugle.com.

From this, the name will be looked up and the mail will be delivered to that host.

There are two entities to this system, the *sender* SMTP and the *receiver* SMTP, that are used to transport mail between two systems. The sender SMTP will establish communications with a receiver SMTP. Attachments are allowed with Internet email but not directly with the protocol used in SMTP (sendmail protocol). The Internet email mailer program

SMTP Functions

- A message is created, properly addressed, and transmitted using SMTP sender, which transmits it to an SMTP receiver, which stores the file.

- Address has the format of:
  - local-part@domain-name
  - Example: matt@naugle.com
  - Mail service record in DNS:
    - naugle.com IN MX 10 NT1mail_server.eng.naugle.com

- SMTP was set up to handle only text.
  - Based on the history of the protocol

- Email applications convert using a variety of protocols like MIME (Multipurpose Internet Mail Extensions).

SMTP (or more specific, sendmail) can only handle text. Therefore, most email applications convert an attachment to text before sending. A common type is MIME (Multipurpose Internet Mail Extensions, beyond the scope of this book). At the receiver, the email application converts the attachment back to its original format.

The SMTP design is based on the following model of communication:

Once you have filled out the header and body section of your mail message, the sender SMTP establishes two-way communication to a receiver SMTP. The receiver SMTP may be either the ultimate destination or a transient stop on the way to the final destination. Commands are sent to the receiver by the sender SMTP and SMTP replies are sent from the receiver SMTP to the sender SMTP in response to each of the commands.

Once two-way communication has been established, a series of commands (of which you can see operate using some mail applications) are issued. The sender SMTP will send a HELLO (HELO) command identifying who it is using its domain name to the receiver. The receiver acknowledges this with a reply using its domain name. Next, the server issues a MAIL command to the receiver. In this will be the identification of the person (place, or thing) sending the mail. The receiver acknowledges this with an OK. The sender SMTP then sends a RCPT command to the receiver, using the intended receiver name as an argument. Each recipient in the list is sent to the receiver one at a time, and each time the receiver acknowledges with an OK for those recipients that it knows about. For those that it does not know about (different domain name), it will send back a different reply that it is forwarding the message on. For any intended recipients received from the SMTP

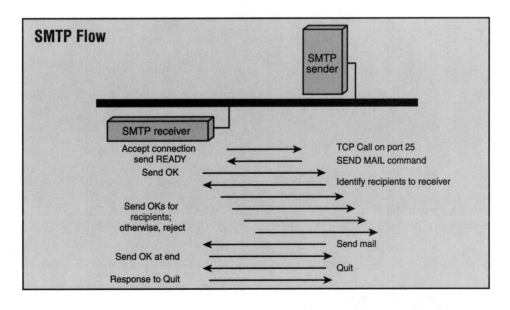

sender for which it has no account, the receiver will reply to the sender that no such user(s) exists. After the intended recipients have been ACK'd or NACK'd, the SMTP sender sends the DATA command and the SMTP receiver will OK this and indicate what the end of message identifier should be. Once this is received (the ending identifier), the SMTP receiver will reply with an OK. Notice that all data is received, the ending identifier is received, and then a reply message is sent by the receiver.

If everything went okay, the sender ends the connection with a QUIT command. The SMTP receiver will reply indicating that the communication channel is closed. The minimum commands that a receiver must support are HELO, MAIL, RCPT, DATA, RSET, NOOP, and QUIT.

Depending on the mail program that you use, the transaction between a recipient and sender of mail has been the same since RFC 821 was written. The interface allows you to complete the mail message, filling in the header (addresses and subject) and the body (text) of the letter. When you press the Send button, the following transaction takes place. Some mail programs actually place the mail commands and state numbers on display while the transaction is taking place. It should be noted here that sending mail is immediate. It may get queued for a small length of time on different routers, and transient mail servers, but not for long. This is for the transport of mail. Most electronic mail today is sent via SMTP and will reside on your mail server host until you retrieve it using POP (discussed next). Today, retrieving your mail does not mean that you have to run the SMTP protocol. A server host will accept mail messages directed to you on your behalf. Then you can sign on any time you want and retrieve your mail.

The following slide shows the interaction with DNS for the mail service.

A record known as the MX record in DNS identifies a mail exchanger for the purpose of identifying hosts for recipients. A mail exchanger is a host that will either process or forward mail for the domain name. Processing means that the host will deliver it the host to which it is addressed or hand it off to another transport, such as UUCP or BITNET. Forwarding means that the host will forward the message on to the final destination or to another mail exchanger closer to the destination.

There can be multiple entries for a mail exchanger in a DNS. Each MX entry will have a precedence number beside it and this signals the sender which mail host it should try first. If the precedence value is equal among MX records, then the sender will randomly pick one from the list. Once the mail sender has successfully delivered the mail to one of the MX hosts, its job is done. It is the job of the MX host to make sure it is forwarded on to its final destination. If there are no MX records for a domain name, it is up to the mailer app as to what happens next. Some will try to deliver it to the IP address of the mail destination.

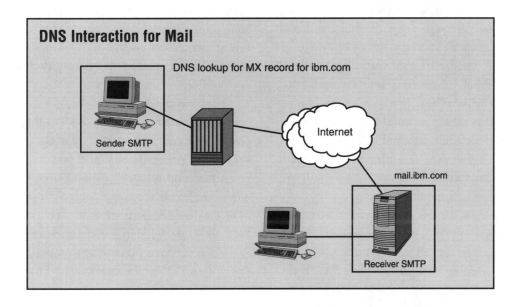

DNS Interaction for Mail

DNS lookup for MX record for ibm.com

Sender SMTP

Internet

mail.ibm.com

Receiver SMTP

265

Post Office Protocol (POP)

The original mail program RFC 821 (which is the one in use today) was set up to send messages directly to a user logged in to a terminal, as well as store these messages to a mailbox. The commands allowed for the receiver to determine if the user was logged on to a terminal (not a PC), if they were accepting messages, and if they were not, is there a mailbox to deliver some mail to. There were no message attachments and messages were sent and received in 7-bit ASCII (8th bit was set to 0); therefore, this would not allow for binary messages to be sent (i.e., no attachments). In fact, the original message was not to exceed 1000 characters (however, implementations that could go beyond this barrier were strongly encouraged to do so).

So, to operate mail, the host must be operational (able to receive) all the time. Today, terminals do exist, but more commonly, personal computers have taken their place. Therefore, the final recipient will be the personal computer. The personal computer will have both SMTP and POP. Even though a personal computer will retrieve its mail via POP, it will still use the SMTP functions to send its mail. Since SMTP expects to be able to deliver mail immediately, this would mean that all users would have to have their personal computers on 100 percent of the time in order to accept mail. Second, to receive and read your mail, you must log on to a specific host.

To operate a mail server generally requires that the mail server is available for a majority of the time, has the ability to store many mail messages, and is able to fully run SMTP and

Post Office Protocol (POP)
■ SMTP is set up to send and receive mail by hosts that are up full time.
■ No rules for those hosts that are intermittent on the LAN
■ POP emulates you as a host on the network.
■ It receives SMTP mail for you to retrieve later
■ POP accounts are set up for you by an ISP or your company.
■ POP retrieves your mail and downloads it to your personal computer when you sign on to your POP account.

accept mail from an SMTP sender. While this may have been feasible for situations like terminal-to-host connectivity, it is not feasible for situations that we have today; namely, personal computers and mobile workers. SMTP is a very robust transaction-oriented protocol and requires the statements previously discussed to operate fully.

What we need is the ability for SMTP to operate (drop off the mail, like a PO Box at the post office), and then another protocol to download to our personal computers (we drop by the post office and retrieve our mail from the post office box.). POP is the protocol to allow for this. Mail can be delivered to a drop-off point and POP allows us to log in and retrieve our mail.

When you sign up with an Internet Service Provider, a POP account is assigned to you; for example, mnaugle@POP3.ISP1.com. You use this when configuring your mail program. Also, when sending mail you must give the SMTP server name to the configuration program as well. The protocol of POP3 is not used for sending mail.

POP Operation 266

POP3 should be viewed only to retrieve your mail from the mail drop-off point. *Sending* mail is a different story. Your personal computer still has the ability to establish a TCP connection to a relay host (intermediate mail host) to send mail. Therefore, you should consider your host as having the ability to be an SMTP sender, and the SMTP protocol explained earlier applies. However, to retrieve your mail, POP3 comes into play.

The client (your PC with a mail application such as Eudora), once established with TCP/IP on its network, builds a connection to the POP3 server. The POP3 server configuration is built during the installation of your mail program on the PC. The connection between your PC and the POP3 server is a TCP connection on TCP port 110. Similar to SMTP, once the connection is established, the server will respond with a greeting like "POP3 server ready."

The POP3 protocol then enters the authentication state. During this phase, you must identify yourself with a username and password. The RFC does not indicate which authentication mechanism you should use. The most common is the simple username/password combination. However, other options are available, such as Kerberos and APOP, which are beyond the scope of this book. Once you have been "authenticated," the POP3 server puts an exclusive lock on your mailbox, ensuring that no other transactions take place on the messages while you are retrieving your mail.

The server now enters the transaction state in which each of the messages in your mailbox is assigned a number. This allows your client POP to indicate how many messages are in your mailbox. Each message can be retrieved one at a time or all can be retrieved. Furthermore, you can instruct your client POP to delete messages as they are retrieved. This can be good and bad. It would be nice to hold on to your messages as a backup on the server, but this requires disk space that can be depleted quickly.

From here, you retrieve your messages and, depending on how you configured you PC mail program, the messages are marked for deletion after your session. After you retrieve your messages, your mail program will send the QUIT command, which closes the POP3 session down. Then the UPDATE process begins on the server, which is housekeeping work on the server (deleting messages, etc.).

From here, you can read your messages locally on your PC. You are now disconnected from the POP3 server and you can manipulate the messages locally. There are many other options available for POP3 which may or may not be implemented; however, from a users' point of view, they are not noticed.

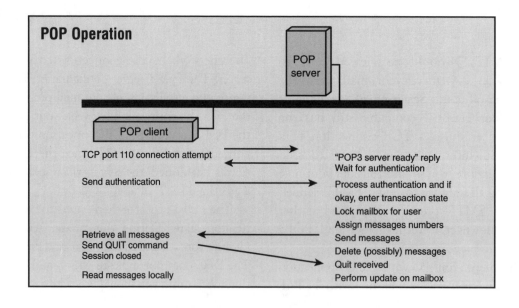

POP Operation

POP server

POP client

TCP port 110 connection attempt → "POP3 server ready" reply
Wait for authentication

Send authentication → Process authentication and if okay, enter transaction state
Lock mailbox for user
Assign messages numbers

Retrieve all messages ← Send messages
Send QUIT command Delete (possibly) messages
Session closed → Quit received

Read messages locally Perform update on mailbox

The following slide shows the relationship between SMTP, DNS, and POP. In this example, mail is sent from your PC to Joe's PC. In order to accomplish this, the send mail (SMTP) program is established to the SMTP server on your ISP. A DNS lookup is accomplished using the root DNS server to find the domain of the intended recipient. A call is made to recipients DNS to find the mail server (which could be the same server as the DNS). Once the mail server is found (its IP address is found), mail is sent to that server. The POP function delivers it to your mail box on that mail server so that when Joe's PC retrieves mail, your mail message will be waiting.

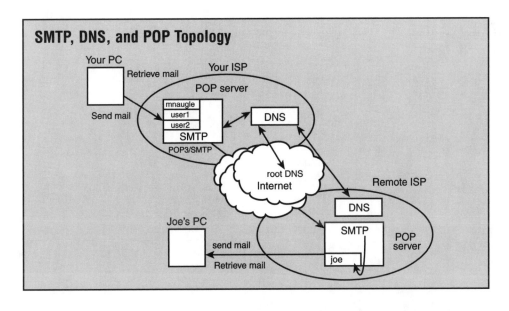

Part Five

IP Multicast

268 Introduction

With addressing, as I have mentioned before, there are three types with IPv4: point-to-point (unicast), point-to-multipoint (multicast), and point-to-all-multipoints (broadcast). But multicast as it pertains to IP is much more than a simple address; it's what enables IP to deliver multimedia over a packet switched network with very little bandwidth consumption (relative to pushing the data to the same recipients using unicast).

You will often hear the pseudo-technical term *push* or *pull* technology. This means you have to go and get the information off the Internet (pull), or the information comes to you (push). There is a vast array of information in the Internet and finding it can be a daunting task. Push technology means that information is sent to you. An example of this can be an information news service that retrieves infor-

mation on certain subjects throughout the day. A lot of readers have probably heard of PointCast. This is an example of a pseudo-push technology that will eventually be a full-blown push technology. Whenever information changes on that news server, stories related to your requests are pushed down to your workstation, saving you the trouble of finding and downloading the information.

Another exciting evolution is the ability to have voice and video run over an IP network. I know, it can be accomplished today, but I am not fond of viewing a 2" × 2" fuzzy screen that has incredible delay and non-lip sync audio. It is like watching an old Japanese movie that has been converted to English. Frame reception at 5 fps is not great. It is fun to experiment, but until it appears like CATV (cable TV), users

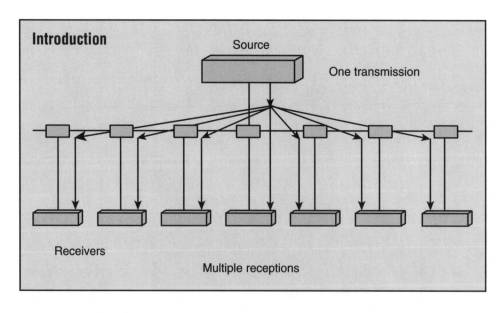

will not consider it as a serious requirement for the LAN infrastructure.

Another advancement on the Internet is voice and video over IP. Replicating a separate stream of data for every user request to a single video source would easily overload the Internet. The ability to transmit one packet and have it replicated at certain points along the many paths to separate destinations is a much more efficient system of distributing data, voice, and video. Multicasting allows this as well.

Multicast Components 269

There are four components to a multicast network: multicast-enabled host NIC, multicast-enabled TCP/IP software, multicast-enabled infrastructure (routers, switches, etc.), and multicast-enabled applications.

Do not confuse the operation of IP multicast as a standalone application. This operates on the very same workstation that you are using today to access IP applications and/or the Internet. IP multicast peacefully coexists with your IP applications.

IP multicast usually does not operate alone; there are other protocols that are used in conjunction with it to provide for VVD (voice, video, and data) over IP. Such protocols are Real Time Protocol (RTP) and the Real Time Control Protocol (RTCP), Real Time Streaming Protocol (RTSP), and Resource Reservation Protocol (RSVP). Similar to this is IP. There are many components to the TCP/IP network and IP is simply one of the components. It provides for datagram delivery. IP multicast is also a component of many. IP multicast is based on a few protocols, but it is all the other necessary components that really make it work.

Berkeley Sockets for Multicast provides an API set that easily enables most Unix hosts to become multicast ready, and Microsoft is supporting multicast in its sockets interface known as WinSock 2.0. With the APIs in place, multicast applications can be built.

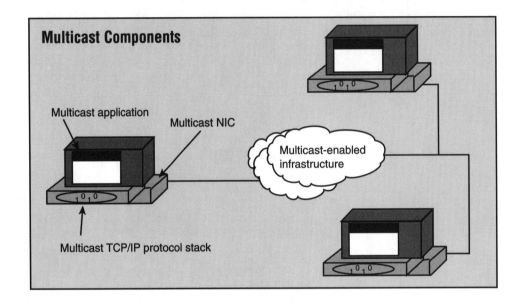

Multicast Caveats

- Multicast is not simply a "turn it on and it works" protocol.
  - Much thought must go into implementing a multicast network

- There are many protocols that run with multicast.

- Multicast requires as much thought to implement as OSPF.
  - Many different types of protocols can be implemented and some are still experimental

- WAN networks as well as LANs must be considered.
  - Frame relay is still only partially multicast ready
  - The Internet is not multicast ready

- There is a learning curve with multicast.

Multicast transmission and reception can take place anywhere it is enabled. There are, however, a few obstructions in the path to widespread implementation of multicast: routers and switches must be multicast ready; the backbone of your internet must be multicast ready; the WAN must be multicast ready; and so on and so on. Add to this the general lack of knowledge and ample studies on the effects of multicast and you should be able to see why implementation is slow. The Unicast forwarding Internet currently plays a part in multicast, but only as a transport between multicast-enabled networks. Tunnels can be built across the Internet using the loose source routing feature of IP. In this way, two "islands" of multicast can be connected together to provide connectivity. Otherwise, the Internet (at the time of this writing) is not multicast-enabled and probably won't be for some years to come.

Many corporate networks have moved to frame relay as their WAN protocol, which consists of the customer device (called the CPE for customer premise equipment, usually a router) and the frame relay provider's equipment (frame relay switches). Making the frame relay cloud multicast ready, however, is not that easy. There are many studies and tests that have to be performed to see how multicast reacts to an existing network that has many customers already enabled who expect 99.999 percent uptime. The frame relay providers will multicast-enable their WAN networks, but it may not happen for a while.

Corporate networks are not multicast-enabled either. These environments have just redone their topologies to allow for ATM and LAN switches to be employed and are now looking at multicast. Most corporate environments do not even realize that their routers are multicast-ready and believe that new equipment must be purchased before multicast is enabled. All routers support the multicast protocol of IGMP. Most routers support the multicast routing practice of DMVRP, PIM, and a few support MOSPF. These will be discussed in detail later but suffice it to say, these are software features that can be turned on, but very carefully. Multicast may be an extension of the IP protocol, but routing multicast packets is a different story.

Unicast (versus Multicast)

For example, let's say that the end of the month sales report is complete and needs to be transmitted to 200 file servers around the country. With unicast addressing, one could write a simple script that would initiate a file transfer to each of the 200 file servers. If the file is 2 MB in length, you now have a 400 MB file transfer that will unnecessarily consume both time and bandwidth.

Enabling multicast would push that one file to the 200 file servers simultaneously, reducing the number of file transfers from 200 to 1, and the size of the file from 400 MB to 2 MB.

One example in which multicast file transfer is used extensively is software distribution. Microsoft and other application companies upgrade their software at least twice a year—a daunting task in large environments. If the upgrade is 20 MB and must be distributed to 50,000 desktops, it would require 1000 billion bytes to be delivered. Assuming the transfer occurs at 512,000 bits per second, the upgrade would take 180 days to complete. And just when you completed one upgrade, the next one is ready.

However, using reliable multicasting, the file could be delivered to 50,000 desktops as a single stream. This means one transfer looks like 50,000. With multicast, the same transmission would complete in 5.2 hours. (This number assumes no real-time errors such as retransmissions. Retransmission costs are variable depending on the number of clients

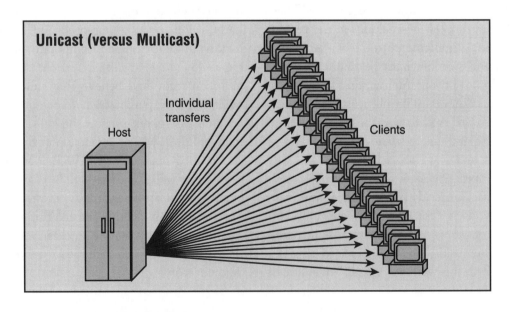

Unicast (versus Multicast)

Individual transfers

Host

Clients

requesting, the status of the lines, etc.) Even so, the worst cost is less than 25 percent of the original pass. The example is theory, but if put into practice I believe that it would be around the number indicated. Even if it took 10 hours to complete, look at the alternative.

Therefore, the advantages to multicast-enabled applications and networks are time savings and scaleable bandwidth.

Multicast (versus Unicast) 272

As noted from the slide, multicast is one stream of packets that is heard by many receivers all using the same IP multicast address as their receiving IP interface. IP multicast places the burden of packet replication on the network via the IP multicast address and routers that are able to forward received multicast packets to more than one port.

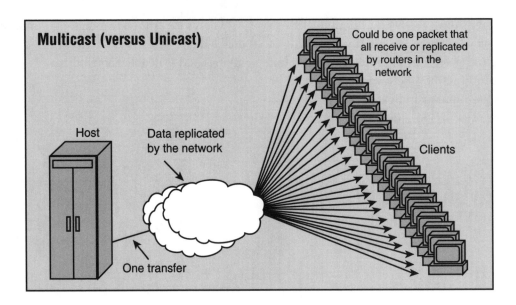

273   Multicasting Type

There are two types of data transmission normally associated with multicasting: *real-time* and *nonreal-time*.

Real-time transmission is the ability to work with the information while it is being transmitted. Two examples of this are video and voice transmissions. Nonreal-time transmission is the ability to transfer the information for use at a later time, directly after the transfer or days later. Examples include CBT files, kiosk, or any type of data file. Both types of transmission have their purposes in the multicast arena. However, nonreal-time trans-

Multicasting Types

- Two types of data multicasting:
  - Real-time and nonreal-time

- Real-time transfers are those that are used as the transfer is occurring.
  - Examples include voice and video such as voice over IP, movies, video conferencing, etc.

- Nonreal-time are those transfers that are multicast but the data is used at a later time.
  - Kiosk, CBI, store-and-forward video

missions are more applicable today because their use is not immediate.

Real-time transfers such as video and voice are still in the experimental stage. Transferring information across a network that is packet switched without some capability for priority is experimental. In some environments, it works rather well (on a single subnet), but when transported across an internet, the quality deteriorates and therefore the interest in the products wanes. There are protocols that are experimental (RSVP) that should assist real-time multicast protocols by providing bandwidth to the application instead of to the network.

Some real-time multicast transfers use a simplex approach that makes it "real near" real-time—they buffer the incoming data for about 30 seconds and start the play. While the information is being used, the application continues to buffer the incoming data for playback. Not perfect, but it's better than nothing.

Addressing Type Review 274

Addressing Type Review

- IPv4 has three address types:
  - Unicast: A one-to-one IP transfer
  - Broadcast: A one-to-all IP transfer
  - Multicast: A one-to-many-but-not-all transfer

The example given in the preceding section is simple, but very real. However, there are many applications today that require a one-to-many or many-to-many type of transmission and reception (e.g., audio and video, stock ticker, workgroup applications, electronic whiteboards, etc.). All of these applications can have one or more senders and one or more receivers. In IPv4, there are three types of addresses:

Unicast: A unique address that allows one host to receive a datagram.

Broadcast: An address that allows every host to receive a datagram.

Multicast: An address that allows a specific group to receive a datagram.

Unicast is the ability to uniquely identify a host on a subnet or internet. The transmission and reception is accomplished in a one-to-one relationship. A broadcast address is exactly that: An address that is received by every host on the subnet. Routers (with exceptions like DHCP and BOOTP) will not forward datagrams that have a local broadcast address. A multicast address is one that allows a specific group of hosts to receive a datagram, while all others ignore the datagram. For this conversation, we will stay with multicasting as it applies to the IP protocol.

275 Introduction to IP Multicast

According to RFC 1112, "Host Extensions for IP Multicasting," the following is the description of IP multicasting:

IP multicasting is the transmission of an IP datagram to a "host group," a set of zero or more hosts identified by a single IP destination address. A multicast datagram is delivered to all members of its destination host group with the same "best-effort" reliability as regular unicast IP datagrams; i.e., the datagram is not guaranteed to arrive intact at all members of the destination group or in the same order relative to other datagrams.

The membership of a host group is dynamic; that is, hosts may join and leave groups at any time. There is no restriction on the location or number of members in a host group. A host may be a member of more than one group at a time. A host need not be a member of a group to send datagrams to it.

As you learn more about IP multicasting, you will realize, that this protocol is simply an extension of the IP protocol itself. It does not

Introduction to IP Multicast

- RFC 1112.

- "IP multicast is the transmission of an IP datagram to a 'host group,' a set of zero or more hosts identified by a single IP destination address."

- Membership is dynamic; hosts may join and leave at any time.

- No restriction on the location or the number of members in a group.

- A host need not be a member of a group to send datagrams to it.

- IP multicast is not a separate protocol, but an extension of the IP protocol.

- A host can provide three levels of support:
  - No support, send only, and send/receive

replace the IP protocol and, in fact, it adds a few functions to the IP protocol to allow a host to send and receive multicast datagrams. This is similar to the way ICMP works with IP.

There are three levels associated with multicast:

Level 0: No support for multicast.

Level 1: The ability to send multicast but not receive.

Level 2: The ability to both send and receive multicast packets.

Extensions to the IP Service Interface

276

The normal IP transmission logic is as simple as:

If the IP destination is on the same local network, send the datagram locally directly to the destination. If not, send the datagram locally to a router.

Since multicasting is nothing more than an extension of the IP protocol, the logic is simply expanded:

If the IP destination is on the same local network or if it is a host group, send the datagram directly to the destination. If

neither, send the datagram locally to a router.

Notice that the multicast host does not specifically look for a router, even though members of the host group may be multiple hops away. Multicast datagrams are not addressed to a router, but multicast datagrams can be reached through an internet—they do not have to remain local. Multicast datagrams that span subnets require routers and these routers must be running a special multicasting protocol (a few of which will be explained next. When a host transmits a multicast packet, it simply transmits the packet out its interface using the normal IP datagram transmission (shown). In this way, all the hosts that belong to the same group on the local network receive and process this datagram. If the TTL field (known as the *scope*) is greater than 1, the multicast routers receive and forward this packet out their interfaces towards all other networks that belong to that group. (How the router determines which interfaces belong to that group is discussed in the section, "DVMRP.") Therefore, the router is also a member of the host group. The receiving router decrements the TTL and forwards the packet as a local multicast on its networks that are participating in that group.

In multicasting, a router is considered part of the group as well as individual hosts.

Extensions to the IP Service Interface

- An addition to the IP interface for sending datagrams is simply looking to see if the destination is a host group.
    - If it is, then forward the datagram to the host group interfaces

- The router is a member of the multicast group.

- A router is simply another multicast interface (a host).

- The router is used to simply make a determination if it should forward the packet based on the group address and not the network address.

- A field in the datagram packet determines how far the packet should be forwarded.

Receiving Multicast Datagrams

- Datagrams are received like unicast datagrams with the exception that a host must "join" a group before it can receive multicast datagrams.

- The IP Service Interface was extended to include two new operations:
  - JoinHostGroup (group-address, interface)
  - LeaveHostGroup (group-address, interface)

- The receiver must join each multicast group from which it wishes to receive multicast datagrams.

- When the station no longer wants to receive multicast datagrams for a group, it issues the LeaveHostGroup.

Multicast IP datagrams are received using the same Receive IP operation as normal, unicast datagrams. However, before any datagrams destined to a particular group can be received, an upper-layer protocol (an application) must ask the IP module to join that group. Thus, the IP service interface must be extended to provide two new operations: JoinHostGroup (group-address, interface) and LeaveHostGroup (group-address, interface).

The JoinHostGroup operation requests that this host become a member of the host group identified by "group-address" on the given network interface. The LeaveGroup operation requests that this host give up its membership in the host group identified by "group-address" on the given network interface. The interface specifies a unique interface for those IP hosts having more than one interface. If you have more than one interface, you can join the same group on each of the interfaces; however, this will allow you to receive duplicate multicast datagrams. More than one application may request to join the same group; the port numbers will differentiate the applications.

The possibility exists for each operation to not work. Since an application can join any group, multiple applications or one application may join many groups, which can lead to resource problems. JoinHostGroup may fail due to lack of local resources. A multicast membership may persist even after an application has requested the LeaveHostGroup, due to the fact that other applications may be using that host group. Remember, a group is a range of hosts that can receive and transmit IP datagrams using a specific IP class D address. A group of hosts all use the same (unique) class D address to indicate the group.

278

Address Format

We know all about the address formats of Classes A, B, and C. The address format that allows for multicast address is known as the Class D address. It is reserved by IANA and has a range of 224.0.0.0 to 239.255.255.255. This allows for 2^{28} bits (groups) for multicast addressing. The base address, 224.0.0.0, is reserved and cannot be assigned to any group. Furthermore, IANA has reserved the range of 224.0.0.1 through 224.0.0.255 for the use of routing protocols, topology discovery, and maintenance protocols. What is interesting is that no router that receives a datagram with this address range is allowed to forward it. It must either consume or discard (filter) the datagram. Other addresses of interest according to RFC 1700 are:

Address Format

■ IP multicast addresses are Class D addresses.

■ They range from 224.0.0.0 through 239.255.255.255.

■ The address of 224.0.0.0 is reserved.

■ The address range of 224.0.0.1 through 224.0.0.255 is reserved for the use of routing protocols.
  ■ Not necessarily generic multicast datagrams. OSPF uses 224.0.0.5 as an AllOSPFRouters multicast address.

■ The reserved ranges are not allowed to be forwarded by a router.
  ■ It must either consume or discard the datagram.

224.0.0.0	Base Address (Reserved)		[RFC1112]	
224.0.0.1	All Systems on This Subnet		[RFC1112]	
224.0.0.2	All Routers on This Subnet			
224.0.0.3	Unassigned			
224.0.0.4	DVMRP	Routers	[RFC1075]	
224.0.0.5	OSPFIGP	OSPFIGP All Routers	[RFC1583]	
224.0.0.6	OSPFIGP	OSPFIGP Designated Routers	[RFC1583]	
224.0.0.7	ST Routers	[RFC1190]		
224.0.0.8	ST Hosts	[RFC1190]		
224.0.0.9	RIP2 Routers	[RFC1723]		
224.0.0.10	IGRP Routers	[Cisco]		
224.0.0.11	Mobile-Agents			
224.0.0.12	DHCP Server / Relay Agent	[RFC1884]		
224.0.0.12–224.0.0.255	Unassigned	[IANA]		

Network interface cards are not interested in any type of Layer 3 addressing. NICs receive and transmit data on the network using MAC (Media Access Control) or hardware addresses. Therefore, some type of mapping must be used to map an IP multicast address to a MAC address. But the NIC plays an important role in receiving multicast packets. Somehow, there has to be a MAC address for multicast, and one for all multicast packets is not efficient. You should note that up to 32 different IP multicast groups may be converted to the same MAC address. The upper 5 bits of the IP address are ignored. It looks like the upper 9 bits, but the first four bits of a Class D address are always 1110 (which converts to a 224 in decimal, the starting number for Class D addresses), and since 9 bits are displaced in this procedure, only the next 5 bits are really

ignored. If you read through RFC 1700 you will see that most of the assigned addresses will not be affected by this procedure.

When used on an Ethernet or IEEE 802 network, the 23 low-order bits of the IP multicast address are placed in the low-order 23 bits of the Ethernet or IEEE 802 net multicast address. The IANA has been allocated a reserved block of MAC layer addresses. Therefore, a multicast MAC address always begins with 01-00-5E (hex).

For example, refer to the slide. The IP multicast address 224.0.1.88 is mapped into a MAC address (converted to hex). First, the IP address must be converted to hex (it is usually written in dotted decimal notation as shown). The address 224 is E0 in hex, 0 is 00 in hex, 1 is 01 in hex, and 88 is 58 in hex. However, only the low-order 23 bits are used. Therefore,

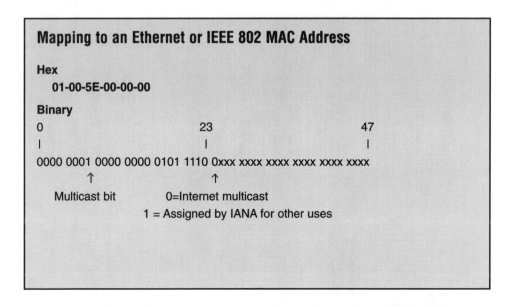

the IP address of 224.0.1.88 converted to a MAC address is 01-00-5E-00-01-88.

In order for the NIC card to receive or transmit multicast packets, the following functions must be invoked to place the multicast address in the NIC card and to remove it.

JoinLocalGroup (mapped group address): Allows the link layer to receive multicast packets for a particular host group.

LeaveLocalGroup (mapped group address): Allows the link layer to stop receiving multicast packets for a particular host group.

The mapped group address is the MAC address that is mapped from the host group multicast address.

The slide shows an IP multicast address and its MAC address equivalent.

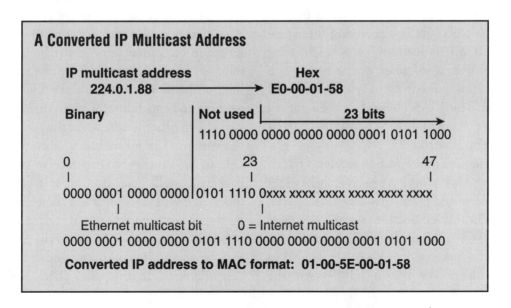

A Converted IP Multicast Address

IP multicast address	Hex
224.0.1.88 ⟶	E0-00-01-58

Binary | Not used | 23 bits ⟶

1110 0000 0000 0000 0000 0001 0101 1000

0   23   47

0000 0001 0000 0000 | 0101 1110 0xxx xxxx xxxx xxxx xxxx xxxx

Ethernet multicast bit   0 = Internet multicast

0000 0001 0000 0000 0101 1110 0000 0000 0000 0001 0101 1000

Converted IP address to MAC format: 01-00-5E-00-01-58

281 Protocols

Review RFC 1112. Naturally, there are a few protocols involved in order to make multicasting work. We will start out with the most prevalent protocols and then work our way into others. No matter which router-router protocol is used, one protocol is used with all of them: the Internet Group Management Protocol (IGMP). To support IGMP, a host must join the "all-hosts" group (address 224.0.0.1) on each network interface at initialization time and must remain a member for as long as the host is active. Therefore, there is at least one multicast address that every multicast host should be a member of.

IGMP is the protocol that runs between multicast hosts and their adjacent multicast routers. (Router manufacturers can choose whether to implement multicast or not. Routers that participate in multicast must run a multicast protocol (beyond RIP2, OSPF, etc.) Most major router manufacturers have or are in the process of implementing these protocols.) IGMP is used to keep neighboring multicast routers informed of the host group memberships present on a particular local network. The IGMP header is used for all multicast communication, whether it is between hosts or routers.

In order for an interface to receive a multicast datagram, it must have previously been set up to receive and process multicast datagrams. Since IGMP does not use a transport layer such as TCP or UDP, the IP Protocol field is set to 2 (as reserved by IANA RFC 1700) in order to identify the process (IGMP) using the

---

Protocols

- IGMP is the framing protocol used with all other protocols to transfer information.

- IGMP runs between hosts and hosts, hosts and routers, and routers and routers.
  - Used to allow hosts to communicate with routers and for routers to communicate with other routers

- To support IGMP, a host must join the all-hosts multicast address of 224.0.0.1.

- IGMP runs on all hosts.

IP service. Therefore, before any multicast packets are received, the upper-layer software must ensure that IP and the MAC layer interfaces are set up to received multicast datagrams.

A host may be a member of more than one group; in fact, there is no upper limit on the number of groups allowed (except for the upper limit of the IP multicast address). NICs have a very limited capability for receiving multicast packets. In other words, when the user installs the version of IP for multicast, it must also be able to set up the NIC to receive multicast packets as well. Each host group will have a different multicast address and therefore it will be mapped to a multicast MAC address as well (discussed previously). But the NIC card may only be able to hold a finite number of multicast addresses. In this case, check with the manufacturer. Some have implemented the ability to receive all multicast packets. In this way, it will be up to the IP layer software to filter out unwanted packets.

IGMP Header 282

The IGMP router places queries to its subnets and the hosts that belong to a group specified in the query response report. The IGMP headers for version 1 and version 2 are shown in the slide (you will find both types on your network). The Type field can be one of four types:

0x11: Membership Query

0x16: Version 2 Membership Report

0x17: Leave Group—for IGMP version 1 compatibility (explained later in the section)

0x12: Version 1 Membership Report—for backward compatibility

IGMP version 2 has a different header than version 1. The Version and Type fields of a version 1 header are combined into one field called the Type field. To allow a multicast router to determine the difference between the two, a new Type field was created for Version 2—Membership Report Message. IGMP version 1 and version 2 routers may coexist. An IGMP version 2 router must be able to act as a version 1 IGMP router. To determine this, the Max Response Time field is set to 0 in all queries (this maps to the unused field in version 1).

The membership query packet has two types: General Query (used to learn group members of any group on an attached network) Group Specific Query (used to learn members of a specific group).

How do you tell the difference between the two? This is determined by the group address in the IGMP header. A general query uses all 0s in the Group Address field and the specific query uses the exact group address. Both of these messages are sent using the IP header address 224.0.0.1 and a mapped multicast MAC address 01-00-5E-00-00-01 (review the conversion method, explained previously).

The Leave Group message is new to IGMP version 2. It allows a router to immediately determine if there are any members of a group left on its interface that received the Leave Group message. This is explained in a moment.

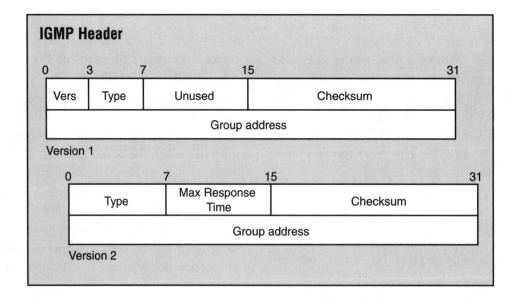

Multicast routers use IGMP to learn which groups have members on each of the routers' interfaces. This information will in turn be used to build multicast trees for forwarding multicast data. It will also have a timer for each of those group memberships. A router that runs IGMP is also a member of any host group that has members on one or more of its interfaces. The multicast router keeps a list of the memberships on its interfaces and not the individual hosts that belong to that group. There really is no need to keep track of the hosts. Simple enough: If only one host on a router interface wishes to join a group, the router has to forward multicast datagrams on that interface. It does not matter if there are 100 hosts or 1 on that interface; the router must be a member of that group as well and forward multicast datagrams out that interface.

The multicast router will know if there are any members of a group left on its interface by sending a query packet out that interface.

For IGMP version 2, a multicast router may assume one of two roles: *querier* or *nonquerier*. All multicast routers, upon initializing, assume they are the querier router. Since multicast routers periodically transmit a query to find hosts for groups, the new router will eventually receive a query if there is another router providing this function. If the router receives another query message from another router and only if that router has a lower IP address, the new router will assume the role as a nonquerier. If the new router has a lower IP address, it will assume the role of querier and the other router will assume the role of nonquerier.

When a host receives a query, it will set delay timers for each group to which it belongs

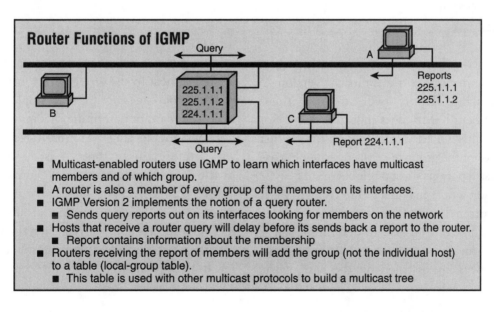

Router Functions of IGMP

- Multicast-enabled routers use IGMP to learn which interfaces have multicast members and of which group.
- A router is also a member of every group of the members on its interfaces.
- IGMP Version 2 implements the notion of a query router.
  - Sends query reports out on its interfaces looking for members on the network
- Hosts that receive a router query will delay before its sends back a report to the router.
  - Report contains information about the membership
- Routers receiving the report of members will add the group (not the individual host) to a table (local-group table).
  - This table is used with other multicast protocols to build a multicast tree

(set between 0 and the timer indicated in the Max Response Time field of the received query). For a host with more than one interface, each interface maintains its own timers. When the time is up, the host responds with a version 2 Membership Report. The TTL field of the IP header will be set to 1. This ensures that the packet will not be forwarded beyond that local network on which it was transmitted. If the host receives a report from another host in the same group, the host will stop its timer and will not send a report. This is to conserve bandwidth and processing time, and avoids having duplicate reports on the network. All of this is accomplished using multi-

cast addressing. 224.0.0.2 is the all-routers multicast address and 224.0.0.1 is the all-hosts address.

If the router receives a report or reports, it will add the group to its internal list, noting the interface on which it received the report. It then sets a timer for the next query message. If it receives more reports for a group, then the timer will be reset to the max value and restarted. If no reports are received before this timer expires, then the router assumes there are no members for that group and it will not forward remotely received multicast datagrams on the interface.

284 HostJoin

When a host joins a multicast group, it immediately transmits a version 2 Membership Report two or three times (remember, IGMP does not use ICMP or TCP). This is done in case that host is the first member of the group and it is repeated in case the first report gets lost or clobbered.

When a host leaves a group (IGMPv2), it transmits a Leave Group message. A host may or may not be able to determine if it is the last member of a group—this is a storage and processing decision on the part of the

implementer. A host that can determine if it is the last host in the group will transmit the Leave Group message. Other implementations that cannot determine this may or may not send this message. The multicast router will determine if any hosts exist for a group by the query message anyway. When a multicast router receives this message, it will send group-specific queries to the group being left. If no reports are received, then the multicast router will assume there are no members left in that group and it will not forward any multicast datagrams for that group out that interface.

IGMPv2 is a preliminary draft specification as of this writing and can be found at the InterNIC (ds.internic.net) under *Draft RFCs*. It mostly contains the ability to conserve bandwidth by allowing a host to elect to receive traffic from specified sources (IP addresses) of a multicast group. Alternatively, it allows a host to specify which sources it does not want to receive information from. What is a source? It is simply a host that originated a multicast datagram. There may be many sources in any one group. With IGMP versions 1 and 2, a host is required to receive all information for a group of which it is a member, no matter which source transmitted it. Also, the Leave Group message is enhanced to allow a host to specify which sources it no longer wishes to receive information from. The multicast router will receive this and possibly stop sending information to that group from that source.

Now that we understand how the host operates with IP multicast and how a host interacts with a multicast router, we need to learn how multicast actually operates. First, we will study the algorithms and then we will take an in-depth look at one multicast protocol: the Distance Vector Multicast Routing Protocol, or DVMRP. The draft RFC used is version 3 of DVMRP.

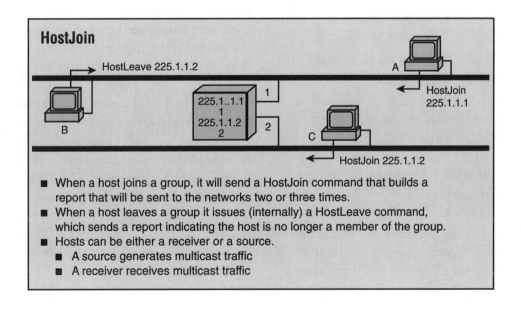

- When a host joins a group, it will send a HostJoin command that builds a report that will be sent to the networks two or three times.
- When a host leaves a group it issues (internally) a HostLeave command, which sends a report indicating the host is no longer a member of the group.
- Hosts can be either a receiver or a source.
    - A source generates multicast traffic
    - A receiver receives multicast traffic

285 Multicast Algorithms

A lot of people do not even realize that they have already worked with multicasting. If you have worked with the Spanning Tree algorithm for bridging or the Open Shortest Path First (OSPF) protocol for IP routing updates, you have already worked with a multicast algorithm.

IP multicasting for subnet routing uses the following protocols:

- Distance Vector Multicast Routing Protocol (DVMRP)
- Multicast Open Shortest Path First (MOSPF)
- Protocol Independent Multicast (PIM)
  - Sparse mode
  - Dense mode

There are essentially three forwarding algorithms that can be used with IP multicasting:

- Flooding
- Spanning Tree
  - Simple Spanning Tree
  - Reverse Path Broadcasting
  - Reverse Path Multicasting (most widely implemented)
- Core-Based Trees (Used in sparse environments [environments that do not have a densely populated environment of hosts], CBT is a type of spanning tree algorithm but different enough to merit its own category).

The purpose of all the algorithms is to build a multicast tree for the forwarding of multicast datagrams. Some algorithms (CBT and sometimes PIM-SM) build only one tree

---

Multicast Algorithms

- IP multicast protocols.
  - Distance Vector Multicast Routing Protocol (DVMRP)
  - Multicast Open Shortest Path First (MOSPF)
  - Protocol Independent Multicast (PIM)
    - Dense mode
    - Sparse mode
- Forwarding algorithm.
- Flooding.
- Spanning tree.
  - Simple spanning tree (one multicast tree for all groups)
  - Reverse path forwarding
  - Reverse path multicasting
- Core-based trees.

---

that all members of the group share, even if the tree does not supply the most efficient (shortest path) route between all members of the group. Other protocols build shortest path trees that allow for the shortest path for all members in the group (DVMRP, OSPF). There can and will be multiple multicast trees built for each source/group on a network. These trees are built dynamically when the first multicast datagram arrives from the source (with the exception of MOSPF).

Multicast datagrams do not necessarily follow the unicast datagram's path. The multicast tree that is built is a dynamic logical tree that a router will build to forward multicast datagrams to its receivers.

A few terms should be explained before we continue. Those familiar with spanning trees already understand about leaves, branches, and the root. For those who are not, read on.

Refer to the slide. It shows the leaves, branches, and the root of a spanning tree. The leaves are simply the endpoints of the tree. If there are no other forwarding paths beyond a router path, then the interface is considered a *leaf* interface. If there are more forwarding paths to a host group, then the interface is considered a *branch*. The *root* is the source of the multicast transmission. There can be many sources for a multicast network.

Picture a tree. A tree has a root, a trunk, branches, and leaves. Leaves are the outermost part of the tree; in fact, they are endpoints. The branches contain the leaves, but leaves cannot contain branches. The root is the source of all life in the tree. Lose the root and the tree dies.

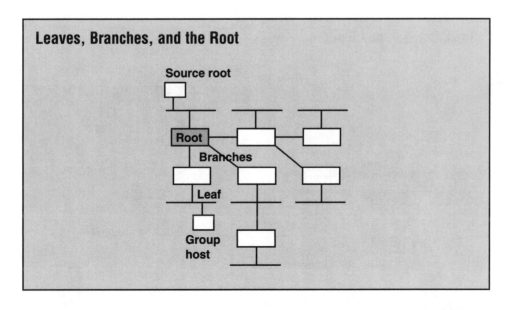

Leaves, Branches, and the Root

Spanning Tree and Flooding

The simplest and most inefficient algorithm for IP multicast forwarding is *flooding*. Essentially, when a multicast router receives a multicast datagram, it will first check to see if it has received this very same datagram before. If it has, it will discard the datagram. However, if it has not, the datagram will be forwarded to all interfaces on the multicast router except for the one on which the datagram was received. You can see how simple this would be to implement. There are not many resources required to implement this algorithm. However, the flooding algorithm does not scale well. As your network grows, the flooding algorithm becomes a resource hog and is very inefficient. It generates a large number of duplicate packets and it forwards out all the interfaces that it has configured, even if there are no hosts downstream that belong to that multicast group. The down-

stream routers have to process the datagram as well, and the router also has to maintain a table for each packet recently received (a timer mechanism would have to be established to clean up the table as well).

Therefore, the spanning tree algorithms look more appealing. They require more logic in the multicast routers, but the trade-off in efficiency is well worth the price. The first algorithm that was invoked was a simple spanning tree. It created one spanning tree out of the current Internet topology.

Once the spanning tree was built, if a multicast router received a multicast datagram, it would forward the datagram out each of its spanning tree interfaces, except the one on which it received the datagram. We have eliminated the loops provided for us in the simplex flooding algorithm and the router is not taxed

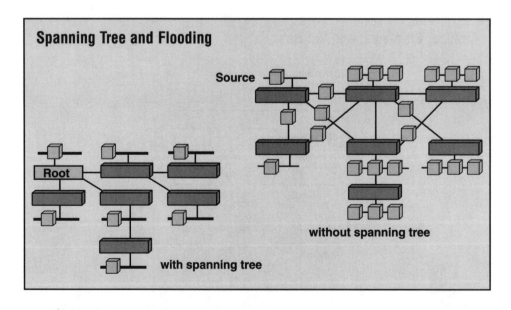

Spanning Tree and Flooding

with maintaining tables for recently forwarded packets (duplicates). Although the spanning tree adds more maintenance traffic on the network (to maintain the spanning tree topology), and has more overhead processing in the router, the efficiencies provided are better than the flooding algorithm. This method has it drawbacks, however, in that it may not provide the best paths to all destinations based on the group address and the source. It simply forwards multicast datagrams out its spanning tree interfaces without regard to group address and the source and whether there are any recipients on any part of the spanning tree. In other words, the complete spanning tree sees all multicasts even if there are no members.

Reverse Path Forwarding (RPF) 288

Since the spanning tree was better but still not efficient or scaleable, many other multicast protocols were tested and experimented, but the protocol that is used with multicasting is Reverse Path Forwarding, or RPF. This algorithm provides a group-specific spanning tree. That is, for each group source (the host that is originating the multicast datagram), a separate distinct spanning tree is built between that source and all the potential host recipients.

This algorithm that you are about to learn may seem backwards, and in a way it is. We know that multicasting is based on a (source, group) pair. If a multicast datagram is received on a router's interface, the router then determines if the interface that the datagram was received on is the shortest path back to the source. Sounds like the opposite of RIP? Well, it is. If the router determines that the interface does provide the shortest path back to the source, it forwards the received datagram on every active interface except the one on which it received the datagram. Otherwise, the router determines that the interface does not provide the shortest path back to the source, and it discards the datagram. The interface determined to be the shortest path back to the source is called the *parent link*. The interface on which the router forwards the multicast datagram is called the *child link*.

Where does the router get this information to allow it to make a decision on what is the shortest path back the source? The routing tables of the router. If you are using a link-state routing update protocol such as OSPF, each router maintains a routing table for whole network, multicast or unicast. If you are using a

distance-vector protocol such as RIP or RIP2, a routing update is needed. We will explain it in further detail in our discussion of DVMRP.

RPF contains many advantages over the mechanism previously described. It is simple to implement. Multicast datagrams are forwarded over multiple links since RDF allows for building separate spanning trees for each source and group pair.

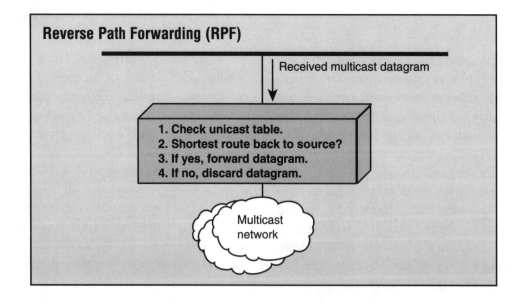

Reverse Path Forwarding (RPF)

Received multicast datagram

1. Check unicast table.
2. Shortest route back to source?
3. If yes, forward datagram.
4. If no, discard datagram.

Multicast network

Some multicast forwarding algorithms, such as DVMRP, broadcast (floods) the first packet that it receives and then waits for Prune messages from the downstream interfaces. The Prune messages come back from multicast routers in response to receiving unwanted multicast traffic at the leaves of the multicast tree; therefore, finding the leaf networks for any multicast tree is important. These routers that connect to leaf networks start the *pruning* process by identifying which downstream interfaces do not belong to the multicast group. Routers that identify these interfaces prune those interfaces. If after pruning its own interfaces, the router finds that none of its interfaces belong to that group, it will send a Prune message upstream to its neighbor. If the router continues to receive multicast datagrams for that source, it will continue to send Prune messages (increasing the delta between them) until the multicast traffic for that group stops.

A prune lifetime is about two hours.

To join new receivers back onto the tree, the *Graft* message is sent. This message is sent hop by hop to each multicast router. Each message is acknowledged between routers to ensure that it was received, thereby guaranteeing end-to-end delivery. Routers that receive Graft messages can make a series of decisions.

If the receiving router has a prune state for the (source, group) pair, then it acknowledges the Graft message and sends a Graft message of its own to its upstream router. If the router has some pruned downstream interfaces but not a pruned upstream interface, it simply adds that interface to the list of downstream interfaces in its routing table. It will also send an acknowledgment to the source of the Graft message. If

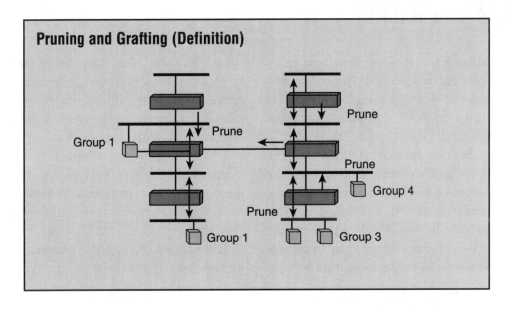

Pruning and Grafting (Definition)

Group 1

Prune

Prune

Group 1

Prune

Group 4

Prune

Group 3

the router has no state (pruned or otherwise) for the (source, group) pair, then any received datagrams for the (source, group) pair should be automatically flooded. A graft acknowledgment is sent to the source of the Graft message as well.

290 Reverse Path Multicasting (RPM)

The algorithm that uses pruning and grafting is how RPM was devised. Actually, a few other protocols were developed, but RPM is used in many multicast algorithms, especially distance-vector such as Distance Vector Multicast Routing Protocol (DVMRP). RPM allows us to trim the tree so that multicast datagrams arrive on those branches and leaf segments that have active participants. The algorithm basically forwards the first multicast packet of every (source, group) pair to all participating routers in the spanning tree (source, group). This algorithm is assisted by the IGMP protocol to determine which segments have active host groups. Using IGMP, multicast routers can determine the group memberships on each leaf subnetwork. In this way, a multicast router can determine whether any of its segments have active host groups. If a host group is not active, the router does not forward a multicast datagram out that interface—it is truncated.

RPM allows the router to transmit a *Prune* message back through the interface on which it received the multicast datagram (its parent link) that allows its upstream neighbor to basically shut off that interface to that downstream router—no need to forward multicast datagrams to the router if it is only going to throw them away. Prune messages are only sent once for each multicast packet the router does not have a group interface for. If that upstream router does not have any leaf networks for a host group and other branch interfaces all sent back a Prune message, then that upstream router may send a Prune message to its upstream router (its parent link) as well. The next upstream router would then shut off its interface to that downstream router. You can prune all the way back to the root.

This cascading of Prune messages creates a true spanning tree topology that will only forward multicast datagrams to those interfaces that have active group hosts. How do we grow back a branch or create leaves? Periodically,

the prune interfaces are removed from the router's table and the branches and leaves grow back. This allows the forwarding of multicast datagrams down those branches, resulting in a new stream of Prune messages to create the true spanning tree.

This algorithm eliminates most problems except for one: scaling. It still does not allow for growing the network to thousands or tens of thousands of routers with hundreds or thousands of multicast groups. The first multicast packet is received by all routers, and then constant pruning messages are needed to keep the spanning tree efficient.

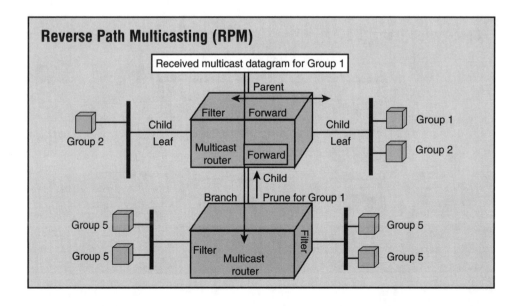

291 Core-Based Tree (CBT)

The previous algorithms build spanning trees based on a source host, and multiple trees can be built from different sources. The source host is basically the root of the spanning tree and the spanning tree branches out from the source. If there are many sources, there are many roots. If there are many multicasts, each has its own multicast tree. CBT builds a single forwarding tree that is shared by all members of a group. The core of this tree (the root) is based on the core router and not the source of the multicast datagram.

CBT works on a concept that builds a backbone consisting of at least one core router. Multicast messages for a group are transmitted in this direction. Any host that wishes to receive multicast information for a specific group transmits a Join message and transmits it towards the core backbone. Each source must be configured with at least one IP address of the core routers. The core consists of at least one router that acts as the core. There can be multiple routers acting as core routers and, if so, the links that connect these core routers become the core backbone.

If there are multiple groups in the network, then multiple trees may be built. It is not the concept of one multicast tree for all groups. However, there is only one multicast tree for each group.

After issuing the Join message, each intermediate router marks the interface and multicast group and then forwards the message towards the core. In doing this, the router is able to forward multicast data towards the core for that group. When the core routers receive this data, they will multicast the data back out all ports, except the one on which it received the data.

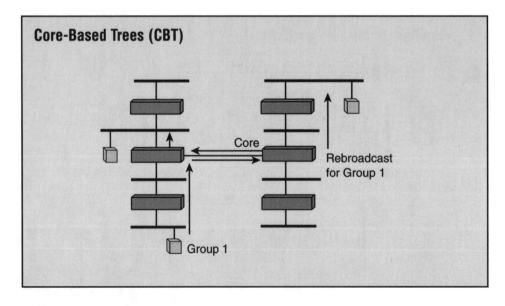

Core-Based Trees (CBT)

This algorithm may simply stay an architecture for which other protocols will be developed. To become a protocol, issues of dynamic selection of the core backbone and management must be settled. The most notable protocol using it is the Protocol Independent Multicast (PIM) Sparse Mode (discussed later). There are advantages and disadvantages of the algorithm: Since each group is based on a single tree rooted at the core, state information on the router is easier to maintain, thereby requiring fewer resources on the router. Information that must be passed between routers to maintain these states is also less, resulting in better efficiency of the bandwidth. However, since all individual data and control messages travel towards a specific core, congestion may be inevitable.

Distance Vector Multicast Routing Protocol (DVMRP) 292

The following text about the DVMRP routing protocol is aligned with the DVMRP version 3 specification, which as of this writing is still a draft RFC. DVMRP uses the Reverse Path Multicasting (RPM) algorithm to dynamically build multicast delivery trees and determine the router's position in the multicast tree in reference to the source subnet of a multicast datagram. DMVRP is a "broadcast and prune" multicast routing protocol. It uses Reverse Path Forwarding to see if a multicast datagram should be forwarded downstream. A multicast forwarding tree is built between a source and all members of the group (receivers). For those familiar with this protocol, it should be noted up front that the latest version of this protocol for UNIX, mrouted 3.5, is also based on RPM, which is significantly different from previous versions in the areas of packet format, tunneling, and so forth.

In order for DVMRP to work, two tables must be built: a unicast route table and a forwarding route table. The unicast route table is used to determine if a multicast datagram was received on the correct port (the upstream interface). The forwarding table is used to determine on which interfaces of a router, a router should forward a multicast datagram (the downstream interface).

To build the unicast routing table, DVMRPs pass route reports to each other containing entries for source subnets. This table is processed like RIP and the shortest distance back to a source is computed and placed in the table. The forwarding table is built by broadcasting the first multicast datagram received and then waiting for other routers to send back Prune and Graft messages to indicate who and who does not want the datagram. Why not simply use the unicast routing table? This is accomplished to allow multicast traffic to follow a different path than the unicast traffic and for the support of a tunnel interface, which unicast traffic does not understand.

DVMRP routers support two types of interfaces: *router* and *tunnel*. The multicast router interface is obvious, but the tunnel interface is not so obvious. To allow for nonmulticast routers to exist in a multicast network, the concept of tunnels is used. Multicast datagrams are encapsulated in unicast IP packets (using IP in IP) and these are send over the unicast routers. Contained in the IP header is a route list that the unicast routers should use. The last entry in this list is the end of the tunnel and is a router that again supports IP multicast. The last router strips off the unicast information and sends the datagram on.

DVMRP is a protocol that uses a distance-vector distributed routing algorithm in order

> ### Distance Vector Multicast Routing Protocol (DVMRP)
>
> - DVMRP uses the Reverse Path Multicasting (RPM).
> - Broadcast and Prune.
> - DVMRP builds two routing tables:
>   - Unicast and forwarding route tables
> - Unicast routing table is built by passing route reports.
> - Two types of interfaces supported:
>   - Router and Tunnel
> - Tunnels exist to allow multicast to live in a nonmulticast world.
>   - An IP multicast packet is wrapped in an IPv4 unicast packet

for each router to determine the distance from itself to any IP multicast traffic source. When DVMRP determines this, it creates IP multicast delivery trees between a source and its distributed group hosts.

The following slide shows the comparison between the multicast routing protocol of DVMRP and the host membership protocol IGMP. The protocol of IGMP runs between the hosts and the routers, and the DVMRP protocol runs between the routers.

However, it should be noted that with IPv4, the encapsulation of DVMRP data is accomplished using an IP encapsulation protocol of 2, which is IGMP. If you place a protocol analyzer on the network you will see DVMRP communicating using IP protocol type 2 for IGMP encapsulation. This does not mean that IGMP is running between routers; it is simply using the IGMP encapsulation to send its data.

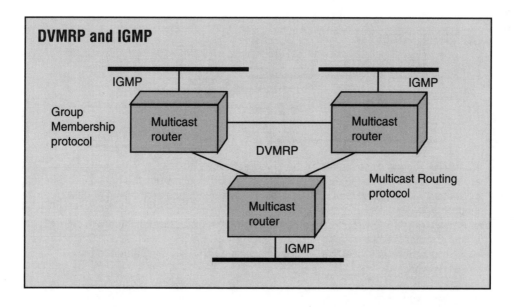

A DVMRP router can and does discover neighbor DVMRP routers through a process known as Neighbor Discovery using the *probe packet*. When a DVMRP router is initialized, it transmits these discovery packets to inform other DVMRP routers that it is operational. These messages are sent periodically (every 10 seconds) to the All DVMRP Routers multicast address. Each of the messages should contain the list of neighbor DVMRP routers that it knows about on that interface. Other routers on other interfaces are not included in this listing; this is local only. Routers should see their IP addresses in their neighbors' messages.

The probe packets allow other DVMRP routers to discover each other and to also detect when a neighbor router no longer exists. If a DVMRP router does not detect this message from a neighbor within 35 seconds, it considers that neighbor to be down.

Contained in this message is a listing of all other DVMRP neighbor routers that the router knows about. If a router does not receive any Probe messages, it considers the subnet to be a leaf network only.

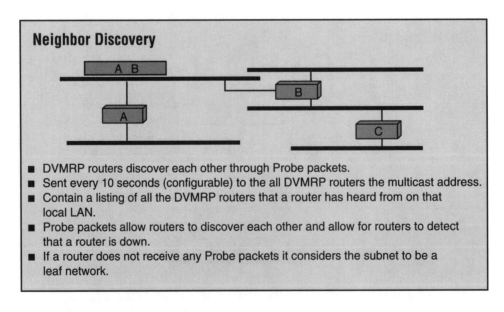

Neighbor Discovery

- DVMRP routers discover each other through Probe packets.
- Sent every 10 seconds (configurable) to the all DVMRP routers the multicast address.
- Contain a listing of all the DVMRP routers that a router has heard from on that local LAN.
- Probe packets allow routers to discover each other and allow for routers to detect that a router is down.
- If a router does not receive any Probe packets it considers the subnet to be a leaf network.

Unicast routing information is sent between neighbors using a special packet called a *route report*. Contained in the route report is a listing of unicast (source) subnets and their masks, and the metric (cost) associated with each subnet. A route learned through route reports should be refreshed within 140 seconds (2 × report interval + 20), after which it can be replaced with the next best route to the same source. If no update and no alternative route exists and 200 seconds have passed, the route is discarded from the routing table.

A route report is sent out every 60 seconds, and any number of route reports can be sent at any time during this interval. In this way, a router is not consumed by a periodic update like RIP that could consist of thousands of routes. At any time during this interval, "flash updates" can be sent. These reports indicate changes in the network but only contain the source subnet that changed. This reduces the loop changes and other catastrophes when paths for source networks change.

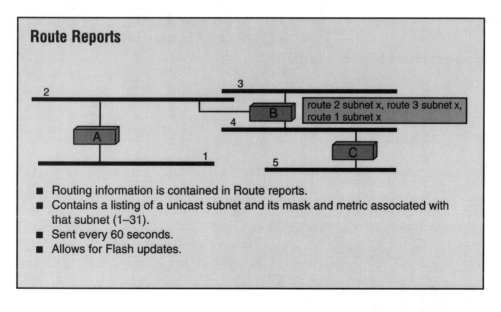

Route Reports

- Routing information is contained in Route reports.
- Contains a listing of a unicast subnet and its mask and metric associated with that subnet (1–31).
- Sent every 60 seconds.
- Allows for Flash updates.

Receiving a route report is a different matter. There are many checks done on the received information. Route reports are processed only by those sent by a known neighbor; otherwise, they are discarded. Generally, two rules are followed: If the route entry is new and the metric is less than infinity, the route is added. That's the simple one. The second rule is tougher and is shown in the table.

If the route entry exists, perform the following checks:

If New Metric < infinity AND New metric > existing metric	If the same neighbor is reporting it, update the entry; otherwise, discard the entry.
If New Metric < infinity AND New metric < existing metric	Update the entry with the route and if necessary, update the reporting neighbor.
If New Metric < infinity AND New metric = existing metric	Refresh the route and if the new neighbor has a lower IP address, update that entry.
If New Metric = infinity AND New gateway = existing gateway	Route is now unreachable, update the entry.
If New Metric = infinity AND New gateway not equal to existing gateway	Ignore
If New metric is between route infinity and 2x infinity	Neighbor considers the receiving router to be upstream for the indicated and that router is dependent on the receiving router for the route indicated. If the receiving neighbor router considers that router to be downstream, the receiving router marks that neighbor as dependent for that route; otherwise, discard the packet, for a dependent router cannot be considered to be upstream.
If the metric is greater than 2x infinity	Ignore

DVMRP Tables

- DVMRP route table contains Source subnets and From Gateways.
  - This table contains entries used to determine if a source's multicast packets were received on the correct interface
- Forwarding table.
  - Used to determine which interfaces a multicast packet should be forwarded on

When an IP multicast datagram is received by a router running DVMRP, it first looks up the source network in its DVMRP unicast routing table. That's right! In order to ensure that all DVMRP routers have a consistent view of the unicast path back to a source, a unicast routing table is propagated to all DVMRP routers as an integral part of the protocol. This is a separate unicast routing table for DVMRP. Actually, there are two tables used in multicast routing: a *routing* table and a *forwarding* table. The DVMRP *routing* table contains Source Subnets and From Gateways. It has the shortest-path source-rooted spanning tree to every participating source subnet in the internet. Compare this with entries from a typical IGP table such as RIP, which contains Destinations and Next-Hop Gateways. The *forwarding* table is created because the routing table is not aware of group memberships. The following table shows a simple DVMRP routing table.

Source Subnet	Subnet Mask	From Gateway	Metric	Status	TTL
150.1.0.0	255.255.0.0	150.1.1.1	5	UP	400
150.2.0.0	255.255.0.0	150.1.2.1	3	UP	350

A simple DVMRP routing table.

Source subnet: The subnetwork that contains a host source.

Subnet mask: The subnet mask of the Source Subnet.

From-gateway: The immediate upstream router that leads back to the source subnet.

Metric: hops (routers) to the source subnet.

TTL (Time to Live): Indicates how long the entry in the table stays before being removed.

Source Subnet	Multicast Group	TTL	Upstream Port	Downstream Ports
150.1.0.0	224.0.1.1	430	1	2,3
150.2.0.0	224.0.1.2			
224.0.2.5	500			

Source Subnet	Multicast Group	TTL	Upstream Port	Downstream Ports
300	1			
3	3			
5				

A DVMRP forwarding table.

Any interface that is designated a leaf network, or any downstream routers for the source group will be included in the downstream ports. The upstream port is determined by the unicast routing table in that if this interface has the shortest route back to the source subnet of this group, it is registered as the upstream interface with that port designation. The forwarding table is created to represent the local router's understanding of the shortest-path source-rooted delivery tree for each (source, group) pair.

298 DVMRP Route Tables

To build a unicast route table, the upstream DVMRP router is dependent on other downstream routers for information. The information that is sent to other DVMRP routers is called a *route report*. The metrics in the route reports are the most important fields of the report. This not only builds the source subnetwork table (indicating the source subnetworks and their reachability), but also allows for the building of a forwarding table that indicates to the router which downstream routers are depending on that upstream router for forwarding multicast datagrams to them. Upstream routers send route reports to their downstream neighbors indicating source subnets and their metrics. Like RIP, the metric to a source subnet is the cumulative cost of all the incoming interfaces so far. The route reports will be sent to a DVMRP's neighbor router. Contained in this list are source subnets and metrics (in the range of 1–31).

If a downstream router wishes to indicate to an upstream router that it is dependent on it for receiving multicast datagrams for a particular

DVMRP Route Tables

■ To build a unicast route table, a DVMRP table is dependent on other downstream routers or information.

■ Metrics are different than those used by typical tables.

■ Relies on the protocol of poison reverse.

■ Metrics range from 1 through 63.

■ Infinity is a route with a hop count of 32.

■ 1–31 is the original metric of the source.

■ 32 is infinity.

■ 33–63 is the poison reverse metric of a downstream router telling its upstream router that it wants to be added to the downstream table.

and 33–63 is the poison reverse metric of a downstream router telling its upstream router that it wants to be added to its table for multicast datagrams of a given source.

Why not just use the existing unicast routing table like a RIP2 table? The reason is that not all routers will be running DVMRP and multicast routers must be able to interact with nonmulticast routers. In order to accomplish this, we must build tunnels across nonmulticast routers. With tunnels, we effectively force the path that the multicast datagram will take. The tunnel may take one route, but a regular unicast packet may take another route path. With this, a router's unicast table may not coincide with a DVMRP router's unicast table. Therefore, we use the unicast information in DVMRP exclusively to determine the shortest route back to the source subnet of a multicast datagram.

source subnet, that downstream router will echo the route back to the upstream neighbor with a metric higher than 32. Infinity for DVMRP is considered to be 32. Therefore, the downstream neighbor will add 32 to the incoming metric and echo this back to the upstream router. This relies on a technique known as *poison reverse*. When the upstream router receives this update, and sees the metric for the source subnetwork in the range between infinity to twice infinity, then the upstream router will add the downstream router to a list of dependent routers for that source. The value of infinity is 32 and indicates that a source network is not reachable. The range of metrics may be between 1–63. The original metric of the source is 1–31, 32 means not reachable,

299

DVMRP Tunneling

RFC 2003 describes IP encapsulation or tunneling. It is not necessary and can be the case many times, to have all routers running a multicast protocol. The question is, how do you get multicast datagrams through the Internet? Most routers on the Internet are not running a multicast protocol. The answer is *tunneling*. With tunneling, you build "islands" of multicast autonomous networks and they communicate with one another over the Internet by tunneling the multicast datagram over the Internet.

DVMRP supports the ability to tunnel a multicast datagram through nonmulticast routers. The multicast datagram is encapsulated in a unicast IP packet and addressed to the routers that do support native multicast routing. In other words, we wrap the multicast packet in an IP header and tell it which path to take to a destination multicast router.

To encapsulate an IP datagram using IP-in-IP encapsulation, an IP header is inserted before the existing IP datagram header. The source and destination address of the outer IP header are described in the input and output of the tunnel or the tunnel endpoints. The original IP header contains the IP source and destination address of the originator and final destination of the datagram.

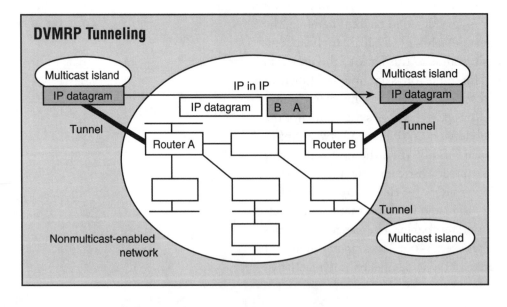

The slide shows IP-in-IP packet encapsulation for tunneling.

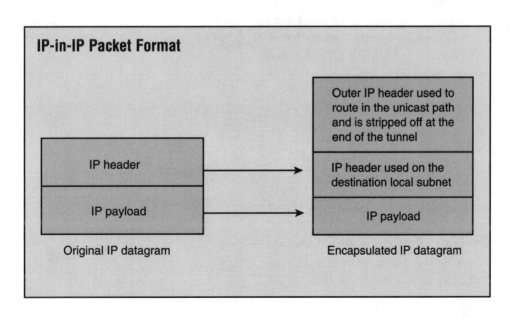

IP-in-IP Packet Format

IP header	Outer IP header used to route in the unicast path and is stripped off at the end of the tunnel
IP payload	IP header used on the destination local subnet
	IP payload
Original IP datagram	Encapsulated IP datagram

301 Protocol-Independent Multicast (PIM)

DVMRP provides great mechanisms for multicasting. Using the latest versions of IGMP and DVMRP, a fully functional multicast tree can be dynamically built and utilized for voice, video, and data. There is, however, a disadvantage to DVMRP: It does not scale well. DVMRP is a distance-vector multicast routing update protocol. DVMRP broadcasts the first multicast packet it receives from the source and then prunes the tree based on feedback from other routers. DVMRP is known as a *dense mode* multicast protocol, and is most efficient when the clients are densely located on the network. It does not scale well when the protocol is being used over WAN links, or when there are simply a few clients scattered throughout the customer's network. This broadcast and prune mechanism, along with multicast routing updates, causes unnecessary overhead over low-bandwidth media types. Furthermore, DVMRP routing tables are based on a RIP-like update. DVMRP also requires the routers to keep state information. This includes group and source information that is used to calculate a tree.

If all the members of a multicast group are located in a bandwidth-rich region (supported by high-speed LANs and not low-speed WANs), then it should be supported by a dense mode protocol such as DVMRP, MOSPF, or PIM-Dense Mode (DM). This can be limiting in that the scope of the group cannot include any members beyond the scope of the domain without placing the unnecessary burden of

---

Protocol-Independent Multicast (PIM)

- DVMRP is a good protocol, but it does not scale well.

- Extra overhead with the RIP-like built routing table.
  - Route reports

- Broadcast and Prune.

- Known as a dense-mode protocol.
  - Inefficient over less densely populated networks

- PIM offers two versions:
  - Dense mode (similar to DVMRP)
  - Sparse mode

Broadcast and Prune messages and possibly multicast routing updates over the link that includes that remote receiver.

PIM offers two versions for multicast routing: *dense mode* and *sparse mode*.

PIM–Dense Mode (PIM-DM)

- Similar to DVMRP but does not build its own unicast routing table.

- Less complex than DVMRP.

- Broadcast and Prune.
  - It will continue to broadcast packets until Prune messages are received

- Accepts duplicate packets in a trade off for efficiency.

- Assumes all downstream interfaces want to receive all multicast packets.

- Three mechanisms used to build a multicast tree:
  - Prune
  - Graft
  - Leaf Network detection

Dense Mode is the easiest to explain, especially if you have read the previous section on DVMRP. It functions similar to DVMRP in that it uses RPM to build source-routed multicast trees. However, unlike DVMRP, PIM does not rely on a independent unicast routing protocol.

When a multicast packet arrives on a PIM-DM interface, it is forwarded to all interfaces until the branches are specifically pruned. Unlike DVMRP, PIM-DM will continue to forward multicast packets until specific Prune messages are received. No tables are build from these prune messages. DVMRP uses a routing table to determine if there are downstream routers that want to receive the multicast datagrams for a specific group. DVMRP, relying on

a routing table that is sent to all multicast routers, is more selective when it forwards messages during the construction of a source-rooted multicast tree. The reasoning behind this is that simplicity and protocol independence are considered a higher priority than additional overhead caused by packet duplication. Building a unicast routing table virtually eliminates duplicate packets. PIM-DM accepts duplicate packets as an alternative to not become dependent on a unicast routing protocol, and therefore avoids building yet another routing database. PIM-DM assumes that all downstream interfaces want to receive multicast datagrams. PIM was actually built for sparse-mode multicast networks and DM was added for simple functionality. PIM-DM does not contain the concept of rendezvous points and there are no periodic joins (however, the Join message is still used). There currently is a draft RFC to allow for "border routers," which allow PIM and DVMRP interoperability. (The RFC can be found at netweb.usc.edu/pim/.)

PIM-DM is less complex than DVMRP. There are three mechanisms that PIM-DM uses to build a multicast tree: Prune, Graft, and Leaf network detection.

303 PIM—Dense Mode Operation

When a multicast datagram is received, its incoming interface is looked up in the unicast routing table; therefore, the router must be running some type of unicast routing protocol (remember the name, *Protocol Independent* Multicast). If the receiver interface is the one on which the router forwards unicast datagrams back to that subnet, the multicast datagram is accepted and forwarded to all ports except the incoming interface. If not, the datagram is simply discarded without error messages being sent (silently discarded). From here, the router checks for a forwarding state for the group address. If there is not an entry for the group address, the router adds one. The router checks the outgoing interface list to see whether it should forward the datagram. This list contains a listing of interfaces from which the router has heard group membership or PIM router messages. The PIM-DM router's messages can be Hello, Prune, Join, or Graft. If there is an active interface(s), the router forwards the datagram out those interfaces. If no interfaces are indicated, a Prune message is sent.

The intended receiver router of that Prune message will be placed in the message (not in the IP header). The downstream router knows this address by doing an RPF lookup in the unicast routing table. When the receiver router receives this Prune request, it will schedule a deletion of that LAN interface for that group, which means it inserts a delay before deletion. It is waiting to see if any other routers respond. Other routers on the subnet will also receive this Prune message and will in

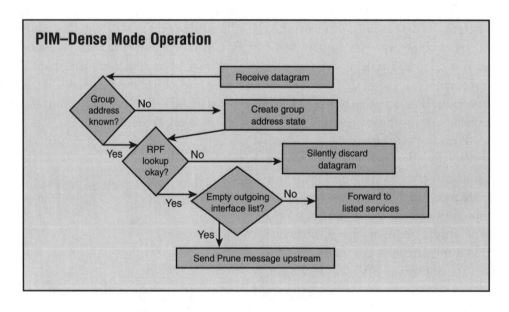

PIM–Dense Mode Operation

turn send a Join message to that router, forcing it to cancel the deletion of the LAN interface for the (source, group) pair. Just because one router prunes doesn't mean there aren't other routers on that same LAN that want to continue receiving information for the group address.

No entries in the outgoing list could be a result of no group members on the interface and the router not receiving any PIM-Hello messages from other routers located on that subnet (this allows for leaf network detection, in that in absence of these messages, only multicast hosts reside on a subnet). A router will keep track of the leaf members (local-group database built by IGMP) and will also contain a listing of routers as well. When a router is not heard from within a specified amount of time, the router deletes that router's entry from the list.

Pruned states for any multicast entry are eventually timed out, forcing all multicast datagrams to be forwarded on all interfaces again, until the multicast trees are pruned.

304 Adding Interfaces

A router can add interfaces for which it received a Graft message (rejoin a branch for a group) or an IGMP membership report. If the router already has state information about a group (it has built an entry for the group), it simply adds or refreshes the interface entry on which the IGMP message or Graft message was received. If the outgoing list entry is empty, the router will send a Graft message upstream towards the source. Any router that receives this message will use that received interface as the outgoing interface for the existing (source, group) pair.

If the router has no state information at all for the (source, group) pair, it will do nothing, for it knows that PIM-DM routers will deliver a multicast datagram to all interfaces when creating a state for the group.

PIM-Graft messages are positive acknowledged. A PIM-Graft message is unicast to the upstream router. The upstream router changes the Graft message into a Graft ACK and sends it back to the originating router.

Adding Interfaces

- Routers add interfaces by using the Graft message.

- When a router receives a Graft it will make one of the following decisions:
  - If the router already has information about the group, it simply adds or refreshes the interface for that group.
  - If the outgoing list is empty (but it knows about the group) that router will send a Graft message upstream.
  - If the router does not know about the group, it will do nothing with the received Graft message knowing that multicast datagrams for an unknown group will always be forwarded and it will wait for those frames.

- Graft messages are acknowledged by each router to the source of the Graft message.

- It is unicast to upstream routers.

PIM–Sparse Mode (PIM-SM)

- Used in sparsely populated multicast networks.

- Uses the concept of a rendezvous point:
  - A places where all sources and destinations meet each other

- Routers find RP for a group address and unicast datagrams to the RP to be redistributed.

- All PIM routers find each other.

- One router is selected the Designated Router (DR) by IGMPv2.

- When a new neighbor is found, the RP address is sent to it by its DR.

- The DR is also responsible for sending Join/Prune commands for its local receivers and sources.

PIM-SM was designed to restrict multicast traffic only to those routers that have a need for the multicast packet. In PIM-SM, a specific router (for redundancy and scalability, some PIM-SM implementations allow for more than one rendezvous point, but that is beyond the scope of this book) is known as the *rendezvous point* (RP). Senders and receivers join a multicast group by registering at the rendezvous router. Routers find out their RP (explained later on slide 313) and then send received multicast datagrams as unicast datagrams to the RP. The RP router redistributes multicast datagrams out the group trees that it has built. A rendezvous point is simply an IP address of a single router and is used by senders to announce themselves and for receivers to find out about new senders for a group.

All routers running PIM periodically (every 30 seconds by default) transmit Hello messages to each other, for the purpose of discovering other PIM routers using 224.0.0.13 (ALL_PIM_ROUTERS group address). This is local multicast that is in the range of not being allowed to traverse a router. When a PIM router receives this message, it stores the IP address for that neighbor. Each PIM router entry will have its own timer for repeat Hello messages. This time is included in the received Hello message and the router will note this time in its table (set to 3.5 * Hello Period (30 seconds) or default to 105 seconds). If the router does not periodically hear from the neighbor, it will time-out and delete that neighbor from the table. When the DR (selected by IGMPv2) receives a new entry (a new router), it unicasts its most recent RP address information to the new neighbor.

A router known as the *designated router* (the DR, usually an IGMPv2 function) is responsible for sending Join/Prune commands to the RP on behalf of its local receivers and sources. The choice of the DR is not based on the IGMP querier, nor is it based on the long-term, last-hop router for the group. The router with the highest IP address within all the received Hello messages is elected DR. The last-hop router is the last router to receive multicast messages before they are delivered to the local receivers. If this is the case, then this router will be the DR.

306

Types of Multicast Trees Using PIM-SM

Multicast trees are still built using PIM, but there are two types:

Shared Tree (Rendezvous Point (RP) rooted trees): Indicated by a (*,G) in the routing table, which indicates a shared tree for the multicast Group G.

Source-Rooted Tree (or SRT tree): Indicated by a (S,G) in the routing table. A source-rooted tree has been built for the multicast Group G and is sourced by the IP address(es).

Like all other multicast routing protocols, PIM conveys its messages in IGMP header data packets. If a host (receiver) wants to join a group, it will convey its membership information through IGMP. When a PIM router receives this IGMP message, the DR looks up the associated RP. The DR creates a "wildcard" entry for the group, which is written as (*,G). The DR creates a Join/Prune message (both Join and Prune entries are included in the same message). The flowchart for this process is shown in the slide. PIM works in conjunction with IGMP.

For a given (source, group) a multicast tree is initially built around the RP router. This initial tree is called a *shared tree* in that all members of the group converse using this single shared tree (albeit, it may not be the shortest path between a source and a host). It is easy to construct, reduces the amount of overhead in the router (tables, state information, etc.), and is easy to implement; however, it may not be efficient. Shared trees are built based on

> **Types of Multicast Trees using PIM-SM**
> - Two types of trees can be built:
>   - Shared Tree (RP rooted trees)
>   - Source Rooted Trees

the center point rendezvous router. This shared tree may not allow for the shortest tree to be built between a source and some receiver hosts.

The PIM protocol can adapt here as well. Based on the data rate, after the shared tree is constructed (after meeting at the rendezvous point) between a host receiver and a source, it can change from being a shared tree to a shortest-path tree. The router sends a Join command directly to the source and a multicast tree is built. The original path through the rendezvous router is torn down.

An important point needs to be brought out here: PIM, like other multicast algorithms, uses RPF. Since PIM-SM uses both source-rooted trees and RP-rooted trees (explained later), the RPF check is done differently for source trees and shared trees. If a PIM router has a source-root tree state, it does the RPF check from the source IP address of the multicast packet. If the router has a shared-tree state (and no explicit source-tree state), it does the RPF check on the RP's address (which is known when members join the group).

PIM-SM uses the RPF lookup function to determine where it needs to send Joins and Prunes.

Joining a Group 307

A router with directly connected neighbors must first join the shared tree. When the DR gets a membership notification from a host, it looks up the associated RP for that group (more information on the RP is coming up). The DR creates a wildcard multicast entry for the group in the form of (*,G). If there is not a specific match for the group, the packet is forwarded according to this entry. The RP address is contained in a special field in the route entry and is included in periodic Join/Prune messages.

The DR sends a Join message to the primary RP. The (*,G) entry indicates a (any source, group) pair. The intermediate router (B) forwards the unicast PIM-JOIN message. Router B also creates a forwarding cache entry for the (*,G) pair, so that they will know how to forward multicast datagrams for the group.

The slide shows the sequence of joining a group.

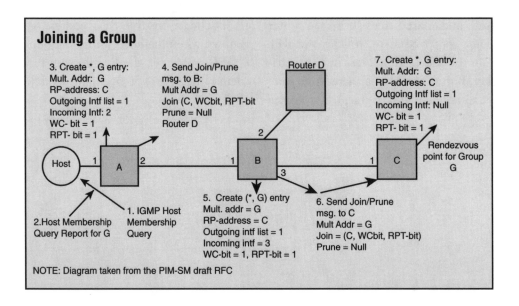

Joining a Group

3. Create *, G entry:
Mult. Addr: G
RP-address: C
Outgoing Intf list = 1
Incoming Intf: 2
WC- bit = 1
RPT- bit = 1

4. Send Join/Prune
msg. to B:
Mult Addr = G
Join (C, WCbit, RPT-bit
Prune = Null
Router D

Router D

7. Create *, G entry:
Mult. Addr: G
RP-address: C
Outgoing Intf list = 1
Incoming Intf: Null
WC- bit = 1
RPT- bit = 1

Host   1   A   2   1   B   1   C

2

3

Rendezvous
point for Group
G

2.Host Membership
Query Report for G

1. IGMP Host
Membership
Query

5. Create (*, G) entry
Mult. addr = G
RP-address = C
Outgoing intf list = 1
Incoming intf = 3
WC-bit = 1, RPT-bit = 1

6. Send Join/Prune
msg. to C
Mult Addr = G
Join = (C, WCbit, RPT-bit)
Prune = Null

NOTE: Diagram taken from the PIM-SM draft RFC

308   A Host Sending to a Group

When a host transmits a multicast packet to a specific group, the designated router (chosen by IGMPv2) forwards the multicast datagram as a unicast datagram to the RP. This unicast datagram is the multicast datagram encapsulated as a PIM-SM-Register packet. This type of packet informs the RP of a new source. The RP strips off the encapsulated (register) headers and redistributes the multicast datagram out the delivery tree. The active RP for that source transmits PIM-JOIN messages back to the source station's DR. The

routers lying between the source's DR and the RP maintain the path information by the received PIM-JOIN messages. This is done so that when nonregistered encapsulated packets are received, they will know what interfaces to forward them on. The RP will send the unicast datagram back out as a multicast datagram across the group's multicast tree. The source's DR will continue to encapsulate the multicast datagrams and send them to the RP. When the DR receives a Register-Stop message from the RP (the RP sends these messages if the RP has no downstream receivers for the group or for that source) it will also send Register-Stop messages if the RP has already joined the (S,G) tree and is receiving the data packets natively (unencapsulated). A timer is used by the DR and if this timer expires, it will start to resend the multicast datagrams encapsulated in Register messages.

The slide shows the sequence of a host sending to a group.

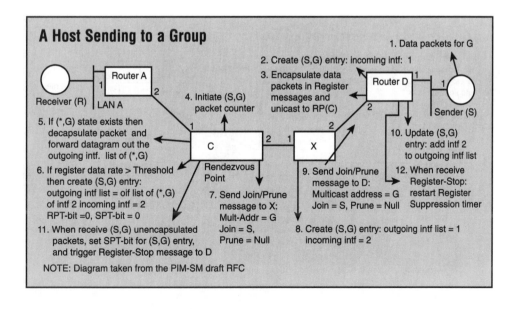

309

Converting to a Source-Rooted Tree

The initial tree built in PIM-SM is the shared RP-tree. However, based on data thresholds that are relative to time, the tree can be converted to source-rooted trees.

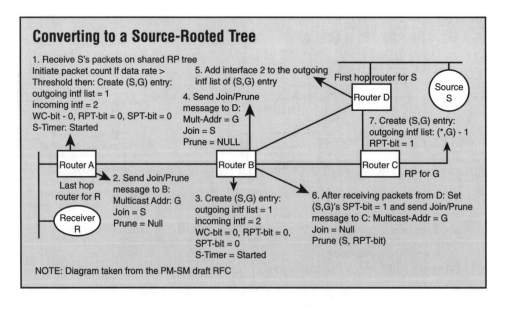

Converting to a Source-Rooted Tree

1. Receive S's packets on shared RP tree Initiate packet count If data rate > Threshold then: Create (S,G) entry: outgoing intf list = 1 incoming intf = 2 WC-bit - 0, RPT-bit = 0, SPT-bit = 0 S-Timer: Started

5. Add interface 2 to the outgoing intf list of (S,G) entry

4. Send Join/Prune message to D: Mult-Addr = G Join = S Prune = NULL

First hop router for S

Router D

Source S

7. Create (S,G) entry: outgoing intf list: (*,G) - 1 RPT-bit = 1

Router A

Router B

Router C

RP for G

Last hop router for R

Receiver R

2. Send Join/Prune message to B: Multicast Addr = G Join = S Prune = Null

3. Create (S,G) entry: outgoing intf list = 1 incoming intf = 2 WC-bit = 0, RPT-bit = 0, SPT-bit = 0 S-Timer = Started

6. After receiving packets from D: Set (S,G)'s SPT-bit = 1 and send Join/Prune message to C: Multicast-Addr = G Join = Null Prune (S, RPT-bit)

NOTE: Diagram taken from the PM-SM draft RFC

PIM-SM uses specific routers known as the *rendezvous point* (RP) to start out the shared tree. Senders and receivers join a multicast group by registering at their rendezvous router. A rendezvous point is simply an IP address of a single router. These points are used by senders to announce themselves and for receivers to find out about new senders for a group.

Where and how is the RP found? There is one router in a single PIM domain (a contiguous set of routers that all implement PIM) called the *bootstrap router* (BSR). This router is responsible for sending out Bootstrap messages. The BSR is dynamically elected and distributes information about the RP. BSR information is sent to each router in the PIM domain. To find out about RPs, all routers within a PIM domain collect Bootstrap messages and store the information contained in the BSR messages.

If a router wishes to work as an RP, it becomes a *candidate* RP (C-RP). C-RPs send out Advertisement messages to the BSR for the domain. Inside the advertisements are the Group Address and the Group Mask (prefix) fields for which it can become the RP; in other words, what group address ranges it can support as an RP. This range can be one group to all groups. This allows the BSR to distribute RP information to other PIM routers in the domain using the All-PIM-Routers message.

Rendezvous Points

- PIM-SM uses specific routers known as RP to start out a shared tree.

- Senders and receivers join a multicast group by registering the group address with their RP.

- RP is simply one or more routers associated with a multicast address.

- One router in the PIM-SM domain is known as the Bootstrap Router (BSR).
  - A simple election process is used to determine the one BSR
  - The BSR distributes information about the RP
  - PIM routers collect and store BSR information

- A router that wishes to become an RP sends out messages indicating this and for what groups.

- The BSR distributes this information.

311

Comparison of Sparse- and Dense-Mode Protocols

Sparse Mode	Dense Mode
Requires explicit joining of senders and receivers. Does not send packets where they have not been requested.	Sends and stores explicit prune state information in response to unwanted packets.
Stores shared-tree join information in anticipation of data packets.	Stateless until data packets are sent.
Relies on an RP initially for senders and receivers to meet and build a shared tree.	No RP, the broadcast nature of the protocol builds the tree.
Unicast protocol independent.	Unicast protocol dependent.
Requires periodic refreshing of explicit Join/Prune messages.	No periodic updates on Prune messages, event driven.

PIM-Sparse Mode is modeled after the Core-Based Tree algorithm. However, the difference between the two is that CBT uses one tree, centered at a core router, instead of at the source of a multicast datagram. CBT builds a single tree for all members in a group.

Comparison of Sparse- and Dense-Mode Protocols

Sparse Mode	Dense Mode
Requires explicit joining of senders and receivers	Sends and stores explicit prune state information in response to unwanted packets
Does not send packets where they have not been requested	Broadcasts the first multicast packet
Stores shared-tree join information in anticipation of data packets	Stateless until data packets are sent
Relies on an RP initially for senders and receivers to meet and build a shared tree	No RP, the broadcast nature of the protocol builds the tree
Unicast protocol independent	Unicast protocol dependent
Requires periodic refreshing of explicit Join/Prune messages	No periodic updates on Prune messages; event driven

Multicast Open Shortest Path First (MOSPF)

Review RFC 1584. If you are not familiar with the OSPF (RFC 1583) protocol, please review the section on that protocol. There are assumptions about that protocol that are made here.

Modifications have been made to the OSPF routing protocol that have enabled the protocol to route IP multicast datagrams. There are three types of routing provided: intra-area routing, inter-area routing, and inter-autonomous system routing.

Intra-area routing is the most basic routing algorithm provided. It runs in a single OSPF area and supports the forwarding of multicast datagrams within a single area. This could be a single area in a multiple area of an OSPF autonomous system, or it could be a single autonomous system when there is only one area in the OSPF topology.

Inter-area routing is an OSPF topology that is split into several routing areas connected through a common area known as the *backbone* area. Decisions on forwarding multicast datagrams are still determined as in the intra-area routing; the information contained in the forwarding cache is used. The difference between the two is the method of forwarding group membership information and the method of constructing the inter-area multicast tree. Selected Area Border Routers (ABRs) are configured to perform a function known as inter-area multicast routers. These routers are responsible for the forwarding of group membership information and multicast datagrams between areas.

Inter-autonomous routing involves a source and destination path that is outside at least one autonomous system (AS). Selected

---

Multicast Open Shortest Path First (MOSPF)

- An extension of OSPF [RFC 1584] March 1994.

- A new LSA [group-membership-LSA] is used to describe the location of multicast destinations.

- A multicast packet's path is calculated using a shortest-path tree based on the IP datagram's source and destination.
    - It is not based on a Broadcast and Prune

- Multicast Hosts join/leave via IGMP [RFC 1112] facilities.

- Branches of the tree not containing multicast members are pruned from the tree.

- Vendor specific implementations can do "route pruning" for better member administration.

- Three types of routing are provided:
    - Intra-area, inter-area, and inter-autonomous system routing

Autonomous System Boundary Routers (ASBRs) are selected as inter-AS multicast forwarders. MOSPF makes the assumption that each inter-AS multicast forwarder is running a multicast routing protocol (such as PIM or DVMRP) that uses the RPF forwarding mechanism. This is the method used by MOSPF to leave its AS and route to another AS that could be running another routing protocol, or to get across the unicast Internet (since MSOPF does not support tunnels).

313   MOSPF Differences

MOSPF differs from DVMRP and PIM is many ways, but it should be noted right up front that MOSPF does not broadcast the first multicast packet it receives. The protocol builds a source-rooted, shortest-path tree "on demand" when it receives the first multicast packet and then prunes the branches not associated with this group. Also, MOSPF does not allow for tunneling as DVMRP does. Multicast datagrams are sent in native mode and are not encapsulated (DVMRP uses IP-in-IP encapsulation for tunneling).

A difference between OSPF and MOSPF is that MOSPF does not allow for equal-cost multipaths. There are tie-breaking rules that have been identified for paths that are found to be equal when calculating the shortest-path tree. One of these rules is that, given an equal-cost path to a destination, the router or LAN with the higher IP address will be chosen. The second tie-breaking rule is that a broadcast-oriented network is always chosen over WAN routers (point-to-point links).

MOSPF Differences

- MOSPF differs from DVMRP and PIM:
  - It does not broadcast the first multicast packet it receives

- Multicast is an integral part of the protocol.

- The protocol builds a source-rooted tree on-demand and then prunes branches.

- Multicast members are part of the link state database.

- Routes are computed like real routes and they are put into the forwarding cache.

- MOSPF does not allow for equal cost multipath:
  - Tie-breaking algorithms have been put into place

- MOSPF routes should be the DR and BDR in any mixed (i.e., non-MOSPF) environments.

OSPF allows for an autonomous system to be split into areas. Problems may occur when using MOSPF in a multi-area OSPF topology, for the ability of a router to have complete knowledge of the entire autonomous system is lost and incomplete shortest-path trees are built. Multicasts will still get through, but they may take the most efficient paths.

MOSPF Caveats

- MOSPF only operates effectively in pure OSPF environments, whereas most networks combine:
    - Different IGPs, such as RIP with OSPF
    - IGPs with EGPs, such as BGP-4 with EGPs

- MOSPF assumes network topology in a multi-area topology.

- MOSPF is known as a dense-mode multicast protocol.

- MOSPF can scale to large numbers of multicast groups but it comes at a cost of processing resources.

- MOSPF has been implemented by a few vendors.

- No ability to "tunnel" multicast datagrams through nonmulticast routers (MOSPF routers can forward unicast).

MOSPF provides for the ability to forward multicast datagrams from one IP subnet to another. A new OSPF link-state advertisement (group-membership LSA) has been added to accommodate this by allowing a source-rooted, pruned, shortest-path tree to be built. This new LSA augments the link-state database; therefore, the MOSPF database is the link-state database of OSPF but with entries that pertain to multicast networks.

The new LSA places the location of multicast destinations in the database. Using this information, MOSPF can build a shortest-path tree for a source group. MOSPF is an extension of OSPF and MOSPF routers will interoperate in nonmulticast routers when forwarding unicast datagrams.

An MOSPF router bases its forwarding decision on the contents of a data cache known as the *forwarding cache*. Each entry in the cache represents a source/destination combination (and possibly ToS). This forwarding cache is built from two components: a local group database (built by IGMP) datagram's shortest-path tree.

The local-group database keeps track of the local membership for the routers directly attached to networks. These entries are paired in the form of (group, attached network). The attached network is the IP address of the network, and the group is the IP multicast address of the multicast group. All we have to have is one host on that network indicating membership and the router will place an entry in the local-group database. Similar to the other multicast routing protocols, this database allows the router to determine which port(s) it should forward a received multicast datagram. The IGMP protocol assists in building this database.

To allow for multicast datagrams to be forwarded to all members of the group in an area, the local-group database is flooded throughout the area (including being received by ABRs) using the group-membership LSA. There is a separate group-membership LSA for each multicast group in the router's group database. The router's group-membership LSA for a specified group lists those local router ports (i.e., the router itself and/or any directly connected transit networks) that should not be pruned from the group's datagram shared trees.

Local-Group Database and the Group-Membership LSA

- New LSA devised:
  - Group-membership LSA
  - Based on IGMP reports
  - Augments the link-state database:
    - There is not a separate database for these LSAs

- Separate group membership LSA sent for each group to which a host belongs.

- Multicast tree is developed from this table.

- Entries are paired (group, attached network).

- Local-group database is flooded throughout the area.

- Router interfaces are included as part of a group.

- ABRs also receive these LSAs.

- ABRs are included in almost all multicast trees:
  - Wildcard feature to ensure that they know about all multicast trees, which enables them to build summary information to send to the backbone

Role of the DR and the BDR

- The DR issues Host Membership queries for the networks attached to it for which it is the DR.

- An MOSPF that is not the DR ignores reports.

- Prevents unnecessary replication of packets.

- The BDR performs the same functions as the DR except that it does not transmit queries until the DR goes away.

- Set non-MOSPF routers with a priority of 0 to ensure they do not become the DR or BDR.

It is the designated router (DR) that issues the Host Membership Queries for the networks attached to it. An MOSPF router ignores reports for those networks not elected the DR. Any responses (IGMP reports) received from the networks builds entries based on groups, in the database. A group address (member) in this database will be deleted when the DR does not receive a report from that member. In a multicast environment, it is very important that the DR is a multicast-enabled router.

Having the DR become the querier prevents unnecessary replication of packets. This prevents multicast datagrams from being replicated as they are delivered to local-group members. This allows for different entries in the local-group database for the DRs in the autonomous system, which means that each router in the autonomous system has a different local-group database. However, the MOSPF link-state database and the datagram shortest-path trees are identical in each router belonging to the autonomous system.

The backup designated router (BDR) performs the same functions as the DR. It does not send out a query, but it processes the IGMP reports (host responses) so that it will contain a complete picture of the DR. In case the DR fails, the BDR can take over. One word of caution: You never want an non-MOSPF router to become the DR or BDR. To disable these routers from becoming the DR or BDR, set their priority to 0. Without the DR or BDR being an MOSPF router, MOSPF cannot operate properly.

When an IGMP report is received, the DR (all other routers except for the BDR discard this message) does some simple error checking (making sure the address is not in the local use range of 224.0.0.0– 244.0.0.255). If there is not an entry in the local-group database, it creates one (using the format of IP group address, attached network number) and sets the age entry to 0. In the local-group database, there is only one entry per multicast address, even if multiple hosts report membership. The DR may transmit a new group-membership LSA. Group-membership LSAs are only flooded to those neighbors that have indicated (through their database description packets) that they are multicast ready. This is accomplished by setting the MC (Multicast Capable) bit in the OSPF Options field of all Hello packets, Database Description packets, and all link-state advertisements.

317

The Local-Group Database

The local-group database consists of three components:

Multicast group: A Class D IP address.

Attached network: The IP address of the attached network that contains the multicast group.

Age: The number of seconds since an IGMP Host Membership report has been seen.

Other routers find out about local-group members through the group-membership LSA. There is one LSA for each multicast group that has one or more entries in the local-group database.

The link-state database indicates which routers/transit networks have attached group members.

The Local-Group Database

- Built in the DR and BDR.

- Consists of three components:
    - A multicast group—a Class D address
    - Attached network—the IP address of the attached network that contains the multicast group
    - Age—the number of seconds since an IGMP Host Membership report has been seen

- Flooded throughout the AS (or single area).

- Assists in building the link-state database and the shortest-path tree.

- Facilitates in the delivery of local multicast datagrams.

Operation

- When the first multicast datagram (containing the source net, multicast destination) is received by a router, it will find the source subnet in the link-state database.

- A source-rooted multicast tree is built using the Router LSAs and the Network LSAs and the Dykstra algorithm.

- Once the tree is built, it is pruned using the information from the group-membership LSAs.

- Final result of the Dykstra algorithm is the pruned shortest-path tree that is rooted at the source.

- Based on this, an entry is made in the forwarding cache of the router.

The local-group database enables the local delivery of multicast datagrams. The datagram's shortest-path tree enables the delivery of multicast datagrams to distant (i.e., not directly attached) group members. Both of these are used in the calculation of the forwarding cache.

The following are standard assumptions when using MOSPF:

- All MOSPF routers within the same area calculate the same shortest-path tree for a given multicast datagram. This is accomplished via synchronized link-state databases.

- Link-state databases can be synchronized using the new group-membership LSA. With each router in an area having the same database, each router should be able

to build a source-rooted, shortest-path, multicast tree without having to broadcast the first multicast packet.

- The shortest-path multicast tree is built "on demand." This means that the tree is built when a router receives a multicast datagram for the first time for a given multicast group. An MOSPF router does not automatically forward the first multicast datagram like DVMRP does. Since the synchronized link-state database contains group-membership LSAs, this allows a MOSPF router to perform "broadcast the first datagram" in its memory and the tree is built on demand. The routers already know where the active group memberships are and can build the tree without forwarding the first datagram and then waiting for Prune messages.

When the first multicast datagram arrives (at any router), the source subnet (IP address of the source) is located in the link-state database. This is sometimes called the MOSPF *link-state database*, but the single database (link-state database) contains entries for both unicast and multicast. A source-rooted multicast tree is calculated using the router LSAs and the network LSAs using the Dykstra algorithm (same as unicast OSPF). Once the tree is built, it is pruned (to eliminate links that do not contain at least one member of a group) using the group-membership LSAs. The final result of the Dykstra algorithm is the pruned shortest-path tree that is rooted at the source (remember, OSPF calculates its shortest-path tree using itself as the root). This shortest-path tree is used to understand which ports should be used for the forwarding of multicast datagrams that are distant (i.e., no local-group membership, but there are members of the group downstream from this router), and which ports should receive which multicast datagram (source).

Now we have two sources of information: the source-routed shortest-path tree and the local-group database. Both of these are used to determine the forwarding cache, which is the only place the router will look to determine forwarding of a multicast datagram.

319 Forwarding Cache

The forwarding cache is used to determine how to forward a multicast datagram. A multicast datagram may be delivered locally or it may be forwarded on a branch to another multicast router. I mentioned before that upon receipt of a multicast datagram, Dykstra runs and the result is a pruned, source-rooted tree. The forwarding cache is built using the shortest-path tree built by the Dykstra algorithm and the entries in the local-group database. The router first finds its position in the shortest-path tree. Once the router discovers its position,

Forwarding Cache

- Used to determine the correct path on which to forward a multicast datagram.

- Entries are placed here by the shortest-path tree built using the Dykstra algorithm and the local-group database.

- Router must find its position in the shortest-path tree.

- Router creates an entry that consists of the (source, group) pair, the upstream node, and the downstream interfaces.

it will create a entry in the forwarding cache that contains the (source, group) pair, the upstream node, and the downstream interfaces.

The following entries are placed into the forwarding cache:

Source network: The network number of the source.

Destination multicast group: A known destination group address to which multicast datagrams are currently being forwarded.

Upstream node: The interface that datagrams addressed to (source, group) should be received on.

List of downstream interfaces: The interface(s) that a multicast datagram (indexed by source, group) should be forwarded on.

List of downstream neighbors: To assist in the forwarding of multicast datagrams in a hybrid (mixed OSPF and MOSPF) network.

TTL: The number of hops the datagram will travel to reach any outlying group members. This provides for efficiency in that the router can discard a multicast datagram if the received TTL is less than this TTL.

TTLs are used by transmitting hosts to restrict the forwarding of a multicast datagram. This allows for efficiency in that a multicast datagram will only be forwarded (over routers) the number of hops indicated by the TTL of the received datagram. Notice that in the forwarding cache, each of the downstream neighbors is labeled with a TTL (Time to Live) value. The is an optimizing feature in that if a MOSPF router receives a multicast datagram whose TTL is lower than the entry in its routing table, the router will discard the datagram. The information contained in the cache remains stable until one of two things happens: An OSPF topology change forces the cache to be flushed (all entries are deleted and are not placed back into this cache until receipt of a multicast datagram which will build a new entry); or a group-membership LSA is received that contains a change in the members of a group. A new tree will have to be constructed based on this information.

320   Inter-Area MOSPF Routing

The basic algorithm for MOSPF works in a single area. Inter-area routing for multicast involves a source and one or more destination groups in different areas. The forwarding of multicast datagrams between areas is still decided by the information contained in the forwarding cache. The problem is the ability to accurately build a complete shortest-path tree because detailed information about the other area's topology is not known (in OSPF it is summarized, in MOSPF it is not known). Furthermore, since LSAs are not flooded to different areas, the group LSA is not propagated to other areas. To compensate for this "unknown" information, estimates are made by using the wildcard feature of the Area Border Router (new to MOSPF) and the summary link advertisements provided by the ABR. After a few introductions, how MOSPF overcomes these limitations is explained.

In a multicast topology that is represented by multiple areas, a new function within the ABR, called *inter-area multicast forwarders*, is implemented. These forwarders pass group information and allow for the ability of multicast datagrams to cross areas. It is the ABR that is configured to perform this function. Forwarders runs as a separate function of the ABR and are used only for multicast datagrams.

ABRs implementing the multicast forwarder summarize their area's group information (how is explained in a moment) and send it to the backbone area through the use of group-membership LSAs, which are "injected" into the backbone area. The backbone routers

> ## Inter-Area MOSPF Routing
>
> - Basic algorithm for MOSPF works in a single area.
>
> - Topologies that include multiple areas have a new function in the ABR known as the "inter-area multicast forwarder":
>   - Passes group information and allows for the ability of multicast datagrams to cross areas
>
> - ABRs summarize their area's group information and inject this information into the backbone.
>
> - Backbone routers record this information in their link-state database and the router from which they received this information.
>
> - Information is asymmetric.
>
> - Inter-area multicast forwarders are ABR wildcard receivers.

receive this information and include it in their link-state database by group and the router it received it from. The backbone routers process this information but do not forward any multicast information on to any other multicast ABRs. Furthermore, no information regarding the backbone's group membership is forwarded to any area. It is asymmetrical. Information flows into the backbone, but the backbone does not flow the information into other areas. So how does information flow between areas, or from the backbone to an area? So how does the multicast forwarder know of the groups in its area and know when to pass information from the backbone to an area? This involves the concept known as the *wildcard receiver*.

MOSPF routers may indicate they want to receive all multicast datagrams regardless of the destination. They can indicate this through their router-LSA using a newly defined bit in the rtype field known as the *W bit*, or *wildcard bit*. This bit is used with inter-area multicast forwarders (ABRs) and permits a MOSPF router to receive all multicast traffic in an area regardless of the group. MOSPF routers that employ this function ensure that they remain on all pruned multicast trees, thus allowing them to receive all multicast datagrams regardless of group membership. By default, all multicast forwarder ABRs are wildcard receivers.

Inter-Area Multicast Example 321

Having the multicast forwarders as wildcards enables them to receive multicast datagrams from the backbone and any multicast forwarder to be included in any multicast tree built in their area. When a multicast datagram is to be forwarded, it is received by the ABR (multicast forwarder) for forwarding to the backbone. The backbone routers know which groups are active in which areas, and since the ABR is part of the backbone they can receive the information from the backbone to be forwarded to their area.

The backbone routers do not implement the wildcard function, for these routers inherently know about all multicast groups through the multicast ABRs flowing summary information into the backbone, which is received by the backbone routers.

How is the forwarding cache built based on these assumptions? It depends on whether the source and a router building the tree are in the same area or not. The forwarding of multicast information is still accomplished using the forwarding cache, but an accurate picture cannot be drawn.

If the source and the router performing the calculation are in the same area, the wildcard feature of the ABR comes into play. This forces the router to be included in all multicast computations, which allows for the branches of the ABR to be included in the shortest-path tree. The ABR will not be pruned.

If the source and the router performing the calculation are in different areas, then the summary link advertisements are used. This forces the inter-area multicast forwarders of the ABR to be included in the calculated tree.

A final note: Area Border Routers have separate link-state databases for each area they attach to—this is a normal OSPF process. For multicast, however, this means that each multicast forwarder must build a separate forwarding tree for each area they attach to. But all of the area's forwarding information is contained in one forwarding cache and as soon as this is built, the shortest-path trees for each area are dismantled. There is no need for them once the forwarding cache contains all the information needed for forwarding multicast datagrams.

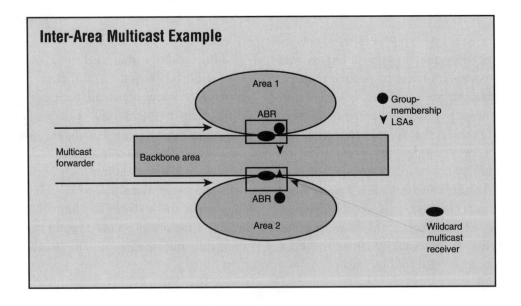

Inter-Area Shortest-Path Tree

The following slide show the path between areas. Notice that the ABRs are wildcard receivers. This allows them to be included in all trees that are built.

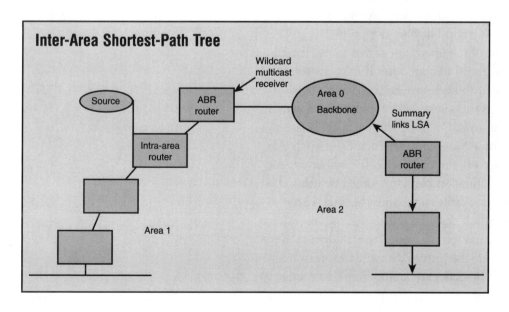

323

Inter-Autonomous System Multicast

This type of multicast routing involves a source and destination that reside in different autonomous systems. This includes the ability of routing between an MOSPF domain and a DVMRP domain, but within the same AS. This is similar in the way OSPF treats RIP. Both OSPF and RIP can be used in the same AS, but they are treated as separate routing domains.

Just as in the inter-area multicast routing, configured Autonomous System Boundary Routers are configured to perform the inter-AS multicast forwarder function. This works under the assumption that each inter-AS multicast forwarder employs a multicast forwarding protocol that uses Reverse Path Forwarding, such as DVMRP or PIM. The multicast ASBRs use the wildcard capability. With this, each ASBR acts as a multicast wildcard receiver for each of its attached areas. This ensures that the inter-AS multicast forwarders are included in all multicast trees. They are not pruned.

Most of the operation of this router is similar to the inter-area multicast forwarder. However, there is one case in which it is different: If the source of the multicast datagram and the router making the calculation are in different ASs. Again, the details of each AS topology will not be known. To compensate for this, information can be assumed by using the Summary-ASBR link and the AS External links, which describe the source subnet. After the calculation is done, the multicast tree begins at the inter-AS multicast forwarder, with all branches stemming from this router.

Inter-Autonomous System Multicast

- Involves source and destinations that reside in different autonomous systems.

- ASBRs perform a new function known as Inter-AS multicast forwarder.

- ASBRs use the wildcard mechanism:
  - Allows ASBRs to be included in all multicast trees

Multicast Conclusion

- MOSPF requires that you run OSPF or MOSPF network.

- MOSPF converges instantly.

- MOSPF does not support tunnels directly.

- MOSPF scales well.

- MOSPF works in sparsely populated areas as well as dense.

Multicasting is coming and it is taking many forms on an internet or the Internet. We have voice, video, and data multicasting. There is one common protocol message format, and that is IGMP. PIM and DVMRP use this framing for their messages as well. MOSPF uses its own LSA for communicating between routers. However, all multicast applications conform to IGMP to register themselves on the local subnet.

All of the protocols have their own advantages and disadvantages. MOSPF requires that you are running OSPF. A RIPv1 or RIPv2 network cannot simply install MOSPF. If the site chooses to use RIP, it must use PIM or DVMRP. MOSPF converges instantly, whereas PIM and DVMRP may have routing loops during a slow convergence. However, installing MOSPF is not a simple task, for MOSPF is OSPF with multicast extensions; therefore, all of the rules with OSPF still apply. MOSPF does not support tunnels. It expects some type of other protocol such as DVMRP to be running on the M-ASBR routers. DVMRP does not scale well and neither does PIM without some tuning. DVMRP and MOSPF work better in densely populated environments, whereas PIM has two modes of operation: sparse and dense mode. PIM allows for duplicate packets in dense mode, in favor of a simpler protocol that is not dependent on a unicast routing mechanism. You really must consider all the options before placing a multicast protocol on your network.

One of the things you must think about with multicast is not only receiving data, but how to respond that data. Yes, multicasting does allow for one station to send one datastream to be received by literally tens of thousands of receivers. But what if there is a need for acknowledgment of that data? This poses a considerable problem: one sender, multiple receivers. If the number of receivers is 2000 and they all need to send some type of Receiver Status message back to the sender, the sender must be able to handle this type of back-channel information flow—especially if the status is long. The inability to handle this is called *implosion*, during which the originator is overrun by the back channel.

325

RFCs to Be Reviewed

2236 Internet Group Management Protocol, Version 2. W. Fenner. November 1997. (Format: TXT=51048 bytes) (Updates RFC1112) (Status: PROPOSED STANDARD).

2201 Core Based Trees (CBT) Multicast Routing Architecture. A.Ballardie. September 1997. (Format: TXT=38040 bytes) (Status: EXPERI-MENTAL).

2189 Core Based Trees (CBT version 2) Multicast Routing. A. Ballardie. September 1997. (Format: TXT=52043 bytes) (Status: EXPERIMENTAL).

2117 Protocol Independent Multicast-Sparse Mode (PIM-SM): Protocol Specification. D. Estrin, D. Farinacci, A. Helmy, D. Thaler, S. Deering, M. Handley, V. Jacobson, C. Liu, P. Sharma, L. Wei. June 1997. (Format: TXT=151886 bytes) (Status: EXPERIMENTAL).

1700 ASSIGNED NUMBERS. J. Reynolds,J. Postel. October 1994. (Format: TXT=458860 bytes) (Obsoletes RFC1340) (Also STD0002) (Status: STANDARD).

1584 Multicast Extensions to OSPF. J. Moy. March 1994. (Format: TXT=262463, PS=426358 bytes) (Status: PROPOSED STANDARD).

1469 IP Multicast over Token-Ring Local Area Networks. T. Pusateri. June 1993. (Format: TXT=8189 bytes) (Status: PROPOSED STAN-DARD).

1458 Requirements for Multicast Protocols. R. Braudes & S. Zabele. May 1993. (Format: TXT=48106 bytes) (Status: INFORMATIONAL).

1112 Host extensions for IP multicasting. S.E. Deering. Aug-01-1989. (Format: TXT=39904 bytes) (Obsoletes RFC0988, RFC1054) (Updated by RFC2236) (Status: STANDARD).

1075 Distance Vector Multicast Routing Protocol. D. Waitzman, C.Partridge, S.E. Deering. Nov-01-1988. (Format: TXT=54731 bytes) (Status: EXPERIMENTAL).

Multicast drafts—these can be obtained from many sources. The one that I used is:

http://info.internet.isi.edu:80/in-drafts/id-abstracts.html

"Distance Vector Multicast Routing Protocol", T. Pusateri, 08/11/1998, <draft-ietf-idmr-dvmrp-v3-07.txt,.ps>. This document is an update to Version 1 of the protocol specified in RFC 1075.

"Domain Wide Multicast Group Membership Reports", Bill Fenner, 08/07/1998, <draft-ietf-idmr-membership-reports-01.txt,.ps>. Domain Wide Multicast Group Membership Reports allow this information to be learned in a fashion similar to IGMP at the domain level.

"Internet Group Management Protocol, Version 3", Steve Deering, B. Cain, A. Thyagarajan, 12/03/1997, <draft-ietf-idmr-igmp-v3-00.txt>. This document specifies Version 3 of the Internet Group Management Protocol, IGMPv3. Version 3 of IGMP adds support for "source filtering."

"PIM Version 2 DR Election Priority Option", L. Wei, 03/05/1998, <draft-ietf-idmr-pimv2-dr-prior-ity-00.txt>. This draft specifies the DR Election Priority Option in PIM version 2 Hello messages.

"IGMP Multicast Router Discovery", B. Cain, Shantam Biswas, 03/12/1998, <draft-ietf-idmr-igmp-mrdisc-00.txt>. Companies have been proposing "IGMP snooping" type schemes for layer-2 bridging devices. A method for discovery multi-cast capable routers is necessary for these schemes.

"Core Based Trees (CBT version 3) Multicast Routing—Protocol Specification—", <draft-ietf-idmr-cbt-spec-v3-01.txt>. This specification supercedes and obsoletes RFC 2189.

RFCs to Be Reviewed

- 2236 Internet Group Management Protocol, Version 2. W. Fenner. November 1997. (Format: TXT=51048 bytes) (Updates RFC1112) (Status: PROPOSED STANDARD).

- 2201 Core Based Trees (CBT) Multicast Routing Architecture. A.Ballardie. September 1997. (Format: TXT=38040 bytes) (Status:EXPERIMENTAL).

- 2189 Core Based Trees (CBT version 2) Multicast Routing. A. Ballardie. September 1997. (Format: TXT=52043 bytes) (Status: EXPERIMENTAL).

- 2117 Protocol Independent Multicast-Sparse Mode (PIM-SM): Protocol Specification. D. Estrin, D. Farinacci, A. Helmy, D. Thaler, S. Deering, M. Handley, V. Jacobson, C. Liu, P. Sharma, L. Wei. June 1997. (Format: TXT=151886 bytes) (Status: EXPERIMENTAL).

- 1700 ASSIGNED NUMBERS. J. Reynolds,J. Postel. October 1994. (Format: TXT=458860 bytes) (Obsoletes RFC1340) (Also STD0002) (Status: STANDARD).

- 1584 Multicast Extensions to OSPF. J. Moy. March 1994. (Format: TXT=262463, PS=426358 bytes) (Status: PROPOSED STANDARD).

- 1469 IP Multicast over Token-Ring Local Area Networks. T. Pusateri. June 1993. (Format: TXT=8189 bytes) (Status: PROPOSED STANDARD).

- 1458 Requirements for Multicast Protocols. R. Braudes & S. Zabele. May 1993. (Format: TXT=48106 bytes) (Status: INFORMATIONAL).

- 1112 Host extensions for IP multicasting. S. Deering. Aug-01-1989. (Format: TXT=39904 bytes) (Obsoletes RFC0988, RFC1054) (Updated by RFC2236) (Status: STANDARD).

- 1075 Distance Vector Multicast Routing Protocol. D. Waitzman, C.Partridge, S. Deering. Nov-01-1988. (Format: TXT=54731 bytes). (Status: EXPERIMENTAL).

Multicast drafts—these can be obtained from many sources. The one that I used is: http://info.internet.isi.edu:80/in-drafts/id-abstracts.html

"Distance Vector Multicast Routing Protocol", T. Pusateri, 08/11/1998, <draft-ietf-idmr-dvmrp-v3-07.txt,.ps>. This document is an update to Version 1 of the protocol specified in RFC 1075.

"Domain Wide Multicast Group Membership Reports", Bill Fenner, 08/07/1998, <draft-ietf-idmr-membership-reports-01.txt,.ps>.

"Internet Group Management Protocol, Version 3", Steve Deering, B. Cain, A. Thyagarajan, 12/03/1997, <draft-ietf-idmr-igmp-v3-00.txt>.

"PIM Version 2 DR Election Priority Option", L. Wei, 03/05/1998, <draft-ietf-idmr-pimv2-dr-priority-00.txt>.

"IGMP Multicast Router Discovery", B. Cain, Shantam Biswas, 03/12/1998, <draft-ietf-idmr-igmp-mrdisc-00.txt>.

"Core Based Trees (CBT version 3) Multicast Routing — Protocol Specification —" <draft-ietf-idmr-cbt-spec-v3-01.txt>.

Web Sites

www.ipmulticast.com
www.mbone.com

Part Six

BOOTP, DHCP, RSVP, and SNMP

326

Boot Protocol (BOOTP)

This protocol has been around a long time. It was most often used with diskless workstations. It enabled these workstations to get their configuration and boot files to remotely boot over the network. The best example of this was SUN workstations and their Network File System (NFS). These diskless network stations could boot over the network (using a small bootstrap protocol found in a PROM). With this they could get their configuration parameters such as their IP address and subnet mask and then perform the boot sequence to boot up their machine from a remote server.

The Bootstrap Protocol (BOOTP) is a UDP/IP-based client-server application originally promoted to allow diskless clients to boot remotely from a server on the same network or from a server on a different network for the purpose of obtaining the name of a file to be loaded into memory and executed, an IP address, and the address of its boot server. The RFC for BOOTP is RFC 951, but there have been a few supplemental RFCs since then to clear up some "loosely defined" features of the protocol that can lead to misinterpretation and eventually incompatibilities between vendors supporting the protocol. The most recent one is RFC 1542, "Clarifications and Extensions for the Bootstrap Protocol." Other configuration information such as the local subnet mask, the local time offset, the addresses of default routers, and the addresses of various Internet servers can also be communicated to a host using BOOTP.

Boot Protocol (BOOTP)

- RFC 951.
  - Updated by RFCs 1395, 1497, 1532, and 1542
- Originated many years ago as a method of booting diskless workstations on a LAN.
- Works as microcode in a PROM.
- Workstation boots a simple operating system.
  - Just enough to send out Boot messages to a BOOTP server
- Usually operates in two stages:
  - First, it gets its IP address
  - Next, it uses the TFTP protocol to boot its full operating image

The basic operation is as follows:

There is a single packet type exchanged between the client and the server. One field in the packet is called the *opcode* and can have one of two values: BOOTREQUEST or BOOTREPLY. The client broadcasts a BOOTREQUEST packet that contains the client's hardware address and its IP address if known. The BOOTREQUEST may contain the name of the server the client wishes to respond. This is to force the BOOTREQUEST packet to a particular server from which to obtain its information. This may occur if there are many servers on the network or if there is more than one image (older/newer) version that could be sent to the client. Inside the BOOTREQUEST may be a generic filename to be booted. Simple names like ipboot or unixboot are used. When the server replies with a BOOTREPLY, it replaces this entry with the full pathname by which the file can be located on that server.

If the client does not know its IP address, the server must possess a database of MAC-to-IP address mappings. Once a match is found, this IP address is placed in a field in the BOOTREPLY packet.

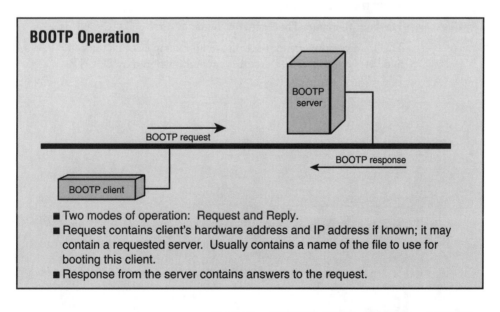

BOOTP Operation

- Two modes of operation: Request and Reply.
- Request contains client's hardware address and IP address if known; it may contain a requested server. Usually contains a name of the file to use for booting this client.
- Response from the server contains answers to the request.

BOOTP Field Definitions

Field	Bytes	Description
op	1	Packet operation code/message type. 1 = BOOTREQUEST, 2 = BOOTREPLY
htype	1	Hardware address type, same as ARP section in "Assigned Numbers" RFC. For example, "1" = 10 Mb Ethernet.
hlen	1	Hardware address length. For example, "6" (bytes) for 10 Mb Ethernet.
hops	1	Client sets to 0 and optionally used by gateways in BOOTP Relay.
xid	4	Transaction ID. A random number used to match this boot request with the responses it generates.
secs	2	Filled in by the client, indicating the number of seconds that have elapsed since the client started trying to boot.
ciaddr	4	Client IP address; filled in by client in BOOTREQUEST, if known.
yiaddr	4	"Your" (client) IP address; filled in by the server if the client doesn't know its own address (i.e., ciaddr was a 0).
siaddr	4	Server IP address, returned in the BOOTREPLY by the server.
giaddr	4	The gateway's IP address of the port that received the first BOOTREQUEST. It is used in the BOOTREPLY function.
chaddr	16	The client's hardware (MAC) address. It is filled in by the client.
sname	64	Optional. The server hostname being requested by the client. All other servers would then ignore this packet.
file	128	The boot filename. The "'generic" name in the BOOTREQUEST.
Vend	64	This is an optional vendor-specific field. Examples of its use could be a serial number, version number, etc. It is generally ignored by BOOTP.

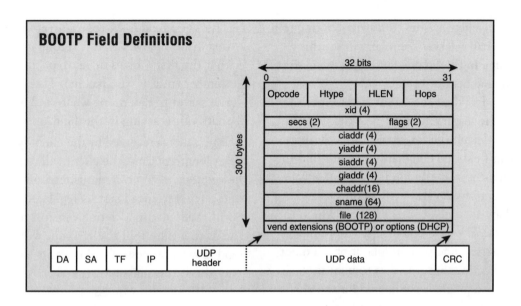

Client Side (BOOTREQUEST)

329

The following is the series of steps taken by the client to build a BOOTREQUEST packet:

1. The IP destination address (in the IP header, not the BOOTP fields) is set to 255.255.255.255. Optionally, it may set the address to the server's IP address, if it is known.

2. The IP source address is set to its IP address (if known); otherwise, it is set to 0.

3. The UDP port numbers are set to 67 for UDP destination port (the server) and 68 for the UDP source port (the client).

4. The op field is set to 1 (BOOTREQUEST).

5. The htype is set to the hardware address type (bit length) and the HLEN is set to the length of the hardware address.

6. xid is set to a random number.

7. secs is set to the number of seconds that have elapsed since the client started booting.

8. The ciaddr is set to an IP address of the client (if known); otherwise, it is set to 0 and the chaddr is set to the client's hardware address.

9. If the client wishes to restrict booting to a particular server name, it will set this name in the Sname field; otherwise, the Sname field is set to 0.

10. The File field can be set to 0 to indicate to the server that it wishes to boot from the default file for its machine. Setting this field to 0 could also indicate that the client is interested in finding out client/server/gateway IP addresses and does not care about a file from which to boot. The field could be set to a simple generic name such as ipboot or unixboot, indicating that it wishes to boot the named program configured for the client. Finally, the field can be set to the full pathname of the server on which the boot file resides.

11. The Vend field is set to whatever the vendor wishes. However, it is recommended that the first 4 bytes be set to a "magic" number (that is, you pick it). This allows the server to determine what kind of information it is seeing in this field.

If no reply is received by the client within a preset length of time, the client will retransmit the request up to an administered amount of times. The retransmission is regulated in that it will randomly send retransmission requests. This is to ensure that the network will not be flooded with requests should clients somehow sync their transmissions (purely by coincidence). Before retransmission, the Secs field is updated.

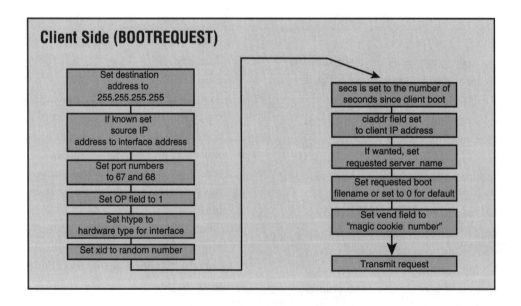

When the server receives the packet, a series of decisions takes place:

- If the UDP destination port is not set to 67, then the server will discard the packet.
- If the Server field (sname) is set to 0 or matches our name, further process the packet.
- If the server name does not match our name, but the name is local on the network, then discard the packet.
- If the server name is not on the local network, the server may choose to forward the packet to that server. Usually, this is accomplished via the BOOTP relay service (explained in a moment).
- If the Ciaddr field is 0, then the client does not know its IP address, so the server will look this up in its database If no match is found for this chaddr, then discard the

packet. Otherwise, the Yiaddr field is filled in on the response packet.

- The Filename field is then checked. If this field contains a 0, then the client is either not interested in a boot file or wishes to use the default boot file. If there is a filename specified, or a default file is found, or the field contains a full-length pathname, then the File field is replaced with the full-length pathname of the selected boot file. If the field is set to a non-0 and no match is found for this field on this server, then the client is asking for a file that the server does not have, and the server will discard the packet.
- Finally, the Vend field is checked and if a recognized type of data is provided, client-specific actions should be taken and a response from these actions is placed in

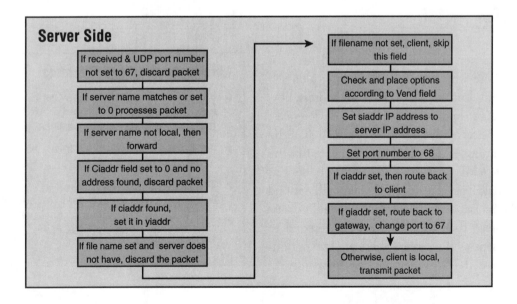

Server Side

- If received & UDP port number not set to 67, discard packet
- If server name matches or set to 0 processes packet
- If server name not local, then forward
- If Ciaddr field set to 0 and no address found, discard packet
- If ciaddr found, set it in yiaddr
- If file name set and server does not have, discard the packet

- If filename not set, client, skip this field
- Check and place options according to Vend field
- Set siaddr IP address to server IP address
- Set port number to 68
- If ciaddr set, then route back to client
- If giaddr set, route back to gateway, change port to 67
- Otherwise, client is local, transmit packet

the Vend Data field of the Reply packet. This field, for example could contain configuration options that can be passed to the boot file that will be transmitted to the client after the BOOTP is finished.

- The Siaddr field is set to the server's address and the Op field is set to a BOOTREPLY. The UDP destination port is set to 68 (BOOTP client).

- If the Ciaddr address of the BOOT-REQUEST is set to a non-0 address, then the packet is IP routed back to the client. However, if the Giaddr is set to a non-0, then the BOOTREPLY is sent directly to this router and the UDP destination port is set to BOOTPS (67). Otherwise, the client is local and the BOOTREPLY is send back to the client on the local LAN.

331   Chicken-or-the-Egg? Dilemma

A question should come to mind here for those who have been following along: If the client does not yet know its IP address, how is it going to respond to the server's ARP request when the server decides to respond? Well, if the client knows its IP address (as indicated in the Ciaddr field), the BOOTREPLY can be sent as a normal IP packet, since the client will respond to ARPs. But if the client does not yet know its IP address, then the client cannot respond to ARPs sent by the server. There are two options available: If the server has the capability to

Chicken-or-the-Egg? Dilemma

- If the client does not yet know its IP address, how does it respond to ARP requests during a server response?

- If the client knows its IP address, this is not a problem.

- Two options:
    - Simply send the reply set to broadcast
    - The server can manually construct the ARP entry using the fields in the received request

manually construct an ARP entry in its table for this client, it will do so using the Chaddr and Yiaddr fields that it is responding with in its BOOTREPLY (BSD Unix has this capability). The server will then reply using IP services and

skip the ARP process. If the server does not have this capability, then it simply sends the BOOTREPLY with the IP address set to Broadcast (B). This event is shown in the table.

ciaddr	giaddr	B	UDP Destination	IP Destination	Link Destination
non-0	X	X	BOOTClient (68)	ciaddr	normal
0.0.0.0	non-0	X	BOOTPServer	giaddr	normal
0.0.0.0	0.0.0.0	0	BOOTPClient (68)	yiaddr	'chaddr'
0.0.0.0	0.0.0.0	1	BOOTPClient (68)	255.255.255.255	broadcastX

BOOTP Relay Agents (or BOOTP Gateway)   332

The BOOTP operation also considers the possibility that clients and servers may not be on the same IP network or subnet (those network segments not separated by a router). Therefore, some kind of relay agent is needed to forward the BOOTP messages. This type of service is most commonly found as part of the router function; however, it is more than a router simply receiving a BOOTP message and forwarding it on to the next segment. Basically, the router receives the message, processes it as if the message was addressed to

it, and then sends out a new BOOTP message to the appropriate forwarded port.

The forwarding (scope) of a BOOTP or DHCP packet can be limited by configuring the router to limit the scope. Each router increments the TTL field. If the received packet has its limit already set in the TTL field, the packet will be discarded. Also, the router must be configured as to which ports the router should forward this packet on. It is not simply forwarded to one port. When the router forwards the packet on, if it is the first router to do so, it will place its address in the Giaddr field of the packet. It knows that it is the first router because this field is set to 0.0.0.0. When a router forwards the packet, it forwards it set to Broadcast.

Cisco enables this feature as IP helper-address. This feature allows for more than just BOOTP packets to be forwarded across the router. Basically, any UDP broadcast address can be forwarded across the router.

**BOOTP Relay Agents
(Or BOOTP Gateway)**

■ Used when requests and servers are not on the same network.
  ■ Separated by a router

■ Need some type of agent that can forward these requests over a router:
  ■ Router must be aware of this because routers do not forward messages addressed in broadcast

■ Router receives a message and resends it as if the router had sent it:
  ■ Places its address in the Giaddr field

■ Can set the scope field to limit the forwarding of the request.

---

333 Dynamic Host Configuration Protocol (DHCP)

Which came first, BOOTP or DHCP? Which one does both? Why do you hear about BOOTP every time something is written about DHCP? Since the protocol is based on a broadcast mechanism, why and how do these protocols operate in a routed environment? In fact, why do we need another configuration mechanism when we have DRARP (Dynamic Reverse Address Resolution Protocol) and ICMP (Internet Control Message Protocol)? DRARP addresses the problem of IP address assignment and hosts can use ICMP to find out the subnetmask for a network and to dynami-

---

Dynamic Host Configuration Protocol (DHCP)

■ DHCP builds on the BOOTP protocol.

■ Probably best known for its IP address leasing capability.

■ Configured as:
  ■ DHCP Client
  ■ DHCP Server
  ■ BOOTP Relay Agent
  ■ Binding

cally discover routers, right? And, since we consider a router to sometimes be a host, does DHCP provide configuration information for a router? Or, have you forgotten about those capabilities?

DHCP is gaining considerable attention due to a number of factors: tight address allocation restrictions, which requires efficient assignment or reassignment of IP addresses (IP addresses are in short supply and are handed out very carefully. DHCP offers us the capability of handing them out statistically based on probability. Therefore, we can have many users and not as many IP addresses.).

This chapter explains the DHCP protocol. The DHCP protocol for the purposes of this

writing can fully interoperate with BOOTP servers and clients.

Terms used in the DHCP protocol are as follows:

DHCP Client: A host that is requesting configuration information.

DHCP Server: A DHCP hosts that supplies configuration parameters to a requesting host.

BOOTP Relay Agent: The protocol that allows BOOTP and DHCP packets to traverse a router.

Binding: Configuration parameters, including an IP address, that are "bound to" a host.

DHCP 334

DHCP provides a transport mechanism for passing configuration information (that is located on a server) to requesting hosts on a TCP/IP network. What kind of parameters are used for this information? The parameter information is based on the host requirements RFCs (RFCs 1122, 1123, 1112, etc.) After being supplied with this configuration information, the host should be able to communicate with any other host on the Internet.

It is true that DHCP is based on BOOTP, but it adds much more functionality including

the ability to "lease" IP network addresses. DHCP also uses some of the features of BOOTP (relay agent, for forwarding the messages across routers) and is interoperable with existing BOOTP clients (RFC 1534 describes the interoperability functions of BOOTP and DHCP). The DHCP messages are in the exact same format as BOOTP. Refer to the slide. DHCP adds the ability to support "leased" IP addresses and other functions. This allows requesting stations to get their IP addresses from a server and then return them when they are finished. These added functions are described in RFC 2132.

DHCP consists of two parts: a protocol for delivering host-specific configuration parameters, and the ability to allocate IP addresses. It is based on a client/server model in which the host requests information from a server. A host can ask a specific server to supply information to it, or it may simply rely on any server to relay information to it. A server must be preconfigured to handle a specific client's request, or the server will ignore the request.

The first service provided by DHCP is static storage of network parameters for requesting clients. This information is stored in a database (or table) on a host server. The entries are "keyed." This means that a unique identifier is used to single out the parameters of a requesting host. This identifier is stated as the "client identifier" (or Chaddr), and the assigned network address, and uniquely identifies the lease between the client and the server for DHCP.

DHCP

- Provides a transport mechanism for passing configuration information to requesting hosts.

- Configuration information is based on that specified in RFCs 1112, 1122, and 1123.

- DHCP and BOOTP are interoperable.

- DHCP messages are in the same format as BOOTP.

- DHCP is considered to do two things:
  - IP address allocation
  - Delivery of configuration information

- Configuration information is stored in a database table on the DHCP server:
  - Client specifies which parameters it is looking for in the Vendor Extensions field of the request packet

IP Address Allocation

- Automatic Allocation: permanently assigns an IP address to a station.

- Dynamic Allocation: assigns an IP address to a requesting station for specified amount of time.

- Manual Allocation: preconfigures the server to give the requesting station the same IP address every time it requests it.

The next service that DHCP provides for is IP address allocation. Three methods are supported: automatic allocation, dynamic allocation, and manual allocation.

Automatic allocation permanently assigns an IP address to a requesting host. Dynamic allocation gives an IP address to a requesting host for a specific amount of time. Manual allocation is the ability to reconfigure an IP address for a host, and the server simply relays that information when the host requests its IP address. This differs from automatic allocation in that with manual allocation, the IP address is preconfigured for the host by the system administrator, whereas the automatic allocation gives an arbitrary address (from a pool of IP addresses) to a requesting host. In other words, the host is not preconfigured with the IP address for that host.

The following message types are used with client/server interaction:

- **DHCPDISCOVER**: This is a client broadcast that is used to locate available servers. It may be forwarded by routers to allow for server segments.
- **DHCPOFFER**: This is a server-to-client response to a DHCPDISCOVER message with an offer of configuration parameters.
- **DHCPREQUEST**: This is a client message to servers for:
    - Requesting offered parameters from one server and implicitly declining offers from all others.
    - Confirming correctness of previously allocated addresses, (e.g., system reboot).
    - Extending the lease on a particular network address.
- **DHCPACK**: This is a server-to-client message that contains configuration parameters, including a committed network address.
- **DHCPNAK**: This is a server-to-client message indicating the client's notion of network address is incorrect (e.g., client has moved to new subnet) or a client's lease has expired.
- **DHCPDECLINE**: This is a client-to-server message indicating a network address is already in use.
- **DHCPRELEASE**: This is a client-to-server message relinquishing a network address and canceling the remaining lease.

DHCP Messages

- DHCPDISCOVER
- DHCPOFFER
- DHCPREQUEST
- DHCPACK
- DHCPNAK
- DHCPDECLINE
- DHCPRELEASE
- DHCPINFORM

- **DHCPINFORM**: New with RFC 2131, this is a client-to-server message asking only for local configuration parameters; the client already has an externally configured network address.

First, a client transmits a DHCPDIS-COVER message on its local physical subnet. Both the IP destination address and the MAC destination address are set to broadcast. The IP source address is set to 0x00000000 and the MAC source address is set to Chaddr, or the client's hardware address.

The client may place in this message some options that include an IP address and the lease duration. If the client has placed a "suggested" IP address in the Options field, the client has been previously configured using DHCP and is now restarting and would like to use that address again. If the client was manually configured with an IP address, the client should use the DHCPINFORM message instead of the DHCPREQUEST message. One feature that the client may use is to obtain a specific list of parameters. The client may indicate this by using the "parameter request list," which indicates to the server which parameters, by tag number, the client is specifically interested in. See RFC 2132 for more information on DHCP options.

This message will be picked up by the routers that implement the BOOTP relay agent and forwarded to other network segments. Again, you can limit the scope (how many routers it can traverse). The Hops field (set to 0 by the client) is incremented (usually by 1) with each router and the administrator of the router sets the maximum hop count. If the received packet has a hop count of 2 and the Max Hops parameter configured in the router is 3, the router will set the Hops field to 3 and forward the packet. If the received packet already has a 3 in the Hops field, the router is not allowed to increment the field to a 4 and it will discard

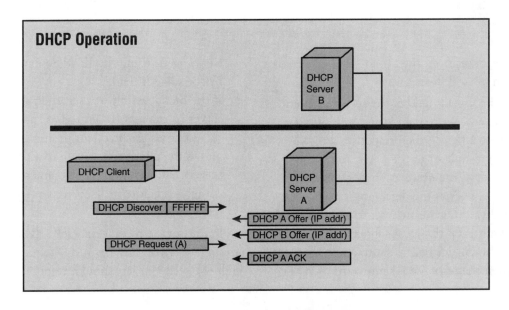

DHCP Operation

the packet. This is known as the *scope* (range) of the DHCP packet.

Each active server that receives this message may respond with a DHCPOFFER message that includes an IP address in the Yiaddr field of the packet. Not all servers will respond. Some may be preconfigured to not respond to certain requests, and others may not have the binding for that client. It may also appear in various Option fields as well. The server does not have to take the offered IP address off the available list, but it does help when the server does remove this offered IP address from its availability pool. At this time, the server may check for current use of the offered IP address by sending an ICMP ECHO request using the offered IP address. This is configurable.

338   DHCP Responses

Responses from the server can be addresses in a few different ways:

- If the Giaddr field of the received client packet is set to 0 and the Ciaddr field is set to a non-0, then responses are to be sent as unicast to the client using the yiaddr as the destination IP address and the chaddr as the destination MAC address. (Giaddr field set to 0 indicates the client is on the local subnet).
- If the Giaddr field is set to a non-0 value, then the response is sent to the BOOTP Relay agent using the IP address indicated by the Giaddr field.
- If the broadcast bit was set, then the server broadcasts (IP and MAC addresses) its responses to the client. Using the B bit allows the client to indicate to a potential server that it cannot receive unicast IP datagrams before its TCP/IP configuration has been set.

If the server receives a DHCPREQUEST messages with an invalid "requested IP address," the server should respond to the client with a DHCPNAK message and report this error in a log.

The client may receive one or more offers from different servers. The client will select one of the servers from the responses that closely match its original request parameters. If the client does not receive a response to its DHCPREQUEST, it will time-out, and retransmit a DHCPREQUEST message.

To respond to a DHCPOFFER, the client transmits a DHCPREQUEST. In the Options field of this message is the server identifier (the server's IP address) indicating which server the client has selected. All other servers will partially ignore this message. However, those declined servers do use this message to indicate that the client will not be using their services, and this releases the offered IP address back to the available pool.

The selected server commits this binding to a place in memory where it will be stored. (A binding is a key that is used to look up information. For example, the preceding entry could be an IP-address-to-client-hardware address.) The server will respond to the client with a DHCPACK message containing all the client's configuration parameters. This binding is indicated as the *client identifier*, and the assigned IP address.

When the client receives the DHCPACK, it will perform some final checks, such as ARPing for the newly assigned IP address to ensure that no one else is assigned to this address. If there are any inconsistencies, the client will send a DHCPDECLINE message to the server and after waiting 10 seconds (it should wait at least 10 seconds), it will restart the configuration process. Also, if the server transmitted a DHCPNAK message to the client, the client will restart (after 10 seconds).

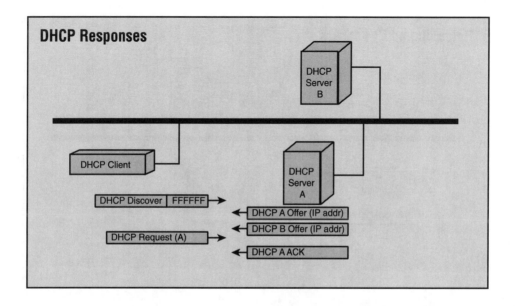

Releasing an IP Address

To "gracefully" stop using the assigned IP address, the client should transmit a DHCPRELEASE message to the server (using the same keyed binding that it used to get the address from that server). This may occur before the lease duration is up.

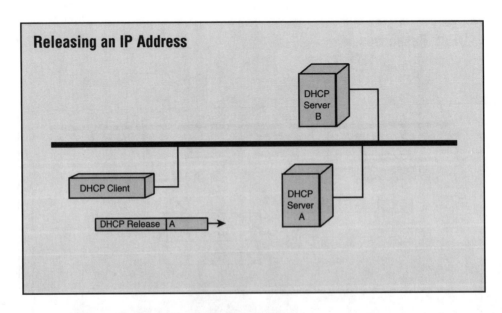

Releasing an IP Address

DHCP Shortcuts

- A client may skip the DHCPDISCOVER if it knows the server address that it wants to talk to.

- Server will respond with a DHCP ACK.

- If the server responds with a DHCPNAK, the client cannot use the parameters it specified in the DHCPREQUEST:
  - Restart with DHCPDISCOVER

- DHCPINFORM message can be used by a client to inform a server that it has an IP address but would like some parameters.
  - Reply is in unicast

some configuration parameters that may be set for it in the server bindings. The reply from the server is unicast (a major difference from all of the other DHCP messages, which are broadcast) directly back to the client.

A simpler approach is used for those clients that were previously serviced by DHCP. The client may skip the DHCP Discover message and instead transmit a DHCPREQUEST message. A server will then respond with a DHCPACK message to fill in the client's configuration parameters. If any of the consistency checks come back as invalid, the server will respond with a DHCPNAK message, meaning that the client may not reuse the requested IP address. The client will restart the process using the longer method (i.e., starting with DHCPDISCOVER).

The DHCPINFORM message can be used by the client to inform a server that it already has an IP address (through a manual configuration process) but it would like a download of

341

Lease Duration

Timers between the server and client may be different. There is not a synchronization of timers between clients and servers using DHCP. This may lead to a problem in that the server assumes the lease is up before the client does (because of the possibility of the inaccuracy of the clocks). To compensate for this, the DHCP server may return a lease smaller than requested by the client. But this is only in response to the client. The server writes the original time into its bindery. This may or may not be accomplished; it depends on how the developer interpreted the RFC.

A client transmits a DHCPREQUEST for the use of an IP address for a certain period of time. The server guarantees not to hand out an allocated IP address that is in use by another client. Furthermore, the server will try to reallocate the same IP address to a requesting client each time it requests an IP address. The length of time that a client uses an IP address is known as the *lease*. If a client needs to extend the lease, it may submit these requests to the server. It is understood between the client and the server that if the server does not receive a message from the client indicating that the client would like to extend the lease, the server assumes that the client is no longer using the IP address, and the lease expires. However, a DHCP server does not automatically reuse expired leased IP addresses. The server will continue down the number of IP addresses and assign those that have not been assigned until it exhausts its list of IP addresses. When this occurs, the server will reallocate an

> ## Lease Duration
>
> - The length of time that a client has sole use of an IP address is known as a lease.
>
> - Lease duration is negotiated between the client and the server during the Request/Offer protocol.
>
> - There is no synchronization of timers between the server and a client:
>   - A server may grant a smaller time than requested to the client, but write the original time in its database.
>
> - To extend the lease, the client must request this of the server:
>   - If there is not an extension request, the lease expires.
>
> - Times are based on a 32-bit integer:
>   - Different implementations allow for different maximum lengths.

IP address that was previously assigned but has expired. The server may probe the network to see if the address is still being used by simply sending an ICMP ECHO request and waiting for a reply. As another consistency check, the host with the newly assigned address may issue an ARP to see if the address has already been assigned to another host. Notice, however, the RFC places these checks as "SHOULD," which means the implementer of the protocol should implement the feature, but it is not required. You may want to ask before implementing a specific vendor's DHCP code.

DHCP implementations may vary, but the lease time is a 32-bit unsigned integer. This number is expressed in seconds, which allows for a lease time in the range of 1 second to (approximately) 136 years—longer than *I* plan to be in this business! According to RFC 2131, there is no minimum lease time requirement.

Efficiencies   342

Clients usually do not need all the configuration parameters that are available using DHCP. To build some efficiency into this protocol, the protocol assumes defaults. Host requirement RFCs (1122, 1123) name the default for the parameters. When the client receives the DHCPNAK packets that contain configuration information, a lot of the information will not be included. The host assumes that default value for anything not contained in the DHCPNAK message.

Another question should have come into your mind by now (if you were paying atten-

tion). If a host is using DHCP for its initial configuration, how does it know to accept TCP/IP packets when TCP/IP has not been fully initialized in the host? To work around this problem, DHCP uses the Flags field. The field is 16 bits in length, but only 1 bit is used. The other 15 must be set to 0. The bit that is used is called the *Broadcast bit*, or *B bit*. Any station that cannot receive unicast datagrams (usually sent by BOOTP Relay agents and servers on DHCPOFFER, DHCPACK, and DHCPNAK messages) must set this bit on DHCPDISCOVER and DHCPREQUEST messages. DHCP servers processing the request will mark this bit and transmit their responses as broadcast in both the IP header and the MAC header.

If the broadcast bit is set to 0, the responses of the server will be transmitted as unicast, with the IP address set to Yiaddr and the MAC destination address set to Chaddr.

Finally, a client may use the DHCPRE-LEASE message to gracefully shut down or to indicate to the DHCP server that the client no longer needs the IP address assigned by the server. The client does not have to use this message and may simply let the lease expire.

Efficiencies

- Not all parameters are needed:
  - Extensive use of defaults
  - Set according to the Host Requirement RFCs 1122, 1123

- Host assumes the default value for anything not contained in the DHCPACK message.

- DHCP makes use of the Flags field to work around the chicken-and-the-egg problem of IP address and ARP responses.

Operational Tables

- The page contains the DHCP fields and the processes that set or reset the fields.

Field	DHCPOFFER	DHCPACK	DHCPNAK
op	BOOTREPLY	BOOTREPLY	BOOTREPLY
htype (From RFC **1700**,"Assigned Numbers")			
hlen (Hardware address length in octets)			
hops	0	0	0
xid	xid from client DHCPDISCOVER message	xid from client DHCPREQUEST message	xid from client DHCPREQUEST message
secs	0	0	0
ciaddr	0	ciaddr from DHCPREQUEST or 0	0
yiaddr	IP address offered to client	IP address assigned to client	0
siaddr	IP address of next bootstrap server	IP address of next bootstrap server	0
flags	flags from client DHCPDISCOVER message	flags from client DHCPREQUEST message	flags from client DHCPREQUEST message
giaddr	giaddr from client DHCPDISCOVER message	giaddr from client DHCPREQUEST message	giaddr from client DHCPREQUEST message
chaddr	chaddr from client DHCPDISCOVER message	chaddr from client DHCPREQUEST message	chaddr from client DHCPREQUEST message
sname	Server hostname or options	Server hostname or options	(unused)
file	Client boot filename or options	Client boot filename or options	(unused)
options	options	options	(unused)

> **Operational Tables (continued)**
>
> ■ The page contains the DHCP fields and the processes that set or reset the fields.

Field	DHCPDISCOVER DHCPINFORM	DHCPREQUEST	DHCPDELCINE DHCPRELEASE
op	BOOTREQUEST	BOOTREQUEST	BOOTREQUEST
htype	(from **RFC 1700**, "Assigned Numbers")	(from **RFC 1700**, "Assigned Numbers")	(from **RFC 1700**, "Assigned Numbers")
hlen	(Hardware address length in octets)	(Hardware address length in octets)	(Hardware address length in octets)
hops	0	0	0
xid	Selected by client	xid from server DHCPOFFER message	Selected by client
secs	0 or seconds since DHCP process has started	0 or seconds since DHCP process has started	0
ciaddr	0 (DHCPDISCOVER) or client's network address (DHCPINFORM)	0 or client's network address (bound/renew/rebind)	0 (DHCPDECLINE) or client's network address (DHCPRELEASE)
yiaddr	0	0	0
siaddr	0	0	0
flags	Set Broadcast bit if client requires a broadcast response	Set Broadcast bit if client requires a broadcast response	0
giaddr	0	0	0
chaddr	Client's hardware address	Client's hardware address	Client's hardware address
sname	Options, if indicated in sname/file option; otherwise, unused	Options, if indicated in sname/file option; otherwise, unused	(unused)
file	Options, if indicated in sname/file option; otherwise, unused	Options, if indicated in sname/file option; otherwise, unused	(unused)
Options	Options	Options	(unused)

RFCs to Be Reviewed

- 951: "Bootstrap Protocol (BOOTP)"
- 1534: "Interoperation between DHCP and BOOTP"
- 2131: "Dynamic Host Configuration Protocol (DHCP)"
- 2132: "DHCP and BOOTP Vendor Extensions"

951: "Bootstrap Protocol (BOOTP)." This includes information on the Relay Agent.

1534: "Interoperation between DHCP and BOOTP."

2131: "Dynamic Host Configuration Protocol (DHCP)." (obsoletes 1541)

2132: "DHCP Options and BOOTP Vendor Extensions." (obsoletes 1533)

Resource Reservation Protocol (RSVP)

QoS (Quality of Service) is currently limited to manual items such as filters, protocol prioritization (fancy filters), compression, network design, and fat pipes. Most of these techniques are applied to WAN ports. While these interim solutions work well, many applications such as voice and video are running on LANs and WANs. There is another step to providing QoS with broadcast networks—RSVP. RSVP provides a general facility for creating and maintaining distributed reservation states across unicast or multicast environments. It is not supposed to be the QoS that rivals ATM's guaranteed QoS. It shows promise as the first of many entries into building QoS for existing broadcast-oriented networks without having to tear out a network and replace it with ATM.

Quality of Service has never been built into most protocols that are currently running on networks today. When Ethernet was invented in the late 1970s, 10 Megabits seemed a huge-enough pipe to give any bandwidth-hungry application more than enough room. However, a bandwidth-hungry application is not the culprit; the culprit is millions of bandwidth-hungry *users*. Personalizing the computer was not thought to have a great impact on the business world. Mainframes and minicomputers were expected to continue to be the computing source of choice; however, the PC changed that. After a few years, the personal computer became able to handle sophisticated graphics, and many different options of voice and video soon became available. Connection to the Internet became a must-have as well.

Resource Reservation Protocol (RSVP)

- QoS abilities on most IP networks are usually about filters, protocol prioritization (fancy filters), compression, and fat pipes (fast or gigabit Ethernet).

- QoS never seemed like a pressing issue until the Web.

- Cannot continue to simply provide for fatter pipes.

- We must find a way to allow multimedia to work on the existing infrastructure.

- ATM is not an alternative for most implementations.

Shared Ethernet and Token Ring networks could not provide the bandwidth necessary to support not only bandwidth-intensive applications that are network aware, but the millions of personal computer users as well. Ethernet has since scaled to 100 Megabits per second and Gigabit Ethernet is making inroads as well. The virtually limitless scalability of the ATM protocol is the first commercial protocol that has QoS scaleable parameters built in; however, ATM is still less than 1 percent of all desktop installations. And there are many consumers that will not tear down their Ethernet or Token Ring networks and replace it with ATM just to get QoS and scaleable bandwidth. Consumers want QoS, but they want it with their existing networks.

Alternatives

- Ethernet allows us some scaling with three speeds.

- ToS offers different paths based on an application request.

- RSVP is a protocol useful where improved Quality of Service (QoS) would enhance transmission of an application's datastream and create higher reliability of its reception at the receiving endstation(s).

- An example where RSVP would be appropriate would be an application for streaming video to the desktop, in a multicast environment, in a routed infrastructure.

Since its inception, IP has had a field known as Type of Service (ToS). The ToS is for internet service quality selection and is specified along the abstract parameters of precedence, delay, throughput, reliability, and cost. These abstract parameters are mapped into the actual service parameters of the particular networks the datagram traverses. File transfers could take a high-delay network while terminal access could take one with low delay (refer to Part III, the IP Protocol). In order to provide for this, router vendors have to provide for ToS in their routers, and application vendors have to build this into their applications. For routers, this can require the maintenance of multiple routing tables for each ToS. The application program is the program that sets these bits and in the past, most application programs moved data and there really was no demand for ToS. Over the years, we simply came up with faster networks to compensate for the millions of new users and bandwidth-hungry applications—the easy way to support QoS is to manipulate the bandwidth.

Gigabit Ethernet now allows us three choices for Ethernet: 10, 100, or 1000 Mbps. This allows for scaling but not for data QoS. Bandwidth is simply one factor in the equation. Also, what comes after gigabit Ethernet (the current Proposal is 10 gigabit Ethernet)? After this we are finally moving into the capabilities of ATM; however, we still run into customer resistance to ATM conversion. They will place ATM on the backbone and possibly use it for the WAN, but not to the desktop. We cannot keep producing more bandwidth without giving some consideration to taming the applications.

RSVP is the first widely known protocol to allow for some type of QoS on an existing broadcast-oriented network. As of this writing, it is still an RFC draft, with the latest version being the functional specification of May 1997. It can be used with IPv6 or IPv4. RSVP covers the QoS portion of protocols optimized for real-time, streaming, multimedia issues. It operates directly on top of IP and supports both unicast and multicast protocols. The operation of RSVP appears to have far greater advantages when used in a multicast network. It is not a transport protocol, but a control protocol like ICMP or IGMP. With IPv4, RSVP operates with UDP, but with IPv6, it will operate on top of IP using the extension header concept.

348 Where It Will Be Used

Let's be up front: RSVP is not designed to provide QoS for the entire Internet. Its original design was to allow QoS for multimedia applications on smaller networks. It is designed to allow applications to choose among multiple, controlled levels of delivery service for their data packets. It reserves network resources along the transmission path of a datastream. It communicates between sending and receiving hosts, but the creation of the reservation is accomplished by the receiving host and only in one direction for data flows. Once the reservation is made, routers between the sender and receiver maintain the reservation. Finally, it is not a replacement for any of the QoS offerings in ATM. Many see it as the migratory step in moving to ATM.

Like ToS in the IP header (IPv4), applications must be RSVP aware. The user application is the one that makes use of RSVP. As of this writing, there are just a few applications that make use of RSVP; for example, WinSock (the API for Windows applications) is QoS aware starting with WinSock 2. Applications that are not RSVP aware may be able to use RSVP tool-kits or dialer programs, which are secondary applications that can make a request for you before starting your application. Applications such as those that are making use of other Internet protocols (such as Real Time Protocol (RTP), and the Real Time Streaming Protocol (RTSP) are better suited to RSVP.

Where It Will Be Used

- RSVP covers the QoS portion of protocols optimized for real-time, streaming, and multimedia issues:
  - RTSP: Real-Time Streaming Protocol— App Layer
  - RTP: Real-Time Transport Protocols (RFC 1889)
  - RTCP: Flow/Control Mechanisms (RFC 1890)
  - RSVP: IETF Draft-14 (QoS)

Operation

- A basic RSVP reservation request (Resv message) consists of a *flowspec* and a *filter spec* that together are called a *"flow descriptor."*

- *flowspec* defines:
  - Service class desired (Guaranteed or Controlled-load)
  - Reservation requested (Rspec)
  - Description of the data flow (Tspec)

- *filter spec*, with the session specification, defines the data "flow" to receive the QoS defined by the *flowspec*.

Reservation requests are made by the receiver, not the sender. Why? The receiver better understands its local parameters (such as LAN type) and is better able to make an intelligent request than a server; otherwise, we would have to configure the server to know every aspect of its possible receivers. For example, if a server must make a bandwidth reservation, how would it know that a receiver is on Ethernet, Token Ring, FDDI, or ATM? How would a server know the type of computer making the reservation? Why does this matter? Speed. An ATM station should be able to make a request larger than an Ethernet station simply because the bandwidth is available. An application on a host uses RSVP to request specific QoS from the network for particular datastreams or flows from the application.

The operation of RSVP is based on two concepts: *flows* and *reservations*. RSVP reserves resources based on a flow. Flows are traffic streams (data) from a sender to a receiver, or possibly to multiple receivers. The flow is defined by the destination IP address and, optionally, a destination port. RSVP may also define the flow by using the Flow Label field in the IPv6 header in conjunction with the source IP address. In combination with the flow, RSVP determines the QoS that a flow requires. QoS determines the network resources for the flow. RSVP does not interpret the flowspec, but it does give that information to hosts and routers along the flow's path. Those systems can examine the flowspec to see if they have the resources to accept the reservation, and if they accept it they use the flowspec to reserve the required resources.

As stated before, the receivers using RSVP actually make the reservations. This is to alleviate the server from being the overall administrator of all the possible receivers. Some receivers are located on Ethernet, others on Token Ring (speed differences). Some may want to leave the flow at any time. Receivers have better independent control over themselves and this allows for flexibility in RSVP.

The reservation is split into two functions: one is performed by the sender, and one is performed by the receiver. Having the receiver make the reservation leads to a question: How does the receiver know the path by which the flow will be forwarded?" The sender will send Path messages that will follow a path from the sender and be propagated by routers. The Path message describes the flow to any possible receivers, and allows routers to get prepared for a possible flow. It identifies the flow to the routers and alerts the routers to the possibility of incoming reservation requests. For multicast, a Path message is sent to a destination multicast address.

350   Path Messages

When a sender transmits a Path message, it will be received by routers along the path. A router inserts its own IP address as the message's last hop. As the Path message is propagated through the network, each router notes the previous router's address and then inserts its own IP address before forwarding the Path message on. Having each router note the last router's IP address, for a flow, allows a router that receives a reservation request to know how to forward that request back in the direction of the sender. This ensures that the receivers will take the correct path for a particular flow. Why? Most network designs have more than one path and a receiver may make a reservation in a path that the sender did not specify.

Path messages can be sent at any time and routers maintain the path state in what is known as a *soft* state. Routers maintain the path information only for a certain period of time, after which they will delete the state. This allows for dynamic flexibility in the path. A new path (via topology changes) may

Path Messages

- Two fundamental RSVP message types: *Path* and *Resv* messages.

- *Path* messages describe:
  - Previous hop IP (RSVP_HOP or "PHOP")
  - Format of the data to come (Sender Template w/filter spec)
  - Traffic characteristics of the datastream (Sender Tspec) and *Adspec* (OPWA)

- Sent end-to-end from *app host sender* to *app host receiver*, along existing routes, with the same addressing as data packets.
  - *Path* messages store *path state* in each node along the way (used by *Resv* messages)

be set up that renders the old path obsolete. A router may fail in the path and no alternate path is available; therefore, the path information is obsolete and needs to be deleted.

RSVP and Routers 351

RSVP also runs in routers and works in conjunction with the requests being transmitted by a network application. RSVP is used in routers to forward QoS requests to all stations along the path or paths of that particular flow. It is also up to the routers to establish and maintain an RSVP state. In other words, if an application makes an RSVP request, each router must forward it to another router en route to the source; yes, the reverse path, receiver to sender.

An RSVP process uses the local route table to obtain routes.

QoS is implemented by a collection of mechanisms known as *traffic control*. This includes three mechanisms:

Packet classifier: Determines the QoS class and possibly the router for each packet.

Admission control: Determines if resources are available to accept or reject a request.

Packet scheduler: Achieves the promised QoS for each outgoing interface.

The slide shows a block diagram for RSVP. Two modules within RSVP known as *admission control* and *policy control* are utilized by a RSVP request. Admission control determines whether the node has the available resources to accept the request (sounds like Call Admission Control under ATM, right?). Policy control determines the permission rights of the requester. If either of these checks fail, the request is discarded and a message is sent back to the requester (the application that made the request) indicating the type of failure. If both of these checks clear, then parameters are set in the packet classifier and the packet scheduler in hopes of obtaining the resources required by the request.

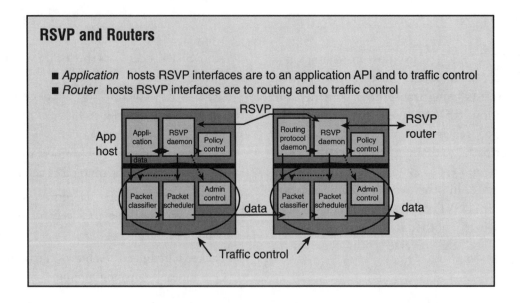

RSVP Requests

- Resv messages: reservation requests sent hop by hop from *host receiver(s)* to *host sender* along the reverse path.

- Each RSVP-speaking receiver node forwards a Resv message to the unicast address of the previous RSVP hop.

- Resv messages create and maintain reservation states in each node along the path(s).

The most basic RSVP request consists of a flow descriptor. A flow descriptor contains:

flowspec: A reservation request that defines a desired QoS and is used to set parameters in a node's packet scheduler.

filter spec: Used to define the set of packets to receive QoS as defined in the flow spec and to set parameters in the packet classifier.

RSVP is based on sessions and defines a session as a data flow with a particular destination and transport-layer protocol. Each session is maintained independently. It is defined by a combination of:

Destination address: A multicast or unicast destination address.

Protocol ID: (Protocol ID is 46)

Destination port: TCP or UDP port number or an application-specific port number. This may be omitted when the destination address is multicast.

There are two message types sent between senders and receivers for reservation of resources. These messages are not sent reliably because the program uses IP directly:

Path: Sent downstream by the RSVP sender host. This message is forwarded by routers using the unicast/multicast routing table. These messages store path state in each forwarding node. This information includes the unicast IP address of the previous hop node. This is used to route the Resv (sent by a receiver in response to a Path message) messages in the reverse path. In addition, the Path message contains information on the format of data packets that the sender will generate, the traffic characteristics of the dataflow, and may carry advertising information known as One Pass with Advertising (OPWA). This is known as an Adspec and allows Path messages to gather information en route to the receiver that the receiver can use to predict end-to-end service.

Resv: Sent upstream by the receiver to the sender. They can either be distinct or shared, allowing for unique reservations to occur for receivers or a single shared reservation that is shared among all packets of selected senders. These messages are sent upstream along the tree until it reaches a point where an existing reservation is equal or greater than that being requested. At that point, the reservation is already in place and does not need to be forwarded any further.

353 Reservation Style

In this reservation request is a set of options that are collectively known as the *reservation style*. These options allow for *shared* or unique (*distinct*) reservations. Examples of shared reservations are for those invoking the use of multicast. Video and audio apps that make use of multicast are great examples of this. Why have multiple reservations for these receivers when one guaranteed pipe will do? The distinct type of reservation is for one-on-one applications such as a small desktop-to-desktop videoconference or when some other type of high-priority, low-loss data stream is needed.

Reservation Style

- RSVP uses several reservation "styles" to fit a variety of applications within Resv messages:
  - *Styles* are collective sets of options included in the Resv request message
  - One option concerns the treatment of reservations as *distinct* or *shared*
  - Another option controls the selection of senders, be that an explicit list or a wildcard implementation:
    - Wildcard-Filter (WF) style
    - Fixed-Filter (FF) style
    - Shared- Explicit (SE) style

A receiver may request a confirmation and will indicate this in the Resv message along with its address. One the reservation is confirmed either unique or merged, a confirmation message is sent.

The basic reservation is completed in one pass. This means that the Resv message is sent from one router to another in the reverse path to the sender. Each router along the way has the right to reject an Resv request.

RSVP Control   354

These options also allow for the control of the selection of senders: *explicit*, which allows for a selected group of senders (each filterspec must match exactly one sender); or a *wildcard* that implicitly selects all the senders to the session (no filterspec is needed). These styles define how reservations are treated from different senders within the same session, and if the requests need to meet a specific criteria or not. There are three types:

Wildcard filter type: Implies both the shared reservation and the wildcard sender selection. This creates a single reservation shared by flows from all upstream neighbors. You can think of this as a big pipe, completely independent of the number of senders using it, which is shared by multiple inputs to the pipe. The size is simply the largest of the resource requests from all receivers; it automatically extends to new senders as they appear.

Fixed Filter: Implies distinct reservation and explicit sender selection. This allows a reservation to be set up for packets from a particular sender, which are not shared with other senders' packets, even from the same session. This style can quickly use up all available resources.

Shared Explicit: This implies shared reservation and explicit sender. It creates a single reservation shared by selected, not all, upstream neighbors.

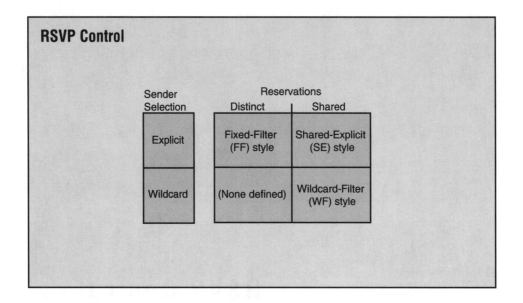

Disabling a Reservation

- PathTear: Received by all receivers downstream and deletes the path state in each node.

- ResvTear: deletes the reservation state and travels upstream towards all senders from its point of initiation:
  - This message specifies styles and filters
  - Flowspecs are ignored

Reservations are removed by *Teardown* messages. This is not required, but is recommended. If a reservation is not removed by the application, it will eventually be removed by the routers—a Refresh message has not been received and within a certain amount of time, the reservation must be removed. There are two types of Teardown messages:

PathTear: Received by all receivers downstream (from the point of initiation, not necessarily the sender) and deletes the path state (in routers, for example) and all dependent reservation state in each node that receives this information.

ResvTear: Deletes reservation state and travels upstream towards all senders from its point of initiation (again, not necessarily the final receiver). This message specifies style and filters. Any flowspec is ignored.

356 Handling Errors

RSVP messages are sent unreliably because the program uses IP directly, similar to IGMP or ICMP. The error messages that RSVP uses are PathErr and ResvErr. This is a simplex process in that an error message is sent upstream to the sender that created the error.

Handling Errors

- RSVP messages are unreliable.
- Error messages are sent using the PathErr and ResvErr.
- Simplex process that is sent upstream to the sender that created the error.

357 Merging Flowspecs

One last statement should be made here, a point that should have come up as a question about multiple reservations being made and the availability of resources to handles such requests. Given the state of today's routers, wouldn't we simply run out of resources within a short amount of time? The question is hard to answer and depends on the manufacturer of the router. Some routers are high performance, possess multiple processors (some of them on the I/O card), and have lots of memory, high-speed interfaces, and so on.

Merging Flowspecs

- RSVP will accommodate transparent operations through non-RSVP-capable devices or clouds.
- One Pass With Advertising (OPWA) is an RSVP enhancement that may be used to predict end-to-end QoS.
- RSVP will merge reservations as they travel upstream to optimize network resources.
- RSVP uses "styles" to define specific options desired by the application.

Some router vendors do not support this. Therefore, it is hard to tell how this control protocol (RSVP) is going to work on routers.

There are some efficiencies in the RSVP protocol itself. One of them is called *merging flowspecs*. Multiple reservation requests from different next hops for the same session and with the same filter spec will have only one reservation on that interface. Contained in the Resv message forwarded to a previous hop is the "largest" of the flowspecs requested by the next hops to which the data flow will be sent. In other words, flowspecs can be cumulative or merged.

A Simple Example 358

An RSVP multicast example is given with the thought of real-time and nonreal-time. Multicast tends to be a bandwidth hog and as so, is the first example used.

Before a session can be created, it must be identified. This is accomplished using the DestAddress, ProtocolID and DestPort [optional], which must be propagated to all the senders and receivers. The following occurs during a session setup:

- The receiver joins a multicast group using IGMP.

- An RSVP-aware application starts to send Path messages to the multicast destination address, which will be received by all receivers in the multicast group.
- A receiver sends a Resv message, specifying the desired flow descriptors. These will be received by the sender.
- The sender starts sending the data packets.

Once the request has been accepted and processed, the resources are reserved, but they are in a *soft state*. A soft state is one that has an entry, but requires some maintenance to stay alive. If this maintenance is not applied, the entry will be deleted. This soft state maintains the reservation, and it is the Path and Resv messages that are used to maintain this soft state. This means the resources established can be modified dynamically as changes occur. This soft state is maintained by RSVP sending refresh messages along the path to indicate to the routers and nodes to keep the resources maintained. If these Refresh messages are not received, an RSVP resource times out and is deleted.

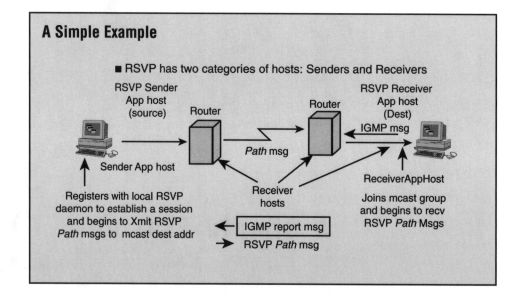

This slide shows the flow of the actual reservation message from the RSVP App host.

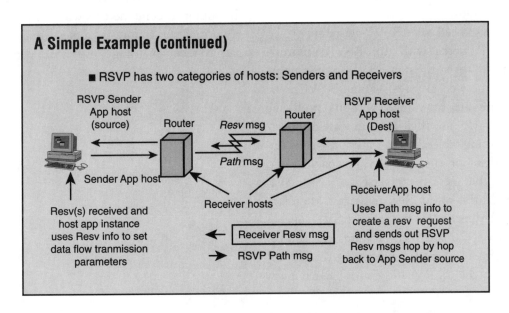

360 Issues

Won't a router become overwhelmed with each receiver making RSVP requests?

No. First, any router has the capability of rejecting a request. Second, RSVP is maintained in the router via a soft state. A reservation will be torn down when it is not needed. Third, RSVP allows for the concept of *merging*. This allows requests to be merged together (shared) when a reservation equaling the size of the request is already in place.

Will RSVP work in areas that do not support it?

Yes. The ability to simply "flip a switch" and all routers on the Internet are RSVP capable is not a reality. In 1983, we did "flip a switch" and all routers (IMPs) and hosts were running the TCP/IP protocol, but today we have millions of routers connected to the Internet, and moving slowly is the method. Therefore, RSVP will be implemented slowly on the Internet.

We also need some RSVP-aware apps.

RSVP works with non-RSVP environments; however, the non-RSVP environments cannot provide any reservation. RSVP Path messages are forwarded without problems because they use their local unicast of multicast routing tables. In the Path message is the IP address of the last RSVP-capable node before the message traversed a non-RSVP node. In this way, a Resv message is then forwarded directly to the next RSVP-capable router on the path back towards the source. Furthermore, there is a bit setting that RSVP sends to the local traffic control mechanism

---

Issues

- Routers have the capability of rejecting a request and requests can be merged.

- Works in areas that are not supporting it.

- To make use of RSVP, applications must be RSVP aware, and there are few:
  - Apps may be rewritten to use QoS-sensitive APIs such as WinSock 2
  - Existing apps may use RSVP Dialer programs or toolkits instead

- Intranet versus Internet usage.
  - Internet ISPs coming up with billing procedures for clients who desire QoS capabilities

---

when it knows that there are non-RSVP nodes hops in the path to a given sender. This allows the router to combine this with other sources of information to forward a message along the path to receivers using Adspecs.

RSVP Summary

- Resource ReSerVation Protocol (RSVP) is a protocol used to reserve network resources along the transmission path(s) of a datastream:
  - The goal being to obtain optimal QoS for that application instance
- RSVP communicates between sending and receiving hosts with the receivers creating the actual reservation for the session:
  - Reservations are made by receivers *upstream* back towards the sender(s)
  - The focus of reservations is on Network layer resources in interconnecting devices (i.e., routers, or devices acting as routers)

The following slide summarizes the chapter.

The following slide is a continuation of the summary.

RSVP Summary (continued)

- RSVP operates on top of IP, occupying the place of a Transport protocol and works as an *internet control* protocol similar to ICMP.

- Supports unicast and multicast protocols:
  - Designed to accommodate large, heterogeneous groups of users with dynamic memberships and topology

- RSVP is unidirectional, or only makes reservations in one direction for data flows.

- Once a reservation is made, it's maintained by using "soft state" in the routers:
  - Soft state provides graceful support for membership changes and adaptation to routing changes

---

363

Conclusion

Individual user demands for better IP service are driving the need for some type of bandwidth reservation. Most of us continue to use the phone as the standard to compare to. The Internet continues to delivery any type of data based on a first-come-first-served basis. The Internet routers still drop an extraordinary amount of packets over the Internet, causing retransmissions. More applications are running over the Internet every day. Multimedia applications are the ones that require QoS only because the users demand it. We have

expected it due to the telephone and cable TV networks. RSVP will allow for this to exist, but it will remain only in pockets of networks and not throughout the Internet. RSVP will place great demands on the routers. Today's routers have yet to prove they can handle anything more than simple data forwarding, and they are not doing *that* very well. Faster routers are coming onto the market and will help alleviate the problem.

The Internet is becoming channelized, which means that there will be streams of data

---

> ### Conclusion
>
> - RSVP is one area addressing QoS issues that are driving forces for future networking requirements:
>   - Web-based everything—wave of the future
>   - Real-time video apps and protocol availability
>   - Integration of voice and data capabilities, availability of multimedia technology, multicast networks—all only increases the demand for QoS features
> - Specifications such as RSVP will only aid in bridging the gap between Layer 2 and Layer 3 QoS capabilities.
> - View www.isi.edu/rsvp.

ATM as some Ethernet zealots would have you believe. ATM and other software and hardware technologies will continue to integrate. RSVP is the first attempt to provide for some type of Quality of Service based on a user-by-user need.

The RSVP homepage can be found at: www.isi.edu/rsvp

running across the Internet that a user can "tune in to." The point that I am trying to make here is that QoS is made up of many factors, and RSVP is simply one of the factors. Do not think that by applying RSVP, all your troubles will disappear. You must continue to apply the other factors as well, such as compression, filters, protocol prioritization, network design, OSPF, IP address summaries, and so forth. One more thing: Multimedia really requires (for best operation) that multicast be enabled. Only recently have ISPs started to multicast enable their networks (even with the entire Internet being non-multicast). Streaming real-time data across the Internet is not very efficient.

Lastly, you should be aware that RSVP is not an attempt to recover lost ground from

364 Simple Network Management Protocol (SNMP)

Network Management can be broken down into five distinct categories:

Account management: Gathers information on which users or departments are employing which network services.

Fault management: Includes troubleshooting, finding, and correcting failed or damaged components, monitoring equipment for early problem indicators, and tracking down distributed problems.

Security: Includes authorization, access control, data encrypting, and management of encrypting keys.

Configuration management: Tracks hardware and software information. Included with this are administration tasks, such as day-to-day monitoring and maintenance of the current physical and logical state of the network, as well as recognition and registrations of applications and services on the network.

Performance: The monitoring of traffic on the network.

Simple Network Management Protocol (SNMP)

- Network management is divided into five categories:
  - Account management
  - Fault management
  - Security
  - Configuration management
  - Performance

There are several elements that comprise SNMP and they all must work together in order for SNMP to operate.

Management server: The network station that runs the management application to monitor or control the management clients.

Management clients: The network station that contains the agent (a software component), which enables the management server to control and monitor them. The agent can be located in any directly attached network device such as router, a PC, a switch, etc.

SNMP: A Request/Response protocol that allows for the exchange of information between the server and an agent. This protocol does not define the items that can be managed.

MIB: The Management Information Base. A collection of objects that contain information that will be utilized by a network management server. It contains all of this information under an entity known as *object*. Similar objects are placed together to form groups. In other words, the MIB is a database. It is a collection of objects formed into groups, each of which contains information that will be given based on a request from a management station.

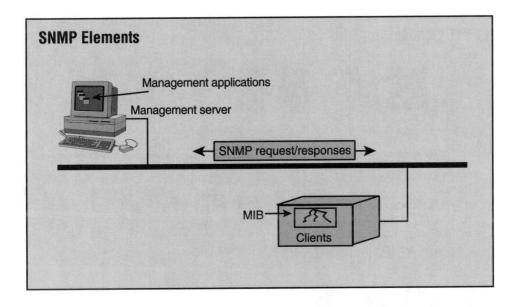

SNMP Elements

Management applications
Management server
SNMP request/responses
MIB
Clients

SNMP Manager

An SNMP manager is a software application that queries the agents for information, or sets information on the client agent. The returned information is then stored in a database to be manipulated by other application software that is not defined by SNMP. The information gathered can be used to display graphs of how many bytes of information are transmitted out a port, how many errors have occurred, and so forth. SNMP simply sets or gathers information in a node.

Therefore, the server will be comprised of two things:

Management applications: Applications that can receive and process the information gathered by the SNMP manager. These applications are the ones that have some type of user interface to allow the network manager to manipulate the SNMP protocol; for example, set the SNMP node that it would like to talk to, send that node information, get information from that node, and so on.

Databases: The information that is stored in the database is from the configuration, performance, and audit data of the agents. There are multiple databases on the server: the MIB database, the Network Element database, and the Management Application databases (Topology database, History Log, Monitor Logs).

All of this runs on top of SNMP. It is not necessary for SNMP to operate, but it does allow for the human factor to fit in.

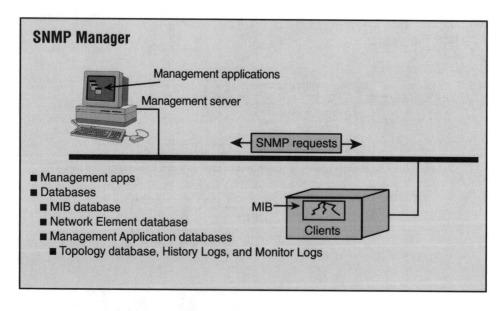

SNMP Manager

- Management apps
- Databases
  - MIB database
  - Network Element database
  - Management Application databases
    - Topology database, History Logs, and Monitor Logs

Agents are simple elements that have access to a network's elements (router, switch, PC, etc.) MIB. Agents are the interface from the network management server to the client MIB. They perform server-requested functions. When a server requests information from a client, it will build its SNMP request (explained in a moment) and send it, unicast, to the client. The agent receives this request, processes it, retrieves or sets the information in the MIB of the client, and generates some type of response to the server. Usually, agents only transmit information when requested by a server. However, there is one instance in which an agent will transmit unsolicited information. It is known as a *trap*.

There are certain things on a network station that may force it to immediately notify the server. Some of these traps are defined by the RFC. Things such as cold/warm start and authentication failure are traps that are sent to the server. Most agent applications today permit the use of user-defined traps. This means that the network administrator of an SNMP compliant device can configure the router to send traps to the server when certain conditions are met. For example, a router may send a trap to the server when its memory buffers constantly overflow or when too many ICMP redirects have been sent.

Another type of agent is known as the *proxy agent*. This allows one station to become an agent for another network station that does not support SNMP. Basically, proxy agents server as translators between servers and non-SNMP capable clients (for security, limited resources, etc.).

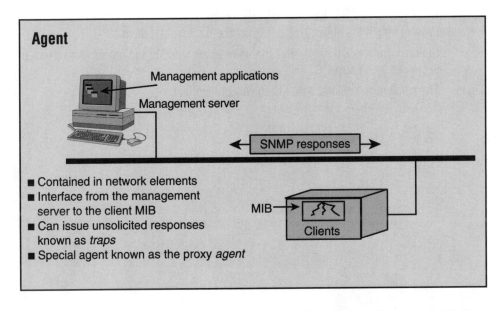

Agent

Management applications
Management server

SNMP responses

MIB

Clients

- Contained in network elements
- Interface from the management server to the client MIB
- Can issue unsolicited responses known as *traps*
- Special agent known as the proxy *agent*

368 Management Information Base (MIB)

The MIB is a collection of objects that contain specific information that together form a group. You can think of a MIB as a database that contains certain information that was either preset (during configuration of the node) or was gathered by the agent and placed into the MIB. Simply stated, the MIB is a database that contains information about the client that is currently placed on it.

The structure of management information is defined in RFC 1155 and defines the format of the MIB objects. This includes the following:

Management Information Base (MIB)

- Collection of objects that contain specific information that together form a group.

- Structure of Management Information is specified in RFC 1155.

- The objects contain the following:
  - Syntax
  - Access
  - Status
  - Description
  - Index
  - DefVal
  - Value notation

Syntax	Required. The abstract notation for the object type. This defines the data type that models the object.
Access	Required. Defines the minimal level of support required for the object types. Must be one of read-only, read-write, write-only, or not accessible.
Status	Required. The status of the MIB entry. Can be mandatory, optional, obsolete, or deprecated (removed).
Description	Optional. A text description of the object type.
Index	Present only if the object type corresponds to a row in a table.
DefVal	Optional. Defines a default value that may be assigned to the object when a new instance is created by an agent.
Value Notation	The name of the object, which is an Object Identifier.

Example MIB Entry

Object:
IfOperStatus {ifEntry 8}

Syntax:
INTEGER {
up (1) — ready to pass packets
down(2),
testing (3) — in some test mode
}
Definition:
The current operational state of the interface. The testing (3) state indicates that no operational packets can be passed.
Access:
Read-only.
Status:
Mandatory.

Object:
----
ifOperStatus { ifEntry 8 }
Syntax:
INTEGER {
up(1), — ready to pass packets
down(2),
testing(3) — in some test mode
}
Definition:
The current operational state of the interface. The testing(3) state indicates that no operational packets can be passed.
Access:
Read-only.
Status:
Mandatory.

The Protocol of SNMP

370

SNMP is the protocol that is used between a manager and a client. SNMP uses a series of SNMP commands and protocol data units (PDUs) to send and receive management information. SNMP was eventually to be migrated to the OSI management scheme (which never came about). Therefore a encoding scheme known as Abstract Syntax Notation, or ASN.1, was used. Only the INTEGER, OCTET, STRING, OBJECT IDENTIFIER, NULL, SEQUENCE, AND SEQUENCE OF are used. There are more encodings, but they are not used.

SNMP uses UDP as its transport layer.

The following are the SNMP protocol data unit (PDU Packet) types:

GetRequest. Requests an agent to return attribute values for a list of managed objects.

GetNextRequest. Used to traverse a table of objects. Since the object attributes are stored in lexicographical order, the result of the previous GetNextRequest can be used as an argument in a subsequent GetNext-Request. In this way, a manager can go through a variable-length table until it has extracted all the information for the same types of objects.

GetResponse. Returns attribute values for the selected objects or error indications for such conditions as invalid object name or nonexistent object.

SetRequest. Used to change the attribute values of selected objects.

Trap. Used by the agent. Traps are used to report certain error conditions and changes

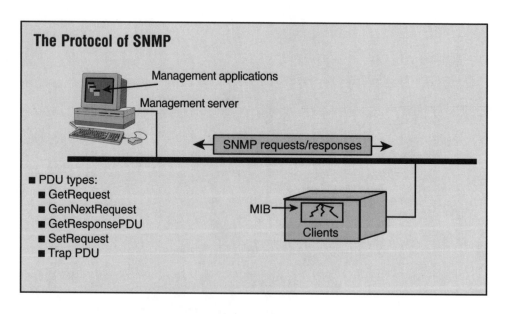

The Protocol of SNMP

Management applications

Management server

SNMP requests/responses

- PDU types:
  - GetRequest
  - GenNextRequest
  - GetResponsePDU
  - SetRequest
  - Trap PDU

MIB

Clients

of state to the managing process. The conditions are cold-start, warm-start, link-up, link-down, EGP neighbor loss (not much use for this one anymore), and authentication failure.

SNMP provides for a simple authentication process between the client and the server. This is known as the *community string* and it must match between a client and the server. This string is embedded in the protocol packet and if either side has a different entry, the received SNMP packet is discarded. This community string is manually configured on the server and the client. The problem is that it is not encrypted in any way when it is transmitted. Any protocol analyzer that is on the same link as this packet can see the community string name. It is plain text.

371

SNMP Encapsulation

The following slide shows the encapsulation of an SNMP packet. The community string is a simple password protection mechanism. Most are set to "public" for read access and "private" for read-write access. This field is established at set up time.

The variable binding indicates which groups or which objects in the groups are being requested for information.

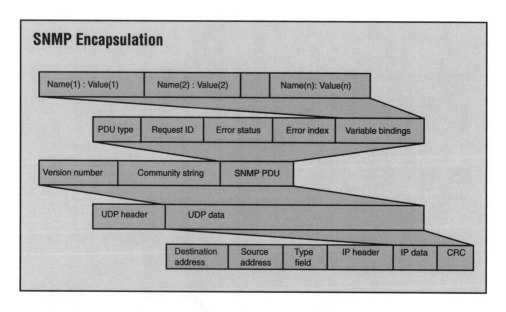

Index

CUSTOMER NOTE: IF THIS BOOK IS ACCOMPANIED BY SOFTWARE, PLEASE READ THE FOLLOWING BEFORE OPENING THE PACKAGE.

To use this CD-ROM, your system must meet the following requirements:

Platform/Processor/Operating System. Windows 3.1 or higher
RAM. 16MB
Hard Drive Space. 2MB
Peripherals. PowerPoint 97 (or viewer)